Bicycling
America's National Parks

Bicycling America's National Parks

ARIZONA & NEW MEXICO

The Best Road and Trail Rides from
the Grand Canyon to Carlsbad Caverns

SARAH BENNETT ALLEY

Foreword by Dennis Coello

 WOODSTOCK, VERMONT

With time, road numbers, signs, park regulations, and amenities referred to in this book may be altered. If you find that such changes have occurred along the routes described in this book, please let the author and publisher know, so that corrections may be made in future editions. Other comments and suggestions are also welcome. Address all correspondence to:

Backcountry Guides
P.O. Box 748
Woodstock, VT 05091

Library of Congress Cataloging-in-Publication Data
Alley, Sarah Bennett.
    Bicycling America's national parks. Arizona and New Mexico : the best road and trail rides from the Grand Canyon to Carlsbad Caverns / Sarah Bennett Alley ; foreword by Dennis Coello.
        p. cm.
    Includes index.
    ISBN 0-88150-481-5 (alk. paper)
    1. All terrain cycling—Arizona—Guidebooks. 2. All terrain cycling—New Mexico—Guidebooks. 3. National parks and reserves—Arizona—Guidebooks. 4. National parks and reserves—New Mexico—Guidebooks. 5. Arizona—Guidebooks. 6. New Mexico—Guidebooks. I. Title: Arizona and New Mexico. II. Title.
GV1045.5.A6 A44 2001
917.89—dc21   00-047402

Maps by Inkspot: A Design Company, © 2001 by The Countryman Press
Interior photographs by Dennis Coello and Sarah Bennett Alley
Cover photographs by Dennis Coello
Cover and interior design by Bodenweber Design
Series editor, Dennis Coello

Published by Backcountry Guides
A division of The Countryman Press
P.O. Box 748
Woodstock, VT 05091

Distributed by W.W. Norton & Company, Inc.
500 Fifth Avenue
New York, NY 10110

Printed in the United States of America

10 9 8 7 6 5 4 3 2 1

For my parents, who brought me west, where I had the chance to be young, and to grow, in wild country.

Many thanks are due to the people who assisted me over the weeks and months I was on the road gathering information for this project. The enthusiasm and encouragement I received from family, friends, and strangers, who all share a love of adventuring on two wheels, kept me rolling when I was far from home and more than a little road weary. Whether it was a shower and a bed, directions, or simply a smile and a few comforting words, their generosity and kindness helped make this book possible.

My respect and gratitude go out to the men and women of the National Park Service who are committed to preserving and sharing some of this country's most fantastic natural and historic treasures. They are under a great deal of pressure to accommodate the needs of a growing number of visitors to our parks each year. Cyclists who care about riding safely in our national parks and would like their presence considered in future park transportation funding need to seek out park service employees and make themselves heard. Let's give them our input and help them do the best job they can.

I also tip my helmet to the dedicated folks who work for the National Forest Service and the Bureau of Land Management, the agencies that manage the road and trail systems in the country surrounding the parks that make for such great cycling. They are responsible for building and maintaining many of the trails and routes in this book and deserve our cooperation and respect.

The riders who appear in the pages of this book, many of them complete strangers who were more than willing to pull over, smile for my camera, and share their tales of the road or trail, are greatly appreciated for their spirit of adventure and love of cycling. And to my family and friends who took time to travel, camp, explore the trails, and pose for my pictures—thank you!

Last, but not least, I would like to thank my editor and friend, Dennis Coello, for offering me the chance to do this project and the opportunity to, once again, wander and revel in the spectacular country of the American Southwest.

Bicycling America's National Parks: Arizona

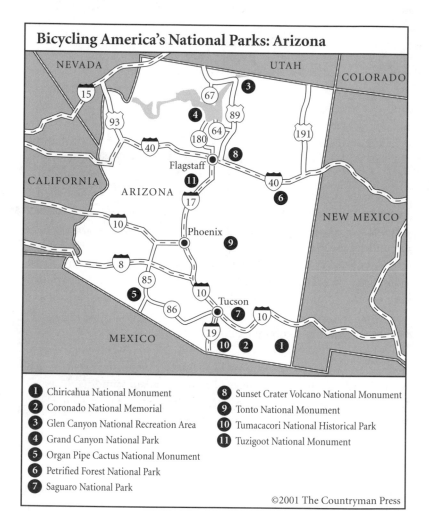

1. Chiricahua National Monument
2. Coronado National Memorial
3. Glen Canyon National Recreation Area
4. Grand Canyon National Park
5. Organ Pipe Cactus National Monument
6. Petrified Forest National Park
7. Saguaro National Park
8. Sunset Crater Volcano National Monument
9. Tonto National Monument
10. Tumacacori National Historical Park
11. Tuzigoot National Monument

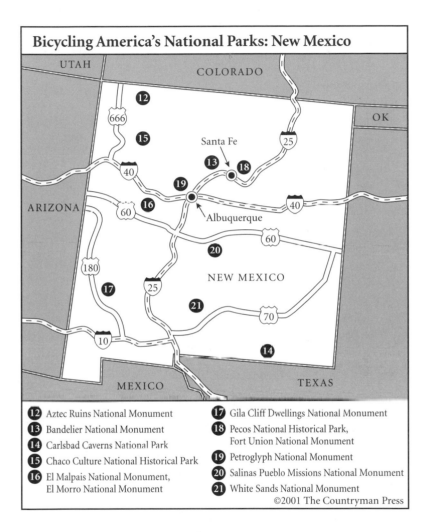

Bicycling America's National Parks: New Mexico

UTAH

COLORADO

OK

12

666

15

Santa Fe

25

ARIZONA

40

13

18

19

60

16

40

Albuquerque

180

60

20

NEW MEXICO

17

25

21

70

10

14

MEXICO

TEXAS

12 Aztec Ruins National Monument

13 Bandelier National Monument

14 Carlsbad Caverns National Park

15 Chaco Culture National Historical Park

16 El Malpais National Monument,
El Morro National Monument

17 Gila Cliff Dwellings National Monument

18 Pecos National Historical Park,
Fort Union National Monument

19 Petroglyph National Monument

20 Salinas Pueblo Missions National Monument

21 White Sands National Monument

©2001 The Countryman Press

Bicycling America's National Parks: Arizona & New Mexico
Map Legend

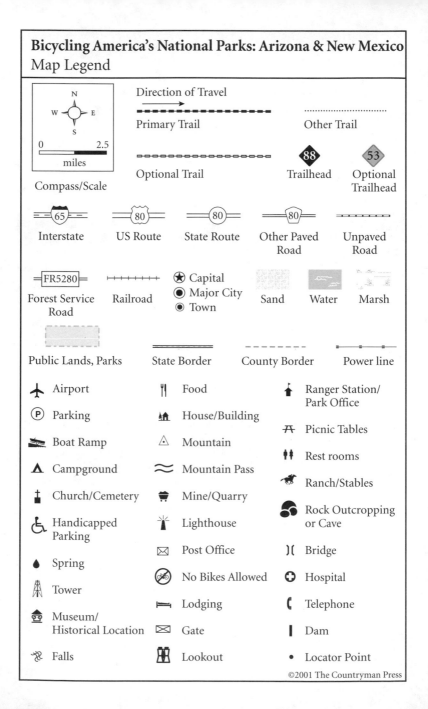

Compass/Scale

Direction of Travel

Primary Trail

Other Trail

Optional Trail

Trailhead

Optional Trailhead

Interstate

US Route

State Route

Other Paved Road

Unpaved Road

Forest Service Road

Railroad

★ Capital
◉ Major City
◎ Town

Sand

Water

Marsh

Public Lands, Parks

State Border

County Border

Power line

✈ Airport

Ⓟ Parking

⛵ Boat Ramp

▲ Campground

⸸ Church/Cemetery

♿ Handicapped Parking

◆ Spring

⛨ Tower

⌂ Museum/Historical Location

⤳ Falls

🍴 Food

🏠 House/Building

△ Mountain

≈ Mountain Pass

⛏ Mine/Quarry

⛯ Lighthouse

⊠ Post Office

🚳 No Bikes Allowed

🛏 Lodging

⊠ Gate

⛨ Lookout

⛫ Ranger Station/Park Office

⊼ Picnic Tables

⚺ Rest rooms

🐎 Ranch/Stables

⬤ Rock Outcropping or Cave

)(Bridge

✚ Hospital

(Telephone

▌ Dam

• Locator Point

CONTENTS

Part One ARIZONA

CHIRICAHUA NATIONAL MONUMENT 30

CORONADO NATIONAL MEMORIAL 58

GLEN CANYON NATIONAL RECREATION AREA 81

GRAND CANYON NATIONAL PARK 107

SOUTH RIM RIDES

Part Two NEW MEXICO

The problem isn't too many people, it's too many cars." So says Interior Secretary Bruce Babbitt when discussing how we Americans are loving our national parks to death. You're skeptical? Then take a look at the statistics: Each year there are more than 287 million "recreation visitors" (non-service or ranger personnel) to the parks. That's right—more than our entire population. Great Smoky Mountains National Park leads the list with almost ten million visitors annually. Grand Canyon is next with four million-plus. Yosemite, Yellowstone, Rocky Mountain, and Olympic all host more than three million visitors every twelve months. Wyoming's Grand Teton, Maine's Acadia, Zion in Utah and Kentucky's Mammoth Cave each sees more than two million people every year, most of them motoring in between May and September. Drive to the Grand Canyon on any summer weekend and you and six thousand other drivers will spend much of your time competing for the two thousand parking spaces. You have better odds at the local mall.

And with the cars come noise, and air pollution, and the clogged roads you thought you left back home. It's gotten so bad in some parks (Grand Canyon, Yosemite, and Zion) that most cars will soon be banned from particular areas or left outside the park entirely, with propane-powered buses and, in time, light-rail systems shuttling people to central dispersal sites. How you see the park from there, by boot or bike or another ride on an "alternatively powered bus" to some distant location and then a hike or bike ride from there, will be up to you. It will be a different, and for some a disturbing change in the way we experience our parks. And that's where this new series steps in to help.

Most national park bookstores are filled with hiking guides, and handouts are available for the shorter walks to the most popular attractions. But not until the Bicycling America's National Parks series did in-depth guides exist for those wishing to see our country's grandest scenery and most important historic sites from the saddle. Whether you're peering through a windshield in those parks that still allow personal cars or through the window of a bus you are sharing with thirty others, it doesn't begin to compare with the wide-screen, fresh-wind-in-the-face feeling of a park viewed over the handlebars. It is an intimate experience, a chance to sense exactly those conditions that created what you are there to see. Zion's towering white and red walls are even more imposing, Organ Pipe's weirdly shaped cactus even odder, Hovenweep National Monument's ancient Indian towers and dwellings even more dramatic when you ride up to them to say hello. Pedal Gettysburg's hills and you'll gain a soldier's appreciation of topography. Be forced to stop to let the buffalo pass in Yellowstone, or in North Dakota's Theodore Roosevelt National Park, and you will see how much larger, how much more magnificent these beasts appear when viewed face-to-face. And—for some this is the best reason of all to pedal a bike—you can pull over and park almost anywhere.

Sarah Bennett Alley, the author of this guide, tells road cyclists and fat-tire bikers alike where to ride to see the sights, when to go for the least traffic and best weather, how to select a route to suit your mood and energy that day, and even whether there's good outside-the-park cycling. There's information on camping, on lodging in the parks and in nearby towns, on flora and fauna, and on where to refuel (as in food, not gas)—even the location of the nearest laundromat. Sarah has logged the miles, interviewed the rangers, and kept both seasoned cyclists and beginning bikers in mind during her research. She's done her part.

Now is the time for all of us to do our part in saving these places of stunning beauty and important history. Our national parks—hundreds of them across America—are our natural, secular cathedrals. It's time to get the cars out of church.

Dennis Coello
Series Editor

INTRODUCTION

When people think about hitting the road and getting out to see the West's national parks in summer, their initial enthusiasm is often dampened by the seemingly endless stream of news reports about overcrowding and vehicle traffic clogging park roads and detracting from the overall park experience. This is especially true for those hoping to see the parks from the seat of their bicycle. After all, who wants to try to pedal alongside an idling column of vehicles, breathing in noxious fumes while trying to take in one of our country's great natural wonders?

In fact, the growing problem of vehicle congestion in the parks and all the negatives it generates has begun to work in cyclists' favor. Parks all across the country, including Yosemite National Park in California, Zion National Park in Utah, and Grand Canyon National Park in Arizona, have taken steps to limit the number of private vehicles on their roads while developing alternative transportation plans that consider bicycle use. These changes include mass transit systems, bike lanes, and new bike and pedestrian pathways. All of these changes are aimed at improving the quality of visiting our national parks and will immeasurably improve the amount and quality of biking opportunities in parks in the future. Someday a paved bike trail will wind along the 35-mile length of the south rim of the Grand Canyon, providing spectacular car- and crowd-free views the entire way. Once this system of trails is completed on both rims, Grand Canyon National Park will become a cyclist's paradise.

Another trend that has aided in the development of transportation plans that include bikes is the surge of interest in biking over the last few decades. This is due in large part to the popularity of mountain bikes. Faced with an ever-increasing number of Americans who travel with their bicycles on their cars, the park service has begun to realize that bicycles are not only a fun, low impact, and energy efficient way to tour parks, they are also one of the best ways to enjoy a rewarding park experience. Some parks are now welcoming cyclists by sponsoring group rides and encouraging local riding clubs to pedal scenic drives on group outings. White Sands National Monument, near Alamogordo, New

Mexico, hosts an annual full moon ride that draws bikers from around the state; it is a fantastic opportunity to see the beautiful shapes of snow-white dunes illuminated by the moon. Great Smoky Mountains National Park in Tennessee hosts a similar event. As parks free up their roadways they will undoubtedly try to find more ways to attract cyclists.

Cycling opportunities in the national parks of Arizona and New Mexico vary considerably depending on each park's focus. Many of the parks and monuments in these two states are centered around the incredibly rich archaeological remains of the ancient cultures that once flourished in the Southwest. These parks tend to be smaller, with limited acreage and few roads open to cyclists. Much of the country that surrounds them, however, is usually wild and scenic, offering plenty of trails and dirt roads for the mountain biker. Lonely, wide-open stretches of paved roads often found nearby will delight skinny-tire fans. While most of the parks that are archaeological in nature can be seen in a day, Mesa Verde National Park and Chaco Cultural Historic Park are two that are best taken in over two or more days.

Some parks have large geologic or geographic features as their focus, including Grand Canyon National Park and Glen Canyon National Recreation Area. Here the scale of everything is bigger, including the time required to get around and see the sights. These parks encompass hundreds of thousands of acres and offer at least a week's worth of biking on both paved roads and dirt backcountry roads inside their boundaries.

Grand Canyon National Park, one of the crown jewels of the national park system, is also one of the most popular, receiving close to 5 million visitors each year. People from all over the world come to this spectacular chasm; most descending on the park during the summer months. Planning your visit to the Grand Canyon during off-peak times will greatly enhance the quality of your stay. At the many other smaller Southwestern parks summer crowding is less of an issue. As you travel further south into the warmer deserts, summer visitation is somewhat lighter because of the extreme temperatures of that season. Visiting then, especially if you are riding a bike, is not recommended. At most parks crowding is a problem only around the visitor center and at the overlooks. Once you get onto your bike, you can move at your own pace, glide in and out of overlooks without worrying about where to park (but

Cyclists explore New Mexico's Chaco Culture National Historical Park.

always cautious of drivers gawking at the scenery), and take in unobstructed views of the surrounding country, the impact of crowds seem to melt away. Mountain bikers will find that they have backcountry roads in and around the parks almost entirely to themselves anytime of year.

One consideration that might discourage cyclists from embarking on a tour of parks in these states is the perception that most of the region is a hot, barren desert that is a less than perfect place to enjoy a cycling adventure. While it is true that the Sonoran Desert in southern Arizona can get brutally hot during the summer months, much cooler temperatures prevail at the higher elevations in Arizona's numerous mountain ranges and high plateaus. The lower, warmer deserts of both southern Arizona and New Mexico provide an ideal climate for cycling during the winter months when much of the rest of the country is experiencing cold and snow. The variety of environments and climates throughout these two states provide cyclists with myriad riding possibilities year-round, but the spring and fall, when temperatures are more moderate and summer crowds have abated, are the very best times of year to plan a cycling vacation to the parks and monuments of the desert Southwest.

The generally arid climate of the region allows cyclists to enjoy riding almost any time of year without the threat of long rainy periods, but staying well hydrated and energetic when exerting yourself on a bike can be a challenge. The strong sun and dry air work quickly to evaporate perspiration, accelerating the loss of precious fluids your body needs to stay healthy and function smoothly. Replacing those fluids with a combination of water and sports drinks is the best way to ward off dehydration and the exhaustion and muscular fatigue that accompany it. Sports drinks work to replace the glucose, salts, and potassium that are lost during exercise and help you retain fluids. They also work to recharge electrolytes, substances that allow your body to metabolize fuel into energy. Covering up with a lightweight, long-sleeved shirt when it's hot will help your body keep cool while also helping to prevent sunburn.

Becoming dehydrated not only zaps your energy, it can lead to heatstroke. Heatstroke is a serious condition characterized by muscle cramps, dizziness, nausea, and vomiting. If left untreated heatstroke can be fatal. Whenever you are riding in the desert, and especially if you are on a long or strenuous ride, it is important not to let thirst regulate your fluid intake; *drink often to avoid becoming dehydrated.* (The same holds true for hunger. By the time you are hungry you are already experiencing an energy deficit. Energy bars, nuts, and dried fruits are a good choice for quick, high-energy snacks.) Begin hydrating before you start to ride and continue to replace fluids after you're done to insure that you'll feel fresh and ready to ride the following day. Also, don't forget to stay hydrated when riding in cooler temperatures at higher elevations or during the winter months.

Although the southwestern deserts are arid by definition, they do experience periods of intense and often violent thunderstorms. These thunderstorms can flood dry arroyos and low-lying areas in a matter of minutes and turn normally hardpacked dirt roads into a sticky, gooey mess, making them difficult for even four-wheel-drive vehicles to negotiate. While the higher elevations receive a good deal of their moisture in the form of snow, most of the region receives the bulk of its precipitation during the summer monsoon season. Beginning around the Fourth of July and running through early September, daily thunderstorms are a common occurrence. These storms form when warm, moisture-laden air in the mid- and upper levels of the atmosphere begin moving up from more tropical latitudes to the south. When this air collides with warm air rising off the mountains and plateaus of the Southwest and is carried skyward to mix with colder air aloft, big, billowing cumulonimbus clouds begin to form. Within a matter of hours these beautiful towers of fluffy white clouds can turn into dark, threatening storm clouds that can generate lightning—a serious danger. If you plan a long ride when this type of weather pattern exists it is a good idea to get an early start so that you're done before these storms let loose.

With the above considerations in mind, you are ready to explore dozens of parks and monuments in one of the wildest and most beautiful regions of America. The many natural and historic sites celebrated in the Southwest's parks and monuments exist within a stunning variety of natural environments, including the redrock canyons, cliffs, and mesas of the Colorado Plateau; sprawling lava fields dotted by extinct volcanoes; isolated "sky islands"—mountain ranges surrounded by barrier-forming deserts where rare and endemic plants and animals thrive; and the Sonoran Desert, where cactus of every size and description, some towering over 50 feet, dominate the landscape. Two other deserts, the Chihuahuan and Great Basin, are also found in these states, as well as alpine forests of mixed spruce and fir, and sensitive riparian woodlands dominated by cottonwoods, Arizona sycamores, and black walnut. The number and variety of bird and animal species that live in these environments is astounding.

The rich human history of this region celebrated at the majority of parks in these states adds a whole other dimension to traveling in this part of the country and imbues the landscape with an air of mystery and romance. Exquisitely constructed stone villages tucked into canyon walls were built by cultures whose successors are today's Pueblo Indians. These ruins are found throughout the region and are the focus of almost a dozen parks covered in this book. Ancient cultures such as the Anasazi, Mogollon, and Hohokam came together from across the region and eventually coalesced into thriving agricultural communities along the upper Rio Grande River drainage. Here they built sprawling, freestanding stone cities that housed thousands. Many of these dwellings were occupied when the Spanish began arriving in the late 16th and early 17th centuries. The fascinating story of Spanish exploration and colonization etched on the Southwestern landscape is joined by stories of Pueblo revolts and migrations, Mexican occupation and war, the American Civil War, and the eventual settlement of the country by Euro-Americans. All make for a thrilling on-the-ground course in the history of the American West that is sure to capture the imagination of even the casual tourist.

How to Use This Book

In putting this book together I've tried to present riding options for different ability levels and kinds of bikers (road and mountain), while maintaining a focus on the natural resources and natural settings that make each park special. This means you'll find everything from a 2-mile ride on a paved trail suitable for trailers and bikes with training wheels inside a park, to a very strenuous and technical ride to a peak or overlook that encompasses an entire geographic region outside the park. As mentioned earlier, the limited acreage of many of the parks sent me searching beyond park boundaries to find bike routes. I tried to stay as close as possible to each park but in some instances a drive of a half hour or so is required to access a ride.

I have tried to include both road and mountain bike routes in each chapter. However, you will generally find more options for mountain bikers than road riders. This is due to a number of factors. First, many more people own mountain bikes these days than road bikes. Second, the undeveloped character of the country that surrounds many of the national parks in Arizona and New Mexico means there are more dirt roads and trails than paved routes. In some parks, such as Organ Pipe Cactus National Monument and Chaco Culture National Historical Park, the country is so remote that virtually all the roads are dirt. Here, a mountain bike will be your best choice for getting around. The main routes and scenic drives through other parks are almost always paved and make for great road rides. Backroads in the parks and roads accessing country surrounding the parks are usually more primitive and better suited to mountain biking. In some instances a paved scenic drive or other route is relatively short. Here I've indicated that the route is suitable for either road or mountain bikes.

Now to the heart of the matter: what's contained in this book and how to use it. Each chapter is devoted to a single park, what makes it so fascinating and special, and the road and mountain bike opportunities found there. The chapters are grouped by state and arranged in alphabetical order. Within each chapter, rides located inside the park are listed first, and those outside the park are listed last. Each grouping of rides is listed from easiest to most difficult. The size and/or geographical features of some parks have resulted in the grouping of rides that are closest to one another. These groups of rides are arranged as described above.

At the beginning of each chapter is an introduction to the park and a discussion of its historical, geologic, ecological, or archaeological significance. Please note that the term "park" is often used generically to refer to all parks, monuments, memorials, historic sites, and national recreation areas managed by the national park system.

Each chapter introduction is followed by a section titled "Cycling in the Park," in which I discuss the particular geography, climate, and other characteristics of the area and how they impact the riding experience in and around that park. I also identify its general location and difficulty, and remark on its particular attributes: "fun family ride," "great hike along the way," "fantastic overlook at the end," "takes you to a ruin," and so on. Next come the rides. After the ride descriptions you'll find a Trip Planning Appendix that provides information to help make your visit to the park as hassle-free as possible. Sidebars offer nonessential but interesting tidbits of information, such as flora and fauna present in the park, fun facts, nearby sights, a museum or ruin, good hikes, or other opportunities for exploring and learning more about the park and the region surrounding it. The Cycling Options sidebar, located somewhere near the start of each chapter, gives you a quick overview of the rides for that park.

Let's cruise through a typical ride outline:

Sample Ride

Immediately following the trail name and type comes a brief introduction to the ride. With this information you will be able to decide, at a glance, whether or not a ride is right for you and your group. Overall length of the ride, its configuration (that is, an out-and-back, a loop, a cherry-stem loop, or a point-to-point), and general comments about the highlights of the ride are all noted here. In some parks where routes are very long, you may find that a vehicle-supported or overnight trip is recommended. This does not mean that the route can't be ridden as a self-supported adventure with panniers and all the necessary gear, or that portions of the route can't be ridden in a single day. The type of trail and riding surface are also briefly referred to here (singletrack, dirt road, doubletrack; whether it is smooth, rocky, or washboarded). Level of difficulty will be identified both in terms of the physical demands and technical riding skills required. Suggestions for trail options, which may include riding shorter portions of the trail, extending it beyond the given turnaround point, riding an additional spur, or changing the configuration of the route, may also appear here.

Starting point: The exact place the ride begins will be given with instructions on how to get there if it is somewhere other than the park's main visitor center. Parking areas are also identified.

Length: The total distance in miles is listed here, sometimes with mileages for portions of the ride or optional spurs. Mileages listed are approximate—they're close to exact, but differences in the calibration of each person's cyclometer may result in slightly different readings. A rough estimate of the amount of time in hours that it will take to ride the route is also listed.

Riding surface: The trail type (singletrack, dirt road, doubletrack) and trail surface (rocky, smooth, rutted, and so on) are described under this heading.

Difficulty: Terms for difficulty include *easy, moderate, difficult*, and *strenuous*. Again, both the physical demands and technical riding ability or bike handling skills required are factored into this rating and are explained. Any other significant aspect of the ride—a long climb or a rocky surface for example—factored into the difficulty rating will also be mentioned here.

Scenery/highlights: Whatever is significant about this ride in terms of how it relates to the park's geology, history, or other natural resource is described here. Scenery, points of interest, or other relevant information is also listed. Sometimes the riding and the physical qualities of the trail are commented on, and any hikes that might be included will be noted.

Best time to ride: Here I identify the time of year and the time of day that is best for this ride. One ride in a chapter might be at a higher elevation than the others so riding it later in the spring or summer may be recommended. Spring and fall are often recommended for riding in southern deserts of Arizona and New Mexico because of the hot summer temperatures. Riding in the morning or evening is also suggested in these areas for the same reason, but also because these tend to be the times of day when wildlife is most active and light is best for viewing the scenery. You may also find that certain kinds of weather might be referred to here, like wind in the spring or thunderstorms on summer afternoons.

Special considerations: In this section you will find information designed to make your ride as safe and enjoyable as it can be. The water and rest rooms nearest the trail or trailhead are always listed here. Safety considerations relating to traffic, weather, trail surface, or anything else, are discussed here. I also remark upon the remoteness of the country, the difficulty of route-finding, or any other consideration that you should keep in mind when preparing for your ride. If there are some good hiking opportunities or particular points of interest along the route that are away from the road or trail, I will recommend that you bring a lock to secure your bike.

Directions for the ride: Here you will find a general description of the route, including its heading and changes in direction, major geographic features traversed by and seen along the route, changes in trail surface, and approximate mileages at points along the way. At the end of the ride description you will find options for amending the route.

Sidebars

Cycling options: A very brief rundown of all the rides listed in the chapter is listed in this sidebar.

Flora: Here you will find a general classification of the habitat type (such as Sonoran Desert, pinyon-juniper woodland, shortgrass prairie, and so forth), found in and around the park. Dominant tree and shrub species are listed for all habitat types, which are generally determined by elevation and the presence of water. The most common and showy wildflower species are also listed and grouped according to the time of season in which they bloom. These lists are not complete but designed to give cyclists a basic idea of what is seen in the park.

Fauna: Listed here are a number of different kinds of animals, including birds, mammals, reptiles, and amphibians. Special attention is given to species found in the park that are either endangered, endemic, or unique to the ecosystem of the region. Raptors, songbirds, hummingbirds, and other notable bird species are listed and their resident or migratory status given. These lists will give you a good idea of the fauna that resides in the park, either seasonally, occasionally, or year-round.

It's interesting to know . . . : In this sidebar you will find some tidbit of information: some historical background on the park or monument, basic information on the native peoples who formerly lived in the area, or some piece of folklore that relates to the park or history of the surrounding area.

Don't miss: Although this is a biking guide, there are hikes and other things to do and see in and around the parks that deserve your attention. A particularly spectacular hike, a beautifully constructed ruin, or a unique geologic feature not accessible by bike may be listed in this sidebar. You might also find a museum, state park, or some other entity outside the park that can provide even more insight into the resources of the park and general region.

Trip Planning Appendix

Camping: Here you will find information on park campgrounds, the facilities they offer, and the procedure for obtaining a campsite. Availability of campsites and any other pertinent information on staying and camping in the park is also listed.

Private campgrounds that have both tent and RV sites are also usually listed. Private campgrounds make a good stopover for tent campers because they often have showers and laundry facilities. I have made an effort to include private campgrounds with those types of facilities.

State parks often spring up next to national parks and can be a great alternative to camping in the park. They usually have more facilities and a greater number of sites. Where state parks are found next to national parks, information on their amenities and how to contact them is provided.

I also make suggestions for primitive camping on adjacent public lands. The agencies that manage those lands and have more information on campsites and procedures are listed at the end of each chapter under "Further information."

Please note: Because prices for campsites both inside and outside the national parks tend to fluctuate, no rates are given.

Lodging: I've provided very basic information about the kinds and locations of lodging options in the area surrounding the park or monument. Chain hotels, motels, B&Bs, and a few out-of-the-way lodges are listed. These are not complete lists; for a more thorough description of your choices you will need to visit the local chamber of commerce or visitor center.

Food: The dining options listed are similarly basic. I make suggestions for where to find a good cup of coffee and a good breakfast, and different kinds of food, be it Mexican, Chinese, continental, steaks, and so on. Again, a more complete list will be available at the local chamber of commerce or visitor center.

Laundry: The closest place to do a load of laundry is listed. Private campgrounds often have laundry facilities, but they're usually reserved for paying guests.

Bike shop/bike rental: Here you will find a listing of the nearest bike shops, an indication of which shops rent, and what specialties they might have (some shops are more devoted to road riders than mountain bikers or vice-versa). While any of these shops should be able to take care of basic repairs and gear needs it is always a good idea to call ahead to make sure there is someone there to help you and they have what you need. Business hours for shops are not listed because they tend to change seasonally.

For further information: Here you will find how to contact the park and obtain any park-related information, as well as the address and phone numbers of nearby chambers of commerce and visitor centers. You will also find a list of public land management agencies that oversee surrounding lands.

Remember, it is always best to supplement this, or any guidebook, with topographic maps and to use a compass when adventuring outside park boundaries. Riding a bike is an activity that has inherent risks; use your best judgement, always wear a helmet, and don't overdo it your first day out. Don't forget to play by the rules: stay on designated roads and trails, do not climb on or disturb archaeological sites, and never remove any naturally occurring or archaeological object from federal lands. Federal fines and penalties are routinely assessed for these types of violations, most of which occur unwittingly. We're not just visitors, we're also part owners of America's parks and monuments and we need to help the many dedicated folks who manage them do the best job they can do. Give them your input and let them know you are there as a cyclist and as a caring member of the populace the parks are designed to benefit.

Visiting and riding in and around our national parks is an incredible opportunity for a rewarding learning experience. Take your time, take some pictures (or maybe just mental snapshots), and leave only tire tracks. You'll be sure to gain a wealth of memories that you'll treasure for a lifetime. Happy trails!

Part One ARIZONA

1

CHIRICAHUA NATIONAL MONUMENT

Located at the northern end of the Chiricahua Mountain Range in the southeastern corner of Arizona lies a fantastic display of sculpted stone pinnacles, pedestals, and balanced rocks celebrated and protected inside Chiricahua National Monument. Chiricahua (pronounced "chee-ree-KAW-wah") is an Apache word meaning "Land of the Standing-up Rocks" and was the homeland of the Chiricahua Apache, some of the very last Native Americans to submit to reservation life.

These mountains are as wild and rugged as they are beautiful, rising over 5,000 feet above surrounding desert valleys. Like other isolated mountain ranges in southern Arizona, the lofty peaks and ridges of the Chiricahua Mountains are referred to as a "sky island." The cooler, wetter conditions found at higher elevations and the constant water supply coursing through the lush canyon bottoms have created a rich variety of habitats for bird and wildlife species, some of which are more commonly found south of the border in Mexico. The harsh, dry desert that surrounds the Chiricahuas has acted like a castle moat over the eons, keeping exotic predators out while sheltering plants and animals unique to these mountains.

The story of the incredible rock formations found inside the monument began 25 to 30 million years ago during a period of dramatic volcanic eruptions. Nearby Turkey Creek Caldera is thought to have been the source of much of the extremely hot ash that spewed out across the landscape in at least eight major volcanic events more violent than anything witnessed in recent times. Glowing avalanches of superheated ash swept downhill in great torrents. As the ash came to rest it fused together into a type of rock referred to as *welded tuff*—the rock responsible for the monument's formations. More ash rained down out of the clouds produced by the eruption, but much of this was cooler and did not bond together as firmly, creating weaker layers that would later play a role in the formation of the pillars.

The sculpting of the magnificent totem pole–like pillars in the monument began later, after a period of mountain building in the region, and has taken place almost exclusively in an 880-foot-thick layer of rock that was laid down in a single eruption. Wind and water have worked with cycles of freezing and thawing, seeking out and widening tiny fissures and cracks existing between poorly consolidated rock layers. Vertical cracks have also been created by shifting faults beneath the mountains. Differences in the hardness of the layers have enabled erosional forces to create the interesting shapes and textures of the pillars. Wind puts on most of the finishing touches and is the principle sculptor in the creation of the many balanced rocks found in the monument. These forests of standing rocks are fascinating and can delight the imagination for hours. The gorgeous mountain scenery, rich natural environments, lack of crowds, and astonishing variety of bird life all help to make a visit to the Chiricahuas and the surrounding country an unforgettable experience.

Cycling in the Park

Although the monument itself is quite small and bikes are limited to one paved road, the beautiful canyons of the Chiricahua Mountains, the forest service roads that access ridge-top vistas, and pretty foothills surrounding the monument, all offer excellent biking opportunities. Both mountain and road bikers shouldn't pass up the chance to pedal through Bonita Canyon to Massai Point inside the monument. This route climbs just over 1,200 feet, among fanciful rock pillars and spires, to gain fantastic views of the Chiracahuas and surrounding countryside. The Pinery Canyon Loop just outside the monument is a wonderful excursion for mountain bikers into cool mountain altitudes. This route climbs to a high saddle and loops around several lower peaks and is suitable for mountain bikers of all abilities in excellent physical condition. The pedal up Cave Creek Canyon is an easy to moderate ride that both mountain and road bikers will enjoy. This canyon is a fantastically scenic area featuring a lush riparian woodland, towering cliffs, and great views to surrounding peaks. The Portal-Paradise Loop and the ride up Whitetail Creek provide more excellent opportunities for exploring by mountain bike and are a good introduction to the mining history of the area. More serious road riders won't want to miss the pedal out across the Sulphur Springs Valley described in the Cochise Magic Circle ride. Three different route choices, including one that is almost a century, provide options for all levels of riders.

While the highest altitudes of the Chiricahua Mountains receive snow in the winter and remain much cooler than the valley floor below in summer, it can still get broiling hot in this part of Arizona. Daytime temperatures frequently flirt with the century mark during the summer months, when the air can become sticky with humidity moving north from the Gulf of Mexico. Moisture high in the atmosphere begins affecting weather patterns in early July and regularly causes daily thunderstorms that can lash these peaks with heavy rains, high winds, and lightning. Be aware of weather forecasts while in these mountains and if afternoon thunderstorms are

A cyclist begins the ride up Bonita Canyon from the park entrance station.

predicted plan to be off high or exposed places and near shelter by late in the day. Dirt roads and trails can become muddy and slick with heavy rains and should be avoided until they can dry out. Fall and spring are the nicest time of year to visit and ride, and is also the time when the greatest variety of resident and migrant birds are present. The Chiricahuas are world famous among avid birdwatchers for the many neotropical species that visit from south of the border. Daytime temperatures can reach into the 60s during the winter months but at night usually dip to right around freezing. If there has been rain or snow, freezing nighttime temperatures can often leave patches of ice or snow on the roads.

Another thing to consider when heading out to this corner of Arizona is that conveniences are few and far between. Camping is a good idea, as it will alleviate the need for spending hours in the car each day driving back and forth to your hotel. Even if you just plan to spend the day, come prepared with plenty of food, drinks, water, and extra clothing. This will ensure that you stay comfortable and refreshed throughout the day no matter what you decide to do. Driving between points may be farther than you think; make sure your gas tank is full. Also, because bike shops are scarce your bike should be in good working order before heading out this way. Always carry a pump, spare tubes, and enough tools to make a few basic repairs.

---

1. BONITA CANYON (See map on page 35)

For road or mountain bikes. The ride up Bonita Canyon on the monument's only paved road provides a tour of the beautifully sculpted rock pillars for which this park is famous. This route climbs steadily for 6 miles, from the visitor center to the end of the road at Massai Point, gaining just over 1,200 feet. Riders of all levels of experience in good to excellent condition will enjoy this wonderfully scenic ride.

Starting point: Monument visitor center.

Length: 6 miles one-way, 12 miles total distance. Add one mile to your total distance if you ride the spur out to Sugarloaf Mountain Trailhead and Picnic Area. Allow at least 3 hours to complete this ride. For a

1 · Bonita Canyon

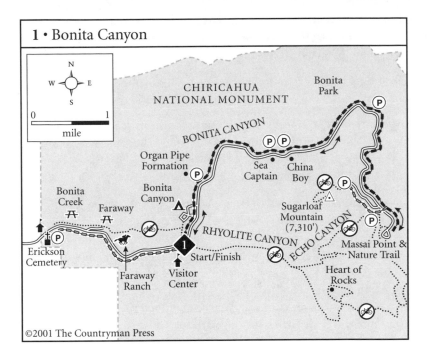

N
W E
S

0   1
mile

CHIRICAHUA
NATIONAL MONUMENT

Bonita
Park

BONITA CANYON

Organ Pipe
Formation

Sea
Captain

China
Boy

Bonita Creek

Faraway

Bonita
Canyon

Sugarloaf
Mountain
(7,310')

RHYOLITE CANYON

ECHO CANYON

Massai Point &
Nature Trail

Erickson
Cemetery

Faraway
Ranch

Visitor
Center

Start/Finish

Heart of
Rocks

©2001 The Countryman Press

slightly longer ride, start pedaling from the pullout just across from the park entrance station and ride the 2 miles of rolling terrain from the mouth of the canyon to the visitor center.

Riding surface: Pavement; rough in spots.

Difficulty: Moderate to difficult. The gain in elevation and length of the climb make this route more challenging.

Scenery/highlights: Bonita Canyon, as the name suggests, is wonderfully scenic, however some of the best views of the pinnacles can be had by taking a few hours to walk one of the many trails that can be accessed from the main road and from the Sugarloaf Mountain spur near the end of Bonita Canyon Drive. Echo Canyon and Heart of Rocks are two of the most popular trails. You might also want to get a bird's-eye view of the monument from Sugarloaf Mountain. It's a quick 1.8 miles to the top— the monument's highest point at 7,310 feet. Views from here are superb. The trail up Sugarloaf can be accessed from the end of the spur road that is near the end of the ride. Bring a bike lock and a trail map (available at the visitor center) if you are interested in hiking among the pinnacles or to the top of Sugarloaf Mountain.

Best time to ride: Fall through spring. Be aware of icy spots on the road in winter.

Special considerations: Water and rest rooms can be found at the visitor center. The road is narrow and winding; please use caution. Also, keep an eye out for wildlife—it is not uncommon to see wild turkeys, deer, and other creatures dashing across the road.

Directions for the ride: To begin this ride, simply go right out of the parking lot at the visitor center and begin pedaling in a north-northeast direction. In approximately 0.6 mile you will come to the short spur road accessing Bonita Canyon Campground. Past the campground the route enters Bonita Canyon, where stands of whimsical rock pillars begin to appear. A pullout on your left 0.4 mile past the campground lets you take a gander upward at the Organ Pipe Formation. In another 0.5 mile the road swings to the right and heads east up the canyon. Approximately 1.3 miles past the Organ Pipe you will come to the first of two pullouts; both are on the left side of the road. At the first turn and look down and across the canyon to a formation known as the Sea Captain. At the second, 0.2 mile beyond, look in the same direction to another known as the China Boy.

The road climbs more steeply over the next 1.3 miles before making a sweeping turn and heading south. At the elbow of this turn is another pullout offering views north to Bonita Park and beyond to Dos Cabezas Peaks. From here it is another 2.2 miles to the end of the road at Massai Point. (About 0.5 mile before you reach the end of the road you will come to the spur road on the right leading to the Sugarloaf Mountain Trailhead and Picnic Area. A few hundred yards along this spur is the trailhead for the Echo Canyon Trail and a picnic area. At the end of the spur road is the trail that leads to the top of Sugarloaf Mountain.) Continue out to Massai Point (6,870 feet), take a break, and enjoy your surroundings. When you're done having a look around or have finished with your hike along the short Massai Point Nature Trail, saddle up and head back down the way you came.

A view of the eastern slope of the Chiricahua Mountains and the buttes flanking the mouth of Cave Creek Canyon.

2. PINERY CANYON LOOP (See map on page 38)

For mountain bikes. This route is a wonderfully scenic tour of one of the Chiricahua Mountains' most beautiful canyons while looping around rock formations that offer clues to the geologic history of the region. Total distance for this cherry-stem loop is approximately 14.5 miles. An alternate starting point near the entrance to the monument will let super-fit riders add another 11 miles of easy, undulating terrain. Beginner to advanced riders in good to excellent physical condition will love this ride.

Starting point: The intersection of Forest Road (FR) 42, the Pinery Canyon Road, and FR 356. Park at a pullout or at a nearby campground. To get there go south on the Pinery Canyon Road from where it leaves the pavement 0.1 mile before the monument entrance station and drive 5.5 miles to the starting point.

Length: 14.5 miles total distance. Allow 4 hours to complete this ride.

Riding surface: Gravel and dirt road. Some are graded and maintained while other sections are rocky.

2 • Pinery Canyon Loop
3 • Cave Creek Canyon
4 • Portal-Paradise Loop
5 • Whitetail Creek

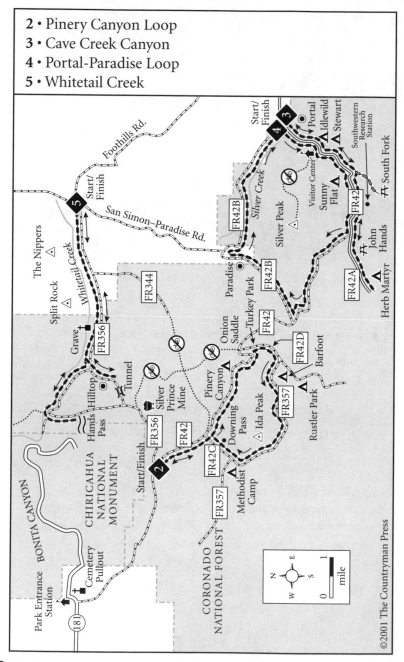

©2001 The Countryman Press

Difficulty: Although the riding surface isn't technical (for the most part), the sustained climbs and almost 2,000 feet of elevation gain make this ride more difficult. A short rocky section on the way down requires some technical riding skills.

Scenery/highlights: Pinery Canyon is gorgeous and the views along the way are fantastic. The broad mouth of this canyon is open, grassy terrain dotted with the rounded shapes of piñon and juniper trees. Farther up the canyon cottonwoods, sycamores, and large oaks grace the banks of Pinery Creek. These trees, characteristically found in riparian areas of upper Sonoran life zones, give way to ponderosa, Chihuahua, and yellow pine as you get higher. Near Onion Saddle fir and spruce are present.

Views on the way up are equally astounding. The basin-and-range geologic province, characterized by small, isolated mountain ranges and broad valleys, stretches away to the west. Neighboring "sky islands," including Dos Cabezas, the Swisshelms, and Dragoon Mountains, encircle the sprawling Sulphur Springs Valley. The rocky heads of Dos Cabezas and the jagged ridgeline of Cochise Stronghold in the Dragoons are some of the most prominent landmarks in the region.

This area was the home range of Chiricahua Apache. The infamous Apache warrior and medicine man Geronimo was a Chiricahua Apache, and countless attacks and raids were launched from the safe haven of these mountains. The Apaches fought long and hard for their freedom and their land and were some of the very last Native American tribes to submit to reservation life.

Best time to ride: Spring and fall.

Special considerations: Private property exists on either side of Pinery Canyon Road; please stay on the main road until reaching the start of this ride. Go prepared with plenty of your own water and snacks.

Directions for the ride: From the intersection of FR 356 and FR 42 ride almost due south on FR 42, following the road as it ascends Pinery Canyon. FR 356 follows the North Fork of Pinery Canyon and is the old road leading to the Silver Prince Mine. At 1.9 miles from the start you will encounter FR 42C coming in on the right. This is where you will finish the loop portion of this ride. To your left, a hiking trail heads north, up Horsefall Canyon. Continue past this intersection as FR 42 (also called

One of many species of agave found growing in the foothills of the Chiricahuas.

the Pinery Canyon Road) climbs more steeply, making several switchbacks as it nears Onion Saddle (7,600 feet). Arrive at Onion Saddle 3.8 miles from the intersection with FR 42C and almost 6 miles from the start. Near the saddle is Pinery Canyon Campground, a beautiful spot that is a nice, cool place to stay during the warmer months.

At Onion Saddle look for FR 42D, signed for Turkey Park and Rustler Park. Go right onto this road, heading south for approximately 1.3 miles to FR 357. Go right onto FR 357 and head west, downhill. In a few hundred yards you will pass a fire lookout on your right; Buena Vista Peak and Rattlesnake Peak are ahead of you, Ida Peak is to your right. The road drops steeply and becomes rocky in spots before descending into the top of Pine Canyon. Descend through Pine Canyon for 4.5 miles before reaching the rustic buildings of a Methodist camp. Just past the Methodist camp is another intersection. Go right onto FR 42C, climbing up and over Downing Pass before dropping into Pinery Canyon. This last push over Downing Pass is 1.1 mile in length. Along this last stretch you'll ride by some beautiful rocky outcrops formed during the volcanic explosions responsible for the pillars inside Chiricahua National

Monument. When you reach Pinery Canyon Road (FR 42), go left and ride the 1.9 miles back to your car.

Option #1: If you would like to make this ride longer, begin at the pullout near the monument's entrance station. Riding from this starting point will add approximately 11 miles to your total ride distance.

Option #2: If you are feeling super adventurous, or have a shuttle driver that is willing to drive around to pick you up, you may wish to continue on FR 42 down the east side of the mountains into Cave Creek Canyon to the small settlement of Portal 12 miles distant.

---

3. CAVE CREEK CANYON (See map on page 38)

For road bikes. This ride is a delightful pedal up one of the prettiest canyons in Arizona. Riders of all abilities should try this moderate, 14-mile route that features towering cliffs pocked with caves, pinnacles, and a riparian corridor that supports a dazzling array of bird species. This route gains approximately 1,700 feet in elevation by the time it ends at the boundary of the Chiricahua Wilderness.

Starting point: Portal, Arizona, on the east side of the Chiricahua Mountains. To get there from the monument go north and west on AZ 186 for 36 miles to the town of Willcox. Go east on I-10 for 42 miles to Exit 382, about 2 miles past the town of San Simon. Go south on the mostly gravel San Simon Paradise Road (also called the Portal Road) for 18 miles. Bear left onto Foothills Road, following the signs for Portal when the road splits. It is 5 more miles to Portal.

Length: 7 miles one-way, 14 miles total distance. An additional 1.5-mile spur that accesses the South Fork Campground will give you a total distance of 15.5 miles. Allow at least 3 hours to complete this ride and enjoy your surroundings.

Riding surface: Pavement. The road is narrow and in poor condition in some spots.

Difficulty: Moderate. The increase in elevation makes this ride more difficult.

FLORA

Because of the Chiricahua's location at the margins of both the Sonoran and Chihuahuan Deserts, elevations that range between 4,000 and 9,400 feet, and a fairly even distribution of moisture throughout the year, a unique mosaic of biomes or habitats has evolved. These habitats include riparian forest, which form a corridor along the range's year-round and intermittent streams, desert grassland, oak woodland or encinal woodland, chaparral, madrean woodland, and conifer forest. The riparian forests of the canyon bottoms include large, stately trees such as the Arizona black walnut, Arizona sycamore, Fremont cottonwood, and velvet ash. The Arizona cypress and several varieties of oaks, including the Arizona white, Emory, silverleaf, wavyleaf, and netleaf are also found here. Other trees you might see include the eastern redbud and American elm. In the drier desert grassland areas away from water sources you'll find a mix of grasses and shrubs as well as agave, banana yucca, Schott's yucca, prickly pear, cholla, and hedgehog cactus. In the slightly higher oak woodland areas you'll find a variety of grasses plus piñons, junipers, and Emory, Arizona, and Mexican blue oaks. Chaparral—a mix of plant species, including one-seed juniper, mountain mahogany, and pointleaf manzanita—tends to dominate on steep slopes. Madrean woodlands are characterized by the presence of Arizona madrone trees but also include Mexican piñon; Arizona, netleaf, and silverleaf oaks; Chihuahua and Apache pines; and alligator junipers. At the highest elevations of the Chiricahuas you will find coniferous forests that include Arizona pine, southwestern white pine, Douglas fir, and Gambel oak.

Scenery/highlights: Cave Creek Canyon is absolutely gorgeous. Tall deciduous trees, including Arizona sycamore, Arizona walnut, velvet ash, Emory oak, and Fremont cottonwood, line a year-round stream that sends its burbling melody skyward to dance among towering cliffs. The deep canyon shadows are cool on a hot day and offer shelter for a stunning variety of birds and animals. This canyon is legendary among avid birdwatchers who come to catch a glimpse of the prized elegant trogon, a native of Mexico who is a seasonal resident of these canyons. Several species of hummingbirds who also live most of the year south of the border can also be seen here.

Along the way you will pass the American Museum of Natural History's Southwestern Research Station, a facility where scientists and students study the creatures and ecology of this unique desert environment. Several enticing campgrounds are also scattered throughout the canyon.

Best time to ride: Spring and fall. This deep canyon is shady and stays somewhat cooler during the summer. The road sometimes closes in winter due to snow. If you do attempt a wintertime ride, be careful of icy spots that can develop in the shadows.

Special considerations: While there is a small lodge with a café and a store in Portal, it is best to come prepared with a full tank of gas and a cooler of drinks, water, and food. Bring any bike supplies you might need. Conveniences are few and far between in this lonesome, high-desert country.

There is a forest service information and visitor center located 1.5 miles up the canyon from Portal. Water and rest rooms are available here.

Directions for the ride: From Portal, simply ride west on the Cave Creek Canyon Road (FR 42). The first few miles are some of the most spectacular. Approximately 1.5 miles from Portal you will come to the forest service visitor center (open from Easter through Labor Day) where you can get information on your surroundings, a weather report, and the history of the area. Approximately 1.5 miles past the visitor center the road forks; to the left the road follows the South Fork of Cave Creek to South Fork Campground. This is a very pretty 3-mile side trip that is well worth the effort.

To the right the road continues up Cave Creek Canyon. Open meadows splashed with sunlight give way to the leafy canopies of sycamores and cottonwoods. Two miles past the fork in the road you will find a collection of buildings belonging to the American Museum of Natural History's Southwestern Research Station. Just past the research station FR 42 turns to dirt and begins its climb to Onion Saddle and beyond, to

A cyclist on the return trip from Massai Point coasts down through Bonita Canyon.

Pinery Canyon and the west side of the range. Continue pedaling onward, up the paved road, now labeled FR 42A, another 2 miles to where it ends at the Herb Martyr Campground at the Chiricahua Wilderness boundary. Take a break, a good drink of water, and a moment to enjoy your surroundings. When you are ready to head back simply ride back the way you came.

---

4. PORTAL-PARADISE LOOP (See map on page 38)

For mountain bikes. This loop route begins in Portal, heads up the spectacularly scenic Cave Creek Canyon, then turns north and descends along Turkey Creek to the small town of Paradise. The route loops back to Portal, making a complete circuit of Silver Peak. Novice- to advanced-level riders in good to excellent physical should have little trouble on this route which presents few technical riding challenges but climbs 1,600 feet in elevation.

Starting point: Portal, Arizona, on the east side of the Chiricahua Mountains. To get there from the monument go north and west on AZ 186 for 36 miles to the town of Willcox. Go east on I-10 for 42 miles to

Exit 382, about 2 miles past the town of San Simon. Go south on the mostly gravel San Simon–Paradise Road (also called the Portal Road) for 18 miles. Bear left onto Foothills Road, following the signs for Portal when the road splits. It is 5 more miles to Portal.

Length: 17 miles total distance. Allow 4 to 5 hours to complete this loop.

Riding surface: 4 miles of pavement, graded dirt and gravel roads on the remainder.

Difficulty: Moderate. Although the riding surface doesn't require many bike handling skills, the distance and elevation gain require a good base of physical fitness.

Scenery/highlights: The scenery, bird and animal life, and remote nature of this area combine to make a day pedaling this route really enjoyable. Cave Creek Canyon, the historic mining towns of Paradise and Portal, and the excellent views to Silver Peak, the Portal Peaks, and the broad, lonely San Simon Valley are wonderful.

Best time to ride: Spring and fall when temperatures are more moderate. You can ride this route year-round, although you're likely to roast in summer. The dirt and gravel sections of this route can become impassable any time due to mud.

Special considerations: While there is a small lodge with a café and a store in Portal, it is best to come prepared to this area with a full tank of gas; a cooler of drinks, food, and plenty of water; and any bike supplies you might need.

Water and rest rooms are available at the forest service information and visitor center located 1.5 miles up the canyon from Portal.

Directions for the ride: From Portal ride west, up Cave Creek Canyon on FR 42. The forest service visitor center, housed in a historic 1920s home, will come up on your right 1.5 miles from the start. In another 1.5 miles the road forks; the left fork accesses South Fork Campground. Stay right and continue pedaling up Cave Creek Canyon. In 2 miles you will come to a collection of buildings belonging to the American Museum of Natural History's Southwestern Research Station.

Just past the research station FR 42 branches right, off the main Cave Creek Canyon Road, and turns to gravel. From here the road continues

Sculpted out of soft volcanic rock by wind, weather, and time, the pillars in Chiricahua National Monument come in many fascinating shapes.

to climb for another 4 miles until reaching Turkey Creek and the road to Paradise. Go right onto FR 42B and descend along Turkey Creek for approximately 3 miles to the historic mining town of Paradise. Have a quick look around as you slide through town heading north, and then go right onto FR 42B as it continues on to Portal. The views across the San Simon Valley, up to Silver Peak, and to the cliffs in Cave Creek Canyon as you approach Portal are great. In approximately 5 miles you will reach the town of Portal where you might want to stop in at the store or café and slake your thirst.

---

5. WHITETAIL CREEK (See map on page 38)

For mountain bikes. This up-and-back route is a more demanding mountain bike adventure that will reward you with great scenery, views, and a visit to an old ghost town with an amazing story. It begins on the east side of the Chiricahua range and ends close to the monument boundary. Intermediate to advanced riders in good condition are best suited to this ride, however, route options exist for both the less experienced and long distance rider.

FAUNA

This area is renowned for the colorful feathered celebrities that visit during the warmer months. The most famous is the elegant trogon, a neotropical summer resident who prefers the canyons' dry oak and pine forests. Parrotlike in shape and about 12 inches long, the males have bright red breast feathers and green feathers on their back; coppery highlights can be seen on the tail. Their call is a distinctive series of short, odd croaking sounds.

Other notable Chiricahua visitors include three varieties of hummingbirds: the blue-throated, black-chinned, and magnificent. Songbirds include dusky-capped and sulphur-bellied flycatchers, solitary vireos, hepatic tanagers, northern and Scott's orioles, rufous-sided towhees, Bewick's wren, yellow-eyed junco, and Virginia's, black-throated gray, Grace's, and redfaced warblers. Whip-poor-wills, scaled and Montezuma quail, whiskered and western screech-owls, and several varieties of hawks also make their home here. The visitor center has a bird list for the monument, as well as a good selection of field guides.

Mountain lions, black bears, and bobcats are all residents of the Chiricahua but are rarely seen. More commonly seen are white-tailed deer, cliff chipmunks, cottontail rabbits, rock squirrels, and the endemic Chiricahua fox squirrel. Secretive coatimundi, ringtail cats, and raccoons do most of their foraging at night. Javelina also make their home here, as do striped and hog-nosed skunks.

Lizards are some of the most commonly seen wildlife in the monument. Less commonly seen are the black-tailed and banded rock rattlesnakes. Given the chance, they are happy to slither out of your path. The nonpoisonous Sonoran mountain kingsnake is brightly banded black, red, and yellow, and is strikingly similar to the poisonous coral snake not found here. The Chiricahua leopard frog is another rare endemic species that has evolved in isolation in these mountains.

Starting point: The San Simon–Paradise Road and FR 356. To get there from the monument go north and west on AZ 186 for 36 miles to the town of Willcox. Go east on I-10 for 42 miles to Exit 382, about 2 miles past the town of San Simon. Go south on the mostly gravel San Simon–Paradise Road (also called the Portal Road) for 18 miles to where the road divides; the left fork goes to Portal and the right fork goes to Paradise. Bear right. Almost immediately after this intersection will be a road on the right signed for Whitetail Creek. This is FR 356. Park here.

Length: 8 miles each way, 16 miles total distance. Allow 3 to 4 hours for this ride.

Riding surface: Dirt road, steep and rocky in places beyond Hilltop.

Difficulty: Moderate to difficult. Several steep, loose, rocky sections will require some technical riding skills. The 1,000-foot elevation gain also adds an element of difficulty.

Scenery/highlights: A short spur takes you to the ghost town of Hilltop, an old mining town 5 miles up Whitetail Canyon Road (FR 356) from the main road. The tiny town of Hilltop actually existed at two different sites. The original location of the town was on the northwest flank of Shaw Peak (7,730 feet), the mountain that dominates the view to your left as you head west. In 1917 a mile-long tunnel was excavated through the mountain, allowing for the town and mine operations to be moved to their present site.

The new location was a better town site and deemed more practical for ore transportation. At the original site, near the southwest end of the tunnel, stood a machine shop, the superintendent's house, and a handful of other buildings that were dismantled and taken through the tunnel piece by piece. The buildings further down in the canyon are what remains of the residential section of Hilltop. Some of the buildings are still in use. The finest among these is the former mine superintendent's home, moved through the mountain in three parts.

Whitetail Canyon is another favorite locale of birdwatchers who come to this corner of Arizona annually to observe its feathered celebrities.

Best time to ride: Spring through fall.

Special considerations: There is a lodge, café, and small store in Portal where you can find drinks and a rest room, but otherwise you will find little in the way of conveniences out here. It's best to come prepared with plenty of your own water and supplies, including any you might need for your bike.

Directions for the ride: From the intersection of the San Simon–Paradise Road and FR 356 pedal west, toward the mountains. To your right as head up Whitetail Canyon are a number of rock formations known as the Nippers. Split Rock is the most distinctive of these formations. Much of the land on either side of the road for the first 5 miles is private property so please be considerate and stay on the road. The first 4 miles of the route crosses open, grassy terrain, providing great views in all directions. As you enter the canyon the road begins to climb more steeply.

Approximately 4 miles from the start you will come to an old grave-yard where miners who toiled long hours in dangerous conditions undoubtedly lie. Another mile up the road a 0.5-mile spur to the left leads to the old town of Hilltop. These buildings are also on private property; please do not enter or disturb anything you might find lying around these structures.

Past the spur to Hilltop, continue to climb through the heart of the canyon, reaching an intersection 2 miles later. FR 356 goes left here, heading due south, continuing to climb toward Hands Pass before dropping into Pinery Canyon on the west side of range. Straight ahead the road continues for only another 0.5 mile before ending at the monument boundary. Continue to the left for 2 more miles on FR 356 up to Hands Pass where you can enjoy commanding views in all directions.

Option #1: If you're short on time and you would like to shorten this ride, simply pedal as far as the old town of Hilltop and return, giving you a total distance of approximately 11 miles.

Option #2: If you are up for a day-long distance adventure and have the strength and stamina to make it enjoyable, consider continuing on FR 356 past Hands Pass, dropping into Pinery Canyon, passing the old town site and workings of the abandoned Silver Prince mine on your way, and heading back up over to the east side of the range via FR 42 and Onion Saddle. From Onion Saddle descend almost 3 miles to where FR 42B heads down Turkey Creek. In 3 miles you come to the small town of Paradise, and 6 miles beyond that you arrive at the intersection where you left your car. This entire loop gives you a ride distance of nearly 30 miles.

6 . COCHISE MAGIC CIRCLE (See map on page 51)

For road bikes. The broad expanse of Sulphur Springs Valley, rimmed by the Dos Cabezas, Chiricahua, Mule, and Dragoon Mountains, is the setting for this road ride which is well suited to those who like empty roads and wide open spaces. This route can actually be broken down into three rides—a near-century (approximately 92 miles), a 73-mile ride, and a 30-mile ride. These options are offered as the Magic Circle Bike Challenge every fall by the Willcox Chamber of Commerce and are sure to please road riders of all abilities.

Starting point: Begin this ride, whichever version of it you plan to do, in the town of Willcox, just off I-10. You many want to park and ride from Keller Park on Bisbee Avenue just off AZ 186 near the interstate, or park near a restaurant or convenience store where you can get a cold drink when you're through.

Length: The longest option here is approximately 92 miles (allow 6 to 8 hours), the intermediate distance is 73 miles (5 hours), and the shortest option is 30 miles (3 hours).

Riding surface: Pavement.

Difficulty: Moderate to very strenuous—you choose. There is one climb up to the settlement of Dos Cabezas that is included in all three routes. Despite the level terrain along most of the ride, elevations in this part of Arizona are quite high. Elevations range between 4,100 and 5,500 feet, which adds an element of difficulty.

Scenery/highlights: The sweeping views of the mountains, rambling open country, and empty roads make these routes a road rider's delight.

Best time to ride: Road riding in this country is ideal in spring and fall, when the temperatures are more moderate.

Special considerations: Water and rest rooms can be found in Willcox, at the monument, and in the town of Sunizona along the way. There are very few bike shops in this neck of the woods so come prepared. The nearest shop able to service a road rider's needs is more than an hour away in Sierra Vista, but you might try the family bike shop in Benson.

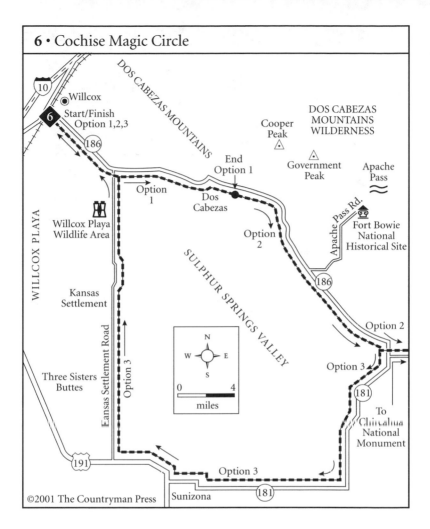

6 · Cochise Magic Circle

If you are riding the shortest option offered here, simply ride out of Willcox in a southeasterly direction on AZ 186. For the first 10 miles you will glide across the valley floor until reaching the toe of the Dos Cabezas Mountains. The road climbs gently for the next couple of miles, but then gets steeper as you near the settlement of Dos Cabezas. After approximately 15 miles of climbing you will reach this small settlement. This is your turnaround point; simply reverse direction and go back the way you came.

Remnants of adobe walls are all that remain of Fort Bowie, an important outpost during the Apache campaigns and settlement of the Southwest.

For the intermediate-length ride, follow directions as above but continue past the settlement of Dos Cabezas for 8 miles, climbing, then descending, then climbing slightly again before passing the turnoff for Apache Pass and Fort Bowie National Historical Site. It is another 9 miles to AZ 181 and the turnoff for Chiricahua National Monument. Go left and ride another 4.5 miles to the monument visitor center, where you can fill your water bottles and rest up before heading back the way you came.

The longest route follows the same directions as above but continues past the turnoff for the monument, heading south on AZ 181. Continue on this heading, skirting the western flank of the Chiricahua Mountains, for approximately 11.5 miles to where AZ 181 makes a 90-degree turn to the right and heads due west. Continue heading west back across Sulphur Springs Valley for 13 miles until you come to the town of Sunizona. Approximately 2 miles past Sunizona you will intersect AZ 191. Go right onto AZ 191, riding for approximately 6 miles to Kansas Settlement Road. Go right onto this road, now pedaling due north. You will ride past Three Sisters Buttes, and reach Kansas Settlement 12.5 miles from where you turned off AZ 191. From Kansas Settlement it is another 10 miles to AZ 186. Go left onto AZ 186 and ride a final 7 miles back to the town of Willcox. Congratulations! You made it!

CAMPING

Bonita Canyon Campground is the only campground in the monument. There you will find 25 campsites managed on a first-come, first-served basis. This one is equipped with flush toilets, water, and picnic tables. There are no hook-ups or showers. A per-night fee is required.

There are many semideveloped campgrounds in nearby Coronado National Forest, several in Pinery Canyon, only a few minutes from the monument. Most of these have vault toilets and fire pits but little else. Inquire about camping on national forest lands in the Chiricahua Mountains at the Douglas Ranger District office in Douglas, Arizona.

RV parks with hook-ups for campers can be found in Willcox, 36 miles north of the monument. The **Magic Circle RV Park** has space for both tenters and RVs and has showers and a swimming pool. **Lifestyle RV Park** (622 N. Haskell Avenue) has an indoor pool and spa, fitness center, restaurant, laundry, and showers.

Both of these are just north of I-10 off exit 40. There are a handful of others in town, call or stop by the chamber of commerce to find out more. RV parks can also be found in the small town of Sunsites, about 35 miles west of the monument, or in Douglas, 50 miles to the south.

LODGING

You will find a good selection of hotels and motels near exit 340 just off the interstate in Willcox, among them **Best Western, Days Inn, Motel 6, Super 8,** and several smaller, non-chain motels. If you're looking for something different, try the **Sunglow Guest Ranch** (520-824-3334 or www.soarizona.com/sunglow), just 10 miles south of the monument. They have weekly rates, kitchenettes, meals, and even horse rentals. The **Cave Creek Ranch** on the east side of the range offers cabins right on the banks of Cave Creek just outside the town of Portal. The managers are noted naturalists who can answer any questions you might have or even take you on guided bird-watching excursions. You can call them at 520-558-2334, visit their website at www. cavecreekranch.com/, or e-mail them at info@cave-creekranch.com. The **Portal Peak Lodge,** located in Portal, has rooms, a café, and a store where you can buy picnic provisions, beer, and birding guides. You can find them at www.portalproductions.com/portalpeaklodge/ or call 520-558-2223.

FOOD

There is no place to buy food at the monument. Your best bet for buying a meal is in the town of Willcox, where there are at least a dozen restaurants. Although most are fast food, you can get a sit-down Mexican or American meal at the **Plaza Restaurant** (1190 W. Rex Allen Drive) or a more up-scale dining experience at the **Solarium Restaurant,** inside the Best Western Plaza Inn. The **Regal Restaurant** (301 N. Haskell Avenue), in downtown Willcox, is another option.

LAUNDRY

Laundromats aren't plentiful in these small towns. The only self-service laundry in Willcox is **A.E.'s Laundromat,** 174 S. Haskell Avenue; 520-384-2251.

BIKE SHOP/BIKE RENTAL

There are a couple of good bike shops in the town of Sierra Vista, and a small one in Benson, but those are an hour or more away from the monument. It is best to have your bike in good working order when you visit this remote corner of Arizona, and to have a few spare tubes and a basic tool kit that can get you by in a pinch.

FOR FURTHER INFORMATION

Chiricahua National Monument—Superintendent, Fort Bowie National Historical Site, Dos Cabezas Route Box 6500, Willcox, AZ 85643; 520-824-3560; http://www.nps.gov/chir/

Coronado National Forest, Douglas Ranger District, 3081 N. Leslie Canyon Road, Douglas, AZ 85607; 520-364-3468

Cochise Visitor Center & Willcox Chamber of Commerce, at AZ 186 and Circle I Road, 1500 N. Circle I Road, Willcox, AZ 85643; 520-384-2272 or 1-800-200-2272; http://www.pinkbanana.com/willcoxchamber

IT'S INTERESTING TO KNOW . . .

For several hundred years the Chiricahua Mountains were home to several loosely affiliated bands of Apache Indians, who came together under pressure from settlers wanting their land. They eventually became known as the Chiricahua Apache.

Apache Indians are Athabascan-speaking peoples who are thought to have migrated into the Southwest from the north about the time Columbus landed in the New World. Fourteen distinct Apache tribes are recognized; they share many of their customs and religious world-views with the Navajo of the Four Corners area. The Apache were traditionally a seminomadic people who gathered wild plants and hunted game over a large part of what is now Arizona, New Mexico, and northern Mexico. Despite their image as a violent, marauding warrior culture, a reputation created by Hollywood, the Apache were peaceful and did not believe in killing. Honor was earned through raids that supplied their families with horses and food, not by taking scalps.

During the 1870s and '80s the Chiricahua Apache were led in their efforts to defend themselves, their homeland, and the resources on which they depended from white settlers by two of the era's most famous Indian leaders: Cochise and Geronimo. Their guerrilla raiding techniques and ability to disappear into the mountains were so successful that for a time the government closed the area to settlement. Eventually the unending flood of settlers demanding access to the country and protection from the U.S. Army resulted in a full-scale war against the Apache people and one of the darker chapters in American history. *Indeh: An Apache Odyssey,* by Eve Ball, is a fascinating and well written story of the Apache people and is highly recommended for anyone interested in the history of the American West and its native peoples.

DON'T MISS

While visiting Chiricahua National Monument, take time to visit Fort Bowie National Historical Site at Apache Pass. Here the past and future of the Southwest collided, and the era of freedom for this country's native peoples came to an end. A reliable spring near the pass where Fort Bowie was eventually built was extremely important for the Chiricahua Indians and also drew all manner of travelers, emigrants, prospectors, and soldiers. Early Spanish travelers called it Puerto del Dado, the Pass of Chance, while those who came later called it Puerto de la Muerte, or Pass of Death, because violence so often erupted there.

The water source was so plentiful and reliable that when John Butterfield established his Overland Mail Company and Butterfield Stagecoach line between St. Louis and California, in 1858, a station house was built here. Cochise and his band of Chiricahua warriors allowed the stagecoach to operate and use the spring for more than two years, but in the winter of 1861 that was all to change.

In January a renegade band of Apache unknown to Cochise raided a ranch nearby, took some cows, and kidnapped a Mexican woman's son. The rancher was convinced that Cochise and his band were to blame and demanded that military authorities confront the Apache leader and secure the return of the boy and his stock. The army responded by sending 54 men and a young, exuberant 2nd lieutenant by the name of George Bascom to try to resolve the situation. Bascom and his men set up camp about a mile from the Butterfield station and then lured Cochise in. As he entered Bascom's tent, Cochise was seized, accused of the crime, and told he would be held hostage until the boy and cattle were returned. Cochise was infuriated. Drawing his knife he slashed his way out of the tent, escaping past the officers stationed outside. Cochise's warriors and army troops fought sporadically for the next two weeks, taking and killing hostages, and entrenching hatreds that would feaul open warfare for the next ten years.

In July, 1862, Brigadier General James Carleton and his California Column were on their way to confront a Confederate threat to New Mexico when their advanced detachment, under the command of Captain Thomas Roberts, was attacked at Apache Pass. Roberts and his men were able to fend off the attack, but the need for a fort became evident. The fort was established within three weeks and named for their commanding officer, Colonel George Washington Bowie. First there were tents, then primitive stone structures, but it wasn't until 1868 that the more substantial adobe barracks, storehouses, officer's homes, store, hospital, and corrals were built.

In 1872 Cochise made peace in return for reservation lands. But further deceit by the army, mismanagement of the reservation, and the death of Cochise resulted in a deterioration of the truce. A charismatic figure named Geronimo and a band of warriors left the reservation and resumed raiding, often disappearing deep into Mexico and frustrating pursuing soldiers. In 1886 Geronimo and his men finally surrendered, ending the Apache Wars and Ft. Bowie's usefulness as a military installation.

When it was abandoned in 1894, Ft. Bowie consisted of 38 structures; only ruins remain today. The modern visitor center building houses a fascinating collection of photographs from the period and a wonderful assortment of Indian and military artifacts. The fort and nearby historic sites are accessible by a 1.5-mile-long foot trail that starts on the Apache Pass Road. It is a 22-mile drive from Chiricahua National Monument to the trail. Take AZ 186 north to Apache Pass Road, drive up and over the pass, parking at the trailhead on the left. There are 8 miles of dirt road, so avoid this trip if heavy thunderstorms are in the area. The trailhead can also be reached from the east by exiting I-10 at the town of Bowie and heading south for 12 miles on Apache Pass Road. Although the trail is only 1.5 miles long, the elevation, aridity, and strong sun make it more strenuous. Water is available at the fort, but be sure to carry some with you on the walk in.

2

During the first half of the 16th century a wealthy and powerful Spanish kingdom rapidly colonized Central and South America. Interested primarily in the New World's mineral riches, the conquerors penetrated as far south as Peru and beyond present-day Mexico City to the north, forcing entire populations of native peoples to work in mines that produced enormous quantities of gold and silver. This treasure was shipped back to Spain, providing the funds and incentive to support additional expeditions to the New World. Fantastic tales of riches beyond the northern frontier fired the Spanish imagination. One such tale was told by Cabeza de Vaca. In 1536 he and three companions stumbled into Mexico City after surviving the shipwreck of an expedition to Florida eight years earlier. While trying to find their way back to the Spanish outpost they wandered through the wilds of what is now Texas and northern Mexico where they said they had seen entire cities ornately decorated with gold and gems. Antonio de Mendoza, the viceroy of New Spain, anxious to confirm de Vaca's stories, immediately sent Fray Marcos de Niza and several guides north. The father returned alone after a year, his guides having been killed by Indians, with reports of an enormous stone city he did not dare enter. He called the city Cibola. This report, combined with the stories of de Vaca, led to sensational rumors and, eventually, to the fabled Seven Cities of Cibola, or the Seven Cities of Gold. The father's report was enough for Mendoza, who put together an expedition of 336 Spanish adventurers, including at least three women, four Franciscan priests, more than a thousand Indian "allies" (most likely conscripts), and over fifteen hundred horses and other live-stock. Although he was tempted to lead the expedition himself, Mendoza appointed the young and ambitious Francisco Vazquez de Coronado, who would go on to claim much of the territory of the American Southwest for Spain. Hoping to find vast riches of gold and silver, and the rumored cities of fabulous wealth, Coronado set off in 1540 to explore the unknown territory to the north on a mission that is recognized as the first European exploration of the American West. Although he did not find the riches his predecessors had found in Peru and Mexico, Coronado was able to establish a base among Pueblo Indian farmers liv-ing along the Rio Grande, and for the next two years explore parts of Arizona, New Mexico, Texas, Oklahoma, and Kansas. His efforts opened the way for further exploration and missionary efforts that resulted in the colonization of the Southwest and the rich cultural heritage and his-tory still celebrated throughout the region to this day.

Cycling in the Park

The Coronado National Memorial shares its southern boundary with the U.S.-Mexico border and encompasses the southern end of the Huachuca (pronounced "wa-CHOO-ka") Mountains, a small, isolated range sur-rounded by expansive valleys typical of the fault-block ranges sprinkled across southern Arizona. Like the Chiricahua Mountains to the east, the Huachucas are spectacularly scenic with deep, forested canyons, home to an amazing variety of bird and animal life, and high rolling ridges that provide sweeping views that reach far into Mexico. From the top of Montezuma Pass, a short but steep pedal for mountain bikes, you can look east, over the San Pedro River Valley, to where Coronado and his expedition of almost fifteen hundred souls passed through on their northward journey more than four and a half centuries ago. Summertime is hot in this neck of the woods and should probably be avoided, however, temperatures are moderated somewhat by elevations that range between 4,000 and 6,500 feet. Afternoon thunderstorms occur frequently over the Huachucas during the monsoon season, July through September. Pay attention to weather forecasts and stay well off high or exposed areas when these storms threaten.

There are biking opportunities galore in the Huachuca Mountains and surrounding country and a couple of excellent bike shops in the town of Sierra Vista, located 20 miles north of the memorial. Several of the canyons between Sierra Vista and the memorial offer top-notch mountain biking adventures, while the wide-open valleys and interesting historical towns in the area make for a road biker's dream. A trail network along the San Pedro River allows families to get out and enjoy some time in the saddle together; the more adventurous can explore almost 14 miles of trails and old roads heading south, all the way to the border. *Bicycling Magazine* has consistently voted Sierra Vista and the surrounding area as one of the top ten cycling sanctuaries over the last decade; a few days spent exploring on two wheels while you are visiting will surely show you why.

CYCLING OPTIONS

Inside Coronado National Memorial you can ride the 3-mile dirt road to the top of Montezuma Pass, a fairly rigorous but nontechnical climb that affords astounding views that reach deep into Mexico. An option lets stronger, more adventurous riders continue west, over the pass, to Parker Canyon Lake. The road ride through Fort Huachuca to Garden Canyon is an excellent 18-mile pedal to one of the prettiest canyons in southern Arizona. An option for mountain bikers lets them explore the upper reaches of the canyon and visit two pictograph sites. Brown Canyon Loop is a five-star mountain bike adventure that fat tire fanatics will love. At San Pedro House, 3 miles of wide, flat, dirt trails within the San Pedro National Conservation Area traverse the wooded banks of the San Pedro River and are ideal for exploring with the whole family. The almost 14-mile long San Pedro Trail, built on old rail- and roadbeds, also traverses the conservation area and offers stronger riders the chance to do some exploring along the river's unique riparian woodlands where a stunning variety of resident and migratory birds can be seen. The 38-mile road ride from Sierra Vista to Tombstone and back requires a strong set of legs and is a favorite among local riders.

7. MONTEZUMA PASS (See map on page 62)

For mountain bikes. The pedal from the visitor center up through Montezuma Canyon to Montezuma Pass and Overlook is a short but fairly demanding ride. Both the views and the effort it takes to get up there are heart-pounding. You can access Coronado Peak (6,864 feet) from the pass via one of the hiking trails that run along these ridges for an even more commanding view of the area. An option for making this ride an all-day adventure is offered at the end of the ride description.

Starting point: Begin this ride at the visitor center.

Length: Approximately 3 miles one-way, just over 6 miles total distance. Allow at least 2 hours to do the ride and to spend time enjoying the view from the pass.

Riding surface: Pavement and narrow, but maintained, dirt road that is washboarded in spots.

Difficulty: Moderate. Although the mileage is minimal you will climb over 1,300 feet in 3 miles, making a solid level of physical fitness a necessity. Technical riding skills are not necessary.

Scenery/highlights: At these elevations, the Upper Sonoran Desert presents a wonderful variety of vegetation dominated by oak woodlands. The views west from the pass to the Canelo Hills, the upper Santa Cruz River Valley, and beyond to the Patagonia Mountains, and east, out Montezuma Canyon to the ribbon of forest that flanks the San Pedro River are something to marvel at. The views get even better from atop Coronado Peak. There you can gaze south, into the mountains of Mexico.

Best time to ride: Spring and fall are ideal. Summertime is hot; in winter the road up to the pass closes occasionally due to snow. Afternoon thunderstorms are common July through September.

Special considerations: Water and rest rooms are available at the visitor center. If you are interested in hiking up to Coronado Peak you should plan on bringing a lock to secure your bike while you are gone. Be wary of afternoon cloud buildups in late summer and early fall; they can quickly become violent thunderstorms with a lot of dangerous lightning.

7 · Montezuma Pass

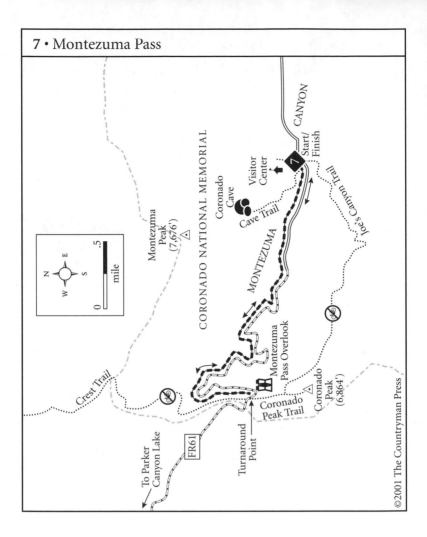

©2001 The Countryman Press

Directions for the ride: After spending some time at the visitor center, with its displays of old Spanish infantry wear and weapons, and gathering information on the natural environment of the memorial, simply ride out of the parking lot and head west up Montezuma Canyon. For the first mile the climb is steady but not too steep. The road makes several switchbacks as it nears the back of the canyon and then one big switchback as it gains the pass. Have a good look around, hike the half-

There are many excellent options for both road and mountain bike adventures around Sierra Vista. Mountain bikers should inquire about the Perimeter Trail, a low-elevation trail linking Coronado National Memorial with Sierra Vista, which was still in the planning stages as this book goes to press. The trail traverses the beautiful, open, oak woodlands of the foothills and almost all of the incredibly scenic canyons that drain off the east side of the Huachuca Mountains. There are also numerous possibilities for mountain bike explorations on the west side of the Huachuca range. Stop in and talk to the folks at the Coronado National Forest office for more information.

Serious road bikers will find plenty to do in this area, beginning with a ride that takes you through Fort Huachuca to the base's west gate, around the northern end of the Huachuca range. Another excellent and very popular ride for the super-fit and well-seasoned cyclist leads to the historic mining town of Bisbee, formerly the route for a road race called La Vuelta de Bisbee. This ride can be done from either the memorial or from Sierra Vista. Visit one of the local bike shops for additional routes.

mile-long trail up to Coronado Peak if your legs can manage it, and when you're ready, head back down the way you came.

Option: The road dipping away off the pass to the west is enticing and can make for a great, all-day out-and-back ride if you have the time and the stamina. If you choose to continue you will be leaving the memorial and riding into the Coronado National Forest on Forest Road (FR) 61, still referred to on many maps as the Montezuma Canyon Road. This route skirts the south and west slopes of the Huachuca Mountains, as well as the boundary of the Miller Peak Wilderness Area, arriving at beautiful Parker Canyon Lake 15 miles from Montezuma Pass and 18 miles from the visitor center. After dropping off the pass the road rolls along between 5,500 and 5,700 feet. You will need to save some energy for gaining the pass on the return trip before coasting back to the visitor center after a 36-mile day.

---

8. GARDEN CANYON (See map on page 66)

For road bikes. The ride through Fort Huachuca and up Garden Canyon is a stellar 18-mile road ride that takes you on a tour of one the prettiest canyons in Arizona and is an introduction to one of the most famous chapters in Western American history. An option for mountain bikers that explores the unpaved upper reaches of the canyon is offered at the end of the trail description.

Starting point: Begin this ride at the main gate of Fort Huachuca, located at the intersection of Buffalo Soldier Trail and Fry Boulevard in Sierra Vista. Be sure to stop at the gate and pick up a free visitor's pass and map of the fort. You may be asked to show your driver's license to the guard.

Length: 9 miles each way, 18 miles total distance. Allow 3 to 4 hours to do the ride and spend some time enjoying your surroundings in Garden Canyon.

Riding surface: Pavement. The road is narrow and in poor condition in some spots.

Difficulty: Moderate.

Scenery/highlights: Fort Huachuca was established on the site where U.S. Army troops made camp in 1877 to help defend settlers and protect travel routes from raiding Apache Indians. By 1886 it had become a permanent fort and headquarters for the campaign against the Chiricahua Apache leader Geronimo. While many of the outpost forts of the settlement period did not survive, Fort Huachuca was kept open to deal with renegade Indians, Mexican bandits, and American outlaws seeking to escape over the nearby Mexican border. Today the fort's mission is to test and develop electronic and communications equipment, and is home to the U.S. Army Intelligence Center and training school.

While at the fort, take time to visit the museum, where a fascinating collection of late-nineteenth-century photographs, memorabilia, and Native American artifacts are on display. One of the most interesting

The higher reaches of Garden Canyon in the Huachuca Mountains.

exhibits, called the Black Experience, chronicles the lives of the African American men who served during the Apache wars. The historic buildings and parade grounds nearby all date from the late 1880s.

Garden Canyon is a well-recognized paradise for birdwatchers and a beautiful spot to take in the scenery and experience the rich natural environment of Arizona's sky islands.

Best time to ride: Spring and fall. Summertime is hot; temperatures frequently soar past the century mark. Snowstorms during the winter months are not uncommon.

Special considerations: Water and rest rooms are available at the picnic areas in Garden Canyon; start off with your water bottles filled. There are no visitor facilities at the fort unless you visit the museum. You are on a military reservation here, and many areas and side roads are closed to the public; obey all signs and stay on the main road.

Directions for the ride: From the parking area just beyond the main gate begin by riding west on Winrow Avenue. It becomes a divided road in 0.5 mile. Continue riding toward the mountains and the heart of the fort. In 2 miles you will come to a T intersection. Make a left at this intersection

8 · Garden Canyon
9 · Brown Canyon Loop

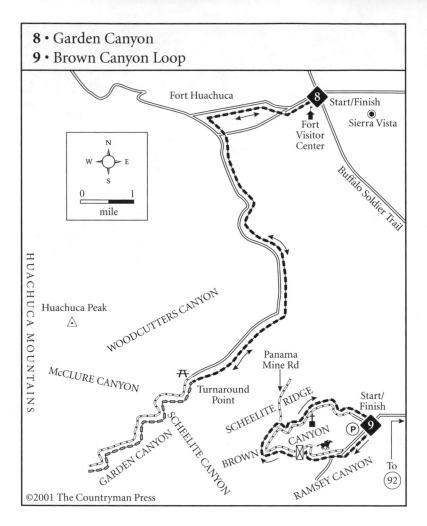

onto a road signed for Garden Canyon and simply referred to as the Garden Canyon Road. Head south, along the eastern flank of Huachuca Peak, following the road as it rolls through open grassy foothills, passing several clusters of army buildings and a shooting range, before turning right and heading west toward Garden Canyon approximately 4 miles from the T intersection. From this westward turn to the end of the pavement at the farthest picnic area in the canyon it is another 3 miles. After you've spent some time enjoying your surroundings, perhaps taking note of some of the rare and colorful bird species that visit this canyon, mount up and return the way you came.

Option: Fat-tire enthusiasts interested in exploring the upper reaches of the canyon should drive the route described above, park at either of the two picnic areas, and begin riding from there. The upper canyon is truly stunning and there are two pictograph panels and a waterfall to see along the way. The road is hardpacked dirt, although rough and washed out in spots, for the first 3 miles. The last mile is extremely steep and rocky and ends atop a pass at a gate. Total trip distance is 8 miles.

---

9. BROWN CANYON LOOP (See map on page 66)

For mountain bikes. The 5-mile loop from Ramsey Canyon over to Brown Canyon and back is considered by locals to be one of the best mountain bike rides in the Huachucas. Gorgeous scenery similar to that found in the famed Ramsey Canyon Preserve, managed by the Nature Conservancy just up the canyon, and fun, fast-paced singletrack make this a five-star ride.

Starting point: The trailhead is located in Ramsey Canyon. To get there drive south from Sierra Vista approximately 7 miles to Ramsey Road. From the memorial, drive north 8 miles from where the park road meets AZ 92. Drive west on Ramsey Road for just over 2 miles to a parking area on the right, directly across from a group of mailboxes.

Length: 5 miles. Allow 2 hours to complete this ride.

Riding surface: A short section of pavement, dirt road, and singletrack.

Difficulty: Easy to moderate. Short, but several climbs and loose, rocky sections make it more difficult.

Scenery/highlights: Beautiful scenery, great bird-watching, an excellent ride in general. Remnants of several old miner's cabins built during the 1800s in Brown Canyon, and an old miner's grave are testament to the hard life faced by some of the earliest settlers to this area. Please do not disturb any of the old structures or relics you might find lying around.

Best time to ride: Fall through spring.

FLORA

Within the 5,000-acre confines of Coronado National Memorial are four distinct biotic communities hosting a variety of plant and animal life. At lower elevations a mixture of grama grass, bunch grasses, and shrubs common to Chihuahuan deserts dominate. Several species of agave and yucca also grow here, as does desert broom. Occurring at lower elevations is a riparian life zone characterized by the presence of Western honey mesquite, a tree commonly found in the Sonoran Desert. Also found are wild grape, cat claw acacia, and trees such as Arizona sycamore, Arizona walnut, and Fremont cottonwoods. At higher elevations oak woodlands dominate, but Emory, Arizona white, and Mexican blue oaks, as well as piñon pine, alligator juniper, mountain mohogany, and the red-barked manzanita tree are also present. The higher elevation riparian zone along the bottom of Montezuma Canyon features Emory and white oaks, Arizona sycamore, Arizona walnut, and several species of willows.

Wildflowers in the memorial and surrounding mountains are timed to bloom in response to specific conditions throughout the year. Several cactus varieties bloom after spring rains. They include the long, whiplike stalks of ocotillos, with firey red blooms; hedgehog cactus, low to the ground with pink and red blooms; and prickly pear cactus, who's blooms are mostly yellow. Several types of yuccas send up tall stalks covered with creamy white flowers in early spring. At least three types of penstemons bloom spring through early summer in shades that range from reddish-orange to purple. Mexican star, a lily, emerges in late spring with a white blossom made up of thin, long-stemmed petals. The large, white, trumpet-shaped blooms of sacred datura can be found in summer; the very large flowers of the pink-throated morning glory emerge only after late summer or early fall rain. The monsoon season, lasting from July through September, often coaxes another show from the area's wildflowers. Rabbitbrush, a regular fall bloomer, is crowned with masses of tiny golden flowers.

Special considerations: Come supplied with water and whatever else you'll need for a couple hours in the saddle. A gas station at the corner of Ramsey Road and AZ 92 should have the necessary supplies. Please stay on the main route; there is private property along sections of this trail.

Directions for the ride: From the parking area ride back out to Ramsey Road and go right, continuing west up Ramsey Canyon. Ride for approximately 0.5 mile to Brown Canyon Road, a dirt road on the right just past another group of mailboxes. Turn right. At 0.8 mile you pass the Discovery Ranch, at which point you begin to climb in earnest toward a pass between two mountains. At 1.5 miles go through a gate; please leave it as you found it (either open or closed) and continue climbing, reaching the top of the climb 2 miles from the start. After a rolling, 0.4-mile descent the road comes to a water trough; pick up the singletrack on the right here. Approximately 2.5 miles from the start the Pamona Mine Road is on the left, and shortly after that the trail crosses through a water ditch. Just beyond is a rocky section. The trail then dips and weaves its way east, encountering the Old Brown Trail on the left 3.2 miles from the start. At 3.7 miles is a gate; leave it as you found it and continue as the trail climbs steeply, reaching another trail taking off on the left 4.0 miles from the start. In another 0.2 mile you reach the top of the hill. From here the trail heads southeast, alternates between singletrack and dirt road for a short distance, and then becomes a dirt road that delivers you back to your starting point 5 miles from the start.

---

10. SAN PEDRO HOUSE TRAIL SYSTEM
(See map on page 70)

For mountain bikes. The San Pedro House Trail System is a wonderful network of wide, hardpacked dirt trails that wind along the banks of the San Pedro River and the tall, stately cottonwoods and willows that make up this unique riparian woodland. With just over 3 miles of trails, the area is well suited for family outings and offers a great introduction to the encompassing San Pedro Riparian National Conservation Area and the extremely important habitat it protects. Birdwatchers and wildlife enthusiasts will be thrilled with the incredible variety of species that make their home here.

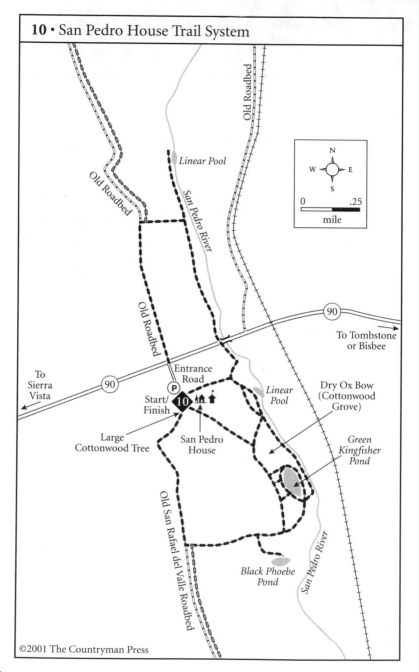

10 · San Pedro House Trail System

Linear Pool

San Pedro River

Old Roadbed

Old Roadbed

Old Roadbed

N
W E
S

0   .25
mile

90

To Tombstone
or Bisbee

To
Sierra
Vista

90

Entrance
Road

P

10

Start/
Finish

San Pedro
House

Large
Cottonwood Tree

Linear
Pool

Dry Ox Bow
(Cottonwood
Grove)

Green
Kingfisher
Pond

Old San Rafael del Valle Roadbed

San Pedro River

Black Phoebe
Pond

©2001 The Countryman Press

Petroglyphs decorate the recesses of an overhang in upper Garden Canyon.

If you are looking for more of a ride, the San Pedro Trail, which runs south from the San Pedro House along old road- and rail beds for 8 miles through the conservation area to Hereford Road and north for 3.5 miles to Escapule Road, is an excellent option

Starting point: Begin this ride at the San Pedro House, a historic ranch house restored by the Friends of the San Pedro River (you will need to stop in and pay a fee). There is a very nice gift shop and bookstore here.

Length: 3 miles total distance, more if you choose to explore some of the other trails. Take some time to sit by the river, explore the riparian forest, or watch for visitors to Green Kingfisher Pond. You can ride for almost 14 miles on the San Pedro Trail, which will someday extend along almost 40 miles of conservation area's river corridor.

Riding surface: Hardpacked dirt that can become soft and a little sandy in spots during dry weather. The old roadbeds of the San Pedro Trail can be loose with sand and gravel in places.

Difficulty: Easy. More moderate if you are riding a longer distance on the San Pedro Trail.

Scenery/highlights: The San Pedro National Conservation Area includes over 56,000 acres of Cochise County, Arizona, encompassing the San Pedro River corridor for almost 40 miles from the Mexican border northward to the town of St. David. This preserve represents the most extensive riparian ecosystem remaining in the Southwest, harboring over 100 species of breeding birds and providing precious habitat for another 250 species of migrant and wintering birds. A bird list and literature on the conservation area are available at the San Pedro House.

Other points of interest along the longer San Pedro Trail include the historic town site of Fairbank, located north of AZ 82 on the east side of the San Pedro bridge. Fairbank was a depot town that sprang up in 1881 with the building of the railroad. The booming mines and mills in the nearby town of Tombstone generated plenty of freight and passenger business for the town that today is completely abandoned. Several structures now maintained by the BLM still stand.

Another worthwhile stop along the San Pedro Trail is the Murray Springs Clovis Site where scientists have unearthed a prehistoric hunting camp used by people who stalked and killed animals now long extinct, including woolly mammoths and camels. A short walk takes you through the site, located north of AZ 90 and south of the Charleston Road.

Best time to ride: You can ride here almost any time of year, although you may want to avoid hot summer temperatures. Spring and fall are best.

Special considerations: Water and a rest room are available at the San Pedro House and at the town site of Fairbank at the north end of the San Pedro Trail. Be sure to bring plenty of your own water as you will quickly become dehydrated in the dry air and warm temperatures of this desert environment.

Directions for the ride: After stopping in at the San Pedro House, paying the fee, cruising the gift shop, and picking up any information that is offered on the trails, birds, and points of interest, simply head out in any direction to explore the San Pedro House Trails. Ride them in any combination for as long as you like.

Longer option: If you want to pick up the San Pedro Trail, head southwest, past the big cottonwood tree, and pedal southward on the old San Rafael del Valle Road. You can ride north by heading back out the entrance road and carefully crossing straight over AZ 90 to pick up the old roadbed. There are several spurs to explore going both directions. When you are ready to return simply retrace your outbound route.

---

11. CHARLESTON ROAD TO TOMBSTONE
(See map on page 74)

For road bikes. The 38-mile ride to Tombstone from Sierra Vista via the Charleston Road is a rolling trip out across the San Pedro River Valley and up over the Tombstone Hills that will provide plenty of challenge for the fit and experienced rider. The fabled Wild West town of Tombstone is the site of the famous shootout at the OK Corral between the Earp brothers and the Clantons.

Starting point: Begin in the town of Sierra Vista. The city park, located at 3105 E. Fry Boulevard, is a good option.

Length: 19 miles one-way, 38 miles total distance. Allow at least a half a day to do the ride and spend some time poking around Tombstone.

Riding surface: Pavement.

Difficulty: Moderate to difficult. The length of this ride and the rolling terrain make it more difficult.

Scenery/highlights: The historic mining town of Tombstone, Arizona, is practically synonymous with the idea of the Wild West, its colorful past immortalized in countless dime-store novels and Hollywood westerns. It was here in 1881 that the Earp brothers and Doc Holliday shot it out with the Clantons at the OK Corral in a gunfight that has been retold so many times the actual facts of the event have been lost. In the Boot Hill Graveyard, at the north edge of town, lie the losers of that battle, along with numerous other gunslingers, and a few who met their fate at the end of a rope. More than 250 of the graves in the cemetery are unmarked.

The town was christened Tombstone by a prospector named Ed Schieffelin, who ventured out this way in 1877 looking for silver. His friends told him the only thing he would find, besides rattlesnakes and Apaches, would be his own tombstone, the name he gave his claim. His mine, the Lucky Cuss, was one of Arizona's richest, and brought scores of prospectors, shopkeepers, gamblers, and other characters to Tombstone,

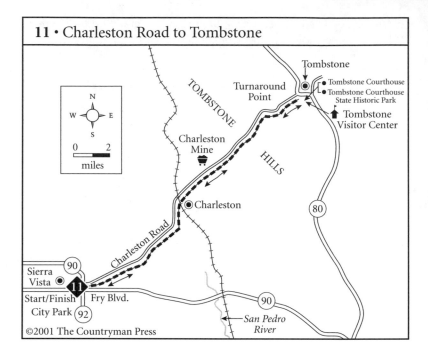

11 · Charleston Road to Tombstone

swelling the population to more than ten thousand by the time it was incorporated in 1879. For every merchant in town it was said there were two saloons, all full of people trying to separate miners from their money. Fire ravaged the town twice, leaving only a few buildings standing, and a freak flood once submerged the mine tunnels, but "the town too tough to die" always bounced back. Although the mines are closed today, Tombstone continues to thrive as a tourist destination that promises a Wild West experience you won't soon forget. You can visit an old saloon, witness a gun battle, watch a show at one of several theaters, or just pedal through and imagine the grit and determination it took to survive in this frontier-era mining town. Stop in at the visitor and information center to find out about all the things to do and see.

Best time to ride: Spring and fall are best for riding across these southern Arizona valleys. Summertime is hot. Beware of thunderstorms July through September.

Special considerations: You will find rest rooms and water at the city

FAUNA

The mountains and canyons of southeastern Arizona are famous for the incredible amount of bird life that thrives in the rich habitats they offer, and the Huachuca Mountains are no different. From fairly common Mexican jays, flickers, and acorn woodpeckers to the far rarer hepatic tanager, cardinal-like pyrrhuloxia, or crested, jet-black phainopepla, the variety of bird species here is sure to delight both the novice and practiced birdwatcher. Numerous species of flycatchers, sparrows, and warblers can be seen as can at least four types of hummingbirds: Anna's, black-chinned, broad-tailed, and Lucifer, which likes to feed on agave blooms. Mockingbirds, curved-billed thrashers, canyon wrens, red-tailed and Coopers hawks, painted redstarts, yellow-eyed juncos, and both Gamble and Montezuma quail are often sighted.

Mammals that make their home in the Huachuca Mountains and are sometimes sighted within the boundaries of the memorial include black bear, mountain lion, Sonoran white-tailed deer, bobcat, javelina, coatimundi, coyote, ringtailed cats, and four species of skunks. At least a dozen species of bats live in the caves and rock crevices found In the memorial, but are nocturnal and so not often seen. Whiptail lizards, Sonoran spotted lizards, Clark's spiny lizards, and short horned lizards are some of the most commonly seen wildlife in the memorial, while diamondback and black-tailed rattlesnakes are some of the most feared. All snakes, including the Sonoran whip snake and Sonoran mountain king snake—similar to the brightly banded coral snake in appearance—are scared of humans and would just as soon stay out of your way.

park in Sierra Vista. Tombstone is a thriving tourist destination and has plenty of places to find refreshments or grab a meal.

Direction for the ride: From Sierra Vista's city park, ride west approximately 0.5 mile to the intersection of AZ 90 and AZ 92. Go left at this intersection, riding north for 0.3 mile to Charleston Road, also known as the Tombstone-Charleston Highway. Go right onto Charleston Road and head east. The road soon angles to the northeast and maintains this heading the entire way to Tombstone. Descend gently toward the San Pedro River and pass the town site of Charleston just after crossing the river. About 2 miles past the former town of Charleston is the turnoff for the old Charleston Mine. Once you cross the San Pedro River the road begins to climb and roll as you pedal toward the Tombstone Hills—the toughest part of the ride. Once you have gained the Tombstone Hills it is just 3 more miles to town. When you're ready to hit the trail again, simply saddle up and head back the way you came.

CAMPING

There are no facilities within the memorial but there are numerous camping possibilities within adjacent Coronado National Forest. The two closest options for semideveloped campgrounds are at the **Reef** and **Ramsey Vista Campgrounds** in Carr Canyon, which lies between the memorial and Sierra Vista. Inquire at the Sierra Vista Ranger District of the Coronado National Forest in Sierra Vista or at the Carr Canyon Administrative Office 2.5 miles up the Carr Canyon Road.

Sierra Vista is well equipped for the motorhome traveler with at least four RV parks to choose from.

LODGING

No lodging is available inside the memorial. Several of the big motel chains are represented in Sierra Vista including **Super 8, Motel 6,** and **Best Western.** There is also a good selection of independently owned motels that offer amenities such as pools, spas, and kitchenettes and are moderately priced. The **Windmere Hotel and Conference Center** is slightly more upscale, as is the **Sierra Suites** hotel.

If you want to get out of town and don't mind paying a bit more there are some excellent options. The **Ramsey Canyon Inn Bed & Breakfast** is located just outside the Ramsey Canyon Preserve, truly a birder's paradise. Both are owned and operated by the Nature Conservancy. **Casa de San Pedro** is an old Spanish-style inn located in Hereford, and the **San Pedro River Inn,** also in Hereford, offers cottages for rent. Check in with the Sierra Vista Convention and Visitor's Bureau to get a complete listing of lodging possibilities.

FOOD

For a town the size of Sierra Vista there are an extraordinary number of restaurants, including Asian, seafood, and Mexican, all kinds of fast food, and of course, the classic American steakhouse. Most are clustered along Fry

Boulevard. A good place to start in the morning is **Caffe O-Le,** where they serve an excellent cup of coffee as well as a good break-fast and lunch. **Connie's Pancake & Steak House** offers a breakfast buffet that is sure to fill you up. There are many excellent Asian restaurants in Sierra Vista; one of the very best is **Tanuki Sushi Bar and Garden** (1221 E. Fry Blvd.) where they serve all kinds of Japanese specialties along with American dishes. **Bunbuku Japanese Restaurant** (297 W. Fry Blvd.) is also quite good, as is **Kim Ba-Woo's Korean Restaurant** (1232 E. Fry Blvd.). **The Shanghai Chinese Restaurant** (1173 E. Fry Blvd.), **Peking Chinese Restaurant** (1481 E. Fry Blvd.), and **A Taste of Asia** (999 E. Fry Blvd.), offering Thai, Korean, and Chinese food, are also worth a try. A good steak is not hard to find in this town; try the **Mesquite Tree Restaurant** (Hwy 92 and Carr Canyon Road), located just south of town, the **Stagecoach Steak House and Saloon,** (4301 S. Hwy 92), or **Cactus Corners** (5043 S. Hwy 92), where they serve pizza and Mexican food as well. If burritos or enchiladas are what you're after, try **La Casita** (465 E. Fry Blvd.), you can wash down your food with 18 different kinds of margaritas. If you're looking for something more upscale try **Schooners' Restaurant and**

IT'S INTERESTING TO KNOW . . .

The name of the Huachuca Mountains, although it suggests Spanish origin, actually comes from the Apache word *Wa-chu-kah,* meaning "Thunder Mountains." The towers of billowing cumulonimbus clouds that form over these mountains during this desert's monsoon season are beautiful but fierce, lashing the peaks with heavy rains and lots of lightning. The season usually begins in July and runs through September, the time when warm, moist air moves north from the Gulf of Mexico and more humid equatorial regions. The warm air hits the mountains of the Southwest and is forced upward, where it collides with colder air at higher altitudes. This gives birth to the majestic, white thunderclouds that so often crown the Huachucas and gave them their name.

DON'T MISS

There are some great opportunities for exploring the scenic and diverse natural environments of Coronado National Memorial; one of them is Coronado Cave. A moderately steep trail begins directly behind the visitor center and climbs 0.75 mile to the cave entrance. There you will find a cavern approximately 600 feet long, 70 feet wide, and 20 feet high with several crawlways. The stalactites, stalagmites, columns, helictites, rimstone dams, and rock draperies that decorate the cave took eons to create. Water seeping through layers of porous limestone and dripping down from the cave walls and ceiling left behind tiny deposits of calcite, the mineral responsible for the cave's beautiful formations. While some of the water sources that created specific formations have dried up, others continue to flow and build. The cave is home to a variety of creatures including several species of bats; please do not disturb their daytime slumber. The cave was also used by the Apache Indians as a hideout when they were being pursued by the U.S. Army during the late 1800s. Visitors to the cave must first obtain a free permit at memorial headquarters and are required to carry a flashlight.

If you'd rather stay above ground to do your exploring, consider hiking to Miller Peak (9,456 feet) via the Crest Trail, leaving from Montezuma Pass (6,575 feet). The Crest Trail is part of the Arizona Trail, which starts at the U.S.-Mexico border inside the memorial and runs south to north through the entire length of Arizona. Hiking from Montezuma Pass north along the Crest Trail, takes you out of the memorial and into the Miller Peak Wilderness Area of the Coronado National Forest. It is approximately 5.3 miles from the pass to Miller Peak via a steep and strenuous trail. You will gain almost 3,000 feet along the way. Check in at the visitor center before you go and make sure there are no afternoon thunderstorms in the forecast. You'll need a sturdy pair of shoes, plenty of water, and some high-energy snacks to munch on along the way. Be prepared for stunning scenery and heart-pounding views.

Oyster Club (2047 S. Hwy 92) or The Grille at Pueblo del Sol (2770 S. St. Andrews Drive).

LAUNDRY

There are several options for doing a load of laundry in Sierra Vista. Try:

Maytag Home Style Laundry, 430 N. 7; 520-459-0565

Sierra Wash-N-Dry, 500 E. Wilcox Dr.; 520-459-5519

Snow White Launderette, 65 S. Garden Ave.; 520-459-4046

BIKE SHOP/BIKE RENTAL

There are two bike shops in Sierra Vista and they are both excellent.

M & M Cycling, 185 C S. Hwy 92 (in Smith's Plaza); 520-458-1316

Sun 'N Spokes Inc., 164 E. Fry Blvd.; 520-458-0685

FOR FURTHER INFORMATION

Coronado National Memorial— Superintendent, 4101 East Montezuma Canyon Road, Hereford, AZ 85615; 520-366-5515; www.nps.gov/coro/

Sierra Vista Convention and Visitor's Bureau, 21 E. Wilcox Drive (1 block south of Fry Blvd.), Sierra Vista, AZ 85635; 520-417-6960; www.visitsierra-vista.com

Coronado National Forest, Sierra Vista Ranger District, 5990 S. Hwy 92, Hereford, AZ 85615; 520-378-0311

BLM San Pedro Project Office, San Pedro Riparian National Conservation Area, 1763 Paseo San Luis, Sierra Vista, AZ 86635; 520-458-3559; www.tucson.az.blm.gov

3

Lake Powell's sparkling expanse and the stunning redrock scenery of the surrounding canyon country are the costars of Glen Canyon National Recreation Area, a spectacle created by both man and nature that draws close to three million visitors each year. Captured behind massive Glen Canyon Dam, the waters of the mighty Colorado River and the smaller San Juan River, have inundated over 200 miles of Glen Canyon and countless side canyons stretching far into southern Utah's desert wilderness. Some 1,960 miles of shoreline (more than in all of New England) were created with the lake, but much was lost.

Many significant prehistoric Puebloan ruins and petroglyph sites, several sites sacred to the Navajo Indians, the Crossing of the Fathers used by Domiguez and Escalante in 1776, the fording place at Hole in the Rock used by Mormon pioneers, and the river glen, or forest, that prompted explorer John Wesley Powell to name the canyon have all disappeared beneath the waves of this reservoir. While Lake Powell and Glen Canyon Dam remain an awesome testament to human's ability to manipulate the environment to suit our needs and have created a paradise for boaters and fisherman, to many in the environmental community the lake and dam are viewed as monuments to human arrogance and destructive excess.

The narrow canyon and towering sandstone walls of Glen Canyon, like those further downriver in the Grand Canyon, are typical of those found throughout the Colorado Plateau and were perfectly suited to building the last of America's big dams. Construction began in 1956 but wasn't completed until 1964. It took another sixteen years for the lake to fill to its current level. Standing 710 feet high and spanning 1,560 feet, Glen Canyon Dam houses eight giant turbines that generate enough electricity to satisfy the needs of most of Arizona, Las Vegas, and Southern California.

Beyond the fluctuating shoreline lie over a million acres of remote desert backcountry traversed by only a handful of dirt roads. The brilliant peach and crimson of the canyon walls and rock formations found throughout the region are unmistakably those of the Colorado Plateau—a giant raft of sedimentary rock layers uplifted some 60 million years ago. Deep canyons, towering buttes, and spires were carved out of the rock over the eons by rivers, wind, and weather. Written in the many different rock layers of the plateau are the stories of shallow seas, shifting sand dunes, river deltas, and the creatures that once lived in these environments. The boundaries of Glen Canyon National Recreation Area encompass an enormous amount of lake and desert terrain with an almost unending network of side canyons, windswept mesas, and fantastic panoramas to discover and enjoy.

Cycling in the Park

While the focus of this national recreation area is Lake Powell and its tributaries, a substantial amount of surrounding desert terrain within the park's boundaries can be explored by bike. Although a few paved roads access points within the park, the majority of routes available to bikes are on dirt roads, some graded and maintained, others quite rough.

Glen Canyon National Recreation Area can be thought of as a sprawling octopus with three main arms stretching away to the north, east, and southwest. The long northern arm stretches all the way to the northern boundary of Canyonlands National Park in southeastern Utah, the eastern boundary reaches almost as far as the town of Mexican Hat on the San Juan River, and the southwestern arm terminates at Navajo Bridge, fifteen miles beyond the dam and the park's headquarters. The central body of the park extends to the northwest, encompassing much of the Escalante River drainage. This central portion of the recreation area

CYCLING OPTIONS

There are five rides listed in this chapter; one is either for road or mountain bikes, the others are for mountain bikes. The first, a loop ride from Carl Hayden Visitor Center at Glen Canyon Dam to the marina at Wahweap and back, can be done on either road or mountain bikes and is a great introduction to Lake Powell and the Page area. A longer option, better suited to road bikers, continues past Wahweap to the town of Big Water. A paved bike and walking trail at Wahweap offers families with little bikers the chance to get out and do some pedaling by the water away from car traffic. The Rim View Trail is a singletrack that encircles Manson Mesa and the town of Page. Views to the lake and surrounding redrock scenery are outstanding. Warm Creek Road takes cyclists into a surreal landscape that has been used by Hollywood filmmakers for decades. This ride follows dirt roads, has many route options, and can be adjusted to suit your time and fitness requirements. Using vehicle support gives the most options and is recommended here. The Hole-in-the-Rock Road used by Mormon pioneers in their efforts to settle southeastern Utah is a ride best suited for intermediate-level riders in good to excellent physical condition. This route is accessed from Escalante, Utah, and is quite remote. The ride out to Panorama Point, near Canyonlands National Park, is also remote but provides a stunning view of the rivers, canyons, and vast, open spaces that characterize the Colorado Plateau.

shares boundaries with Capitol Reef National Park and the newly created Grand Staircase–Escalante National Monument. The entire southern boundary of the park is shared with the Navajo Indian Reservation, which extends east and west along the southern shore of the San Juan River and Lake Powell.

Seeing all of Glen Canyon National Recreation Area from the seat of your bike is no small undertaking, not only because of the vast distances involved, but because of the area's remote nature and the often poor con-

Lake Powell fills an old river meander as seen from the Rim Trail just outside Page, Arizona.

dition of some of the park's back roads. Page, Arizona, home to the recreation area's headquarters, is a good place to acclimate to the desert, get a few rides in, and gather the resources you'll need to explore the park's extensive backcountry. Riding Page's Rim View Trail around the mesa where town sits, or riding the pavement out to Wahweap or Big Water from the visitor center are excellent riding options near the dam, park headquarters, and the conveniences Page offers. Exploring the backcountry on Warm Creek Road, Hole-in-the-Rock Road, or the road out to Panorama Point and Cleopatra's Chair will require a significant time commitment, careful planning, and no small amount of energy. The Hole-in-the-Rock Road is far from anything and could be done as a multi-day adventure. Camping in this area is a good option. The long stretches of empty road through gorgeous red desert scenery make for wonderful road riding in places but are, again, far from a bed and a hot meal if you're not self-supported or simply riding out from one of the small towns in the area. The effort and preparation it takes to really get out there and explore this park on two wheels will be energy well spent, and is sure to reward you with an experience you won't soon forget.

Summertime across the entire expanse of Glen Canyon National

Recreation Area can be scorching; for days on end temperatures can reach 100 degrees or better. Jumping in the lake after a couple of hours on your bike is always a good way to cool off, but not all routes are near the lake. Spring and fall are the best times for riding and tend to be drier. Like much of the Southwest, this region experiences thunderstorms from the beginning of July to around the first week in September. Although they may not be as frequent as they are further south in Arizona, they can be equally severe, with heavy rains and dangerous amounts of lightning. These heavy rains not only turn the dirt roads here into a gooey, sticky mess, they can cause flash flooding in the washes. The dirt roads of the park's backcountry should be avoided when they become saturated, including in winter after snowstorms. While most of the dirt roads that must be driven to access rides are suitable for passenger cars, they can become rutted and rough, especially after wet weather. It is always a good idea to check with a park ranger for road and weather conditions before traveling in this remote country. When you are heading out to explore, go prepared with plenty of fuel, food, water, and any tools or equipment you might need for your bike. This will give you the most options and ensure that your two-wheeled adventure is memorable for all the right reasons.

Note: Glen Canyon National Recreation Area extends far into Utah and shares boundaries with several other national parks in that state. If you are visiting the far reaches of this park and would like more ideas for riding in and around adjacent parks, pick up a copy of *Bicycling America's National Parks: Utah and Colorado* (Backcountry Guides, 2000).

---

12. WAHWEAP–BIG WATER (See map on page 87)

For road or mountain bikes. There are several ride options for this route, allowing all levels and types of cyclists to get out and enjoy a pedal by the lake. The ride from the Carl Hayden Visitor Center at the dam along Lake Shore Drive to Wahweap, where you'll find a marina, lodge, and boating facilities, is a loop that can be done on either a road or mountain bike. A mile-long paved walking and biking trail at Wahweap running along the shore of the lake offers a chance to get out with the kids away from car traffic. And for those who prefer skinny tires and want more of a workout, the ride from the visitor center to the town of Big Water and back is a 32-mile excursion.

Starting point: Carl Hayden Visitor Center at Glen Canyon Dam. If you would like to get the kids out and be away from car traffic you will need to drive to Wahweap and park near the lodge where the paved bike trail begins.

Length: The loop to Wahweap and back is 15.5 miles; to Big Water and back is approximately 32 miles; the paved biking trail at Wahweap is approximately 2 miles out-and-back along the lake's shore. Allow at least 3 hours to ride to Wahweap and back, more if you want to spend time at the shore enjoying the view, and at least 4 to get to Big Water and back.

Riding surface: Pavement.

Difficulty: Easy to more difficult. While the routes to Wahweap and Big Water do have some hills the overall elevation losses and gains are not significant. The bike trail at Wahweap is easy.

Scenery/highlights: Besides providing wonderful views to Wahweap Bay, one of the biggest in the lake, these rides offer the chance to ponder the stunningly beautiful yet incongruous combination of a large, blue body of water in a redrock desert setting.

Best time to ride: The summer months are exceedingly busy around Page and Wahweap, making the shoulder seasons of spring and fall your best choice for a ride.

Special considerations: Because you will be entering the park on your ride to Wahweap you will be required to pay a fee. Rest rooms, water, and food are all available in Page, Wahweap, and Big Water. You may want to bring a suit and go for a swim at Wahweap Beach.

Directions for the ride: After spending some time checking out the dam and the many interesting displays at the visitor center simply head out of the parking lot and go right, climbing west on US 89. If you are riding to Wahweap, and even if you are riding to Big Water, go right in 0.8 mile onto Lake Shore Drive. Pedal another 0.6 mile to the fee station and then head north along the lake shore, passing South Wahweap and several scenic pullouts along the way. As you come into Wahweap, approxi-

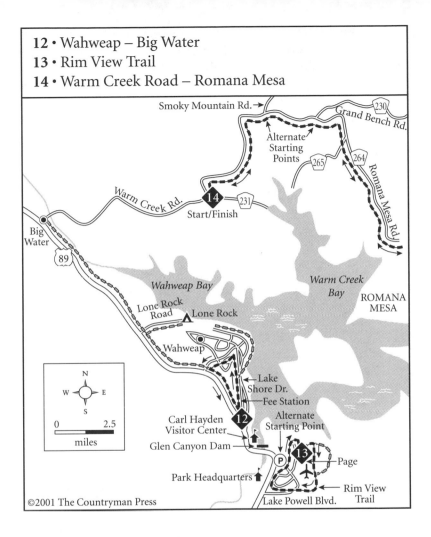

12 • Wahweap – Big Water
13 • Rim View Trail
14 • Warm Creek Road – Romana Mesa

Smoky Mountain Rd. →

Grand Bench Rd.

230

Alternate
Starting
Points

265   264

Romana Mesa Rd.

Warm Creek Rd.

14 231
Start/Finish

Big
Water

89

Wahweap Bay

Warm Creek
Bay

ROMANA
MESA

Lone Rock
Road   ▲ Lone Rock

● Wahweap

N
W   E
S

0   2.5

miles

Lake
Shore Dr.

Fee Station

Carl Hayden
Visitor Center

Alternate
Starting Point

12

Glen Canyon Dam

P   **13**

Park Headquarters

Page

Rim View
Trail

©2001 The Countryman Press

Lake Powell Blvd.

mately 5.5 miles from the visitor center, a road to the right will take you
to the Wahweap Ranger Station, the Wahweap Lodge, the marina, several restaurants, and the start of the paved walking and hiking trail.

You may want to continue straight ahead at this junction, making a
loop past the picnic area, Wahweap Beach swimming area and campground, and an area called the Coves. This road loops all the way around, past the boat repair shop, and comes out on the Wahweap North Road.

If you do not choose to make this loop through Wahweap, go left onto Wahweap North Road and head west to US 89. It is approximately 4 miles from Wahweap to US 89 on the Wahweap North Road. When you reach US 89, go left, riding south along the highway back toward the dam and Page. Approximately 2.5 miles from the point where you turned onto US 89 look for a spur road heading east. This short road takes you up to Sunrise Hill, a fantastic overlook of Wahweap Bay. Back on the main route, continue heading south on US 89, reaching the visitor center and your vehicle in another 3.5 miles.

Option #1: If you want to get out with your kids on the paved bike trail, drive to the Wahweap Lodge following the directions described above, park, and ride from there.

Option #2: If you are riding out to Big Water and back and you do not want to pay the park entrance fee, stay on US 89 at the turnoff for Lake Shore Drive. Approximately 5 miles beyond the Wahweap North Road, as you are heading northwest to Big Water, Lone Rock Road leads to an overlook of the Lone Rock formation. You are almost at the Utah-Arizona border. This side trip will give you a total ride distance closer to 35 miles.

---

13. RIM VIEW TRAIL (See map on page 87)

For mountain bikes. Built by volunteers over a number of years, Page's Rim View Trail is one that fat-tire fiends of all levels will relish. This loop dips and winds around the edge of Manson Mesa, the one on which the town of Page perches. As you encircle the mesa you'll enjoy spectacular views of Lake Powell and the surrounding countryside. If you are in Page, or just passing through, don't miss the chance to pedal this super-fun and incredibly scenic singletrack trail.

Starting point: There are several places to pick up or jump off this trail; one of the best is at the north end of town off North Navajo Drive near Lakeview School. This is the start of the Nature Trail that drops down to meet the Rim View Trail. To get there head south on US 89 from the dam and go left onto Lake Powell Boulevard. As you come up onto the mesa look for Vista Avenue. Go left onto Vista Avenue and follow it until it dead-ends at North Navajo Drive. Turn left and follow North Navajo Drive until it ends. Park here.

FLORA

The enormous expanse of Glen Canyon National Recreation Area encompasses numerous types of habitats and vegetation zones. Starting at the highest elevations and descending to the lake level are piñon-juniper woodlands (7,500'–5,000') and sagebrush shrubland (7,500'–5,500'), shadscale shrubland (5,500'–3,700'), arid grasslands (6,500'–3,700'), sand shrubland (6,000'–3,700'), saltbush barrens (5,000' and lower), and dry riparian washes, Cottonwood-Coyote willow riparian zones, and hanging gardens, all of which occur at the lake level (3,250') or just above.

Wildflowers are many. What you see will depend upon elevation, soil type, time of year, and previous rainfall. Most flower in spring. At the higher elevations the red flowers of Eaton's penstemon, red to orange blooms of Indian paintbrush, large, white evening primrose, and the pink and purple flowers of desert four o'clock are all easy to spot. Utah serviceberry, a common shrub in the park's higher reaches, is covered with creamy-white flowers in spring. At lower elevations you might see the pink sand penstemon, yellow desert trumpet, prince's plume, and yellow or orange globemallow. In fall purple asters and yellow snakeweed will catch your eye. Tamarisk, an invasive shrub found around the lake and in side canyons, is an exotic species that was imported from the Middle East to help prevent streambank erosion. While not unattractive, it is a pernicious pest that has forced out native willows and other vegetation favored by wildlife. A single tamarisk can absorb 40 gallons of water a day and has roots that go extremely deep, reaching seeps and springs that then disappear from the surface. Efforts to eradicate tamarisk in nearby Grand Canyon National Park have been unsuccessful.

Another convenient place to pick up the trail, and one that is easy to find, is the McDonald's parking lot on Lake Powell Boulevard just off US 89 before you climb up onto the mesa. You can also leave your car at park headquarters, located directly opposite the McDonald's on Scenic View

Road, or you can park out at the scenic viewpoint itself and get a look at the Colorado River before starting out.

Length: 9 miles; additional loops and spurs can increase the total distance to 14 miles. Allow 2 to 3 hours to ride this loop and enjoy the spectacular views along the way.

Riding surface: Hardpacked dirt singletrack. Some sections of loose rock and sand may exist.

Difficulty: Moderate. Riders of all levels should give this trail a try. There are a few steep pitches, a few tight turns, and a couple of loose spots requiring some technical riding skill.

Scenery/highlights: Wonderful views of the lake and redrock desert abound; you may want to bring your camera along. Great singletrack riding is also a big plus.

Best time to ride: Spring and fall.

Special considerations: Desert soils and vegetation are extremely fragile, so please stay on the trail at all times; where one track goes others will follow. Be aware of vehicle traffic as you cross over the paved roads. All conveniences can be found in the town of Page but there are none along the trail itself.

Directions for the ride: If you start near the school at the end of North Navajo Drive you will find the trail well marked; if you start from the McDonald's parking lot it is less well marked but still easily visible. At the end of North Navajo Drive begin by picking up what is known as the Nature Trail. This trail accesses the Rim View Trail and, at the point where it meets the main trail, crosses over and makes a loop. This loop is for foot traffic *only.* The Rim View Trail can be ridden in either direction but will described here heading clockwise.

After descending 0.3 mile from the top of the mesa you will come to the Rim View Trail; turn right and begin riding east. You will be looking over Antelope Canyon to Antelope Point Marina, owned and managed by the Navajo Nation. To the north, on the other side of the snake-shaped body of water stretching eastward, is Antelope Island, the largest island on the lake. Just over a mile from where you picked up the Rim View Trail your route swings around to the right and begins heading south along the eastern edge of Manson Mesa. As you pedal southward you'll enjoy expansive views into the Navajo Reservation to the east; Page's airport is on the mesa above to the west. Continue on this heading, following the trail for approximately 3.5 miles to where your route again swings right and heads in a northwesterly direction.

In 0.5 mile the trail intersects Coppermine Road at the southeast edge of the mesa. Cross over the road and continue just below the library and other buildings of Coconino Community College. In another 0.5 mile cross Lake Powell Boulevard and begin riding along the edge of Lake Powell National Golf Course. Approximately 1 mile from where you crossed over Lake Powell Boulevard the trail splits; the lower trail, to the left, takes you on a beautiful tour of a golf course offset by stunning redrock scenery. The right, higher route is used when the lower route is closed because of a golf tournament. As you near the end of the golf course upper and lower routes come together and cross over the northern end of Lake Powell Boulevard. Here the trail continues past the McDonald's and the Arizonainn, heading northward along the western edge of the mesa. You will enjoy another 1.7 miles of trail as it makes its way around the northwestern edge of the mesa and offers spectacular views out to Wahweap Bay. When you reach the intersection with the Nature Trail go right and climb back up to where you left your car.

14. WARM CREEK ROAD–ROMANA MESA
(See map on page 87)

For mountain bikes. This long ride traverses a portion of the Warm Creek Road, taking cyclists out to Crosby Canyon and Alstrom Point where views to isolated Romana Mesa await. This is an adventure into a surreal landscape where many options for creating routes deep into the desert backcountry exist. Several optional starting points will be listed, providing mileages ranging between 14 and 35 miles. The best option is to be accompanied by a support vehicle, but if you are a super-fit rider with good riding skills and are willing to spend a long day in the saddle, there are miles and miles of desert roads to explore.

Starting point: All starting points listed are accessed from Big Water, Utah. To get there from the dam's visitor center drive north on US 89 approximately 15 miles to the town. As you come into town turn right at the Warm Creek Motel onto Ethan Allen Drive. Travel a third of a mile and go right again onto Concord Drive. There will be a sign reading GLEN CANYON NATIONAL RECREATION AREA—STATE HIGHWAY 12; this is the Warm Creek Road. It is also identified as Smoky Mountain Road on some maps.

Drive 9 miles out Warm Creek Road to its intersection with Crosby Canyon Road (County Road 231) and park there for the long version of this ride, another 6 miles to the intersection with the Smoky Mountain Road for the intermediate-length ride, and another 3 miles beyond that to the intersection with the Grand Bench and Alstrom Point/Romana Mesa Road for the shortest version of this ride.

Length: 35, 20, or 14 miles—you choose. Allow most of a day to access and ride any of these routes.

Riding surface: Dirt or clay roads that become rougher and rockier as you go. Note that the spur road out to Romana Mesa is very rocky.

Difficulty: Moderate to strenuous. If you are using a vehicle as support you can ride for as long as you like and simply catch a lift when you've had enough. If you are riding the longest route in a day or continuing on toward Grand Bench on a self-supported trip with panniers, the distances, aridity, and amount of water you must carry will make pedaling out here strenuous.

Scenery/highlights: Much of the scenery along the Warm Creek Road is characterized by barren landscapes in shades of gray and blue that give way to brighter reds as you move toward the lake. The color comes from Mancos shale of the Tropic formation deposited when this area was covered by a warm, shallow sea 64 million years ago during the Cretaceous period. Rich in marine fossils, the landscape's stark, barren appearance has been a draw for numerous filmmakers. Many scenes in *The Planet of the Apes* were shot at locations along this road.

Views to the west of Warm Creek and Wahweap Bays, and to the east of Padre Bay, Gunsight Butte, and Padre Butte are superb. To the south and east, now 550 feet below the lake's surface, is the Crossing of the Fathers, where the intrepid Spanish missionaries Dominguez and Escalante crossed the Colorado River while exploring this country in 1776.

Best time to ride: Fall through spring. Do not attempt riding or driving out this way if the ground is saturated; clay soils turn into a gooey, sticky mess that will mire even four-wheel-drive vehicles.

Special considerations: You will find most conveniences in the town of Big Water or 15 miles away in the town of Page but no water or rest rooms once you leave the pavement. Be sure to carry plenty of water, sunscreen, and snacks, and be prepared to make basic repairs to your bike. If you are using a vehicle for support, carry extra water and other drinks, food, and make sure your gas tank is full.

Directions for the ride: From the intersection of Warm Creek Road (CR 230) and Crosby Canyon Road (CR 231) begin riding north on CR 230 toward Nipple Bench, a toe of the sprawling Kaiparowits Plateau. (It is 4 miles down to the lake on Crosby Canyon Road, a good, shorter ride option and place to take a dip after your ride.) The main Warm Creek Road is to the left. Descend slightly and cross over the Warm Creek drainage; the road then bends around and heads east. Approximately 7 miles from the start you come to the intersection with Smoky Mountain Road (UT 12). Past this intersection the road is signed as the Grand Bench Road. This is the intermediate starting point.

Go right at the next fork, continuing toward Alstrom Point and Romana Mesa. The road to the left (CR 230) stretches for seventy-plus miles across the Kaiparowits Plateau to Escalante, Utah. Another 3 miles beyond this intersection an unnamed pinnacle comes up on your left and soon after a dirt track signed for Alstrom Point will be on the right. Ignore it; a better-used, unsigned road will be on the right a short distance later. This junction is the starting point for the 14-mile (7 miles each way) option out Romana Mesa Road (CR 264).

Continue straight. In 2 miles the road splits again; bear left this time, staying on the main Romana Mesa Road. The road on the right goes to the lake. For the next 5 miles make your way south, down the spine of the mesa on a road that becomes rougher and rockier as you go. Numerous spur roads take off in all directions; remember, bikes must stay on the main, designated roads. At the end of the road you will enjoy sweeping views in all directions. The last 1.5 miles of this route is extremely rough and may require dismounts from time to time. Enjoy the solitude out here, rest up, then reverse the route to get back to your starting point.

15. HOLE-IN-THE-ROCK ROAD (See map on page 95)

For mountain bikes. The Hole-in-the-Rock Road is the route taken in 1879 by 236 Mormon pioneers, 1,000 cattle, and 80 wagons on their way to settle southeastern Utah. Men had to be lowered in barrels over the edge of the cliff at the end of the road to blast a way through the rock to get down to the Colorado River, which they ferried across, and then began the same process to get up the other side. Miraculously, not a single animal, wagon, or life was lost on the six-month journey. The entire length of Hole-in-the-Rock Road, from where it leaves UT 12 just 5 miles east of Escalante, Utah, to its terminus at a notch in the rock above sparkling Lake Powell, is 61 miles. The first 42 miles are well-maintained dirt, easily driven by passenger cars. The last 18.5 miles, beginning at Dance Hall Rock, are rougher, making the rock a good place to begin a cycling adventure. This will be the route described here, although there are many options for making a longer or shorter vehicle or self-supported trips on the Hole-in-the-Rock Road. There are many good places to camp along the way. Intermediate-level riders with a good to excellent level of physical fitness can pedal this route, provided they go prepared and have the stamina to endure a long day in the saddle.

Starting point: Begin at Dance Hall Rock, a large, freestanding mound of sandstone on the left-hand side of the road. One side of the rock is hollowed out into a large cavern. Here, the story goes, pioneers danced to the music of fiddle players days before the harrowing descent through the "the hole-in-the-rock." To get there take UT 12 east from the town of Escalante 5 miles to the start of the Hole-in-the-Rock Road. Go right and drive south 38 miles to Dance Hall Rock. Park there.

Length: 18.5 miles one-way, 37 miles total distance. This is a long, all-day affair if you are not camping along the way.

Riding surface: 12 miles of dirt road with sections of washboard and sand; 6.5 miles of a rough, four-wheel-drive jeep road.

Difficulty: Moderate to strenuous. The distance is by far the most challenging aspect of this ride, although there are several sections over slickrock near the end that require good technical skills.

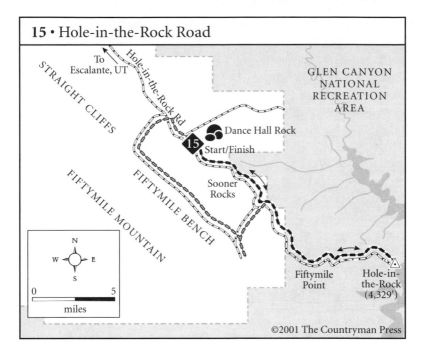

15 • Hole-in-the-Rock Road

To Escalante, UT

Hole-in-the-Rock Rd

STRAIGHT CLIFFS

GLEN CANYON NATIONAL RECREATION AREA

Dance Hall Rock

15 Start/Finish

Sooner Rocks

FIFTYMILE MOUNTAIN

FIFTYMILE BENCH

N
W E
S

0   5
miles

Fiftymile Point

Hole-in-the-Rock (4,329')

©2001 The Countryman Press

Scenery/highlights: When you try to imagine a caravan of 80 wagons and 1,000 head of cattle bumping along this road you begin to appreciate the tenacity and toughness of the early Mormon settlers. Given a directive, or order, from church headquarters in Salt Lake City to settle the fertile lands along the San Juan River in southeastern Utah, they dutifully began preparing for a journey they thought would take six weeks. Time was of the essence; the settlers needed to lay claim to the area both to prevent gentile (non-Mormon) settlers from establishing themselves in the region first and to begin work on administering to, and maybe even converting, the Native Americans living there.

Routes were scouted that would take them south and east through Arizona and far into eastern Utah. The route directly south and across the canyon was chosen because it was most direct. In the fall of 1879 they struck south from the town of Escalante into lands unknown. An advance group of 50 men went ahead to build the route, making way for the wagons. News of the cliffs filtered back to the group, undoubtedly causing a great deal of anxiety. Reports of little water also added to the worries of the group. They pressed on, moving quickly over the first 50 miles, but creeping over the last 6. Sections of rough slickrock and sand slowed them down considerably. A 45-foot drop and almost three-quarters of a mile of steep slickrock down to the Colorado River awaited them at the end of the road. Getting down it and then across the river appeared to be impossible.

Men with picks and blasting powder were lowered over the side and went to work, opening a notch through the rock just wide enough for the wagons. After six weeks of backbreaking labor the road through the cliff down to the river was completed. They ferried across the Colorado River without incident on a large raft that had been built upstream and floated down to the crossing. After struggling up the far side of the canyon, the settlers eventually arrived at the future town site of Bluff, where they dug in and began the work of establishing a new city in the land of Zion.

The vast expanse of desert that surrounds you as you travel south on Hole-in-the-Rock Road is much the same as it was when the pioneers came through over a century ago, with the notable exception of the view at the end. Where the silt-laden Colorado River once burbled along toward the Gulf of Mexico, now stand the quiet blue waters of Lake Powell. To the east extends a great pale pan of rock: Navajo sandstone, sculpted by canyon-forming rivulets feeding the Escalante River. To the west the Kaiparowits Plateau sprawls across the horizon, terminating in a well-defined band of rock jutting southward called the Straight Cliffs. This land is full of visual wonders and thousands of unseen nooks and crannies sheltering the secrets of both nature and the ancient people who once lived in this country. You could spend weeks exploring the many canyons of the Escalante River accessible from this road, or just a day trying to absorb the enormity and beauty of the landscape.

Best time to ride: Spring and fall. This road, and many of the side roads that access camping areas, become impassable in wet weather.

Special considerations: This is very remote country and you will find little in the way of facilities along the way. There are picnic tables and vault toilets at the Devil's Garden pullout and parking area 16.5 miles south of UT 12, but that's it. Make sure you come prepared; start out

Striations from fractures, cracks, and the staining and desert varnish that colors the sandstones of the Colorado Plateau create fascinating patterns and textures.

with a full gas tank and enough food and water to last for several days.

Directions for the ride: As you head south along Hole-in-the-Rock Road you'll want to stop at Devil's Garden, 16.5 miles south of UT 12, and take the short hike to see the fantastic shapes and colors of the hoodoos found there. From Dance Hall Rock, 25 miles further down the road, park and begin pedaling southward on this easy-going dirt road. The phalanx of the Straight Cliffs accompanies you southward to the west, while pale peachy-orange slickrock stretches away to the east. Within the first mile you pass Forty Mile Spring and a few miles later descend through Carcass Wash, site of a terrible accident that claimed the lives of 13 Boy Scouts in June 1963 when the brakes on their truck failed.

The road undulates as it dips through numerous sand washes, descending in 4 miles to the domed shapes of Sooner Rocks. At Sooner Rocks, and again at Cave Point, another 4 plus miles down the road, the road defines the boundary between Grand Staircase–Escalante National Monument and the adjoining Glen Canyon Recreation Area. The road continues to roll and dip over the terrain, becoming decidedly rougher at Fiftymile Point, approximately 12 miles from the start.

At Fiftymile Point the road drops steeply over a ledge and gets rougher as it crosses over sections of slickrock, drops off ledges, and traverses sections of loose, broken rock. At the end of the road, where the cut drops away through the rock, you'll find a visitor registration box. Sign your name as proof you made the journey and then carefully make your way down through the blasted cut, where you can still see drill holes, steps, and wagon-wheel marks, for a quick plunge in the lake. When you're properly refreshed and have had a good look around, remount and head back the way you came.

Option: If you are camping out this way and have a couple of days to ride, you might want to consider riding Fiftymile Bench Road. You can make a 27-mile loop by connecting Fiftymile Bench Road and Hole-in-the-Rock Roads. This loop can be ridden in either direction; Dance Hall Rock makes a good starting point. Pedal south, beyond Dance Hall Rock, approximately 6.5 miles and go right on Fiftymile Bench Road. The road climbs almost 2,000 feet on dirt and jeep roads up the Sooner Slide (a "slide" is an apron of eroded material) and contours the slopes below the Straight Cliffs as you head north. Fabulous views of the Escalante River drainage system, the Henry Mountains, and the sprawl of Glen Canyon National Recreation Area abound from high on Fiftymile Bench Road. The road then drops down Willow Tank Slide to rejoin the Hole-in-the-Rock Road; go right to ride back to Dance Hall Rock.

---

16. PANORAMA POINT (See map on page 99)

For mountain bikes. The out-and-back ride on North Point Mesa to Panorama Point offers a fantastic perspective on Canyonlands National Park and the rivers that have helped shape this region. Beginning and intermediate riders who aren't put off by sand and a few rocky spots will be richly rewarded for the moderate to strenuous effort it takes to get out here. Remember that the 600 feet of elevation loss on the way out to the point will have to be negotiated on the return trip.

Starting point: Begin this ride at the turnoff to North Point Mesa just south of the Hans Flat Ranger Station of Canyonlands National Park. To

16 · Panorama Point

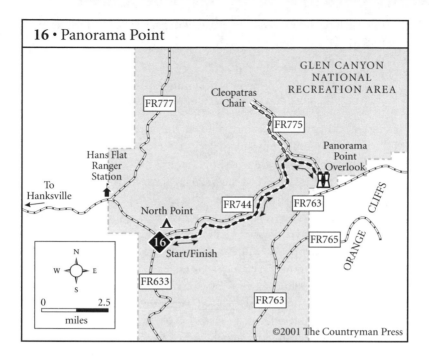

get there from Green River, Utah, travel 12 miles west on I-70 to UT 24. This is exit 147, signed for Hanksville and Capitol Reef. Head south for 25 miles on UT 24. Just past the turnoff for Goblin Valley State Park turn left onto a gravel, two-wheel-drive road, and head east for 46 miles to the Hans Flat Ranger Station. Be aware that this road can become impassable in bad weather.

From the Hans Flat Ranger Station, go southeast, following signs for the Flint Trail. After 2 miles you will pass a fork for French Spring on the left, and immediately beyond that is the start of the North Point Road accessing Panorama Point and Cleopatra's Chair. Park your car at this intersection near the camping area.

Length: 8.5 miles one-way, 17 miles total distance. An optional 2.5 spur out to Cleopatra's Chair will add 5 miles but is well worth the effort. Allow 3 to 4 hours to complete this ride, but an entire day to get out there and back if you are not camping nearby.

Riding surface: Jeep roads comprised of packed sand, broken rock, bedrock, and sand bogs.

Difficulty: Moderate to more difficult. Negotiating the sand and a few of the rocky sections takes some technical skill. A solid base of physical fitness is recommended for this somewhat long ride.

Scenery/highlights: Panorama Point, at the very end of North Point Mesa, juts out from the phalanx of rock referred to as the Orange Cliffs; you will be almost 2,500 feet above the Green River. The tangled maze of canyons that give this area of Canyonlands National Park its name lie to the southeast; directly south is the distinctive shape of Elaterite Butte, and to the east is Ekker Butte. Farther to the east is the glowing outline of the White Rim where euphoric mountain bikers are no doubt gazing in your direction. Junction Butte and Grand View Point, part of the mesa known as Island in the Sky, are also to the east, a mere 40 miles as the crow flies but several hours away by car. Words can't quite describe the sensory experience that awaits you at Panorama Point—you'll simply have to see it for yourself.

The massive sandstone butte known as Cleopatra's Chair is a beautiful, salmon-colored, sheer-wall monolith that is breathtaking in its enormity. Stand against the cool, pink stone of this regal giant with your head tilted back, gazing skyward toward its summit will delight you as your head spins. This distinctive butte can be seen for hundreds of miles on a clear day, and is one of the most easily recognized landmarks in Canyonlands.

Best time to ride: Spring and fall.

Special considerations: This is a remote area where little in the way of conveniences exist. Make sure that you have a full tank of gas, a cooler full of drinks, some food, and at least a gallon of water a day for every person. You may want to consider camping out here so you do not have to drive in and out on the same day. Check in with the ranger at Hans Flat if you are interested in camping. Permits required to camp in the Orange Cliffs area are issued by Canyonlands National Park; call 435-259-7164 for more information. The primitive campgrounds out here have neither water nor bathrooms. Bury all human waste and carry out all garbage.

FAUNA

The most numerous bird here is the common raven, dependably curious and quite bold, often raiding unkempt campsites for food or trinkets. Bewick's wren, black-throated gray warblers, western scrub jays, and the juniper titmouse are also common.

In riparian zones expect to see ash-throated flycatchers, Lucy's and yellow warblers, black phoebes, lesser goldfinches, blue grosbeaks, house finches, mourning doves, and black-chinned hummingbirds. Rock wrens, canyon wrens, and violet-green swallows are drawn to the cliffs. Endangered peregrine falcon populations have increased along with populations of water-loving birds which they hunt. Other raptors include golden eagles and red-tailed hawks. There has been a dramatic increase in the number of water birds in the area since the creation of the lake, over 90 species as of 1999. Most are migratory and are present only in the winter months.

Small mammals are numerous and include white-tailed antelope squirrels, rock squirrels, pack rats, kangaroo rats, desert cottontail rabbits, and jackrabbits. Beaver have also made a comeback in the area with the increase in riparian habitat. Mule deer are found in piñon-juniper forests and in the side canyons; they are the mountain lion's primary food source. Bobcats live here but are not common. Coyotes are quite common. Gray, red, and kit foxes all exist here, as do ringtail cats, a cousin of the raccoon that can be a nuisance to campers.

Lizards, such as the brown side-blotched, western whiptail, desert spiny, eastern fence, desert horned-toad, leopard, and collared, are some of the most often seen wildlife. If you're lucky you may get to see a larger lizard called a chuckwalla. Gopher snakes are quite common, less so are western and faded midget rattlesnakes. In riparian zones you may see the Colorado Plateau canyon treefrog, a red-spotted toad, or a Woodhouse's toad.

In the lake itself, large- and smallmouth bass, striped bass, and carp dominate.

Directions for the ride: From the parking area ride north on the North Point Road across the delicate desert landscape dotted with sage and pygmy forests of piñon and juniper. As you pedal along, descending gently, you will be crossing over a land bridge to another sky island supported by ramparts of Wingate sandstone, referred to here as the Orange Cliffs. Just under 7 miles from the start of this ride you come to a fork in the road. Go right to Panorama Point, left to visit Cleopatra's Chair (you may want to save that excursion for the way back).

Panorama Point is 2 miles past the fork. Breathe deep and try to take it all in. It's easy to imagine being on the wing up here, a lone hawk with only the wind beneath you. When you decide it's time to go, saddle up and ride back to the junction with the spur road to Cleopatra's Chair. If you haven't had enough, take an hour or so to make the 5-mile (total distance) out-and-back spur to get up close to this enormous rock formation. When you're done exploring, ride the North Point Road back to where you left your car.

CAMPING

There are campgrounds at every marina around the lake as well as at Lee's Ferry, on the Colorado River below the dam. Campgrounds at **Lee's Ferry** and **Hite Marina** are managed by the park service; campgrounds at **Wahweap, Bullfrog,** and **Halls Crossing** are run by conscessioners. All operate on a first-come, first-served basis, require a fee, and accept all National Park Service passes. Most have picnic tables, rest rooms, and drinking water.

Primitive camping is allowed along the shoreline at **Lone Rock** (Wahweap area), **Stanton Creek, Bullfrog North & South** (Bullfrog area), **Hite, Dirty Devil,** and **Farley Canyon** (Hite area). These sites have no facilities except for vault toilets. Backcountry camping is allowed throughout the park, although regulations and permitting vary from one district to another. If you are doing a vehicle- or self-supported cycling trip on any of the park's back roads and you intend to camp along the way make sure you check with the district ranger and secure the proper permit. If you plan to camp on BLM lands surrounding the recreation area be sure to check on the regulations and permitting required there.

RV campgrounds are available at **Wahweap, Bullfrog,** and **Halls Crossing.** To reserve RV camping space call 1-800-528-6154.

Coin-operated showers and laundry are available at **Wahweap, Halls Crossing,** and **Bullfrog** and are usually found in the RV campgrounds.

The privately owned **Page– Lake Powell Campground** has both RV and tent sites as well as an indoor pool, store, laundry, and showers. Non-guests can use shower facilities and their dump station for a small fee. They are located southeast of town on Coppermine Road.

LODGING

At each of the marinas around the lake you will find some kind of lodging option, campsites, an RV park, and a store where you can buy basic supplies. Some of the marinas have restaurants; some do not. You can buy gas at all of them. You will also find a ranger station and park information at each marina. Other services are available and include boat tours and rentals.

There are two main lodges inside the park, one at Wahweap and the other at Bullfrog. The **Wahweap Lodge** is priced in the premium range and is the bigger of the two with 350 rooms, two restaurants, two swimming pools, and a jacuzzi. It is recommended that you call four to six weeks in advance to book a reservation (520-645-2433 or 1-800-528-6154). Nearby, at Wahweap Junction on US 89, you'll find the **Lake Powell Motel** with more moderately priced rooms.

Defiance House Lodge at Bullfrog is much smaller than Wahweap Lodge, with only 49 rooms and one restaurant, but is equally as nice. Trailers that sleep up to six are available for rent at Bullfrog and are ideal for families. There is a medical clinic near the lodge. It is difficult to get reservations during the summer months so call well in advance, (435-684-3000 or 1-800-528-6154).

At **Halls Crossing** you will find three-bedroom family units for rent, a store, RV park, and coin-operated laundry and showers. At **Hite** you will find the same, three-bedroom family units in trailers.

There are all kinds of lodging choices in Page including budget motels, B&Bs, at least 10 chain hotels, and a hostel. There is a **Ramada Inn** and a **Marriott Courtyard** with slightly nicer rooms; you can expect to pay more. Stop in at the **Page–Lake Powell Chamber of Commerce** to find out more about accommodations in Page.

FOOD

Inside the park you will find groceries available at each marina, but full-service restaurants at only Wahweap and Bullfrog.

DON'T MISS

Don't pass up the chance to visit Rainbow Bridge National Monument. Rainbow Bridge is the largest natural bridge in the world, measuring over 290 feet high and 275 feet across. This freestanding redrock span could fit the Statue of Liberty or the entire U.S. Capitol building beneath it. The site was designated as a national monument in 1910 by President Taft but has been revered by the native peoples of this country for centuries. The Navajo, whose reservation lands encompass the monument, consider Rainbow Bridge sacred and have fought to maintain some control over visitor numbers and impacts to the site. At one time the tribe sued the federal government to prevent them from flooding the area when Lake Powell was being filled. Rainbow Bridge is not an arch but a natural bridge, formed when a river, instead of flowing around an oxbow, punched through an eroded neck of rock.

Rainbow Bridge is most easily accessed by water. Boat tours leave from Wahweap, Halls Crossing, and Bullfrog marinas. Call the main park information desk to make reservations for one of these boat tours. Several long and extremely rough hiking trails will also take you to the monument from inside the Navajo Reservation. The park service has a published guide to hiking to Rainbow Bridge that can be acquired by calling or writing Glen Canyon National Recreation Area, but they cannot issue the required hiking permits. Hiking permits must be obtained from either the Cameron Visitor Center and Ranger Station (P.O. Box 459, Cameron, AZ 86020; phone 520-679-2303, fax 520-679-2330), or from the Navajo Parks and Recreation Department (P.O. Box 9000, Window Rock, AZ 86515; 520-871-6647).

The **Rainbow Room** at Wahweap Lodge offers fine dining with spectacular views over the lake. They serve three meals a day, have a lounge, and live entertainment during the busiest months of the summer. **Itza Pizza** has more casual fare and an outside deck. Because of the proximity of the town of Page you will find only limited supplies at Wahweap's marina store.

At both Halls Crossing and Hite small stores offering basic picnic supplies and a limited selection of food items. In the Defiance House Lodge at Bullfrog the **Anasazi Restaurant** serves breakfast, lunch, and dinner. You can get basic supplies or mail a letter at **Trailer Village** in Bullfrog, or at the service station, where you can also get service or repairs for your vehicle.

You'll find a wide variety of restaurants in Page: Chinese, Italian, Mexican, and a couple of good cafés and grills. For a good cup of coffee in the morning try **Beans Gourmet Coffee House** on North Navajo Drive.

LAUNDRY

There are possibilities for doing a load of laundry at three of the marinas around the lake and in the town of Page. You'll find coin-operated laundry machines and showers in the RV campgrounds at **Wahweap, Halls Crossing,** and **Bullfrog.**

BIKE SHOP/BIKE RENTAL

Page has had a hard time supporting a bike shop in recent years and when this book went to press the one shop in town had closed. The next closest option for finding bike parts, repairs, or rentals is several hours away. In Arizona the town of Flagstaff has several good shops; in Utah you can find at least half a dozen in Moab, one in Panguitch, a couple in the Cedar City area, and a couple in St. George. If you are going to Zion National Park you'll find a good shop in the town of Springdale.

FOR FURTHER INFORMATION

Glen Canyon National Recreation Area— Superintendent, Rainbow Bridge National Monument, P.O. Box 1507, Page, AZ 86040. General information: 520-608-6404; 24-hour emergency: 800-582-4351; http://www.nps.gov/glca/

Page–Lake Powell Chamber of Commerce, 644 N. Navajo Drive (in the Dam Plaza), P.O. Box 727, Page, AZ 86040; 520-645-2741 or 888-261-PAGE; e-mail: chamber@ page-lakepowell.chamber.org

4

The Grand Canyon is, without question, one of the world's great natural wonders and America's most popular national park. This spectacular chasm, created over millions of years by the uplifting of the Colorado Plateau and the energetic downcutting of the Colorado River, has created a perspective on time and space that is truly awe inspiring. Close to five million visitors a year come from all over the world to experience the canyon's humbling magnificence, taking away a renewed appreciation for Mother Nature's artistry. From Glen Canyon Dam, this river-carved canyon winds through solid rock for 277 miles before it meets the dammed waters of Lake Mead. North and south rims of the canyon are on average 10 miles apart, spanning 18 miles at the widest point. Depth of the canyon, from rim to river, averages over a mile.

The stories revealed in the cliffs and terraces of the canyon walls reach back two billion years to when the earth was half its current age. The oldest rocks are found in the Inner Gorge, the deepest part of the canyon. These schists and granites were once sedimentary rocks similar to the rock layers seen at the canyon rims. Billions of years ago they were twisted and compressed under intense pressure from overlying rock layers, and then heated to melting point by the earth's molten core. Veins of magma oozed into the fractured rock from below. As the rock and magma cooled and recrystallized they became extremely hard, and are the most erosion-resistant rock in the canyon. Above them are stacked almost a mile of shales, sandstones, and limestones masterfully sculpted by erosion over the eons. These layers have provided geologists an unequaled opportunity to study the climates and events that have shaped North America.

Above the Vishnu Group's schists and granites are a group of tilted, crumpled, Precambrian shales and sandstones riddled with faults and ancient lavas. More than 130 million years of erosion produced an enormous gap in the record above this layer. The result of a prolonged period of erosion or perhaps a sequence of cataclysmic events, this gap occurs across much of western North America and is referred to as the Great Uncomformity. On top of these jumbled Precambrian rocks a more consistent record commences in horizontal layers of sedimentary rock. The first layer is evidence of the deepening seas of the Cambrian Period, 500 to 570 million years ago (m.y.). Deposits now recognized as the brownish, ledge-forming Tapeats sandstone, greenish Bright Angel shale, and Muav limestone are the legacies of this period. All of these layers contain a rich variety of early marine fossils.

A gap above these layers indicates that the Cambrian seas receded and another period of erosion began. After this period of erosion a layer of sediment was deposited across a channeled floodplain; the resultant rock is called Temple Butte limestone. Above that is the Missisippian period's (360 to 335 m.y.) Redwall limestone. Hundreds of feet thick in places and fairly erosion resistant, it forms sheer walls in the canyon. Crinoids, brachiopods, corals, and fish all occur in this gray layer that has been stained red by minerals in the layers above. During the following Pennsylvanian period (335 to 290 m.y.), there is evidence of the existence of a large bay that filled periodically with layers of silt, sand, and mud. These red layers are the alternately cliff- and slope-forming Supai Group. A thick band of Hermit shale, deposited during the Permian period (290 to 240 m.y.), lies above the Supai Group and contains dinosaur tracks and fossils of ferns and other plants. Later in the Permian period a desert of blowing dunes swept across western North America, resulting in the light, cross-bedded Coconino sandstone, easily seen higher up in the canyon walls and buttes. Seas then encroached again, erasing the desert and leaving behind tan- and buff-colored Toro-

CYCLING OPTIONS

Road bikers and mountain bikers can ride the spectacular 9-mile long West Rim Drive along the South Rim year-round. This route is closed to vehicle traffic during the summer months but can be busy with car and camper traffic the rest of the year. The longer, 24-mile East Rim Drive is best suited for serious road riders, however, a shorter 11-mile option out to Grandview Point, one of the best overlooks on the South Rim, is sure to satisfy the time and fitness requirements of others. The Tusayan Bike Trails, just outside the south boundary of the park, wind through old-growth ponderosa pines and offer seclusion, a wilderness setting, and several distance options. The Coconino Rim Trail is another option for mountain bikers just outside the park's boundary. This route takes riders past several historic sites and winds along an escarpment or "rim" above a basin, allowing for great views to the Grand Canyon in the north and the Painted Desert in the east.

The higher, cooler North Rim opens sometime in May and closes in late October or early November with the first heavy snow. Here you'll find a long, 23-mile paved route out to Cape Royal, with a shorter 11-mile route option to Point Imperial. The 18-mile trip out to Point Sublime traverses a rough, doubletrack jeep road that will thrill mountain bikers. The newly created Rainbow Rim Trail was designed with mountain bikers in mind and is a fast-paced, rollicking ride along the western edge of the Kaibab Plateau with overlooks over the Tapeats Amphitheater and the Grand Canyon. This trail can be accessed at several points, making it possible to create your own routes and loops using forest service roads.

weap and Kaibab limestones. Both of these layers are rich in marine fossils and resistant to erosion. They are capped throughout the Colorado Plateau by the Moenkopi formation, a layer of red sandstones and siltstones deposited on a river floodplain or tidal flat during the Triassic period (205 to 240 m.y.) of the Mesozoic era. Ripple marks, mud cracks,

An enormous view of the Grand Canyon looking west from Point Sublime on the North Rim.

animal tracks, and even pits from rain drops can be found in this layer. The soft, colorful mudstones and volcanic ash of the Chinle formation, like the Moenkopi layers below it, have been eroded away in many places near the Grand Canyon, leaving the Kaibab limestone to define the canyon rims.

Another 180 million years after the deposition of all these sediments, or about 60 million years ago, faulting and squeezing of the earth's crust began forcing what would become the Colorado Plateau skyward. Within the larger plateau smaller upwarps and plateaus began forming. Streams and rivers draining the Rocky Mountains to the east flowed westward but ran into the plateau and were forced to take a more southerly route. The river that eventually became the Colorado traced the path of today's Little Colorado River, flowing into the Painted Desert. Meanwhile, snowmelt and runoff from the Kaibab Plateau, the crown of the larger Colorado Plateau, began cutting a west-running drainage. Sometime between 2 and 10 million years ago enough sediment and rock were stripped away that this drainage broke through to the east, capturing the waters of the south-bound river. This new river eagerly cascaded down thousands of feet in a headlong rush toward the Gulf of California. A period of planetary warming and increased precipitation then fueled the river, sending torrents of raging water across the plateau, accelerating the canyon's formation. While rain and snow, wind and weather, con-tinue to sculpt the many fantastic buttes and temples in the canyon, the erosional force of the river itself, which works to widen the canyon bottom, was greatly diminished when Glen Canyon Dam was completed in 1964.

Possibilities for exploring the main canyon and its rims and many side canyons are almost limitless and could provide an entire lifetime of adventure. The canyon's size and intricacies, its constantly changing yet always stunning visual beauty, and the palpable sense of the earth's ancient history here are profoundly moving and instill a deeper and more complex appreciation of the natural world and our place in it.

Cycling in the Park

SOUTH RIM

The busy South Rim of the Grand Canyon receives 90 percent of the park's visitors, most of whom come during the summer months. The popular West Rim Drive winds along the canyon rim for 9 miles, ending at Hermit's Rest where you'll find a gift shop, rest rooms, and several hiking trails that access the canyon bottom. During the summer months private vehicle traffic is prohibited and a free shuttle bus takes sightseers out along this drive. Bicycles, however, are permitted year-round. More serious road riders might want to tackle the rolling 24-mile trip out along East Rim Drive from the South Rim Visitor Center to Desert View (48 miles out-and-back); others may want to ride only a portion of the route. Spectacular views from overlooks along both rim drives warrant carrying a panoramic camera and lots of film. For mountain bikers on the South Rim there is a network of easy trails just outside the park in the Kaibab National Forest near Tusayan, and a pedal along the Coconino Rim that is part of the border-to-border Arizona Trail. There are no dirt roads or trails open to mountain bikers anywhere inside the park on the South Rim.

There is little vehicle traffic to worry about when riding off the main roads in the national forest, however, riding on any of the paved roads inside the park on the South Rim can be nerve wracking because of the narrow, shoulderless roads and the number of cars and campers, especially during the summer's peak tourist season. Although having some experience with busy roads will make a pedal here more enjoyable, it is best to plan cycling along the South Rim in spring or fall when it is less crowded. Daytime temperatures climb into the mid-60s atop the rim by the beginning of April and remain comfortable for riding until early November. Getting out in the early morning, or saving your ride for evening when the light in the canyon is at its best, are also good ways to avoid congestion along the road and at overlooks. Other things to keep in mind when planning to do some biking along the South Rim are the high elevations (approximately 7,000 to 7,500 feet above sea level), strong sun, dry air, and quickly changing weather. Start out slow; drink plenty of water before, during, and after your ride; and cover up or wear plenty of sunscreen—all will help you avoid getting overheated, dehydrated, and just plain exhausted.

NORTH RIM

The North Rim is much less crowded than the south, although you can expect some congestion during the busy summer months. Great riding opportunities exist on both paved and dirt roads on this side of the canyon, which is only 10 miles from the South Rim as the crow flies but is 215 miles around and 5 hours driving by road. Possibilities for pedaling on the North Rim begin with the 23-mile long paved road out to Cape Royal, where sweeping views of the park's eastern segment await. This makes for a long 46-mile day that will delight seasoned road riders. A shorter out-and-back ride to Point Imperial from Grand Canyon Lodge and Visitor Center gives a total distance of 22 miles. A primitive 18-mile long jeep road traverses the rim west of Grand Canyon Lodge and accesses several spectacular overlooks, including Point Sublime, where the road ends. The recently completed Rainbow Rim Trail, existing just outside the park in Kaibab National Forest, is a thrilling, 18-mile singletrack that zigzags along the western edge of the Kaibab Plateau with constant views of the Grand Canyon. Avid mountain bikers won't want to miss this one.

As you cycle across the Walhalla Plateau to Cape Royal, or skirt the rim of Crystal Creek drainage on your way out to Point Sublime, you'll notice that scenery and feel of the North Rim is quite different than that of the south. This is because the North Rim is 1,000 to 1,500 feet higher than the south and receives 60 percent more moisture. As a result, temperatures are much cooler. Wintertime brings a 6- to 8-foot deep blanket of snow to the Kaibab Plateau, sometimes closing park facilities and access to the North Rim well into May. Roads and facilities generally stay open until the first big snowfall, sometime in late October. Weather can change quickly up here, causing the mercury to plummet, so it's always a good idea to carry extra clothing when out for a long ride. The summer monsoon season, which begins in July and can run through mid-September, results in daily cloud buildups and violent thunderstorms that lash the North Rim with heavy rains and lightning. If you plan to be out all day, check local weather forecasts and try to avoid getting caught in one of these storms.

Despite the cooler temperatures of the North Rim, the air is still very dry and the sun's rays are fierce; using plenty of sunscreen or staying covered up and drinking lots of water will help you make the most of your day. Also, plan on taking a day or so to acclimate to the elevation *before* a big ride; your body will need some time to adjust to the thinner air.

Note: Grand Canyon National Park is in the middle of developing an extensive, long-range transportation plan that will make this park one of the most bike-friendly in the United States. In addition to a light rail system that will bring visitors into the park at the South Rim and take them out along West Rim Drive, the plan includes a greenway trail system for cyclists and pedestrians. On the South Rim this trail system will extend along the rim from Hermit's Rest at the end of the West Rim Drive almost 35 miles to Desert View near the eastern boundary of the park and south to the town of Tusayan. These 12-foot-wide, paved trails will parallel existing park roads, between road and canyon rim, providing for spectacular views the entire way. There are also plans for building a similar greenway system on the North Rim, resulting in 73 miles of car-free trails for either road or mountain bikes. Construction of these trails will take place on the South Rim first, where the need to offset congestion is greatest.

As of the writing of this book none of these greenways exist, although construction is scheduled to begin in the summer of 2000. The first section of trail will begin near Grand Canyon Village, head north to Mather Point, and extend for a short distance in either direction. This first segment will be designated as pedestrian-only, to get people from the village area to the rim as quickly and easily as possible. Subsequent sections will be built over the next few years as funding becomes available. Find out more about the Grand Canyon Greenway project by going to www. nps.gov/grca/greenway/.

SOUTH RIM RIDES

17. WEST RIM DRIVE (See map on page 115)

For road or mountain bikes. The 9-mile long route along West Rim Drive from the South Rim Visitor Center and Park Headquarters to Hermit's Rest includes some of the South Rim's best views and several dizzying points where canyon walls drop away for more than 3,000 feet. A ban on private vehicles along this route during the busy summer months does not affect cyclists, who can linger at empty overlooks and pedal on when buses full of tourists pull up.

Starting point: South Rim Visitor Center.

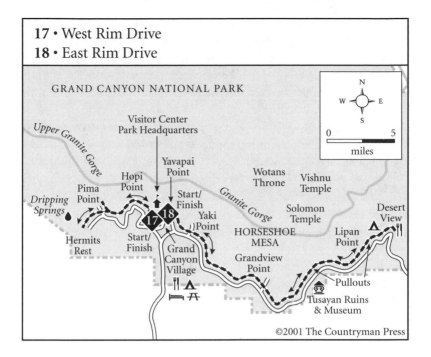

17 • West Rim Drive
18 • East Rim Drive

GRAND CANYON NATIONAL PARK

Upper Granite Gorge

Dripping Springs

Pima Point

Hopi Point

Visitor Center
Park Headquarters

Yavapai Point

Hermits Rest

Start/ Finish

Start/ Finish

Grand Canyon Village

Granite Gorge

Wotans Throne

Vishnu Temple

Solomon Temple

HORSESHOE MESA

Grandview Point

Yaki Point

Desert View

Lipan Point

Pullouts

Tusayan Ruins & Museum

N
W — E
S

0   5
miles

©2001 The Countryman Press

Length: 18 miles total distance. Allow at least a half a day to ride the distance, gaze out over the canyon, and look around at Hermit's Rest.

Riding surface: Pavement.

Difficulty: Easy to moderate. Although this route loses only 200 feet on the way to Hermit's Rest, elevations are high, so you may feel short of breath and more tired than usual after a ride of this length.

Scenery/highlights: Views of the Bright Angel Trail descending the Garden Creek drainage and of the Battleship, a sculpted butte across from Maricopa Point, are some of the highlights as you start out on this ride. Just past Maricopa Point is the Orphan Mine, where copper and uranium were once extracted from the canyon wall. Heart-pounding views await at Powell Memorial, a fitting place to honor the first European to thoroughly study the canyon and navigate its entire length. At Hopi Point you can see the river below and look into the Inferno at the top of the Salt Creek drainage. At the Abyss, the Great Mohave Wall drops 3,000 feet to the head of Monument Creek. At Pima Point the view to the north includes Cathedral Stairs and Cope Butte, which define the boundary between Monument Creek to the east and the massive Hermit Creek drainage to the west. At the end of the road you come to Hermit's Rest, a charming structure designed by famous architect Mary Colter. This place is named for Louis Boucher, a hermit who came to the canyon 1891 to work mining claims in Boucher Canyon. He lived alone near Dripping Springs for 21 years.

Best time to ride: Spring and fall.

Special considerations: Beware of traffic, especially around pullouts. Bikes are not allowed off the main road or on any of the walkways to overlook points. If you want to spend time at any of the overlooks, walking out the Hermit Trail, or in the gift shop at Hermit's Rest, be sure to bring a lock to secure your bike while you are away.

Water and rest rooms are available at the visitor center, at Grand Canyon Village, and at Hermit's Rest.

Directions for the ride: From the visitor center, head west on the access road, past the Shrine of Ages, turning right onto West Rim Drive. In approximately 0.8 mile you come to Grand Canyon Village where you'll find hotels, shops, and the historic railroad station. Past Grand Canyon Village the route loops around through stands of piñon and juniper and heads north along the western edge of Garden Creek drainage, arriving at Maricopa Point approximately 3 miles from the start. For the next 3.2 miles the route hugs the rim, tracing the outline of the Hopi Wall and the Great Mohave Wall, past Hopi and Mohave Points, and around the Abyss, which forms the head of the Monument Creek drainage. The route then leaves the canyon rim, winding through high-desert forests for another mile, reaching the short spur out to Pima Point approximately 8 miles from the start. From there the route heads southwest, along the rim and the eastern edge of Hermit Creek drainage, arriving at Hermit's Rest 9 miles from the start. Take some time here and when you're ready to go head back the way you came.

18. EAST RIM DRIVE (See map on page 115)

For road bikes. Although the overlooks along the 24-mile-long East Rim Drive are fewer than on West Rim Drive, they are no less spectacular. Grandview Point, as the name suggests, is one of the best and is a good turnaround point for those wanting a shorter ride. The rolling nature of the topography along this part of the rim makes this route ideally suited for the seasoned road rider looking for a classic half-century. East Rim Drive doubles as AZ Highway 64. There are no restrictions on vehicles; as a result traffic can get extremely heavy during the summer months.

Starting point: South Rim Visitor Center.

Length: 24 miles one-way, 48 miles out-and-back (without spurs). Spur roads add another 4.5 miles to the total distance. This is an all-day adventure with stops at overlooks and points of interest along the way. Those interested in a shorter excursion can turn around at Grandview Point, 11.6 miles from the start.

Riding surface: Pavement; narrow, limited shoulders.

Difficulty: Strenuous. Overall length, rolling terrain, and elevation make this ride more difficult.

Scenery/highlights: At Yavapai Point and Observation Station you'll enjoy outstanding views into Garden Creek and Pipe Spring drainages. A museum with exhibits on the canyon's geology and a great selection of books, maps, posters, videos, and postcards is located here. This spot is one of the South Rim's best for watching the sunset. Mather Point, the next stop along the route and named after the park's first director, is many people's first impression of the Grand Canyon. From here you can see the inner gorge and numerous stone temples and buttes carved from the earth long ago by the river. The spur road to Yaki Point accesses the Kaibab Trail, which descends along Cedar Ridge and takes hikers to the canyon bottom. Grandview Point is the next, and perhaps most spectacular stop along this route. Hance Creek drainage falls away to the east of this overlook, which is perched directly above Horseshoe Mesa. The awesome views of buttes, thrones, and temples on the far side of the canyon are mind-boggling. Further along you'll come to Moran Point near the

FLORA

There are three main habitat types on the canyon rims: piñon –juniper woodlands, ponderosa pine forests, and subalpine spruce-fir forests. Subalpine forests occur above 8,000 feet on the North Rim and include Englemann spruce, subalpine and white fir, and quaking aspen. Ponderosa pines can be found above 7,000 feet in drainages and on cooler slopes, but occur in pure stands above 7,200 feet. Utah juniper and piñon pine dominate on the South Rim. Gambel oak and mountain mahogany are also found along the rims. Both favor warmer, drier areas.

Around the canyon edges the trees have been stunted and gnarled by exposure to wind and weather. Dominant forest types on both rims often give way to trees and shrubs normally found at lower elevations. This is due to the influence of hot, dry updrafts traveling from the canyon bottom up the canyon walls and over the rims. This "canyon rim effect" is apparent on the North Rim at Cape Royal and Bright Angel Point where piñon and juniper replace ponderosa pine forests.

Shrubs in the park include cliffrose, buffalo berry, cliff fendlerbush, and fern bush. These four like drier areas while Wood's rose (commonly reffered to as wild rose), three-leaf sumac, wax currant, and Utah serviceberry are more likely to be found away from cliff rims in slightly wetter areas.

Wildflowers include scarlet gilia (also called sky rocket), Indian paintbrush, lupine, evening primrose, and globe mallow. Tall Yellow primrose, often 3 to 10 feet tall, is more commonly found on the North Rim. Both sego and mariposa lilies exist in the park, as do Palmer's, thickleaf, and fire cracker penstemon. Golden corydalis, yellow and red blanket flower, goldeneye, longleaf phlox, and Lambert's locoweed are species more likely found on the South Rim, while purple larkspur, Fransican bluebells or mertensia, fireweed, green gentian, and giant helleborine, a member of the orchid family, live in the meadows and wetter areas on the North Rim.

head of Red Canyon, and later Lipan Point, where it is possible to see the entire geologic sequence of the canyon, from the metamorphic rocks of Granite Gorge to the Kaibab limestone that rims the edge of the plateau directly across from you. Between Moran and Lipan Points is the Tusayan Ruin and Museum. This ruin was built by ancestral Puebloans at the end of the 12th century, and was inhabited for only a few decades. The small museum has information on the ruin, the people who lived there, and displays of artifacts removed from the site. At Desert View, the easternmost overlook and turnaround point on the ride, are stunning views up the north-south running portion of the canyon and the Desert View Watchtower, another whimsical structure designed by Mary Colter. An information center, bookstore, gift shop, gas station, and campground can also be found here. Desert View is the highest viewpoint along the South Rim at 7,500 feet above sea level.

Best time to ride: Spring and fall.

Special considerations: Traffic can be extremely heavy along this route; please ride in single file and stay to the right. Rest rooms and water are available at the South Rim Visitor Center and at Desert View. Also found at Desert View is a snack bar and general store where you can get something to eat. Pit toilets are available at several picnic areas along the way.

Directions for the ride: From the visitor center, go left and ride out the short access road you came in on. Pedal due north for 0.6 mile to the short spur to Yavapai Point. If you want to go to the Yavapai Observation Station and see the geologic exhibits and views, turn left and ride 0.2 mile. If not, continue onward to Mather Point, one of the most popular vistas along the rim, another 0.5 mile down the road. Approximately 1.7 miles from the start is the three-way intersection of East and West Rim Drives and AZ 64. East Rim Drive and AZ 64 share the same route, heading east from here. AZ 64/180 continues south to the town of Tusayan, and beyond to Williams, Arizona. A mile past this intersection is the mile-long spur road out to Yaki Point.

Back on the main route, you soon pass a picnic area on the right and another one mile beyond that, also on the right. The route continues south and east through stands of piñon and juniper before coming back to the rim at the head of the three-pronged Grapevine Creek drainage, approximately 6 miles from the start. The road meets the top of each fork of the drainage over the next 3 miles, and then climbs gradually through more high-desert forest for another 2 miles before reaching the turnoff for Grandview Point approximately 11 miles from the start. It is an easy 0.6 mile out to Grandview Point, considered by many to be one of the most spectacular overlooks anywhere along the South Rim. (If you are doing the shorter version of this ride this is your turnaround point.)

Past the turnoff for Grandview Point the route continues southeast for another 2 miles before swinging around to the northeast, climbing a short distance, and then descending Buggeln Hill. As you descend, keep your eyes peeled to your left to catch glimpses into the Hance Creek drainage and the many beautifully sculpted buttes and towers across the canyon. Approximately 16.6 miles from the start is the spur road out to Moran Point, where the Hance Trail descends into Red Canyon. Coronado Butte is directly to the west at this overlook. The road again skirts the canyon rim 2.5 miles past Moran Point; you can peer down into the Papago Creek drainage, and then continue for another 1.5 miles to Tusayan Ruins and Museum. From the ruins the road climbs gradually for 1.4 miles to Lipan Point, and beyond, for another 2 miles to Desert View. When you've had a chance to take in the view, look around at the information center, explore Mary Colter's lookout, and recharge for the pedal back, climb into the saddle and return the way you came.

---

19. TUSAYAN BIKE TRAILS (See map on page 121)

For mountain bikes. The Tusayan Bike Trails area contains a series of three loops on both singletrack trails and old logging roads. These loops wind around through deep, secluded stands of ponderosa pine just outside the south boundary of the park. Riders of varying abilities can enjoy one or a combination of all three loops, easily adjusting the length and time in the saddle. A brand-new trail now extends 16 miles to Grandview Tower, using part of the Tusayan Bike Trail loops as a section of its route.

Starting point: The trailhead for all three loops is located 0.3 mile north of the town of Tusayan, 0.4 mile south of the Tusayan Ranger District offices and ranger station, and 0.6 mile south of the park's south entrance station, on the west side of AZ 64/US 180. The trailhead is well marked.

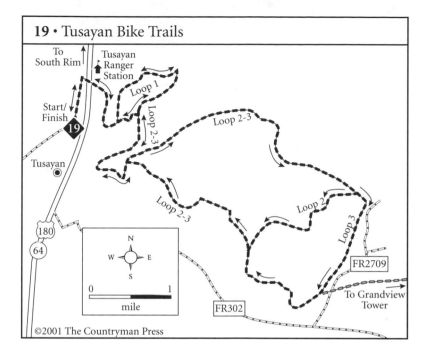

19 · Tusayan Bike Trails

To South Rim

Tusayan Ranger Station

Loop 1

Loop 2-3

Start/Finish

19

Tusayan

180

64

N
W ⬩ E
S

0   1
mile

Loop 2-3

Loop 2-3

Loop 2

Loop 3

FR2709

FR302

To Grandview Tower

©2001 The Countryman Press

Length: Loop #1 is 3.7 miles from the trailhead and back, loop #2, also called Rocky Road, is 10.2 miles, and loop #3, also called the Gumbo Loop, is 11.2 miles. The trail to Grandview Tower from the trailhead is 16 miles one-way, 32 miles out-and-back. Allow anywhere from 1 to 6 hours to ride these trails.

Riding surface: Old dirt logging roads and singletrack with a few rocky sections.

Difficulty: Easy to strenuous, depending on how long you choose to ride.

Scenery/highlights: Although there aren't any canyon overlooks along these trails, they offer the chance to get out and pedal on quiet, secluded trails through forests of ponderosa pine, piñon pine, and juniper. Some of the ponderosa pines along loop #1 are old growth, meaning they have never been logged. These trees are purported to be some of the biggest and oldest ponderosa pines in the world. The forest habitat also provides excellent opportunity for viewing wildlife. Species you might see include elk, mule deer, pronghorn antelope, coyote, porcupine, wild turkey, several hawk species, and golden eagles. Many other resident and migratory birds fly through these woods.

Best time to ride: Spring and fall.

Special considerations: There are no facilities at the trailhead. Water and rest rooms can be found at the Tusayan Ranger District offices and ranger station 0.4 mile north of the trailhead, or in Tusayan 0.3 mile south.

Directions for the ride: From the trailhead, begin by pedaling north a few hundred yards, following the trail as it enters a concrete walkway that passes under AZ 64/US 180. Follow the route, marked by brown stakes with the numbers 1, 2, and 3 on them, for 0.7 miles to the start of loop trail #1. This loop can be ridden in either direction. If you want to bypass loop #1 bear right, and ride a short distance to the spur that accesses loop trails #2 and #3. If you plan on riding loop trail #1, go right, and follow the trail along old logging roads as it loops through some very large, old ponderosa pines.

At 2 miles from the start you will come back to the start of loop #1. Now turn left, ride a few hundred feet, and go right again. It is 1.1 miles from the start to the beginning of loops #2 and #3. These two loops share the majority of the trail, with loop #2 simply taking a shorter route through the middle of loop #3. Go left onto the trail, following the brown markers that take you through the woods and over several rocky sections. You encounter loop trail #2 leaving on the right approximately 3.5 miles from the start of the loop. This option is only about a mile shorter than the longer loop. Whichever way you decide to go, return the way you came once you arrive back at the start of loops 2 and 3.

Option: If you are interested in continuing on to Grandview Tower (trail #4 of the Tusayan Bike Trails), ride loop #3, watching for this signed trail, which takes off on the left 6 miles from the start of loop trails #2 and #3. Follow this trail as it rolls through the ponderosas approximately 2 miles to Ten X Tank. From here the trail heads south, reaching FR 303 in 2.2 miles. The route briefly follows FR 303, continuing south, and then leaves the road 0.4 mile later heading east. A short distance after leaving the road the trail comes to Watson Tank. The trail then follows Watson drainage as it heads east, climbing gently over the next 4 miles to Grandview Tower. Retrace your route to return to your car.

---

20. COCONINO RIM TRAIL (See map on page 124)

For mountain bikes. The Coconino Rim Trail forms part of the border-to-border Arizona Trail and extends for just over 9 miles along the top of an escarpment that rims an area referred to as the Upper Basin. Besides views of the Grand Canyon to the north and distant panoramas of the Painted Desert in the east, you will visit Grandview Lookout Tower and can take a spur out to visit the cabins of the Hull brothers' sheep operation, built in the 1880s. This is a newly constructed trail through an area that is plentiful in both wildlife and wilderness scenery. For an easier option you may return on Forest Road (FR) 310, the Coconino Rim Road, which will save time and 2 miles of pedaling. The adventurous may want to continue south along the Arizona Trail to Russell Tank, the historic Moqui Stage Station along the old stage route to the canyon, or even beyond, to Flagstaff.

Starting point: Trailhead near Grandview Lookout Tower. To get there go east on FR 302 from AZ 64/US 180 near the south end of Tusayan. If you are coming from the south, this dirt and gravel road leaves on the right side just past a sign that marks the southern boundary of the town of Tusayan. Once on FR 302, drive east for 16 miles to the Grandview Lookout Tower and trailhead.

You can also access this trailhead from East Rim Drive, also AZ 64. The turnoff to Grandview Tower and the trailhead is signed for the Arizona Trail leaves 2 miles east of the spur road to Grandview Point overlook on the canyon rim. Follow this road, FR 310, approximately 1 mile to Grandview Lookout Tower and park.

Length: 9.1 miles one way, 18.2 miles out-and-back. Returning via FR 310 will give a slightly shorter total distance of 16 miles. Allow at least a half a day for this ride.

Riding surface: Dirt singletrack. An option allows riders to return via a dirt road.

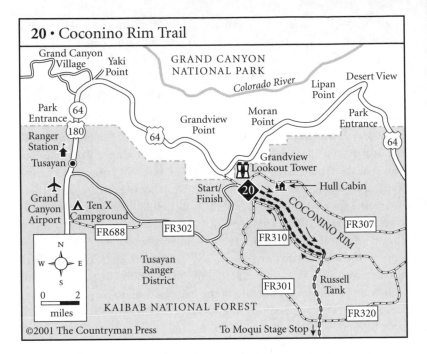

20 · Coconino Rim Trail

Grand Canyon Village Yaki Point GRAND CANYON NATIONAL PARK *Colorado River* Lipan Point Desert View

Park Entrance 64 180

Ranger Station Tusayan

Grand Canyon Airport ▲ Ten X Campground

64 Grandview Point Moran Point Park Entrance 64

Grandview Lookout Tower

Start/Finish 20 Hull Cabin

COCONINO RIM FR307

FR688 FR302 FR310

N W E S 0 2 miles

Tusayan Ranger District

FR301 Russell Tank FR320

KAIBAB NATIONAL FOREST

©2001 The Countryman Press To Moqui Stage Stop ↓

Difficulty: Easy to moderate. There is one steep section of rocky switchbacks, otherwise the trail is smooth and almost level. Elevation and distance will make this route more difficult for some.

Scenery/highlights: Grandview Lookout Tower and a two-room cabin built in 1936 by the Civilian Conservation Corps are near the trailhead. The 80-foot tower was used to detect forest fires burning in the distance during a period when overhead airplane flights were rare.

A side trip to Hull Cabin, 1.5 miles past the lookout tower on FR 307, provides insight into the early ranching history of the area. There are actually four structures that comprise the Hull Cabin Historic District: a residence, a storage cabin, a log barn, and water tank, all set in a small meadow surrounded by old-growth ponderosa pine. Brothers Phillip and William Hull established their sheep ranch at this site in 1884 and built the structures in 1888. The cabins are beautifully constructed from hand-hewn ponderosa logs. Shortly after the cabins were built Phillip died of a heart attack, leaving his brother to carry on the operation alone. William eventually abandoned sheep ranching and began prospecting in the canyon bottom. The cabins became the property of the forest service around the turn of the century and became a ranger station in 1907. They are still owned and used by the forest service and serve as living quarters for summer workers. Please respect their privacy.

In addition to historic sites, this ride visits some gorgeous backcountry away from the busy canyon rim. Views are plentiful, wildlife abounds, and the trail itself is a fun, fast-paced singletrack.

Best time to ride: Spring and fall.

Special considerations: Vault toilets can be found at the trailhead but there is no water available here or anywhere along the route. Be sure to bring plenty of your own for before, during, and after your ride.

Directions for the ride: Begin pedaling southward from the trailhead. Almost immediately you come to a short interpretive loop that identifies mistletoe and its affects on ponderosa pine forests. A few hundred feet beyond, the trail crosses over FR 307, which accesses Hull Cabin. If you are interested in riding to this historic site go left onto FR 307 and ride for 1.5 miles to the group of buildings in a small meadow. If not, continue southward, following the trail as it winds along between the Coconino Rim to the left and FR 310, also referred to as the Coconino Rim Road, on the right.

The trail continues heading south and east as it winds in and out of stately ponderosas and dense patches of Gambel oak and cliffrose. Approximately 3 miles from the start the trail jogs eastward as it skirts Tusayan Mountain (7,486 feet). At this point you can enjoy excellent views of the Upper Basin, the Coconino Rim, and distant views of the Painted Desert, a rosy red glow along the eastern horizon. A little further along the trail views north to the Grand Canyon and the dark brow of the Kaibab Plateau can be had. Scott Trick Tank, where ranchers trapped meager runoff for their cattle, is on the right approximately 6 miles from the start. At 7.3 miles the route follows a series of short, steep switchbacks as the trail crosses a drainage. In another 1.4 miles the route meets FR 310 and continues south to Russell Tank and Moqui Station. This is your turnaround point. You can either return via the singletrack route you rode out, or return on FR 310, the Coconino Rim Road, a fairly well-traveled dirt road that will deliver you back to the trailhead but in less time and over a shorter distance.

If you are interested in continuing along the Arizona Trail, first be sure to pick up information from the Tusayan Ranger District offices in Tusayan. It is about 2 miles to Russel Tank from FR 310, and another 8 to Moqui Stage Station.

NORTH RIM RIDES

21. POINT IMPERIAL–CAPE ROYAL
(See map on page 128)

For road bikes. This route begins at Grand Canyon Lodge, near heart-stopping Bright Angel Point, and traverses the Walhalla Plateau, an enormous terrace, or peninsula, surrounded on every side by the yawning depths of the Grand Canyon. The road out to Cape Royal and Point Imperial serves as the North Rim's scenic drive. It skirts the eastern edge of the plateau, accessing some of the highest and most spectacular vistas on either rim. The gorgeous alpine scenery and thrilling vistas are sure to make the shorter 11-mile trip to Point Imperial, or the much longer 23-mile journey out to Cape Royal, some of your most memorable pedals ever.

Starting point: North Rim Visitor Center next to Grand Canyon Lodge.

Length: 11 miles one-way, 22 miles out-and-back to Point Imperial; 23 miles one-way, 46 miles out-and-back to Cape Royal, or 51.3 miles total if you ride out to Point Imperial on your way to Cape Royal.

Riding surface: Pavement; narrow roads with no shoulders, rough pavement in spots.

Difficulty: Moderate to strenuous. The rolling terrain, the elevations, (7,800 and 8,800 feet), and the length of this route will make it a challenging ride for most. The highest point on the ride is Point Imperial (8,807 feet); the lowest is at Cape Royal (7,865 feet).

Scenery/highlights: Words fall far short of describing the beauty and immensity of the panoramas that can be viewed from these two overlooks. At Point Imperial you'll be looking into the eastern portion of the park and over the north-south running part of the canyon and river. The

Alpine forests dominate on the North Rim, which rises 1,000 to 1,500 feet higher than the South Rim and receives 60 percent more moisture.

enormous natural amphitheater below you was carved primarily by Nankoweep Creek. The overlook itself sits between the northernmost and middle sections of the three-pronged Nankoweep drainage. Woolsey Point and Bourke Point are immediately to your left, while Sullivan Peak and Hancock Butte are directly across on the right. To the southeast stands Hayden Peak, a magnificent single spire of rock. Many other buttes, points, and mesas flood the scene, drawing your eyes into the depths of Marble Canyon and beyond, to the sprawling Navajo Reservation stretching away from the far rim. From Vista Encantada you'll be looking over the same drainage, only further south.

At Cape Royal, Freya Castle to the left and Wotans Throne further out and to the right, are the two closest of the many formations that almost seem to crowd the view. Beyond is a fantastic collection of spires and buttes that includes Vishnu Temple, Krishna Shrine, and Rama Shrine, almost directly south. To the west is Half Butte, Angels Gate, Dunn Butte, and Hawkins Butte. Across the canyon is Horseshoe Mesa with Grandview Point above.

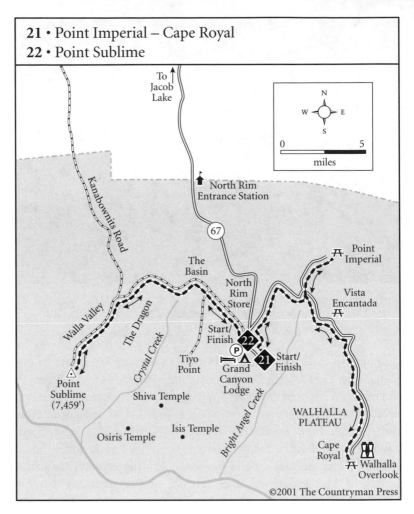

21 · Point Imperial – Cape Royal
22 · Point Sublime

Best time to ride: Mid- to late May, when the road to the North Rim opens, through October or until heavy snows close the road once again.

Special considerations: Water and rest rooms are available at the visitor center. Vault toilets can be found at the two major overlooks. Be sure to bring plenty of water and high-energy snacks to help your body cope with the high elevations and dry air of the North Rim. You may also want to bring a lock to secure your bike while you walk out to viewpoints or to Walhalla Ruins.

Also, check local forecasts; afternoon thunderstorms can be quite violent during the monsoon season up here, with strong winds, hail, and lightning. It is always best to go prepared with a light rain and wind shell, and perhaps a long underwear top for warmth; when storms move in at these elevations temperatures drop substantially.

Directions for the ride: From the visitor center, ride north on AZ 67, the road you drove in on, and pedal for 3 miles, past several spur roads on the left leading to the campground and ranger station, to the Cape Royal Road. Turn right onto this road and begin pedaling up the Fuller Creek drainage. Alpine forests of spruce, fir, and pines mixed with stands of quaking aspen flank the road on either side as you climb toward Point Imperial, the highest point on either rim. Approximately 3 miles from the junction with AZ 67 and the Cape Royal Road the route turns and heads southeast. At 6.7 miles from the start you come to a picnic area on the right. Past the picnic area descend for 1.5 miles to the intersection with the Point Imperial Road 8.3 miles from the start. If you are going to Point Imperial, turn left here and begin climbing, reaching it 2.7 miles later, 11 miles from the start.

Back on the main road, follow the route as it traverses the neck of the plateau and climbs around the top of Bright Angel Canyon, winding in and out of the trees. Periodically you can catch glimpses of this drainage, one of the largest in the greater Grand Canyon. In approximately 4.7 miles you come to Vista Encantada. Another 1.6 miles beyond Vista Encantada the road swings out to the rim at Roosevelt Point; Tritle Peak rises directly across from here while Nankoweep drainage drops away around it. Now begins a long, 7.5-mile, fairly straight, gradually descending pedal, alternating through forest and meadow before reaching the rim again. Just before the road meets the rim, approximately 20.5 miles from the start or 2.5 miles from Cape Royal, is the start to the easy 2-mile hike to Cape Final. The trailhead is at a dirt pullout on the left side of the road. Walhalla Overlook, another mile down the road, is directly over the Unkar Creek drainage and the last pullout before Cape Royal. Directly across the road are the Walhalla Ruins, remnants of a farming community of ancient Puebloans who summered on top of this plateau 800 to 900 years ago. Now it's just over a mile to the end of the road at Cape Royal. Take some time here, rest, drink your fluids, and try to absorb the stunning panorama before you. Angels Window, a massive natural arch, can be seen from here and is accessed by a nearby trail. When ready, remount and return the way you came.

---

22. POINT SUBLIME (See map on page 128)

For mountain bikes. The 18-mile journey out to Point Sublime makes for a long day, but is sure to be one of your most memorable two-wheeled adventures in this or any park. The outstanding views, gorgeous alpine scenery, enormous old-growth ponderosa pines, and serenity found in this backcountry area make this a five-star fat-tire adventure. The route traverses a rough and sometimes muddy four-wheel-drive road that rolls up and down between 8,300 and 7,400 feet, losing elevation as it nears Point Sublime.

Starting point: Begin this ride at the Widfross Trail (hiking only) parking lot and trailhead. To get there drive 2.5 miles north of the North Rim Visitor Center on AZ 67 and go left on a road signed for the Widfross Trail. Drive approximately 1 mile to the parking area.

Length: 18 miles one-way, 36 miles out-and-back. Allow a full day to cover this distance and spend time at the overlooks.

Riding surface: Four-wheel-drive doubletrack jeep road.

Difficulty: Strenuous. The length, elevation, and rolling terrain will make this ride challenging for most. The first 10 miles are a lot of up and down; the last 8 are a steady descent to Point Sublime.

Scenery/highlights: Open, sunny meadows dotted with wildflowers and rimmed with quaking aspen, deep shadowy forests of spruce and fir, and gargantuan ponderosa pine that grow right along the canyon's edge create a fantastic natural setting unique to the North Rim. You may even see a strange looking white-tailed squirrel with large, tufted ears; this is the Kaibab squirrel. It has evolved on this "sky-island," cut off from other squirrel species, and is found nowhere else in the world.

Views from Point Sublime and along the trail are stupendous. The enormous Dragon and Crystal Creek drainages stretch away toward the Colorado in layers of shadowed buttes and cliffs. The two long arms of

Tall, stately ponderosa pines and empty dirt roads crisscross the Kaibab National Forest just outside park boundaries on the North Rim.

FAUNA

Known for its curiosity, gregarious nature, and boldness is the large, jet-black raven. Ravens are undoubtedly the most commonly seen wildlife species in the park. Please do not feed the ravens, chipmunks, or any animal species that might appear tame to you. Feeding them alters their behavior and will eventually result in their death.

Wild turkeys, once over-hunted and quite rare, have made a strong recovery and are now quite common on both sides of the canyon. These large, ground-loving birds were one of the first animals to be domesticated by Native Americans. Gambel's quail, also quite common, can be found scurrying in the underbrush on both sides of the canyon. Violet-green swallows, cliff swallows, and northern rough-winged swallows also migrate here during the warmer months and are a delight to see rocketing back and forth over the rims, catching insects carried skyward on strong canyon updrafts during summer months.

Raptors common to the park include golden eagles, turkey vultures, peregrine flacons, and red-tailed hawks. Several woodpecker species, including flickers, acorn woodpeckers, hairy woodpeckers, and red-naped sapsuckers, thrive in the pine and piñon-juniper forests. Broad-tailed, rufous, Costa's, and black-chinned hummingbirds all make an appearance during summer, as do a variety of warblers, among them Audubon's, Virginia's, yellow-rumped, and Grace's. Cassin's kingbird, horned larks, meadowlarks, piñon jays, scrub jays, and Steller's jays (in the spruce-fir forests of the North Rim), are some of the bigger birds you might see. Western and mountain bluebirds, western tanagers, and the much rarer hooded oriole are some of the more colorful birds that visit the rims. The delightful, descending tune of the canyon wren is joined by that of Bewick's, house, rock, and cactus wrens, among numerous other visiting songbirds. Inquire at the visitor center for a complete bird list.

Large mammals that live near the canyon rims and further reaches of the plateaus include black bear, mountain lion, bobcat, coyote, gray fox, and badger. Grazers such as mule deer, elk, and desert bighorn sheep live in the park. Deer and elk prefer the meadows and pine forests of the plateaus; the shy desert bighorns prefer the more remote and rougher canyon country below the rims. Desert cottontails, blacktail jackrabbits, and several species of skunks live on the rims, along with numerous species of squirrels. Among the squirrel species, Abert and the Kaibab are examples of a single species that at some point became geographically isolated and evolved into genetically distinct species. Both have tufted ears; the Kaibab's ears are larger and its tail white.

these drainages are separated only by a long, sculpted mesa known as the Dragon. At Point Sublime the crenalated fins of Sagittarius Ridge extend from northwest to southeast almost directly in front of you, while Confuscious and Mencius Temple rise in the east.

Best time to ride: Mid-May through October. Stay away if the ground is saturated.

Special considerations: There are no rest rooms and no water along this route. The nearest facilities are located at the North Rim Visitor Center.

There are many roads taking off in all directions out here, although the main road to Point Sublime shows evidence of more consistent use. Still, a good map of the area will help you stay on course and will enhance your knowledge of major land features along the route and at overlooks.

Because this is a long day on the trail you want to go prepared; bring plenty of water, high-energy snacks, sunscreen, and extra clothes. Check with the ranger at the visitor center before you head out; if strong afternoon thunderstorms are forecast you may want to save this ride for another day.

Directions for the ride: From the Widfross Trailhead parking lot, go back out to the road and turn left. This road takes you up a gentle grade, past a refuse dumping area, and then bears right, heading into the woods. There are several dirt roads taking off in various directions as you start out but the more well-used Point Sublime Road will remain obvious. The park has purposefully left the road out to Point Sublime unsigned in order to cut down on traffic across delicate meadows that can become a mud bog when saturated.

For the first mile the route traverses an area referred to as Marble Flats, then begins to dip and climb over several drainages that are not much more than shallow depressions. Approximately 4.2 miles from the start you enter a broad meadow known as the Basin. It can be marshy and wet and the road through here muddy. Just after you enter the Basin you come to a junction where the road heading south to Tiyo Point splits off to the left. (The Tiyo Point Road has recently been gated and closed to bicycles.) Stay right, ride along the edge of the Basin, and then climb, following the road to where it meets the canyon rim at the head of Dragon Creek drainage 2 miles past the Tiyo Point junction.

From there the road rolls up and down over short, but sometimes steep, hills. Approximately 4.6 miles past the Dragon Creek overlook the road meets the rim overlooking the Crystal Creek drainage, offering numerous chances to peer into one of the most fantastic side canyons of the Grand Canyon. The road skirts the rim for the next 0.5 mile before turning and descending toward the junction with the Kanabownits Road another 0.6 mile later. The Kanabownits Road accesses Point Sublime from De Motte Park, further north on the plateau in Kaibab National Forest. This intersection is close to 11.9 miles from the start. For the next 6.2 miles the route trends southwest, staying on top of a low ridge that descends gradually to Point Sublime. Have a look around and when you're rested, saddle up, and get ready for the pedal back.

---

23. RAINBOW RIM TRAIL (See map on page 135)

For mountain bikes. The Rainbow Rim Trail is a newly constructed singletrack that traces the western edge of the Kaibab Plateau just outside the park boundary. This 18-mile trail is quickly becoming one of the most popular trails in northern Arizona, and a few hours spent zipping through mixed forests of ponderosa pine and Gambel oak and peering into the massive Tapeats Amphitheater and beyond into the Grand Canyon will surely show you why.

23 • Rainbow Rim Trail

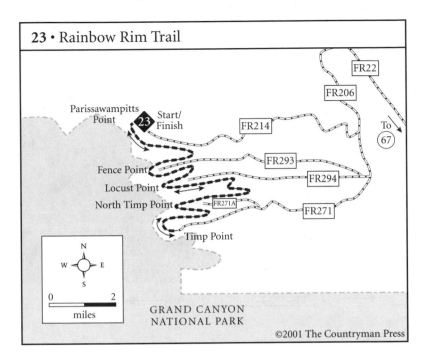

GRAND CANYON
NATIONAL PARK

©2001 The Countryman Press

Starting point: There are 5 different access points along this trail; the most direct is at the northern terminus at Parissawampitts Point. To get there go approximately 18 miles north on AZ 67 from the North Rim Visitor Center to De Motte Park; FR 22 will be on the left. (If you come to the Kaibab Lodge and the North Rim Country Store you have gone too far. Turn around and drive south 0.8 mile.) Follow FR 22, a graded dirt road, for 10.5 miles to FR 206. Go left and continue on FR 206 for 3.5 miles until you come to FR 214. Turn right onto FR 214 and follow it for another 8 miles (passing FR 250 just over 4.5 miles from FR 206) to the Parissawampitts Viewpoint. The trail begins here.

All of the other access points along the trail can be reached from FR 250, which goes south off FR 214 approximately 3.5 miles before reaching Parissawampitts Point.

Length: 18 miles one-way, 36 miles out-and-back. Ride for as far and as long as you like or create your own loops with the forest service roads that access the trail at Fence, Locust, North Timp, and Timp Points.

Close to the edge on the South Rim with weather closing in.

Riding surface: Singletrack trail; some sections are rocky.

Difficulty: Moderate to strenuous. Riding the entire length of the trail out and back makes for a long day, however, it is easy to adjust the length and distance or create loops using forest service roads. Elevations are around 7,500 feet and vary by only a few hundred feet.

Scenery/highlights: Views of the Tapeats Amphitheater and into the canyon are outstanding. Wonderful scenery and a fun, fast-paced single-track all make this trail a don't-miss opportunity for serious mountain bikers.

Best time to ride: Mid- to late May through October. Be aware of hunting seasons and locations in the fall; this area is very popular with deer and elk hunters.

Special considerations: There are no services near the trailhead or anywhere along this route; make sure you are prepared with plenty of gas, water, food, and a cooler full of drinks for after your ride.

A Kaibab National Forest map for the North Kaibab Ranger District or other maps showing forest service road designations is a must for traversing this remote area. Pick one up at the Kaibab Visitor Center in Jacob Lake before you head south toward the rim, or find a map at the North Rim Visitor Center in the park.

Directions for the ride: From Parissawampitts Point, pick up the trail and follow it as it heads south and then swings around and heads east, contouring the Parissawampitts Canyon drainage that has carved a notch into the canyon rim. The trail traces the outline of this drainage arriving at Fence Point (accessed by FR 293) in 5.5 miles. From here the trail again heads east, contouring Locust Canyon, and arrives at Locust Point (accessed by FR 294) in 3 miles. At Locust Point the trail skirts the edge of Timp Canyon and arrives at North Timp Point (accessed by FR 271A) in another 3 miles, or 11.5 miles from the start. The last section of trail follows the convoluted edge of the canyon around another drainage between North Timp and Timp Points, arriving at the latter in 6.5 miles. Timp Point, accessed by FR 271, is the southernmost point along the trail. When you are ready to go, retrace your route, or create a loop with one of the access roads and FR 250. Enjoy!

CAMPING

All park campgrounds tend to be crowded during the summer months. If you are planning to visit call well in advance for reservations; they are accepted as early as 5 months in advance beginning on the 5th of every month. Several campgrounds do reserve "walk-in" space for campers but you'll need to arrive early in the morning to secure one of these sites. These sites can be available even if the sign reads FULL. A fee is charged for all campsites inside the park. Reservations for campsites anywhere in the park can be made by contacting Biospherics at 1-800-365-2267 or at www.reservations.nps.gov.

SOUTH RIM

Inside the park: Mather Campground is located in Grand Canyon Village just south of the visitor center. It has drinking water but no hook-ups and is open year-round. Reservations are accepted for April 1 through November 30th. The rest of the

year campsites are managed on a first-come, first-served basis.

Camping with hook-ups is available in Grand Canyon Village

!

IT'S INTERESTING TO KNOW . . .

There are ten major formations or rock layers that make up the mile of strata in the Grand Canyon; remembering them all can be difficult. "Know the canyon history. See the rocks made by time, very slowly," can help one remember the canyon's major rock layers and the order in which they occur.

Know . . . . . . Kaibab limestone
the . . . . . . Toroweap Formation
canyon . . . Coconino sandstone
history . . . . Hermit shale
See . . . . Supai Group
rocks . . . . . . Redwall limestone
made . . . . . . Muav limestone
by . . . . Bright Angel shale
time . . . . Tapeats sandstone
very slowly . . . . . . Vishnu schist

at **Trailer Village,** which is adjacent to Mather Campground. Call (303) 297-2757 for Trailer Village reservations.At nearby **Camper Services** in Grand Canyon Village laundry facilities, showers, and ice are available.

Desert View Campground is located 25 miles east of Grand Canyon Village and is open mid-April through mid-October, weather permitting. Managed on a first-come, first-served basis, reservations are not accepted.

Outside the park: There are several possibilities for camping in and around Tusayan. You can try the private **Grand Canyon Camper Village,** which has both tent and RV sites. The Tusayan Ranger District of the Kaibab National Forest manages the developed **Ten X Campground** and the **Charley Group Site.** Call or stop by the Tusayan Ranger District offices in Tusayan for more information or to reserve a group site.

There is also the option of primitive camping in the **Kaibab National Forest.** Check in at the ranger station in Tusayan to get recommendations on where to camp and a list of regulations. Campfires are prohibited in certain areas.

NORTH RIM

Inside the park: The **North Rim Campground** is located 1.5 miles north of the Grand Canyon Lodge and the visitor center. It is open mid-May to mid-October but is somewhat weather dependent. There are tent and vehicle sites but no hook-ups.

Outside the park: There is a developed campground at De Motte Park, the **Demotte Park Campground,** located just south of the Kaibab Lodge, 16 miles north of the North Rim facilities. They have drinking water but no showers or hook-ups and no reservations are taken. Even further north, at Jacob Lake, you'll find the **Jacob Lake Campground.** They have drinking water but no showers or hook-ups. **Jacob Lake RV Park** has hook-ups and tent sites but no showers and no reservations are taken.

There are almost unlimited opportunities for camping in Kaibab National Forest, which stretches north from the northern boundary of the park to well beyond Jacob Lake. Pick up a forest service map of the area or stop in at the North Kaibab Visitor Center in Jacob Lake for suggestions and a list of camping regulations.

LODGING

SOUTH RIM

Inside the park: Located in the heart of Grand Canyon Village is the historic **Bright Angel Lodge.** Built in 1935, this popular gathering spot sits right on the rim near the Bright Angel trailhead and offers both cabins and rooms in the lodge. Lodge rooms range from basic and inexpensive to deluxe and pricey. The lodge houses two restaurants, a lounge, snack bar and barber shop. The **Thunderbird** and **Kachina Lodges** are also located right on the canyon rim in Grand Canyon Village and are more expensive. The **El Tovar Hotel** is the oldest, finest, and most expensive of any of the accommodations found on the South Rim. This beautiful building was constructed in 1905 and is now a historic landmark. Each room is different, the conveniences are modern, and the best food on the South Rim can also be found here. The **Maswik Lodge,** located south of the Bright Angel Lodge away from the rim, has cabins set in the woods and rooms in the lodge that range from moderate to expensive. The lodge also houses a cafeteria. The **Yavapai Lodge** is located one mile east of Bright Angel Lodge and is just south of the South Rim Visitor Center. There is a cafeteria-style restaurant on the premises and the rooms are modern and slightly more expensive.

Outside the park: There are lots of options in and around Tusayan, beginning with the **Moqui Lodge**, which is also owned and operated by Grand Canyon Lodges. There's also a **Best Western,** a **Rodeway Inn,** a **Quality Inn** and **Holiday Inn Express. Grand Canyon Suites** and **The Grand Hotel**, which has a dinner theater and Native American performances during the summer months, are also in Tusayan. There are few cheap rooms in Tusayan. If you're looking for something inexpensive drive farther south to the town of Valle and try the **Grand Canyon Motel** or the **Grand Canyon Inn.**

NORTH RIM

Inside the park: The only lodging inside the park on the North Rim is at **Grand Canyon Lodge,** open mid-May through October. You can choose between moderately priced hotel rooms or cabins that sleep up to four people (a bargain). There is also a restaurant in the lodge.

Outside the park: Approximately 18 miles north of Grand Canyon Lodge on AZ 67 you'll find the **Kaibab Lodge.** Cabins that sleep four or more are available at a moderate price. Another 26 miles north in Jacob Lake is the **Jacob Lake Inn,** offering both cabins and basic motel rooms. Both have restaurants serving three meals a day.

FOOD

SOUTH RIM

Inside the park: Both the **Maswik Lodge** and the **Yavapai Lodge** have inexpensive, cafeteria-style restaurants serving breakfast, lunch, and dinner. The **Bright Angel Restaurant** and the **Arizona Steakhouse** are both located in the Bright Angel Lodge. More elegant fare and atmosphere can be found at the **El Tovar Hotel,** where you'll need to make reservations. You'll find snack bars in the Bright Angel Lodge and at the east end of East Rim Drive at Desert View. A general store near the visitor center has a deli counter and sells food, as does the general store at Desert View.

Outside the park: Several of the larger hotels in Tusayan have restaurants that generally serve three meals a day. Other than a steakhouse, your choices are mostly fast-food. There is a general store that sells some food but there is no real grocery store in Tusayan.

NORTH RIM

Inside the park: The **Grand Canyon Lodge** serves three meals a day in an enormous dining room where guests enjoy fantastic views of the canyon. Reservations are required for dinner and recommended for breakfast during peak season. There is also a snack bar in the lodge and a saloon that serves drinks and gourmet coffees.

Outside the park: A restaurant at the Kaibab Lodge 18 miles north of the canyon rim serves three meals a day. You can buy groceries and picnic supplies next door at the **North Rim Country Store.** You'll also find groceries for sale in Jacob Lake.

LAUNDRY

On the South Rim coin-operated laundry facilities are available at **Camper Services** in Grand Canyon Village. On the North Rim coin-operated laundry facilities can be found adjacent to the campground.

BIKE SHOP/BIKE RENTAL

Just over 90 miles from the South Rim, in the town of Flagstaff, are at least half a dozen really good bike shops that offer sales, rentals, and service. In the future, when the Grand Canyon Greenway trail system is completed, the park may even get into the bike rental business, but for now Flagstaff is the nearest option.

On the North Rim your options for bike needs and services are even more distant. St. George, Utah, has a couple of good bike shops, and there is one in Springdale, just outside the entrance to Zion National Park.

FOR FURTHER INFORMATION

Grand Canyon National Park— Superintendent, P.O. Box 129, Grand Canyon, AZ 86023; 520-638-7888; www.nps.gov/grca/
Grand Canyon Association, P.O. Box 399, Grand Canyon, AZ 86023; 520-638-2481; www.grand canyon.org. Offers books, maps, and other information.

Kaibab National Forest, Tusayan Ranger District, P.O. Box 3088, Tusayan, AZ 86023; 520-638-2443; www.fs.fed.us/r3/kai/

Kaibab National Forest, North Kaibab Ranger District, P.O. Box 248, Fredonia, AZ 86022; 520-643-7395; www.fs.fed.us/r3/kai/

Kaibab National Forest, Kaibab Plateau Visitors Center, AZ Hwy 67, Jacob Lake, AZ 86022; 520-643-7298

5

ORGAN PIPE CACTUS NATIONAL MONUMENT

Showcased in Organ Pipe Cactus National Monument, besides the stately cactus for which this park is named, are the many highly adapted and intriguing plant and animal species that characterize the Sonoran Desert ecosystem. The Sonoran Desert is one of four desert types that exist in North America; the other three are Great Basin, Mojave, and Chihuahuan. In the United States the Sonoran Desert is found only in southern Arizona and in a small corner of California but it extends far into Mexico. The combination of low latitude, low elevation, and rainy seasons in winter and late summer allows the Sonoran Desert to support a far greater diversity of life than the other North American deserts.

Although fairly common throughout the Mexican state of Sonora and along the Baja Peninsula, the organ pipe cactus exists only within, and immediately outside of, the boundaries of the monument in the United States. This cactus is enormous, with multiple spiny branches radiating upward from a single base. The largest specimens reach 15 to 20 feet in height and 10 to 15 feet in circumference. This creature seems a glutton for the punishing sun and heat of the Sonoran Desert, preferring the hottest and driest south-facing slopes of the park's mountain ranges. The only places the cactus can survive at this latitude, these exposures provide critical warmth during the winter when severe frosts can kill them.

By May or June, when temperatures soar well past the century mark, the organ pipe cactus is ready to bloom, but waits until evening to open hundreds of small, pale lavender flowers radiating from the tips of its arms. The flowers stay open at night to attract nocturnal pollinators, such as bats and moths, then close the next day as the ravaging rays of the desert sun intensify. Red, juicy, egg-sized fruits mature in July and are an important food source for the animals that live here.

Here, among the sprawling valleys, rocky mountain ranges, solitude, and strange yet beautiful creatures of this desert awaits a wilderness experience that is perhaps best described as magical.

Cycling in the Park

The two scenic drives and the backcountry roads inside Organ Pipe Cactus National Monument offer several excellent riding opportunities. Those who relish wide-open spaces, lonely roads, and empty country will love riding in this park, but before heading out this way there are some important things to consider. Between May and September temperatures often climb to 105°F and above, making it extremely difficult to enjoy yourself or to stay well hydrated while exerting yourself on a bicycle. Becoming dehydrated under a strong sun in that kind of heat can quickly lead to a number of serious, potentially life-threatening conditions. Visiting the park between October and April, when

CYCLING OPTIONS

There are four rides in this chapter; all are for mountain bikes. Alamo Canyon is a short, very scenic 6-mile ride that offers a great introduction to the area and is suitable for all ability levels. The unmaintained Camino de Dos Republicas is slightly longer and takes riders out to the historic Gachado Line Camp and Dos Lomitas Ranch. The 21-mile long Ajo Mountain Drive is longer but can be done in a couple of hours. The route follows a graded dirt road and accesses large stands of organ pipe cacti as well as some of the prettiest areas in the monument. The much longer Puerto Blanco Drive (51 miles) is perhaps best done as a vehicle-supported trip, allowing cyclists to adjust time in the saddle to suit fitness and time constraints.

Saguaro cactus share the monument with the organ pipe. Here the tips of the saguaro's arms are crowned with emerging blooms.

daytime temperatures range between 60 and 80 degrees, is strongly recommended. Even in winter the air is very dry and you should plan on drinking at least a gallon of water a day, more if you spend longer than an hour or two on your bike.

Ajo Mountain and Puerto Blanco are the two main scenic drives in the park. Both routes follow graded, maintained dirt roads. While Ajo Mountain Drive is 21 miles long and can be ridden in a few hours, Puerto Blanco Drive is a 51-mile loop through the park's desert wilderness that requires more time and stamina if you plan to ride unaided by a support vehicle. Quitobaquito Springs, about halfway along the route, is a true desert oasis critical to the survival of the wildlife in this area. These springs also served for hundreds of years as an important water source for travelers along historic settlement and trading routes from Mexico. Riding up Alamo Canyon is an easy 3-mile trip into a beautiful desert canyon where trails lead deep into the rugged Ajo Mountains. Another moderately easy ride on an unmaintained dirt road takes you out to the old Gachado Line Camp and Dos Lomitas Ranch site on Camino de Dos Republicas. Although no off-road riding is allowed in the park, the pedaling possibilities on the scenic and backcountry routes offer something for almost every level of rider in a setting that is uniquely beautiful and historically rich.

---

24. ALAMO CANYON (See map on page 148)

For mountain bikes. This ride is an easy 3-mile (6 miles total distance) pedal up a dirt road that terminates at the base of the rugged Ajo Mountain Range. The road accesses a primitive campground where you can pick up hiking trails to an old line camp and beyond into the enchanting wilderness of this desert.

Starting point: Begin approximately 10 miles north of the visitor center at the start of the Alamo Canyon Road. Park on the side of the dirt road as soon as you leave the pavement.

Length: Just under 3 miles each way, approximately 6 miles total. Allow two hours.

Riding surface: Graded, maintained dirt road.

Difficulty: Easy. A few hundred feet in elevation are gained on the way up.

Scenery/highlights: The route up Alamo Canyon, views to the rocky cliffs of the Ajo Mountains, and surrounding Sonoran Desert scenery make for a great introductory ride to this park's resources.

Best time to ride: October through April.

Special considerations: There are vault toilets at the campground but no water. Be sure to carry and drink plenty of water. If you are interested in hiking to the line camp ruins you should bring a lock to secure your bike while you're gone.

Directions for the ride: From the start of the Alamo Canyon Road where you left your car, simply begin by pedaling east-southeast toward the Ajo Mountains. At first the road follows a simple depression in the desert that begins to feel more like a canyon as you approach the mountains. After approximately 3 miles the road ends at a primitive, four-site campground. Take a break here, have something to drink, and lock up your bike before hiking to the ruins of a turn-of-the-century ranch outpost. When you're done head back the way you came.

25. CAMINO DE DOS REPUBLICAS (See map on page 148)

For mountain bikes. This route follows an unmaintained dirt road 5 miles to the ruins of the Gachado Line Camp and the Dos Lomitas Ranch in operation from about 1900 until sometime in the 1930s. The road parallels the U.S.-Mexico border for a little more than half the way and is a great outing for all levels of mountain bikers.

Starting point: Begin this ride at the start of the Camino de Dos Republicas, directly across AZ 85 from the southern portion of Puerto Blanco Drive that accesses Quitobaquito Springs.

Length: 5 miles one-way, 10 miles total distance. Allow 3 hours to do the ride and visit the historic sites along the way.

Riding surface: This dirt road is not maintained; it may be rough and rutted, especially after heavy rains.

Difficulty: Easy.

Scenery/highlights: The Gachado Line Camp and Dos Lomitas Ranch buildings are remnants of one of this region's early ranching operations, owned and managed by the Gray family. A "line camp" is simply the place where the work of the ranch was done, as opposed to the "ranch," which was the rancher's residence. A small ranching operation continues nearby but there is little ranching taking place in this country today. At these sites you'll find mesquite wood corrals, adobe buildings, and a barn, monuments to the hard work and perseverance it took to make a living here.

Best time to ride: October through April.

Special considerations: Water and rest rooms are available at the visitor center but nowhere along the trail.

This area sometimes sees traffic from illegal immigrants trying to gain entrance into the United States from Mexico. Park rangers advise staying at a distance and reporting anyone who looks like they might be traveling on foot in this area.

Directions for the ride: From the start of the Camino de Dos Republicas (the Way of Two Republics), pedal in a southeasterly direction for just

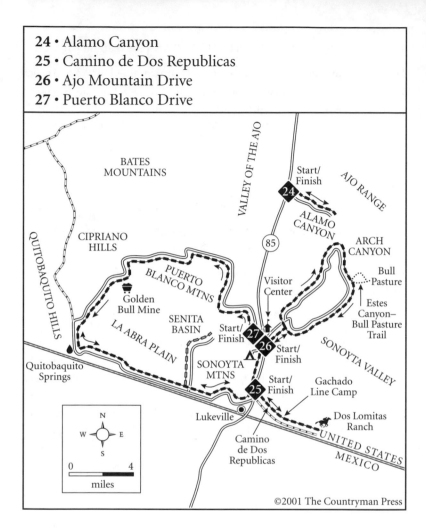

under 2 miles through sparse saltbush flats to Gachado Line Camp. Here you will find an old barn, some mesquite corrals, and a few other signs that the work of cattle ranching actually took place out here at one time. Continue heading southeast; the route now parallels the international border. In another 3 miles you'll come to the abandoned buildings of the Gray family's Dos Lomitas Ranch. Have a look around and when you're ready to go simply head back the way you came.

26. AJO MOUNTAIN DRIVE (See map on page 148)

For mountain bikes. This 21-mile loop crosses over the Diablo Mountains and winds along through the foothills of the Ajo Range, providing spectacular views of surrounding desert landscapes and access to some of the largest stands of organ pipe cactus in the monument. Riders of all abilities who are in good condition are well suited to this ride. While the loop is only open in a one-way, clockwise direction for cars, it can be ridden in either direction by cyclists.

Starting point: Begin at the visitors center.

Length: 21 miles. Allow 2 to 3 hours to ride this route without stopping; more if you plan on taking time to enjoy the view, examine desert plants and wildlife, or perhaps hike one of several trails accessed from this road.

Riding surface: Graded dirt road.

Difficulty: Moderate. Although elevation gains and losses are close to 1,000 feet the grades are gentle and riding surface smooth. The length of this route will make it more difficult for some.

Scenery/highlights: The Ajo Mountains are the highest in this area with Mt. Ajo, just to the east of the northern end of this route, rising to 4,808 feet. Diaz Peak (4,024 feet) and Diaz Spire (3,892 feet) are further south. Tillotson Peak (3,374 feet), to the north or left as you ride toward the Ajo Mountains, is in the smaller Diablo Mountain Range.

The Ajo, like the other small mountain ranges in the monument, are rugged, highly eroded remnants of Tertiary volcanic rocks thrust upward as fault-block ranges. The banded cliffs of lava, tuff, and breccia first oozed out of cracks in the earth's crust between 14 and 22 million years ago, forming a thick layer that was later broken and lifted when faults deep within the earth became active. As the mountains are worn down by rain and weather the resulting sediments form smoothly sloping angles of valley fill. The sediments of these sloping desert plains consolidate to create "desert pavement," a tough layer of armor that protects precious desert soils from further erosion.

Best time to ride: October through April.

FLORA

In early spring this desert landscape hosts a fantastic display that begins with Mexican gold poppies, blue lupines, pink owl clover, orange globe mallow, and a host of other annuals. They are followed by the blooms of numerous species of cacti, including the organ pipe, which flower throughout the spring and early summer in a fantastic assortment of colors and shapes. Some of the other cacti found in the park include ocotillo, with its long, whiplike arms, Engelmann prickly pear, Coville's barrel cactus, teddybear cholla, chainfruit cholla, and the massive saguaro cactus, easily recognized by its single massive trunk and curious arrangement of armlike branches. The saguaro has large, creamy, saucer-sized flowers that adorn the tips of its arms and later turn into juicy red fruits that are collected and made into jelly, wine, and other foods by the native Pima and Tohono O'odham Indians that continue to live in the region. The senita cactus is another rare inhabitant of the monument. Almost its entire U.S. population lives in Senita Basin. It is a much smaller version of the organ pipe with gray whiskery spines that cover the tops of almost bare arms.

Also in Senita Basin is the very rare, subtropical elephant tree. Gray with a short, stout trunk, this tree supports a dense tangle of branches. The foothill paloverde, with its lovely green bark, is the most common tree found in the park but its tiny leaves provide little shade. In the highest reaches of the Ajo Mountains a relic population of junipers left over from wetter times in the past survives, as does a variety of oak found nowhere else in the world.

Shrubs, including creosote bush, bursage, brittlebush, saltbush, jojoba, and Mexican jumping bean, are distributed in the different plant communities in the monument.

Special considerations: Be sure to purchase, for a nominal fee, the park's published guide on the drive before you head out. Numbered points of interest are identified and explained along the way.

Young saguaros dominate in this corner of the monument.

There is a pit toilet available at the Estes Canyon Picnic Area, about halfway along the route, but there is no water anywhere out here. Bring plenty of your own, plus lunch or some high-energy snacks to keep you rolling.

Be wary of occasional car and camper traffic, stay to the right, and observe the rules of the road. Riding in the early morning or evening is a great way to avoid vehicle traffic, enjoy beautiful desert light, and observe wildlife when it is most active.

Directions for the ride: From the visitor center head out to AZ 85, cross over the highway, and begin pedaling in a northeasterly direction on Ajo Mountain Drive. As you head out into the desert, crossing through the sparse vegetation of what is recognized as a mixed-scrub community, it is hard not to be a little intimidated by the vastness of the landscape. In approximately 2 miles the route heads around the toe of a hill and splits; you can ride this loop either way; the clockwise direction will be described here. After bearing left, the road winds, slipping through some hills, following a wash for a short distance before traversing the gently sloping skirt of the Diablo Mountains. Approximately 3 miles from

FAUNA

Less visible but equally as fascinating as the plants of the Sonoran desert are the animals who have developed elaborate survival strategies to cope with high temperatures and periods of drought.

Close to 40 species of birds are year-round residents; another 230 pass through on their migration routes. Quitobaquito Oasis and springs is a magnet for many of the migrants. Some of the birds you are most likely to see in the park include Gambel's quail, the Gila woodpecker, roadrunners, curved-bill thrashers, white-winged doves, and cactus wrens. The red-eyed, jet-black phainopepla also visits the monument and is a favorite of birdwatchers, as is the pyrrhuloxia, a gray-and-red cousin of the cardinal. Red-tailed hawks are quite common, and Harris' hawks, unique to this corner of the country, are regular visitors. The crested caracara is a fierce looking, eaglelike bird that it is quite rare north of the Mexican border but is sometimes seen here. This graceful flier often floats just above the ground, looking for carrion or small prey, and has distinctive black crest with a white neck, large bill, and red or yellow face.

Small mammals regularly seen in the monument include cottontail rabbits, antelope and blacktailed jackrabbits, and antelope squirrels. Numerous smaller species of rodents, including pack rats and kangaroo rats, which get all the moisture they need from the plants they eat, are very common. The javelina, a type of wild pig, also lives in the monument and can meet its water requirements by eating cactus leaves and fruits. Found west of the highway in the wide-open plains of the monument are Sonora pronghorn antelope. They are smaller and lighter in color than their northern cousins, and can, like the javelina, go weeks without drinking water. These fleet-footed animals can sprint at 50 mph and maintain a steady 35 mph run. Desert bighorn sheep are found in the higher, rockier reaches of the Ajo and Puerto Blanco Mountains but are rarely seen. While coyotes are regular visitors around the park and near the campgrounds, the park's other predators—bobcats and mountain lions—keep a lower profile.

Both this region and this monument are rich in reptile species. There are at least 26 species of snakes in the monument, 6 of them rattlesnakes. They, like many other desert snakes, are active mostly at night, but in the morning it is not uncommon to find one stretched out sunning itself trying to warm up. If you happen upon one of these shy and normally unthreatening creatures, simply back away or make a loud noise and wait for them to retreat. Another poisonous but easily recognized resident is the coral snake, brightly banded in black, orange, yellow, and white. The rosy boa is a small, very docile snake that resembles a large earthworm. Nonpoisonous gopher snakes and several species of whipsnakes are the most commonly seen snakes in the monument. Lizards are plentiful and come in all different shapes and sizes. There are several varieties of whiptail lizards, smaller brown side-blotched lizards, larger greenish-blue chuckawallas, and the rarely encountered Gila monster, whose bite is poisonous. Gila monsters are slow moving and easily distinguished by their all-over black and yellow pattern.

where the road forks you will come to a pullout and picnic area among the humble peaks of the Diablo Mountains. These mountains no doubt got their name from the nearby Camino del Diablo, or Devil's Highway, a route traveled for centuries by native people and then later by Spanish explorers making their way between the Colorado River and Sonoyta, Mexico.

The road then dips and rolls through the Diablo Mountains, heading almost due north for another 4 miles before reaching the Arch Canyon picnic area 9 miles from the start. This is the highest point in the ride, approximately 2,600 feet above sea level. From there the route turns and heads due south, along the foot of the Ajo Mountains. Just over 2 miles past Arch Canyon you will come to the Estes Canyon Picnic Area where a pit toilet is available. You are almost directly west of Mt. Ajo, and at the start of the Bull Pasture–Estes Canyon Trail. This 4-mile trail is steep and loose in places but considered by many to be the most spectacular hike in the park.

Continuing southward on your bike, the route climbs gently over a low pass between the foothills of the Ajo and Diablo Mountains before sliding out onto the broad, flat expanse of the Sonoyta Valley. It is another 8 miles around on the loop before rejoining the two-way, 2-mile section of road that will take you back to the visitor center.

27. PUERTO BLANCO DRIVE (See map on page 148)

For mountain bikes. This is a lengthy, 51-mile adventure on a graded dirt road that makes a circle of the Puerto Blanco Mountains and the La Abra Plain. Several interesting sites can be accessed from this road, including the old Golden Bell Mine, Quitobaquito Springs, and Senita Basin. The distance involved makes this ride best suited for the very fit rider who loves nothing better than a long day in the saddle, or a vehicle-supported trip that will allow riders to pick and choose the sections they would like to pedal. Possibilities exist for making this a multi-day adventure or riding out and back to Senita Basin (13 miles each way).

Starting point: Begin at the visitor center.

Length: 51 miles, including the 4-mile spur (one-way) to Senita Basin. This is an all-day, or possibly a multi-day outing. Having a vehicle for support will allow you to adjust time and distance.

Riding surface: Graded dirt road.

Difficulty: Moderate to strenuous. Overall distance is the most challenging aspect of this ride.

Scenery/highlights: A variety of desert environments that include thriving stands of organ pipe and saguaro cactus, a historically important desert oasis, a rare desert flora community at Senita Basin, and several old mine workings are just a few of the interesting sights along Puerto Blanco Drive.

Best time to ride: October through April.

Special considerations: This is a long day; be sure to bring plenty of water and high-energy foods to help you keep pedaling. Possibilities exist for making this a multi-day adventure by camping off the Pozo Nuevo

Like the Ajo Range in Organ Pipe National Monument, many of southern Arizona's ranges have volcanic origins.

Road that heads into the park's backcountry, a little over 2 miles north of Quitobaquito Springs. If you are interested in camping you must obtain a permit at the visitor center. There are vault toilets at Bonita Well and Senita Basin picnic areas but no water.

Because of the proximity to the border with Mexico and availability of water at Quitobaquito Springs this area occasionally sees illegal immigrants passing through. If you see anyone who looks like they may be traveling on foot, park employees advise staying well away and contacting a park ranger. Keep valuables hidden and lock your vehicle and bicycle when leaving them unattended.

Directions for the ride: There are one-way and two-way portions of this loop. The one-way portion begins near the visitor center and travels west, up and around the Puerto Blanco Mountains, to the Bates Well and Pozo Nuevo Junction just north of Quitobaquito Springs. The two-way portion begins at this junction and continues east along the international border to AZ 85 just north of Lukeville. To drive or ride the entire loop, first ride the one-way section in a counterclockwise direction. This is how the route will be described.

Pick up the park brochure with descriptions of sights along the way before you hit the trail. It is available at the visitor center for a nominal fee.

Puerto Blanco Drive begins near the visitor center; start the ride by pedaling north-northwest. Over the first few miles the route traverses a mixed-scrub community of shrubs, scrubby trees, and various types of cacti. Damage to the trees and cacti done by cattle that were once allowed to graze here can still be seen, even though ranching operations were halted more than twenty years ago. As you continue to pedal northward the peaks of the Puerto Blanco Mountains come into focus. Pinkley Peak, at 3,145 feet, is the highest in the range. The Puerto Blanco Mountains are made up of lavas and tuff (hardened volcanic ash); these and other materials indicate extensive volcanic activity in this area during Tertiary times, 15 to 25 million years ago.

Approximately 6 miles from the start the Valley of the Ajo comes into view. This expansive plain is rimmed on three sides by the Ajo, Bates, and Puerto Blanco mountains and was created when these mountain fault blocks uplifted and then eroded. The sediment washed off the mountains has filled this valley and will eventually bury the mountains. At 7.3 miles the road crosses through a wash and passes a picnic table, reaching another important erosional desert landform, a *bajada,* in 8.6 miles. A bajada is a series of overlapping alluvial fans sloping from the side of a mountain and running out to the valley floor. Bajadas create especially good conditions for desert vegetation and wildflowers as is evident here. In another 3 miles the road crosses over the spine of the Puerto Blanco Mountains and what is referred to as the Little Continental Divide. To the north of this divide all the arroyos drain into the Gila River; to the south they drain into Mexico's Rio Sonoyta. At almost 12 miles you pass the start of the Dripping Springs Mine Trail (2 miles up and back). The road then descends gently, crosses through a wash, and continues westward. Away to the north is the jagged outline of the Bates Mountains. The highest point in the range is Kino Peak (3,197 feet), named for Padre Eusebio Francisco Kino, a Jesuit missionary who brought cattle and Christianity to this region in the late 1600s.

Approximately 17 miles from the start is the Golden Bell Mine. Charlie Bell, a local prospector looking for gold, silver, and copper, set up operations here in the early 1930s. At 18.3 miles you come to Bonita Well, where there is a picnic area and rest rooms. A rancher named Robert L. Gray

Clouds and late afternoon sun create spectacular effects against the Ajo Mountains.

developed the well for his cattle in the 1930s. At 22 miles you come to the Bates Well and Puerto Blanco Junction where an unmaintained four-wheel-drive road heads north through the Growler Valley to Pozo Nuevo and Bates Wells. In 2 miles, at Quitobaquito Junction, a 0.4-mile spur heads to Quitobaquito Oasis and spring. This historic oasis has long been an important stopover for travelers. The pond that exists here supports a rare species of fish, an astonishing variety of resident and migratory birds, and a host of desert wildlife. Almost 30 miles from the start the road meets and follows the international border east. At 33.3 miles a 4-mile spur road leads to Senita Basin where the rare elephant tree and senita cactus coexist. Both species are common to subtropical Mexico but are very rare in the United States. Just under 42 miles from the start you rejoin the main road. From here it is another 5 miles of dirt road before reaching the junction with AZ 85. Go left and pedal or drive another 4 miles to the visitor center.

Option: Riding to Senita Basin and back from the visitor center is a shorter option that might appeal to some, and while you can ride out-and back to Quitobaquito Oasis, the total distance (50 miles) is not much shorter than the round-trip distance around Puerto Blanco Drive.

CAMPING

The main campground near the visitor center has 208 sites, is managed on a first-come, first-served basis, and is open year-round. It usually fills up quickly from October through April so plan to arrive early if you want to secure a spot. There are no hook-ups or showers, but drinking water is available. You will also find fire grills, although collecting firewood is prohibited. A fee is required.

There are four campsites at the **Alamo Canyon Primitive Campground,** located 14 miles north of the visitor center. This is a really pretty spot and several good hikes begin here. It is free but you must first acquire a permit at the visitor center. This campground does not accommodate RVs or trailers.

Camping in the backcountry is also allowed but requires a backcountry camping permit, available at the visitor center.

There are a handful of RV parks 22 miles north of the monument in Why, and several more 10 miles further in the town of Ajo. Most of these have tent sites

and offer the use of their shower facilities for a nominal fee.

LODGING

In the vicinity of the monument you will find accommodations in the towns of Lukeville, 5 miles south of the visitor center, Sonoyta, Mexico, 2 miles beyond Luke-

IT'S INTERESTING TO KNOW . . .

The Spanish word *ajo* means "garlic" but it is unlikely the nearby town and mountains and valley in this monument were named for this plant, which does not grow here. *Au'auho* is the Tohono O'odham Indian (also sometimes referred to as Pima or Papago Indian) word for paint and was probably used to identify this region and the red ore pigment they collected here and used to decorate their bodies.

ville, and in Ajo, 32 miles north.

In the tiny town of Lukeville the **Gringo Pass Motel and Trailer Park** is located on AZ 85. There are several motels and restaurants clustered around a charming town plaza in Sonoyta, Mexico. There are at least three motels in Ajo and two B&Bs: the **Mine Manager's House Inn** (520-387-6505) and the **Guest House Inn** (520-387-6133).

FOOD

Lukeville has a supermarket and a café serving three meals a day. In Sonoyta you'll find several restaurants. In Why, 22 miles north of the monument, there are couple of cafés and a gas station that has groceries and a few snack items. Your best choices for dining out are in Ajo. Several restaurants serve Mexican food in town, including the **Copper Kettle** (23 Plaza St.), **Don Juans** (100 Estrella Ave.), **Señor Sancho's** (663 N. 2nd Ave.), and **Chiliville**, just out of town at mile post 38-2 on AZ 85. Other offerings include **Cancun Café & Gift Shop** (320 W. Palo Verde Ave.), **Dago Joe's Family Restaurant** (2055 N. AZ 85), **Bamboo Village** (1810 N. 2nd Ave., serving Chinese food), **Marcela's Café & Bakery** (1117

W. Dorsey St.), and **Plaza Ice Cream & Deli** on the downtown plaza (28 Plaza). A few fast-food restaurants round out the dining options in Ajo.

LAUNDRY

You can do a load of laundry at any of the four RV campgrounds in Why.

DON'T MISS

The Estes Canyon–Bull Pasture Trail, which leaves from the Estes Canyon Picnic Area along Ajo Mountain Drive, is a fantastic opportunity to take in some of the park's best views and scenery. This 4-mile loop trail traverses several habitat types and reaches high points where you can revel at 360-degree panoramas of the surrounding desert. The Estes Canyon section of the trail crosses the canyon of the same name, while the Bull Pasture section climbs a ridge. Both meet at a spur that leads to a high meadow where ranchers once grazed their cattle.

BIKE SHOP/BIKE RENTAL

Bike shops are scarce in this remote corner of Arizona, so it is best to be prepared with a few spare tubes and tools. The nearest place for full-service bike shops and rentals is Tucson, where there are dozens of good shops.

FOR FURTHER INFORMATION

Organ Pipe Cactus National Monument—Superintendent, Route 1, Box 100, Ajo, AZ 85321; 520-387-6849; http://www.nps.gov/orpi/; orpi_information@nps.gov

Ajo District Chamber of Commerce, 321 Taladro, Ajo, AZ 85321; 520-387-7742

A bird's-eye view of the "Big Ditch" looking west from Point Sublime, Grand Canyon National Park. *Photo by Sarah Bennett Alley*

The blue waters of Lake Powell and red rocks of the Colorado Plateau are a stunning contrast as seen from the Rim Trail, just outside Glen Canyon National Recreation Area. *Photo by Sarah Bennett Alley*

Aspens glow in the morning sun near Barillas Peak in the Santa Fe Mountains, not far from Pecos National Historical Park. *Photo by Sarah Bennett Alley*

Craters and a landscape blanketed by cinders in the shadow of the San
Francisco peaks, Sunset Crater National Monument.
Photo by Sarah Bennett Alley

Solitude now reigns over stone cities that once were the epicenter of
Chacoan civilization at Chaco Canyon National Historical Park.
Photo by Dennis Coello

Storm clouds and late afternoon sun make for spectacular lighting over the Grand Canyon. *Photo by Dennis Coello*

A cyclist negotiates the Lime Kiln Trail near Tuzigoot National Monument. *Photo by Sarah Bennett Alley*

The beautifully banded hills of Painted Desert in Petrified Forest National Monument. *Photo by Sarah Bennett Alley*

Columns of volcanic tuff, the soft rock used by the ancients to build their pueblos and to secure them to cliff walls, flank a canyon just outside Bandelier National Monument. *Photo by Sarah Bennett Alley*

The hauntingly beautiful ruins of San Gregorio de Abó church and pueblo at Abó, one of three sites in Salinas Pueblo Missions National Monument. *Photo by Sarah Bennett Alley*

The fossilized remains of giant trees toppled in a volcanic explosion millions of years ago now lie scattered about the desert in Petrified Forest National Park. *Photo by Sarah Bennett Alley*

Petroglyphs etched into a boulder along the volcanic escarpment where more than 20,000 mysterious etchings have been cataloged. *Photo by Sarah Bennett Alley*

A rider appears suspended as she pedals through the sugar-white dunes on Dunes Drive inside White Sands National Monument. *Photo by Tim Alley*

A rider approaches the rugged Ajo Mountains inside Organ Pipe National Monument. *Photo by Dennis Coello*

6

This park can be divided into three sections: the Painted Desert at the north end, the petrified trees in the south, and a wealth of archaeological riches in the middle. The story that gave shape to the landscape and resulted in the preservation of the trees and fossils found in the park began sometime during the Triassic period, between 205 and 240 million years ago. During this time, a forest of gigantic pine-like trees, some reaching 200 feet tall, cloaked the foothills of a volcanically active mountain range. Numerous streams and rivulets crisscrossed a broad floodplain that stretched away from the foot of the mountains. Beneath the canopy of giant trees grew a lush mix of ferns, palms, and other plants that sheltered small but fleet-footed carnivorous dinosaurs, crocodile-like reptiles, and enormous fish-eating amphibians. It was a warm, watery world teeming with life that came very suddenly, and very violently, to an end.

Geologist theorize that a series of catastrophic volcanic eruptions began in the nearby mountains and toppled the great trees. Floods of melting snow and ice from high on the volcanoes became mud flows that hurled the huge logs downward and out onto the floodplain. Layers of fine volcanic particles in the form of mud, silt, and ash continued to fall and settle over the trees, herbaceous plants, and animals that washed onto the mud flats. These layers were impermeable to oxygen and thus prevented the process of decay. Over time, however, water carrying

An incredible palette of pastel hues creates an almost surreal landscape in the Painted Desert.

microscopic bits of silica began percolating down through the layers. Eventually these silica particles began to replace the trees, cell by cell, in a fossilization process that preserved them almost perfectly, right down to their battered bark and broken limbs. Minerals such as iron and manganese leached out of the layers above and began to color the now-petrified logs in shades of blue, yellow, black, white, and red. Natural cavities in the wood filled with glistening quartz crystals.

Word of the petrified wood's incredible beauty spread quickly after its discovery in the late 1850s. The petrified, jewel-like remnants of the ancient past were looted by souvenir hunters, collectors, and craftsmen before President Theodore W. Roosevelt protected the area as a national monument in 1906. While untold tons of fossilized wood have been removed from the park you can still see the fantastic rainbow of agates in the specimens that remain. Pieces of the logs are scattered all over the park, but collecting them is strictly forbidden.

The beautifully banded badlands of the Painted Desert, first called El Desierto Pintado by the Spanish explorers of Coronado's expedition in 1540, are ancient ash and mud deposits painted by the same minerals through a similar process. These poorly consolidated, highly eroded, yet colorful soils, along with the petrified wood, occur in a layer of strata called the Chinle formation, which appears throughout the Colorado Plateau geologic province. Still, there is more to this park than meets the eye. Archaeological evidence suggests that nomadic hunters began moving through and camping in what is now the park ten thousand years ago. Later, these nomads settled and farmed in the area and eventually built permanent stone structures like the one at Puerco Pueblo. Like many of the stone ruins in the Four Corners region, Puerco Pueblo was mysteriously abandoned sometime around 1400.

Cycling in the Park

There is one 28-mile paved scenic drive that extends through the park from north to south, with 20 pullouts and points of interest along the way. The scenic drive is a two-way road connecting I-40 in the north and US 180 in the south. It can be ridden from either end as an out-and-back, making for a long, 56-mile day in the saddle, or you can ride it in one direction and arrange to be picked up at the other end. Another possibility is to simply ride a portion of the route out to chosen points of interest, and then ride back the way you came. An excellent option for a shorter ride begins at the Painted Desert Visitor Center and follows the scenic drive for 5 miles as it loops north and then south before crossing over I-40. This 10-mile ride takes you to 8 different overlooks of the Painted Desert portion of the park. Another option begins at the Rainbow Forest Museum at the drive's south end. From here you can ride north for just over 8 miles to the Agate Bridge pullout, visiting the Long Logs, Agate House, Crystal Forest, and Jasper Forest points of interest along the way. You can always adjust the length of your ride to fit your time and fitness needs if you have a support vehicle.

CYCLING OPTIONS

Cycling options are limited to the one scenic drive stretching between the north and south entrance stations. Riding this route one-way gives a distance of 28 miles, making the out-and-back a long, 56-mile day in the saddle. Options for riding the Painted Desert or petrified log sections of the scenic drive give distances of 10 and almost 20 miles, respectively.

There are a few things to keep in mind when planning to visit and ride in Petrified Forest National Park. Almost a million people visit here every year, more than half of them during the summer months. The scenic drive can become busy with cars and campers and is very narrow; there are almost no shoulders for its entire length. Some experience sharing the road with cars will be helpful here. Also, summer temperatures frequently reach the century mark, making it difficult to stay comfortable and well hydrated while exerting yourself on a bike. For these reasons, a spring or fall visit, when temperatures are more moderate and the crowds have abated, is a far better time to come and take in the sights. Bring along a lock to secure your bike while taking short hikes among the petrified logs and painted hills of this magical desert.

---

28. PAINTED DESERT–PETRIFIED FOREST SCENIC DRIVE (See map on page 165)

For road or mountain bikes. The scenic drive that runs north to south through the park is your only possibility for getting out and doing some pedaling here. The route undulates slightly over several low mesas but loses only 300 feet cumulatively between the Painted Desert Visitor Center at the north end and Rainbow Forest Museum at the south. There are many interesting pullouts along the way and several short, don't-miss hikes that provide an up-close perspective on this park's many wonders. Although the route can be ridden in either direction it will be described from north to south. Options for shorter rides are included at the end of the ride description.

Starting point: Painted Desert Visitor Center, located just off I-40 68 miles west of Gallup, New Mexico, and 24 miles east of Holbrook, Arizona.

Length: 28 miles one-way, 56 miles total. A shorter tour of Painted Desert overlooks is 10 miles total. Another option that takes you to all the major petrified log sites gives a total distance of 20 miles.

Riding surface: Pavement; very narrow road.

Difficulty: Easy to strenuous depending on the distance you decide to ride.

28 · Painted Desert – Petrified Forest Scenic Drive

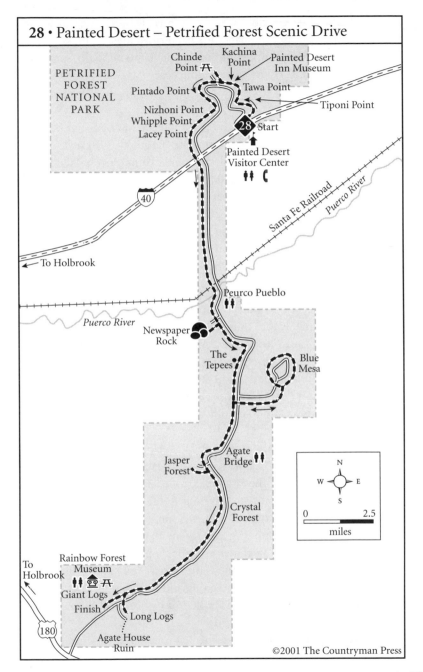

PETRIFIED FOREST NATIONAL PARK

Chinde Point

Kachina Point

Painted Desert Inn Museum

Pintado Point

Tawa Point

Tiponi Point

Nizhoni Point
Whipple Point
Lacey Point

28 Start

Painted Desert Visitor Center

40

Santa Fe Railroad

Puerco River

To Holbrook

Peurco Pueblo

Puerco River

Newspaper Rock

The Tepees

Blue Mesa

Agate Bridge

Jasper Forest

Crystal Forest

N
W · E
S

0   2.5
miles

Rainbow Forest Museum

To Holbrook

Giant Logs

Finish

Long Logs

Agate House Ruin

180

©2001 The Countryman Press

Scenery/highlights: Overlooks of the Painted Desert, ruins of Puerco Pueblo, petroglyphs at Newspaper Rock, petrified logs, and fossils at the Rainbow Forest Museum are the main highlights along a route that offers sweeping views of the surrounding desert.

Best time to ride: Spring and fall.

Special considerations: Water and rest rooms are available at both the Painted Desert Visitor Center and the Rainbow Forest Museum. Additional rest rooms are available at Chinde Point, Puerco Pueblo, and Agate Bridge pullouts spring through fall. You'll also find a gas station and restaurant at the Painted Desert Visitor Center just off I-40.

The Painted Desert Inn, located 2 miles along the route, has cultural displays and a bookstore that also sells Native American crafts, so you may want to bring your wallet. You will also need to pay a fee at the park entrance station beyond the start of this ride.

Directions for the ride: After watching the short film and looking at the various displays at the Painted Desert Visitor Center mount up and go right. In approximately 0.25 mile you will need to pay your park entrance fee at the North Entrance Station. Another 0.3 mile beyond is Tiponi Point, the first of eight stops overlooking the Painted Desert, the largest section of the park, added in 1932 when the monument became a national park. Tawa Point Overlook, at 1.4 miles, is the next stop, where you'll find great views and the trailhead for the 0.25 mile Rim Trail leading to Kachina Point.

Almost 2 miles from the start is the historic Painted Desert Inn and Kachina Point Overlook. The inn was built in 1924 with Indian labor and local materials and was the brainchild of Herbert Lore, who saw an opportunity to offer motorists traveling Route 66 a place to stay and spend their dollars on Indian curios. The inn was acquired by the park service, along with surrounding acreage, in 1936 when it was enlarged and used as an information center and gift shop. Murals on the walls of the inn were painted by the famous Hopi artist Fred Kabotie during the 1940s. Plans were made to tear down the old structure in 1962 after the Painted Desert Visitor Center was built, but its historical value was recognized and the building was saved.

Just 0.2 mile past the inn is the 0.3-mile spur to Chinde Point Overlook and picnic area, the most northerly point along the route. Back

FLORA

While the banded hills and red desert of the park and surrounding area are beautiful, they are a landscape that has been drastically changed. Before settlement this area would be classified as a short-grass prairie, but overgrazing and the encroachment of non-native species, such as tamarisk, have transformed this desert into a relatively barren moonscape, where water is free to carry the soil away. The betonite clays responsible for the colorful banding of the hills is a sticky mess when wet, but turns to a powdery dust that blows away in the wind when dry. Rainfall is meager, only 9 inches per year, most coming in the form of heavy thunderstorms. Only a few plants root and take hold.

Wildflowers are few, but in spring you might find the fiery orange blooms of Indian paintbrush, or the cream to orange blossoms of a mariposa lily. The large, tissuelike flowers of evening primrose also bloom here, and by midsummer you're bound to see sunflowers along the roadside. Orange globe mallow is common in the area around Puerco Pueblo, and is also found along road where extra water drains off the pavement. Brittlebrush and four-wing saltbush exist in isolated areas in the park, and blue sage, which would have been rare 150 years ago, is now common, able to encroach into places were grasses once dominated. Both rabbitbrush and the smaller snakeweed are quite common and become covered in crowns of golden blooms in fall.

on the main road, at 2.7 miles, continue heading west for 0.4 mile to Pintado Point, which sits atop an ancient lava flow that has protected the soft Chinle formation clays below it. At 4.3 miles is Nizhoni Point, where soft selenite gypsum crystals litter the ground. Whipple Point, 0.2 mile farther, is the next stop, named after Lieutenant A.W. Whipple, credited with being the first white man to see the Painted Desert and petrified logs. Lacey Point Overlook, 5 miles from the start, is the last of the Painted Desert overlooks in this section and the turnaround point

Silica particles replaced the cells of these ancient logs in a fossilization process that preserved them almost perfectly.

for the shorter ride option. It is another 6 miles to the next pullout at Puerco Pueblo.

From Lacey Point the road heads almost due south, crossing over I-40 (no access) approximately 6.3 miles from the start. At 10.5 miles the road crosses over a railroad bridge, and 0.4 mile later crosses the bridge over what used to be the Puerco River. Archaeologic evidence suggests that

FAUNA

The ever-present raven, who lives year-round in the park, is surely one of the most often-sighted wildlife species here. It is joined in the warmer months by northern harriers (also called marsh hawks), red-tailed hawks, and the occasional golden eagle. Several species of owls are also known to visit the park, but unless you are out at night and know how to spot them you won't see them.

These raptors feed on the bountiful supply of deer mice, cottontail rabbits, and jackrabbits that thrives in this desert. Coyotes, who also hunt these rodents, are seen fairly regularly. Two herds of desert pronghorn antelope inhabit the park and surrounding area, but have remained artificially cut off from one another by the Santa Fe Railroad. The park has made efforts in recent years to unite the two herds in an effort to keep the gene pool healthy. Mule deer live in the Painted Desert region of the park, and sometimes come down around the Painted Desert Visitor Center in winter to drink from nearby springs. You're more than likely to see several kinds of lizards warming themselves on pieces of petrified log or dashing for cover, among them whiptail lizards, brown side-blotched lizards, and occasionally, the fairly large and regal-looking collared lizard. There are two kinds of rattlesnakes in the park, both of which are rarely seen. The most interesting is the very small, very shy, and very rare Hopi rattlesnake.

this river once ran year-round and supported cottonwood trees, willows, and meadows along its banks. This environment, wetter than it is now, was also able to support the large community of people who lived at Puerco Pueblo and farmed along the river's banks. The grasslands, cottonwoods, and seasonal river flow survived into the 19th century but were wiped out by overgrazing. Now the channel is dry, crusted with salt deposits, and continues to deteriorate whenever floods rumble through. Puerco Pueblo, at 11.2 miles, is a single-story pueblo with 76 rooms, two kivas, and a central plaza. It was occupied between A.D. 1100 and 1400. While one of the kivas remains intact only foundations are left of most of the structures. Numerous petroglyphs are etched into boulders below the pueblo, but they are not as concentrated as those at Newspaper Rock, almost a mile farther south, where hundreds cover a single boulder.

Just over 14 miles from the start you come to the Tepees, cone-shaped Chinle formation hills. Another 1.6 miles brings you to the 3-mile long Blue Mesa spur road. (Riding out this spur will add 6 miles to your total distance.) From Blue Mesa you can enjoy sweeping views in all directions and take a 1-mile interpretive trail among the blue and lavender hills of this area. At Agate Bridge (18.5 miles) a petrified log hangs suspended over a gully carved out by erosion. The log was reinforced with cement in 1917 when it began to show signs of cracking. In 0.2 mile a 0.5-mile spur takes you to the Jasper Forest where you can enjoy views to the west and observe hundreds of pieces of petrified wood that have emerged as the surrounding hillsides. The Crystal Forest Loop Trail (at 21.5 miles) is a paved, 0.5-mile loop that takes you among some of the heaviest concentrations of petrified wood in the park. At 27 miles a 0.5-mile spur leads to the Long Logs Loop and Agate House Trail; both are about 0.5 mile long. Several of the pieces along the Long Logs Loop measure over 100 feet. Agate House is a stone pueblo built entirely out of petrified wood by the ancients who once lived in this area. One of the original seven rooms of the pueblo has been rebuilt. At 28.1 miles you pass a picnic area and just beyond you'll find the Rainbow Forest Museum, Fred Harvey's Gift Shop and Fountain, and the start of the 0.5-mile Giant Logs Trail where one fallen log measures over 6 feet in diameter.

Option #1: If you are interested in a 10-mile pedal that even some of the younger family members might enjoy, try riding from the Painted Desert Visitor Center to Lacey Point and back. Follow the ride description above to that point and back.

Option #2: A slightly longer ride than the option above takes you north from the south end of the drive to Agate Bridge. Follow directions as above in reverse to that point and then return the way you came for a total distance of 19.6 miles.

CAMPING

There are no campgrounds in the park, however, camping in the backcountry of the Painted Desert is allowed for backpackers who obtain a permit. Permits are available at the Painted Desert Visitor Center and they are free.

Tent sites are offered just outside the south entrance of the park by purveyors of a gift store there. Your other options are in Holbrook, located at the junction of I-40 and US 180, about 20 miles west of the park. The **OK RV Park,** north of I-40 at exit 286 has sites for campers, showers, and laundry facilities. A **KOA Kampground** off the same exit also has showers and laundry. Another option 10 miles west of Holbrook is **Cholla Lake County Park.** Here you'll find a lake where swimming is allowed, tent sites and RV sites, and showers that are open March through October.

LODGING

The nearest lodging options are in Holbrook, at the junction of I-40

IT'S INTERESTING TO KNOW . . .

The volcanic eruptions that leveled and preserved the trees showcased in Petrified Forest National Park also preserved, in almost perfect detail, numerous plants and animals. Nowhere in the Chinle formation is the fossil record as rich as it is in the park. The fossils found here are some of the oldest found anywhere in the world and have puzzled the paleontologists who are still trying to classify them. One of the most famous is a small but fierce looking dinosaur dubbed Gertie unearthed in 1984. Some 40 species of plants, including deciduous trees, ferns, palms, and others have been found in the fossil record, as have giant dragonflies. A collection of fossil specimens is on display at both visitor centers.

and US 180 about 20 miles west of the park. Here you'll find a good assortment of chain hotels, including **Budget Inn, Super 8, Econo Lodge, Comfort Inn, Holiday Inn Express,** and **Best Western.** There are also at least 10 inexpensive motels to choose from.

FOOD

The **Fred Harvey Restaurant** at the north end near the Painted Desert Visitor Center has a complete breakfast and lunch menu. At the south end, inside the Rainbow Forest Museum, is a snack bar offering hot dogs, ice cream, and the like.

There are a lot of fast-food restaurants and cafés serving greasy, run-of-the-mill American food in Holbrook. Try the **Cholla Restaurant** (609 W Hopi Dr.) or the **El Rancho Restaurant** (867 Navajo Blvd.) for a selection of Mexican and American dishes. The **Mandarin Beauty** (2218 N Navajo Blvd.) serves Chinese food for lunch and dinner, and the **Mesa Restaurante Italiana** offers an American interpretation of Italian food.

LAUNDRY

You can do a load of laundry at either of the RV parks in Holbrook, or visit

Holbrook Laundry, 1613 E. Navajo Blvd.; 520-524-1630

Leisure Laundry, 2208 Navajo Blvd.; 520-524-6659

DON'T MISS

While visiting this park don't miss the chance to hike into the backcountry wilderness of the Painted Desert. The 4-mile out-and-back trip to Onyx Bridge is a great way to experience the solitude and serenity that lies just beyond the pavement. The route begins just behind the Painted Desert Inn at Kachina Point and ambles across stark yet beautiful hills and washes for 2 miles before arriving at an enormous stone log spanning a wash. Although the trail is not well marked and is often swept away by wind and rain, it is difficult to get lost because the inn remains visible at all times.

BIKE SHOP/BIKE RENTAL

The nearest resource for bike parts and service is at **Cycle Mania** in the town of Show Low, about an hour south of Holbrook on AZ 77 (3051 S. White Mountain Rd. #A, Show Low, AZ 85901; 520-537-8812). Flagstaff, close to 2 hours west of Holbrook on I-40, has at least a half a dozen good bike shops able to satisfy all your biking needs.

FOR FURTHER INFORMATION

Petrified Forest National Park— Superintendent, P.O. Box 2217, Petrified Forest National Park, AZ 86028; 520-524-6228; http://www.nps.gov/pefo/

Holbrook Chamber of Commerce, 100 E. Arizona St., Holbrook, AZ 86025; 520-524-2459 or 1-800-524-2459; www.ci.holbrook.az.us

7

The mighty saguaro cactus, and the Sonoran Desert ecosystem it helps define, are the centerpiece and focus of Saguaro National Park. The park exists as two units, one east of Tucson in the foothills of the Rincon Mountains, and one west of Tucson, in the Tucson Mountains. Both magnificent stands, or "forests," of saguaros, the largest succulent in North America. Able to reach 50 feet tall and weigh as much as 8 tons, this spiny giant is the reigning monarch of the Sonoran Desert and the uncontested symbol of the American Southwest. Expertly adapted to the harsh conditions of the hottest and driest desert on the continent, the saguaro has long played a vital role in the survival of the Sonoran Desert's wildlife and native peoples. The curious arrangement of branches, or "arms," of these cacti give them distinct personalities that continue to delight visitors and longtime desert dwellers alike.

Temperatures that exceed 100 degrees for close to a third of the year and a scant 12 inches of annual precipitation can make life in the Sonoran Desert extremely hard, especially for a young saguaro. Although an adult saguaro may produce as many as 40 million seeds in its lifetime, only a few will survive to maturity. The slow-growing cactus takes 15 years to grow one foot, 30 years to flower and begin to produce fruit, 50 years to reach the height of a tall man, and 75 before the first arms emerge. If the saguaro survives 100 years it may reach 25 feet in height; those lucky enough to survive 150 years or more achieve gargantuan proportions.

Location is a critical factor in a saguaro's survival and success. They have the best chance of thriving if they happen to root near a rock or under a nurse tree, such as a mesquite or paloverde. Here the young cactus is sheltered from the sun's fierce rays, insulated from winter cold, and out of the way of trampling or nibbling animals. Saguaros prefer gently sloping *bajadas,* desert plains that fan out from the foot of mountain ranges, where they can receive runoff but also get good drainage. Hard frosts can kill a saguaro, as can lightning, high winds, and extended droughts. Therefore you will usually find them growing on southern exposures, where they enjoy the warmth of the winter sun, and in wind-sheltered areas. Human impacts, such as livestock grazing and pirating for use in landscaping, have taken a heavy toll in the past. Today state laws that dole out harsh penalties for disturbing saguaros, regardless of where they grow, are helping to protect them.

The saguaro's large, saucer-sized blossoms erupt like a crown from the tips of its arms and center trunk beginning in late April. Blooming lasts for 4 weeks and can extend into early June. The waxy, cream-colored petals open in the evening when the sun's ravaging rays have faded, and stay open at night for pollinators, such as white-winged doves and long-nosed bats, both migrants from Mexico. Moths, bees, and other insects also do their part to pollinate the saguaro's blooms. Ruby-red fruits ripen in June and July and are a feast for desert creatures, including javelinas, coyotes, foxes, and numerous bird and insect species. The Tohono O'odham Indians are native to this area and still collect the fruit to make jams, jellies, and ceremonial wine. Besides its immense size and unique character, the saguaro plays a vital role in the health of the Sonoran Desert community, and is richly deserving of the protection it receives in this park.

Cycling in the Park

Inside the Rincon Mountain District of Saguaro National Park, or Saguaro East, is Cactus Forest Drive, a paved, one-way road that loops through the heart of a large, old saguaro forest. This is a popular ride for locals and is a great pedal on either a road or mountain bike. Mountain

CYCLING OPTIONS

Saguaro National Park is one of the only parks in the country that has a singletrack trail that is open to mountain bikers. The Cactus Forest Trail, which bisects the paved Cactus Forest Scenic Drive in the park's eastern unit, is a super-fun trail fat-tire enthusiasts of all abilities will relish. The paved loop that encompasses the dirt trail is also a great pedal that is very popular with local bikers. Road riders will enjoy the trip out along the Old Spanish Trail to Colossal Cave, and avid mountain bikers will be thrilled with the Chiva Falls Loop and the many other trails in that area.

Inside the west unit of the park mountain bikers can ride the cherry-stem Bajada Loop from the Red Hills Visitor Center, and may choose to adventure further north into the park's backcountry on the Golden Gate Road. The paved McCain Loop Road swings around through a portion of Tucson Mountain Park on a 10-plus-mile route through country similar to what you would see inside the park. Along the way you can stop in and visit the Arizona–Sonora Desert Museum, world renowned for the natural settings provided for the many types of desert plant and animal species on display. An option lets those looking for more of a workout continue south on Kinney Road, past the Old Tucson Studios, to Ajo Road where the route ends.

bikers may want to test their skills on the 2.5-mile Cactus Forest Trail, a dirt singletrack that bisects the scenic drive loop. This fun, rolling trail twists and turns around enormous saguaros and other spiny desert dwellers. More serious road riders will enjoy riding from the park south and east along the Old Spanish Trail to Colossal Cave at the southwestern edge of the Rincon Mountains. Many more mountain biking adventures exist just north of Saguaro East in the Rincon Mountains, in the Coronado National Forest. Chiva Falls Loop, just north of the park in the heart of the Rincon, is one of many in an extensive network of trails that keep mountain bikers in the Tucson area happy.

A mountain biker slides by some of the other spiny desert dwellers that inhabit Saguaro National Park on the Cactus Forest Trail.

On the other side of town you'll find the Bajada Loop, a graded dirt road that serves as the main scenic drive inside Saguaro West. The McCain Loop Road, near the west unit of the park, is a good option for those who prefer the pavement, and is often ridden by serious road riders and racers who come to train in Tucson during the winter.

When thinking about biking in the Sonoran Desert there are several important factors to keep in mind, most importantly the area's seasonal weather patterns. November through March temperatures are comfortable during the day (mid-60s to mid-70s) and chilly at night, but beginning in mid-May temperatures begin to climb up toward the century mark, where they hover until mid- to late September. December through February sees light winter rains that culminate with the beginning of the spring bloom. Riding through the Sonoran Desert in bloom is the experience of a lifetime; the many different kinds of cacti that share the desert with the saguaro put forth masses of eye-dazzling flowers that come in an astounding variety of shapes and colors. This bloom extends through May, usually peaking sometime in March or April. June and July are the hottest months and should be avoided if at all possible. During July and August monsoonal thunderstorms produce heavy rains and lightning and can cause dangerous localized flooding through previously dry arroyos or streambeds.

Average humidity throughout the year in this desert is less than 20 percent, which means your body will constantly be losing precious fluids to the atmosphere. In order to stay healthy and feel energetic you must continually replace fluids by drinking plenty of water—at least a gallon a day when at rest. Drink before, during, and after your ride to prevent dehydration and fatigue. Don't let thirst regulate your fluid intake; by the time you're thirsty your body is already depleted. For long rides it's a good idea to carry some kind of energy drink or mix. These contain salts, glucose, and electrolytes that help your body to retain fluids and convert fuel into energy. Muscle cramps, dizziness, headaches, nausea, and fatigue are all signs of heat-related stress or illness that are serious and can quickly become life threatening.

The desert's unlimited supply of cactus thorns can wreak havoc on your plans for hassle-free, off-road adventure. Local mountain bikers use one of several methods to deal with this prickly situation. A plastic liner can be placed between your tube and tire, preventing the thorn from reaching the tube, or a thick, gooey substance that quickly seals perforations can be injected into your tire's tube. Stop in at one of the many shops in Tucson to get your mountain bike ready for desert riding. Also, it's not a bad idea to add a pair of tweezers to your tool kit while riding here.

SAGUARO EAST

---

29. CACTUS FOREST DRIVE AND TRAIL
(See map on page 180)

Cactus Forest Drive is a paved, one-way road that loops through mature stands of saguaro cactus in the foothills of the Rincon Mountains, providing wonderful views to the peaks above and the sprawling Tucson Basin to the west. Both road and mountain bikes are suitable for this pedal. Mountain bikers can take advantage of the singletrack trail that bisects the loop and ride the gravel road out to Mica View Picnic Area.

Starting point: Saguaro East Visitor Center.

Length: The paved loop is 7.6 miles start to finish, riding the Cactus Forest Trail gives a total distance of 6 miles. Allow 2 to 3 hours to ride these loops and take in the sights along the way.

Riding surface: Paved road and dirt singletrack.

Difficulty: Easy to moderate.

Scenery/highlights: Great riding, beautiful desert scenery, good views of the Rincon Mountains. A good opportunity to get an up-close look at the spiny giants celebrated in this park and for mountain bikers to enjoy one of the only unpaved trails in any national park open to mountain bikes.

Best time to ride: Late fall through early spring. Riding this route in spring when the desert is blooming is best of all.

Special considerations: Water and rest rooms are available at the visitor center.

The paved Cactus Forest Drive Loop is very narrow and has many tight turns and several steep hills; please use caution, ride to the right in single file, and check your speed on the hills.

Directions for the ride: After taking some time to check out the interesting exhibits and displays explaining the life cycle of the saguaro cactus and the curiosities of Sonoran Desert creatures, saddle up and begin pedaling east. Routes divide almost immediately and you must make a choice. If you are on a mountain bike and want to ride the Cactus Forest Trail you need to decide which direction you are going to ride it. To the right is a two-way section of road that will deliver you to the southern terminus of the trail. To the left the one-way road takes you to the northern end of the trail. The loop route is described here in a clockwise direction and the trail section is described from north to south.

Bear left, following the one-way loop road as it heads north. This narrow, winding road dips and rises over numerous hills and drainages, arriving at the turnoff for Mica View Picnic Area approximately 1.8 miles from the start. Those with tires that can handle this gravel road may want to pedal the 0.7 mile to the picnic area, have a look around, and add some distance to your total mileage. Past the turnoff to Mica View Picnic Area the road heads east, continuing around in a clockwise direction. Another 0.4 mile down the road you pass a pullout on the right. A short distance

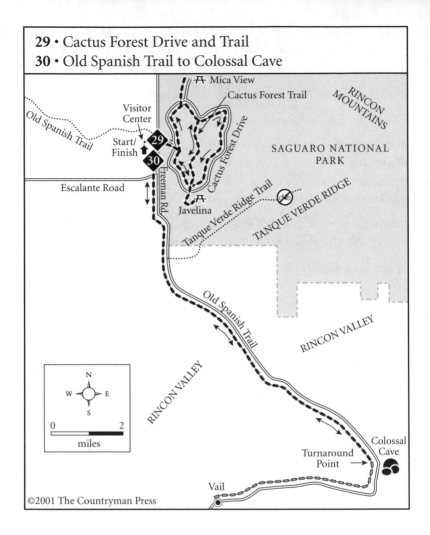

29 · Cactus Forest Drive and Trail
30 · Old Spanish Trail to Colossal Cave

Mica View

Cactus Forest Trail

RINCON MOUNTAINS

Visitor Center

Old Spanish Trail

Start/ Finish

29

30

Cactus Forest Drive

SAGUARO NATIONAL PARK

Escalante Road

Freeman Rd.

Javelina

Tanque Verde Ridge Trail

TANQUE VERDE RIDGE

Old Spanish Trail

RINCON VALLEY

N
W — E
S

0   2
miles

RINCON VALLEY

Turnaround Point

Colossal Cave

Vail

©2001 The Countryman Press

beyond this pullout is the beginning of the Cactus Forest Trail, 2.5 miles from the start.

Go right onto the trail if you are on a mountain bike and begin riding south, following the trail as it winds through the desert on hard, fast desert pavement—compacted desert soils. A mile along the route you come to the remnants of an old lime kiln operation. Past this point are a couple of short, steep climbs and descents before arriving back on the

A lone cyclist enjoys an evening ride on the Cactus Forest Trail inside Saguaro National Park's eastern unit.

main road 2.5 miles from the start of the singletrack and 5.0 miles from the visitor center.

If you are continuing around on the paved route simply follow the loop as it heads east, paralleling Tanque Verde Ridge. At the edge of an arroyo, 0.7 mile beyond the Cactus Forest Trailhead, there is a pullout. Past this pullout the road turns and heads south. In 0.5 mile you come to the Rincon Mountains Overlook, a pullout on the left. The road continues for another 1.9 miles to Javelina Rocks, and another 0.7 mile to the turnoff for Javelina Picnic Area and the short Freeman Homestead Trail 6.3 miles from the start. This turnoff is the southernmost point in the loop; now the road turns and heads north, passing the southern access to the Cactus Forest Trail in 0.3 miles, and a pullout and overlook of the Tucson Basin in another 0.8 mile. In another 0.2 miles, or 7.6 miles from the start, you arrive back at the visitor center.

---

30. OLD SPANISH TRAIL TO COLOSSAL CAVE
(See map on page 180)

For road bikes. The pedal south along the Old Spanish Trail to Colossal Cave is a great spin for road bikers who want to get out and stretch their legs while taking in some beautiful Sonoran Desert scenery. Colossal Cave is a dry limestone cavern filled with interesting formations and delightful 70-degree air. Tours of the cavern leave every half-hour and take about 45 minutes.

Starting point: Saguaro East Visitor Center.

Length: 12 miles one-way, 24 miles out-and-back. Allow at least 3 hours to ride the distance, more if you are interested in touring the cave. An option lets stronger riders extend their ride another 5 miles to the town of Vail, giving a total distance of 34 miles.

Riding surface: Pavement; wide shoulders with a bike lane.

Difficulty: Moderate. This route is mostly level with one climb up to the cave area. The overall distance will make this ride more difficult for some.

Scenery/highlights: This is a great road ride along a route once used by Spanish friars, soldiers, and settlers coming from Mexico City to settle this basin valley. Tucson has a rich and fascinating history and is worth exploring while you are in the area.

Sonoran Desert scenery, views into the Rincon Mountains, and the geologic wonders of Colossal Cave all make this a great ride.

Best time to ride: Anytime but summer.

Special considerations: Water and rest rooms are available at the park visitor center and at Colossal Cave. There is also a snack bar near the entrance to the cave. If you plan to tour the cave be sure to bring a lock to secure your bike while you are away.

Directions for the ride: From the visitor center head back out to the road you came in on and turn left onto Old Spanish Trail. You will stay on this road for the entire length of your ride. For the first 2.3 miles the protected acreage of Saguaro National Park will be on the left, the boundary defined by the road as you pedal south. The route then crosses over the toe of Tanque Verde Ridge and dips across two arroyos over the next mile before angling to the southeast. For the next 6 miles the route traverses the Rincon Valley. Great views into the heart of the Rincon Mountains and the Rincon Mountain Wilderness will be to your left. The road then begins climbing gently toward a ridge extending from the mountains. Near the top of this ridge is the turnoff for Colossal Cave. Ride up the drive to the cave and arrive at the parking lot approximately 12 miles from the start. When you are rested up reverse your route and head back to the park's visitor center.

Option: Stronger riders who want to extend their ride may continue past the turnoff for the cave and ride another 5 miles to the historic rail town of Vail. Riding all the way to Vail and back will give you a total ride distance of 34 miles.

---

31. CHIVA FALLS LOOP (See map on page 184)

For mountain bikes. This loop is in the beautiful Redington Pass area of the Rincon Mountains, north of Saguaro National Park's eastern unit. Just under 12 miles, this cherry-stem loop is a fun, fast singletrack with just a few technical sections that will please both intermediate and advanced fat-tire fans. Gorgeous scenery, including a stream and water-

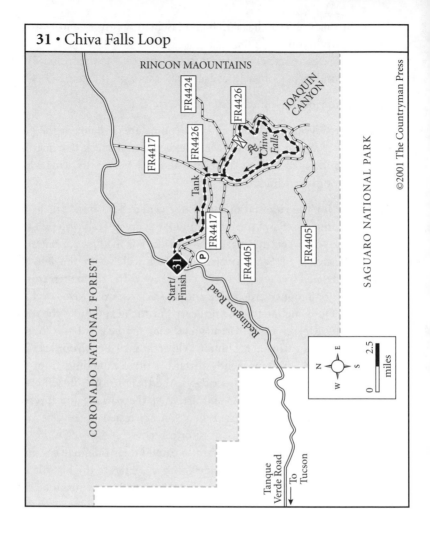

RINCON MAOUNTAINS

FR4424

FR4426

JOAQUIN CANYON

FR4426

FR4417

Tank

Chiva Falls

©2001 The Countryman Press

SAGUARO NATIONAL PARK

FR4417

FR4405

FR4405

31

P

Start/ Finish

Redington Road

CORONADO NATIONAL FOREST

N E S W

0   2.5

miles

Tanque Verde Road

To Tucson

fall, views up to the Rincon Mountain peaks, over the Tucson Basin looking west, and to nearby Mount Lemmon in the Santa Catalina Mountains all make this a spectacular ride.

Starting point: Begin at a parking area and trailhead located on
Redington Road. To get there from the park, go right onto Freeman Road
and follow it north for just under 5 miles to Tanque Verde Road. Go right
onto Tanque Verde Road and follow it east, toward the mountains, until

the pavement ends. Where the road turns to dirt it becomes Redington Road. Drive 4.5 miles up Redington Road to the parking area on the right. The trailhead is at the end of the parking lot.

Length: 12-mile cherry-stem loop.

Riding surface: Dirt ATV-style doubletrack that has a couple of sections that all but the most technically accomplished riders will want to negotiate on foot.

Difficulty: Moderate to difficult. Elevations range between 3,720 and 4,200 feet.

Scenery/highlights: Chiva Falls is a beautiful pour-over into a large pool that is big enough for a refreshing dip on a hot day. The stream that fills it runs late fall through spring and has created an oasis for desert wildlife of all kinds, including the fat-tire variety.

Great views in all directions abound and the high-desert scenery is gorgeous.

Best time to ride: Anytime but summer.

Special considerations: There are no facilities at the trailhead or anywhere along this route so come prepared.

This is one of the most popular rides in the east Tucson area. Plan on an early start to avoid the crowds.

There are many excellent riding options in this area. Pick up a Santa Catalina District map for the Coronado National Forest or check with one of the local bike shops for more information on trails in the Rincon and Santa Catalina Mountains.

Directions for the ride: From the parking lot ride east, toward the Rincon Mountains on Forest Road (FR) 4417. In a few hundred yards bear right. At 0.8 mile from the start is a section of trail known as the Chute. Continue heading south and east on the trail as it rolls over rocks and dips through sections of gravely sand. Approximately 2.8 miles from the start, after passing a stock tank, you come to a junction. Bear right onto FR 4426. In another 0.5 mile is another junction; go left over a cattle guard. A short distance later, just past a corral, go left again, continuing on FR 4426.

FLORA

Besides the impressive saguaro, there are at least 50 other cactus species in the park. Among these you'll find hedgehog, claret cup, barrel, and fishook cactus, so-named because of the curled tips of its spines. There are no fewer than six varieties of cholla. Beavertail cactus and several species of prickly pear have paddle-shaped leaves and put forth large, brightly colored blooms every spring. The elegant, night-blooming cereus also lives here but is harder to spot.

Ocotillo, with long, spiny, whiplike branches that radiate out from a single base and are tufted with brilliant red flowers in spring, is not a cactus but is classified as a tree. Many of the trees in this desert are also covered with spines, including catclaw acacia, white-thorn acacia, and mesquite. Blue and foothill paloverde also occur in this park and are easy to recognize because of their green bark. Shrubs include desert broom, brittlebrush, and creosote bush. Soaptree yucca, agave, sotol, shin dagger, and Spanish bayonet are other spiny plants classified as shrubs.

Herbaceous wildflowers are few in this park and the timing and number of blooms is entirely dependent upon the amount of rain received in the previous season and when it fell. Those you might expect to see blooming beginning in February and running through the spring include anemone, fairy duster, larkspur, fleabane, gold poppy, lupine, owl's clover, and Parry's penstemon. Prickly poppy and desert marigold are opportunistic and will put forth a bloom when desert rains permit.

Now the route begins to climb. In 0.6 mile, 4.4 miles from the start, is a gate. Please close it behind you. The route winds its way southward from here, rolling up and down as it crosses over several drainages, passing a spur road 6.4 miles from the start. There is a junction just 0.2 mile past this spur road. Go right onto FR 4405 and ride a few hundred yards to the top of a steep, dangerous descent. The route then continues to

SARAH BENNETT ALLEY

Chiva Falls is a welcoming desert oasis for both hot, dusty bikers and wildlife. (Do not submerge yourself in these small pools; sweat and lotions pollute the water for the creatures that depend on it.)

descend, reaching the spur road that will take you to Chiva Falls in 1.7 miles or just over 8 miles from the start. Go right to get to the falls and ride as far as you can, about 0.2 mile. Stash your bike, climb through the boulders, and behold the sparkling pool and waterfall before you.

When you've had a snack and are ready to go, head back out to the main route. Go right, back onto FR 4405 and ride 0.5 mile to a junction. You have now completed the loop section of the ride. Go left, back onto FR 4426, and right just after that across the cattle guard. In another 0.5 mile go left onto 4417, stay right at the next junction, and roll into the parking lot 12 miles from the start.

SAGUARO WEST

32. BAJADA LOOP DRIVE (See map on page 189)

For mountain bikes. This cherry-stem loop through the western unit of Saguaro National Park encompasses several peaks of the Tucson Mountains and follows a dirt road through some exceptionally dense stands of saguaro cactus. Riders of almost all abilities will enjoy this pedal, the wonderful views of adjacent Avra Valley, and the solitude that can be found in abundance in this section of the park.

Starting point: Red Hills Visitor Center.

Length: 9 miles. Allow 2 to 3 hours to complete this ride with time to pause at the sights along the way.

Riding surface: Pavement and graded dirt road that can be wash-boarded in some spots and loose in others.

Difficulty: Easy.

Scenery/highlights: Saguaros come in all sizes out here, each with their own individual character. Surrounding Sonoran Desert scenery is wonderful. This is a spectacular tour in March and April when the desert is in bloom.

Best time to ride: Fall through spring.

Special considerations: Rest rooms and water are available at the visitor

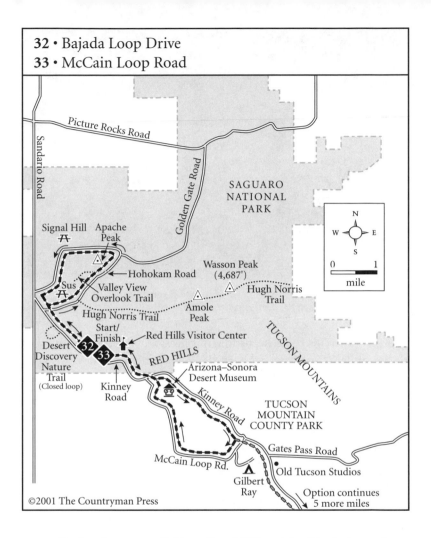

32 · Bajada Loop Drive
33 · McCain Loop Road

Picture Rocks Road

Sandario Road

Golden Gate Road

SAGUARO
NATIONAL
PARK

Signal Hill
Apache Peak

Wasson Peak
(4,687')

Hohokam Road

Hugh Norris
Trail

Sus

Valley View
Overlook Trail

Amole
Peak

Hugh Norris Trail

Start/
Finish

Red Hills Visitor Center

Desert
Discovery
Nature
Trail
(Closed loop)

32

33

RED HILLS

TUCSON MOUNTAINS

Kinney
Road

Arizona–Sonora
Desert Museum

Kinney Road

TUCSON
MOUNTAIN
COUNTY PARK

Gates Pass Road

McCain Loop Rd.

Old Tucson Studios

Gilbert
Ray

Option continues
5 more miles

N
W · E
S

0   1
mile

©2001 The Countryman Press

center. Vault toilets are available at Signal Hill and Sus Picnic Areas along the way.

There are many great hiking opportunities along this route. Several are short and provide excellent views of the park and surrounding terrain. If you are interested in getting off your bike and taking time to hike be sure to bring a lock to secure your bike while you are away.

Directions for the ride: From the visitor center ride out to Kinney Road

An ancient petroglyph in the park strangely resembles our favorite mode of touring the desert backcountry!

and go right. This route heads in a northwesterly direction, arriving at the 0.5-mile Desert Discovery Nature Trail 1 mile from the start. Look for this trailhead on the left-hand side of the road. It is another 0.6 mile to Hohokam Road and the start of the loop portion of this ride.

Go right onto Hohokam Road, 1.6 miles from the start, and begin pedaling along this rolling dirt road in a northeasterly direction. In 0.5 mile from the start of the dirt road you come to Sus Picnic Area. Another 0.5 mile beyond is the trailhead for the Hugh Norris Trail and the start of the one-way portion of this scenic drive. Just 3 miles from the start the trailhead for the 1.5 mile round-trip Valley View Overlook Trail, taking you to the top of the ridge encircled by the ride, will be on the left. From atop the ridge you can see almost all of the park to the east and the sprawling Avra Valley to the west. The route now climbs, and then descends, winding around through forests saguaros, for another mile, reaching the junction where the Golden Gate Road comes in from the east, 4.2 miles from the start. (Riders with stamina and energy to spare may want to go right at this junction and explore this 4-plus mile route that accesses Picture Rocks Road near the north end of the park.)

Bear left onto Golden Gate Road, still continuing around on the

FAUNA

Despite the landscape's stark appearance and the hot, dry conditions that dominate, the Sonoran Desert is full of life. The desert is the busiest between sunset and sunrise, when cooler temperatures coax creatures out to forage, hunt, and move about. You'll notice the birds' constant chatter and activity when riding or walking through a forest of saguaros. The Gila woodpecker and gilded flicker are year-round residents of the park. Both make holes in the saguaro trunks each spring for their nests; many are later used by other birds, including elf and burrowing owls, American kestrels, Lucy's warbler, cactus wrens, western kingbirds, purple martins, and phainopeplas. Inside the saguaro's trunk and branches the eggs or young birds are as much as 20°F cooler when it's hot and 20°F warmer when it's cold. White-winged doves migrate from Mexico to feed on the saguaro blooms' sweet nectar and are often heard cooing on late spring evenings. They are one of the saguaro's primary pollinators, as are several species of bats. Gambel quail can often be seen scampering around the desert floor, taking flight when frightened. Many visitors traveling the backroads of the park are lucky enough to catch a glimpse of a roadrunner.

Small rodents such as the cactus mouse and the kangaroo rat are expertly adapted to living in the desert. The kangaroo rat never needs to drink water but gets all its moisture from the plants it eats. Desert cottontails and several species of jackrabbits, able to disipate heat through their large ears, make their home here, as does the javelina, who eats the leaves and fruits of prickly pear cactus to meet its water needs. The desert tortoise, endangered in many parts of the West, is found here, as is the Gila monster, North America's only poisonous lizard. Both of them feed at dawn and dusk, but perhaps the most feared resident of the park, the Western diamondback rattlesnake, is nocturnal and is rarely seen. Look for them on chilly mornings in spring or fall, stretched out on a trail to warm themselves; they are generally sluggish at these times and want to be left alone.

Bajada Loop, and ride west, arriving at the spur to Signal Hill Picnic Area in 1.2 miles. It is 0.3 mile out to the picnic area. Past this spur the scenic drive continues as dirt for another 1.7 miles before meeting the paved Sandario Road. Go left onto this road, ride south for 0.2 mile, and then bear left onto Kinney Road. You pass the start of Hohokam Road in another 0.2 mile, and then it is another 1.6 miles to the Red Hills Visitor Center.

---

33. MCCAIN LOOP ROAD (See map on page 189)

For road bikes. Cyclists who prefer pavement can start from the Red Hills Visitor Center and do a loop through a portion of Tucson Mountain Park, a county park that features much of the same beautiful Sonoran desert scenery as what you'll find inside Saguaro West. You'll notice plenty of serious-looking road riders in this area; it's a favorite for racers who come to train in Tucson during winter when the rest of the country is cold and wet.

Starting point: Red Hills Visitor Center.

Length: Approximately 10.3 miles. There are several possibilities for longer routes.

Riding surface: Pavement, wide shoulders.

Difficulty: Easy.

Scenery/highlights: The park and surrounding area offer many interesting sights and possibilities for creating your own routes. The Arizona–Sonora Desert Museum, discussed in some detail at the end of this chapter, is a don't-miss stop along this ride. Another good option is to ride further south on Kinney Road to the Old Tuscson Studios, where gunslingers have fought it out again and again for both the big screen and for television series such as *Gunsmoke.*

Best time to ride: Anytime but summer.

Special considerations: Water and rest rooms are available at the visitor center, the Arizona–Sonora Desert Museum, and at the Gilbert Ray Campground, located about halfway through the ride. Be sure to bring along a lock to secure your bike if you are interested in making any of these stops.

Directions for the ride: From the Red Hills Visitor Center ride out to Kinney Road and go left. The route heads southeast for 1 mile to where Mile Wide Road comes in from the west. For the next 0.5 mile the route skirts the Red Hills before arriving at the intersection of Kinney and McCain Loop Roads. You can ride the loop portion of this ride in either direction; it will be described going clockwise here.

Bear left, continuing east on Kinney Road. Approximately 0.7 mile past the junction you come to the museum; pull in to see the many interesting plant, animal, and reptile exhibits here, or save it for later and continue riding southeast. Past the turnoff for the museum the road rolls over several gentle grades, reaching the southern end of the McCain Loop in 2.7 miles, 4.9 miles from the start. Go right and begin your return journey. From the last junction it is 0.4 mile to the turnoff for Tucson Mountain Park's Gilbert Ray Campground. From there you will simply follow the road as it heads south and west, and then north, rejoining Kinney Road 3.5 miles later or 8.8 miles from the start. When you reach Kinney Road go left, and ride 1.5 miles back to the Red Hills Visitor Center.

Option: For those wanting a little more time in the saddle, continue riding southeast on Kinney Road past the turnoff onto McCain Loop Road. In approximately 0.7 mile you reach the junction with the Gates Pass Road, a steep winding road favored by road racers in training. Another 0.3 mile down the road is Old Tucson, a well-used western movie set that you might remember from one of several old feature films or television movies. Kinney Road continues through the Tucson Mountain Park for almost another 3 miles to the main park entrance, and then for another 2 miles to the junction with Ajo Road. This is your turnaround point. This out-and-back option adds 12 miles to your total distance.

CAMPING

There are no campgrounds inside either park unit but there are many campsites in the nearby **Coronado National Forest,** or at one of the dozens of private campgrounds sprinkled around Tucson. **Pima County Parks** also manages several nearby campgrounds, including the **Gilbert Ray Campground** near Saguaro West.

IT'S INTERESTING TO KNOW...

The saguaro's many ridges are actually accordian-like pleats that enable the plant to expand and store water that is gathered through an extensive root system. Spongy flesh in the trunk and branches becomes a reservoir of a gelatin-like substance that helps to retain water and slow the evaporation process.

LODGING

There are hundreds of lodging possibilities in Tucson. You'll find everything from hostels to motels, chain hotels, fancy desert inns, luxury resorts, B&Bs, and guest ranches. Call or visit the **Tucson Accommodation Bureau** to find out more and make reservations at any of the city's major hotels. It is located directly across from the Tucson Convention & Visitors Bureau on 130 S. Scott Ave. and can be reached by calling 1-888-907-1888 or 520-622-2422.

FOOD

There are no restaurants or snack bars anywhere inside the east or west units of the park, but that doesn't mean a good meal will be hard to find. Tucson's rich cultural heritage and its booming economy which has brought people from all over the world, means that there is a wealth of good restaurants to choose from. You'll find virtually any kind of ethnic food, excellent Mexican and Southwestern dishes, as well as a selection of brew pubs and trendy cafés serving nouveau cuisine. Talk to the folks at the visitors and convention bureau in Tucson, where you can pick up a free dining guide.

There are dozens of laundries and self-service laundromats in Tucson; pick up the yellow pages to find one close to you.

DON'T MISS

Don't miss the chance to visit the Arizona–Sonora Desert Museum, located just south of the park's western unit on Kinney Road. This museum is an internationally renowned zoo, botanical garden, and natural history museum that has extensive exhibits and displays of this desert's myriad life-forms. These exhibits have been designed to mimic the surrounding desert and provide a natural setting for the animals and plants on display. Walk-in aviaries, a Life Underground exhibit that reveals what desert creatures are up to when they're out of sight, an aquatic exhibit, butterfly gardens, cactus gardens, gardens pollinated by bats and moths, and many other fascinating exhibits display more than two hundred species of animals and three hundred plants. Endangered animals and plants are also featured at the museum, including the Mexican gray wolf, the ocelot, jaguarundi, and numerous species of desert fish. Great views of the surrounding desert, a fabulous bookstore and gift shop, and special programs that run daily are other draws to this wonderful museum. Allow 2 to 3 hours to tour the excellent exhibits. Because 85 percent of the museum is outside you'll want to cover up or wear sunscreen, bring your sunglasses, and wear comfortable shoes. It is open every day and stays open late on Saturday evenings in summer. There are two restaurants at the museum (one that serves brunch on Sundays), a coffee bar, and a snack bar. The museum is located about 2.5 miles southeast of the park's Red Hills Visitor Center, and about 14 miles west of Tucson. You can get recorded information about museum hours and admission fees at 520-883-2707, or on their web site: www.desertmuseum.org.

BIKE SHOP/BIKE RENTAL

Tucson has one of the largest and most enthusiastic bike communities of any city of its size in the country, and supports more than two dozen bicycle shops that cater to a variety of riders and their needs. You'll find shops that specialize in off-road riding, road racing, tandem cycles, hand-built frames, cyclo-cross, and more. Pick up a phone book, check out their ads, and decide which one is right for you.

FOR FURTHER INFORMATION

Saguaro National Park—Superintendent, 3693 South Old Spanish Trail, Tucson, AZ 85730-5601; 520-733-5153 (Saguaro East, general information); 520-733-5158 (Saguaro West, Red Hills Visitor Center); www.nps.gov/sagu/

Metropolitan Tucson Convention & Visitors Bureau, 130 S. Scott Ave., Tucson, AZ 85701; 1-800-638-8350 or 520-624-1817; www.arizonaguide.com/visittucson

Coronado National Forest, Santa Catalina Ranger District, Sabino Canyon Visitor Center, 5700 N. Sabino Canyon Road, Tucson, AZ 85750; 520-749-8700; www.fs.fed.us/r3/coronado/scrd/

8

Sunset Crater Volcano National Monument

The graceful, uninterrupted lines of this black cone, tinted orange-yellow and red at its crown, and the blanket of cinders that surround it for more than 120 square miles, help to identify Sunset Crater as one of the youngest geologic features in North America. Tree-ring data and archaeological evidence suggesting that the Indian cultures living in the vicinity of the volcano were suddenly forced to flee have helped scientists to identify the exact date of the eruption that created Sunset Crater.

Sometime in the winter of A.D. 1064–1065 the ground began to rumble and shake and molten rock began to spray out of a crack in the earth. Molten material was thrown high into the air, then fell to the ground as cinders, dramatically changing the landscape. As eruptions continued over the next two hundred years heavier cinders built up around the vent, creating the 1,000-foot cone, while lighter and smaller particles were distributed for hundreds of miles across northern Arizona by prevailing winds. Two substantial eruptions flowed out of the base of Sunset Crater in the form of lava; the Kana-a flow in 1064 and the Bonito flow in 1180. Although all living things in their path were destroyed, these flows created a wonderland of fascinating formations, including caves where rivers of molten lava suddenly drained away, bulges and wedges of lava that look as if they were forced out of the ground yesterday, and patterns of cracking that occurred on the surface of the flows as they cooled. What look like heaps of crumbled lava are called spatter cones—young volcanoes created around gas vents that suddenly opened, spraying bits of lava skyward. Around the year 1250, an eruption of material containing high concentrations of sulfur and iron spewed out of Sunset Crater in what was probably the cone's last burst of activity. As these oxidized particles fell back down they colored the rim of the cone in hues that prompted John Wesley Powell to name the feature while he was exploring the region in 1885.

Wupatki National Monument

The Indians living in proximity to the crater before the eruptions that began in A.D. 1064 have been identified by archaeologists as culturally distinct from the groups of Anasazi, or ancestral Puebloans, who once lived in the Four Corners area. They are called the *Sinagua*, the Spanish term for "without water," a name that identifies their ability to survive in a region with almost no available surface water. The Sinagua were living in partially buried pithouses and farming corn and other crops on the

IT'S INTERESTING TO KNOW . . .

Although the term "Anasazi" is still commonly used to identify the ancient culture that lived in the Four Corners and built these beautiful stone cities, the almost two dozen tribes who claim ancestry to these people have collectively rejected this term. "Anasazi" is a Navajo word meaning "Enemies of our Ancestors," or "Ancient Foreigners," names that cast the ancient Puebloans as violent and aggressive outsiders or invaders, when in fact their history speaks otherwise. The park service is working closely with modern Native Americans to gain better insight into their understanding of the ruins, symbols, and artifacts found here, and have agreed to use the terms "ancestral Puebloans," "ancient Puebloans," or simply "Puebloans," in place of "Anasazi."

The many incredible singletrack trails around Flagstaff make this area a mountain biker's paradise

rocky terrain near the present crater as they had for almost four hundred years when the eruptions began. Ash rained down from above, lava flows and deep accumulations of cinders obliterated their fields and the landscape they had once called home.

Within a few decades the Sinagua returned to find that where ash and cinders were evenly distributed and not too deep, their crops flourished. The ash worked to trap moisture, prevent evaporation, and absorbed more heat, lengthening the growing season. Tree rings and other evidence also suggest a climate shift around this time that resulted in more abundant rain. The Sinagua continued to return to the area along with others who perhaps had heard of the fertile growing conditions. Evidence shows that the Kayenta Anasazi from the northeast, the Cohonina from the west, and the Hohokam and Mogollon from the south also migrated into the Wupatki region. Material artifacts and architecture reflect a mix of previously distinct cultural traits resulting in advances in technology, artistic development, and social and religious customs. Together these people built Lomaki, Nalakihu, Citadel, Wupatki, and Wukoki, all beautiful stone pueblos, some as large as one hundred rooms. While the masonry style is that of the Anasazi, the presence of a large, oval ball court suggests Hohokam influence. The pre-Columbian game that was played on these courts was imported from cultures even further to the south such as the Maya, Zapotec, and Aztec. Many other smaller pueblos, grain storage sites, and ruins are scattered throughout the park's backcountry but are off-limits to the public.

Whether these thriving settlements began to experience pressure from invading tribes, started to suffer from overcrowding or possibly disease, or simply exhausted the area's natural resources, they began to leave around 1200 and had completely deserted the area by 1250. A prolonged drought at this time played a role in their disappearance. Archaeologists theorize that they moved south to the Verde Valley and northeast, to the Hopi Mesas. Oral histories of today's modern Hopi Indians trace the origins of at least eight clans to the Wupatki area.

Walnut Canyon National Monument
The ruins protected in and around Walnut Canyon National Monument exhibit some of the same multicultural influences found at Wupatki, but are credited to a group of people living around the canyon that were distinctly Sinaguan. Archaeologists believe that the Sinagua first moved into the volcanic terrain north and east of present day Flagstaff around A.D. 600. They were drawn, as previous Archaic cultures had been, to the area's rich abundance of plants and wildlife, but were also adept at using the region's scant rainfall to cultivate beans, squash, and a particularly hearty type of corn.

Along the rims of Walnut Canyon, a beautiful 350-foot-deep gorge, the Sinagua farmed the deeper pockets of soil and made use of drainage patterns, creating check dams and terraces to catch every bit of available runoff. They hunted deer and small game and made extensive use of the wild plants growing in the canyon for medicine, food, and the material items they needed. At first they lived alongside their fields in partially buried one-room pithouses, structures that used a conical arrangement of branches overhead for roofs. But in the period just after the eruption of Sunset Crater a significant change in Sinaguan architecture occurred.

Beginning around A.D. 1100, the Sinagua began building cliff dwellings in Walnut Canyon, taking advantage of the natural recesses and ledges in the layer of Kaibab limestone just below the rim. Many are built into south- and east-facing caverns to gain the benefit of the sun,

An early season snowstorm and icy fog have frosted the landscape, creating a beautiful but chilly scene for a touring cyclist.

CYCLING OPTIONS

There are five rides in this chapter; two are suitable for either road or mountain bikes, one is for road bikes, and the other two are for mountain bikes. Both mountain and road bikers can ride the short distance from the Sunset Crater Volcano Visitor Center to the Cinder Hills Overlook, while road bikes are probably better suited for the 9-mile trek out to the main group of ruins at Wupatki from that park's visitor center. The short trip out to the Wukoki ruin is better suited for families or those with time or fitness constraints. The ultra-fit and ambitious road rider will love the half-century ride that includes sweeping through both parks and the country in between. The Mount Elden–Dry Lake Hills Trail System has many mountain bike routes and is a don't-miss opportunity for fat-tire enthusiasts who love singletrack. A portion of the Arizona Trail along the rim of Walnut Canyon provides some great mountain biking and a unique perspective on Walnut Canyon National Monument and the Sinaguan culture that once flourished there.

while others, probably used during the summer months, are on north-facing exposures. Archaeologists believe that women were responsible for building these cliff dwellings, using limestone gravels and a gold-colored clay to cement limestone rocks into place. Wooden beams reinforced doorways and the walls were plastered with clay inside and out.

These cliff dwellings, and several pueblo dwellings that dot the rims at Walnut Canyon, were built during the same period as the above-ground villages at Wupatki, a time when the Sinaguan culture and its people were flourishing. Sinaguan settlements and influence extended over a large portion of present-day Arizona and items such as seashells, turquoise, and feathers from tropical birds show they were part of an extensive trade network. The Sinagua lived in the cliffs at Walnut Canyon for over one hundred years, but for reasons that are not entirely understood began to leave the area, completely abandoning their home in the cliffs by the year 1250.

The cliff dwellings remained untouched until the late 1800s, when the area became a popular destination for souvenir hunters. The railroad brought tourists to dig for pleasure among the ancient dwellings, and more serious pot hunters who used dynamite to remove walls and let light in on their excavations. In 1915 the area gained protection as a national monument.

Cycling in the Parks

These three national monuments are located within 30 minutes of each other and within 20 miles of the bike-friendly town of Flagstaff. Each is relatively small, and although there are not many riding possibilities within park boundaries, there are excellent opportunities to ride to points of interest, link the parks, and get out into the country that is part of the stories they share.

Tour the ruins of Wupatki, make the short trip out to Wukoki from the visitor center, or combine that with the longer trip out to Citadel, Nalakihu, and Lomaki ruins. Serious road riders can tour both Wupatki and Sunset Crater Volcano National Monuments by riding the loop road combined with a stretch of US 89, making five-star half-century ride.

Heading past the bluff of Coconino sandstone and cave known as Fisher Point on the way to ride a portion of the Arizona Trail

Riders of all types can ride from the visitor center at Sunset Crater Volcano National Monument east through the park's volcanic terrain. The Mt. Elden Trail System just outside Flagstaff offers mountain bikers miles and miles of some of the best singletrack riding anywhere in Arizona, and is a riding opportunity fat-tire enthusiasts won't want to miss. A section of the Arizona Trail that takes off near Walnut Canyon and winds its way west along the rim of the canyon and adjacent drainages is another excellent adventure for mountain bikers.

The elevation of this area hovers right around 7,000 feet and will take some getting used to before trying to tackle a long ride. This elevation also means cold and often snowy winters, but pleasant temperatures for getting out and riding the rest of the year. The dry air and higher altitudes will work to zap your body of its precious fluids and energy, so start out slow, drink plenty of water, and save longer rides for later in your stay. Because of its high elevations and the San Francisco Peaks, the Flagstaff area receives a good dousing by the afternoon thunderstorms that regularly build up during the monsoon season. Be aware that a day that starts out cloudless and blue can turn dark and stormy by afternoon, beginning in mid-July and running through mid-September. These storms pack a powerful electrical punch, so it is a good idea to be well off high or exposed places when one rolls in.

---

34. WUPATKI RUINS TOUR (See map on page 205)

For road or mountain bikes. Cyclists who want to visit the ruins at Wupatki have a couple of options here: a short route out to Wukoki Ruin starting from the visitor center, or a longer trip out to Nalakihu, Lomaki, and Citadel Ruins clustered on the loop road about 10 miles to the west. It is open, mostly level terrain with a few hills any way you decide go.

Starting point: Wupatki Visitor Center.

Length: 2.8 miles one way, 5.6 miles out-and-back to Wukoki Ruin; 9.8 miles one-way, 19.6 miles out-and-back to the others. Time needed will vary, depending on what route you choose and the amount of time you spend at the ruins.

Riding surface: Pavement; some road shoulders.

34 · Wupatki Ruins Tour
35 · Crater Tour
36 · Craters and Ruins Ride

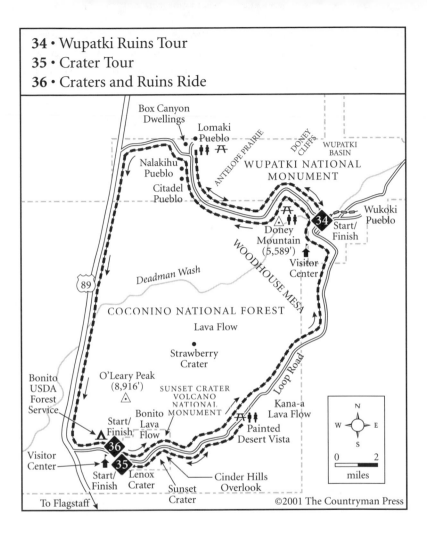

Difficulty: Easy to moderate.

Scenery/highlights: Beautifully constructed stone pueblos, sweeping panoramas of the Painted Desert, and wonderful views up to the San Francisco Peaks abound on this route.

Wukoki is a smaller pueblo but the best preserved in the park. Wupatki is the largest ruin in the park, with over one hundred rooms, a ball court, and a mysterious blowhole, or a fissure in the earth that emits bursts of air. These blowholes occur in several places in this area and probably had some significance for the ancient people who lived and often built their homes near them. The blowhole at Wupatki is located about a hundred yards beyond the ball court. Citadel Pueblo is perched on a volcanic butte and had close to fifty rooms. Nearby Nalakihu, Hopi for House Standing Outside the Village, was smaller, containing only a dozen rooms. Lomaki, or Beautiful House, is a small, two-story pueblo that sits at the edge of a box canyon.

Best time to ride: Spring through fall.

Special considerations: Water and rest rooms are available at the visitor center. Vault toilets are located at the parking area near the cluster of ruins. Be sure to bring along a lock to secure your bike while you are away looking at the ruins.

Directions for the ride: If you are interested in the shorter trip out to Wukoki Ruin, go right out of the visitor center and ride south 0.3 mile to the Wukoki spur road on your left. Turn left onto this road and ride 2.5 miles to a parking lot. Secure your bike at the parking lot and walk 0.3 miles t Wukoki Ruin. When you done having a look around, remount and return to the visitor center.

If you are riding out to the group of ruins located west of the visitor center, go left out of the parking lot and head north and west. The road heads north until dipping through Deadman Wash, 1 mile from the start. For the next 2 miles the road traverses the Wupatki Basin before turning and climbing toward Doney Mountain. You reach a picnic area on the left just over 4 miles from the start. A trail to the top of Doney Mountain leaves from this picnic area. The route then strikes west, extending for almost 3 miles in a straight line before swinging north. You arrive at the parking area for Citadel and Nalakihu Ruin just 9.5 miles from the start. Another 0.3 mile further is the spur road and trail taking you to Lomaki Ruin. When you are ready to return simply head back the way you came.

---

35. CRATER TOUR (See map on page 205)

For road or mountain bikes. This short tour takes cyclists through the center of this slightly more than 3,000-acre park and the lunar landscape created by Sunset Crater and several other cinder cones. Riders with more time and stamina can continue beyond the boundary of the park to the Kana-a lava flow and Painted Desert Vista and complete a tour of the earth's creative power.

Starting point: Sunset Crater Visitor Center.

Length: 3 miles one-way, 6 miles out-and-back to Cinder Hills Overlook; 7 miles one-way, 14 miles out-and-back to Painted Desert Vista and the lava flow. Allow a minimum of 2 hours to complete this route.

Riding surface: Pavement; some shoulder.

Difficulty: Moderate. Although these routes aren't terribly long there are some good hills.

Scenery/highlights: Lenox Crater, Sunset Crater, and Strawberry Crater are the most distinctive of the many cinder cones in this area. Together with the black and red cinders that blanket the landscape, they create a surreal setting that will delight the senses and beg the imagination to conjure images of a fiery landscape. The San Francisco Peaks dominating the skyline to the west and south are the remnants of an enormous volcano and a much larger volcanic field that stretches for miles across northern Arizona. This cluster of peaks, along with the beautiful, young cinder cones of this park, are a reminder that the earth below your tires is alive and only temporarily slumbering.

Best time to ride: Spring through fall. In summer these parks see a lot of tourists heading back and forth to the Grand Canyon; be prepared for more vehicle traffic on the loop road during this time.

Special considerations: Water and rest rooms are available at the visitor center. Vault toilets are available at the Visitor Contact Station and information kiosk at the start of the Lava Flow Nature Trail, and at the Painted Desert Vista picnic area.

If you are interested in hiking the 0.5-mile trail up to Lenox Crater or take the informative walk on the Lava Flow Nature Trail be sure to bring a lock to secure your bike while you are away.

Directions for the ride: From the visitor center, ride out onto the Loop Road you drove in on and go right. The route climbs gradually toward

FLORA

The cinders and lava flows in and around Sunset Crater Volcano National Monument present a very difficult environment for plants, but some, like the ruddy-barked ponderosa pine, seem to thrive. Two species of juniper can be found in the lower areas of the park; curiously, quaking aspen is found only along the lava flow margins. Apache plume, which sends up long dusters of cream-colored flowers, and wax currant are the most common shrubs in the park. Wildflowers such as evening primrose, with its billowy white petals, blazing star, western wallflower, scarlet gilia, Indian paintbrush, purple locoweed, and several species of lupine are also quite common. The field near Bonito Campground is filled with yellow sunflowers in late summer and fall. A bright pink species of penstemon is endemic to the small area surrounding the crater.

Wupatki, 2,000 feet lower than Sunset Crater, presents a much different, more desertlike collage of plant species. Piñon and juniper are the dominant tree species, growing primarily on the west side of the park along with various types of bunch grasses. On the east side you'll find only shrubs. These include four-wing saltbush, rabbitbrush, snakeweed, ephedra or Mormon tea, and Apache plume. There are few herbacous wildflowers, but you might see the red blooms of Indian paintbrush in spring. Both rabbitbrush and snakeweed are crowned with yellow blossoms in fall.

Walnut Canyon contains three habitat types: ponderosa pine forest, piñon-juniper woodland, and riparian forest. Along the rims, ponderosa pines dominate. They are joined by piñon pine, one-seed juniper, Utah juniper, mountain mahogany, and Gambel oak. Piñon-juniper forests dominate below the rim. In the canyon bottom, you'll find deciduous trees such as black walnut, box elder, cottonwoods, and big-tooth maple. Banana yucca, fern bush, snowberry, and Fremont barberry can be found at various elevations, as can Indian paintbrush, lupine, a variety of asters and pickly-pear cactus. The beautiful but rare Rocky Mountain iris blooms in spring.

A tunnel through a fin of volcanic tuff returning from the Inner Basin on the Waterline Road.

the boundary of the park and continues climbing toward the pullout that provides overlooks to the Bonita Lava Flow, just over a mile from the start. Just beyond this pullout, and 1.5 miles from the start, the short spur road taking you to the Visitor Contact Station and the start of the Lava Flow Nature Trail will be on your right. Past this spur the road climbs more steeply, up and around the flank of Sunset Crater; the highest point is reached on its northwest side. Descend and then ride over a few more ups and downs before reaching Cinder Hills Overlook, 3 miles from the visitor center. Reverse your route to return to the visitor center from here if you are doing the shorter ride.

Continuing on from here, toward Painted Desert Vista and Kana-a lava flow commits you to more uphill on the return trip. From the Cinder Hills Overlook continue east and north for 4 miles to the Painted Desert Vista and picnic area. When you've had something to eat and are rested return the way you came.

---

36. CRATERS AND RUINS RIDE (See map on page 205)

For road bikes. Seasoned road riders with plenty of strength and stamina will find the half-century ride around the Loop Road, connecting both Sunset Crater Volcano and Wupatki National Monuments with a section of US 89 is as rewarding as it is challenging. For years this route was the site of a popular race and it continues to be a favorite place for local racers to come and train.

Starting point: Sunset Crater Volcano National Monument Visitor Center.

Length: 51 miles total. Allow at least a half a day to do this ride if you plan to spend time at any of the points of interest along the way.

Riding surface: Pavement. Loop Road has good shoulders, US 89 is a divided highway.

Difficulty: Difficult. The 2,000-plus feet of elevation loss and gain, the relatively high altitude and the length of this ride will make this a strenuous ride for all but the most fit.

Scenery/highlights: The spectacular and ever-changing scenery begins

The striking setting, beautiful stone work, and intriguing features such as the blow holes and ball court found at Wupatki make these ruins fascinating to explore.

with the dark, lunarlike landscape around Sunset Crater, gives way to the open expanse of the Painted Desert, and then disappears into ponderosa pine forests and meadows as you climb back to elevations above 7,000 feet. Constant on the western horizon are the San Francisco Peaks, remnants of an extinct volcano that figures prominently in the cosmology of both Navajo and Hopi Indian tribes.

Best time to ride: Spring through fall.

Special considerations: Water and rest rooms are available at both Sunset Crater Volcano and Wupatki visitor centers. Vault toilets are available at three picnic areas along the way.

This route can be ridden in either direction, but is described here as a counterclockwise loop. The highest point is just a few miles from the start, on the flanks of Sunset Crater; the lowest point is near the Wupatki Visitor Center at Deadman Wash.

Directions for the ride: From the visitor center at Sunset Crater Volcano National Monument head out onto the Loop Road and go right. You will climb gently at first, more steeply as you ascend along the flanks of

Sunset Crater. In approximately 3 miles you pass Cinder Hills Overlook and, just beyond, exit the park at its eastern boundary. The route rolls up and down from here, then begins a steady descent, reaching Painted Desert Vista about 7 miles from the start. Continue heading northeast, sloping across the desert toward Wupatki National Monument. Approximately 18 miles from the start you cross the park boundary into Wupatki and in another 2.5 miles arrive at the Wupatki Visitor Center. From here the route heads north for another mile, dips across Deadman Wash, and then turns and heads west, across the Wupatki Basin, before turning southwest and beginning its climb toward Doney Mountain. After passing a picnic area 4 miles from Wupatki Visitor Center, the road turns and heads almost due west, crossing almost 3 miles of high open desert before swinging north again. You pass Citadel, Nalakihu, and Lomaki Ruins 29 miles from the start, and reach US 89 approximately 33 miles from the start.

Carefully cross US 89 and go left, or south. Once on US 89 it is a long, uphill straightaway for 15 miles to the southern end of Loop Road. You climb out of the desert and into the ponderosas, gaining elevation with every stroke. When you reach the turnoff for Sunset Crater Volcano National Monument go left and ride the almost 3 miles back to the visitor center and your vehicle.

---

37. PIPELINE TRAIL (See map on page 213)

For mountain bikes. The Pipeline Trail is offered here as an introduction to the many excellent singletrack trails of the Mount Elden–Dry Lake Hills Trail System. There are many possibilities for combining this trail with others, such as Fatman's Loop or the Oldham Trail, and for creating your own routes. You can pick up this trail near the Peaks Ranger Station of Coconino National Forest, where information on the rest of the trails in this system is available. Options are given for slightly longer rides.

Starting point: Begin at the Elden Trailhead, just north of the Peaks Ranger Station on US 89 northeast of Flagstaff.

Length: From the ranger station to where the Pipeline Trail meets the Oldham Trail is 3.4 miles one-way, 6.8 miles out-and-back.

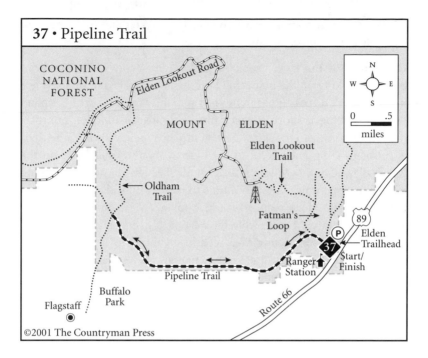

37 · Pipeline Trail

COCONINO NATIONAL FOREST

Elden Lookout Road

MOUNT ELDEN

Elden Lookout Trail

Oldham Trail

Fatman's Loop

Elden Trailhead

Start/Finish

Ranger Station

Pipeline Trail

Buffalo Park

Flagstaff

Route 66

©2001 The Countryman Press

Riding surface: Singletrack trails that are hardpacked and fast; slightly rocky and sandy in some places.

Difficulty: Easy. Only a slight change in elevation.

Scenery/highlights: The trail system here will thrill avid mountain bikers with days of memorable singletrack riding. Mt. Elden is itself an ancient volcano, but much larger and older than those found inside Sunset Crater Volcano National Monument. Along this route you'll be riding through ponderosa pine forests and open grassy meadows. Clumps of Gambel oak and cliffrose form a shrubby understory in places. This is an excellent place to spot wildlife or spend a few minutes bird-watching.

Best time to ride: Spring through fall.

Special considerations: Stop in and pick up information about other trails in the area, as well as information on native plants and animals, at the Peaks Ranger Station before you head out. Water and rest rooms are available at the ranger station.

Directions for the ride: From the parking lot at the Elden Trailhead begin by picking up the main trail heading north and west. In just a few hundred yards a trail comes in on the right; this is a portion of Fatman's Loop. Continue a short distance further to a trail junction approximately 0.3 mile from the start. Go left onto the Pipeline Trail; to the right is Fatman's Loop and access to the Elden Lookout Trail. Once on the Pipeline Trail simply follow it as it winds through the trees, emerging into sunny, open meadows from time to time as it heads west. The trail is fairly straight along sections where it follows a gas pipeline right-of-way. Approximately 2 miles from the start the trail enters into the Mount Elden Environmental Study Area, set aside by the forest service as a field laboratory for schools and environmental groups. A trail will come in from the left about 3.2 miles from the start and at 3.4 miles the Pipeline Trail comes to a junction with the Oldham Trail. This is your turnaround point. Go back the way you came.

Option #1: If interested in doing some exploring and you're up for a more technical challenge, go right onto the Oldham Trail. After 1.3 miles a trail comes in from the left accessing the Mount Elden Lookout Road. Beyond this junction the trail (now called the Upper Oldham Trail) becomes steeper and more technical, eventually emerging onto the lookout road.

Option #2: If you'd like to ride a little further but would rather stay away from anything steep or technical, go left and ride the OldhamTrail for about 1.5 miles to Buffalo Park in North Flagstaff. When you are ready to return retrace your route back to the Elden Trailhead parking lot.

---

38. ARIZONA TRAIL—EQUESTRIAN BYPASS
(See map on page 217)

For mountain bikes. The section of Arizona Trail described here can be accessed just outside Walnut Canyon National Monument and ridden for 9 miles along the rim of the canyon itself. The route consists mainly of singletrack with a few sections of dirt road, and winds west, through deep stands of ponderosa, emerging near Fisher Point, just south of

A rider negotiates a rocky stretch of the Equestrian Bypass portion of the Arizona Trail heading west along the rim of Walnut Canyon.

FAUNA

Birds common to these monuments include the raven, Steller's, piñon, and scrub jays, mountain bluebirds in winter, and turkey vultures spring through fall. Red-tailed hawks, Cooper's hawks, goshawks, and kestrels are raptors commonly found in the area. Hummingbirds, including rufous, black-chinned, and broad-tailed, are ubiquitous spring through fall. You might see a roadrunner scurry across the road in Wupatki or a wild turkey along the rims at Walnut Canyon. Walnut Canyon, with its riparian habitat, offers the best bird-watching opportunity.

Because of its drier, more open terrain, you'll see fewer mammals in Wupatki, but those you might see include jackrabbits, cottontails, antelope squirrels, and mule deer. These same critters plus skunks, racoons, Abert's squirrel, easy to recognize because of its tufted ears, are common around Sunset Crater, and although black bear, cougar, and pronghorn antelope have been sighted there in the past they are rare. Elk and mule deer are quite common in the rim-side forests of Walnut Canyon, where you might get lucky and spot a gray fox, bobcat, or even a black bear.

downtown Flagstaff. There is no requirement for distance or time in the saddle, simply pedal out as far as you like and enjoy the views.

Starting point: Begin at the trailhead located 3.8 miles west of the access road to Walnut Canyon National Monument. To get there, head back out toward I-40 from the Walnut Canyon Visitor Center and drive just under a mile to where Forest Road (FR) 303 leaves from the west side of the road. Turn left onto this dirt road and follow it for 3.8 miles to the trailhead, located on the left side of the road.

Length: 9 miles one-way, 18 miles out-and-back if the entire section of trail is ridden.

Riding surface: Singletrack and dirt roads.

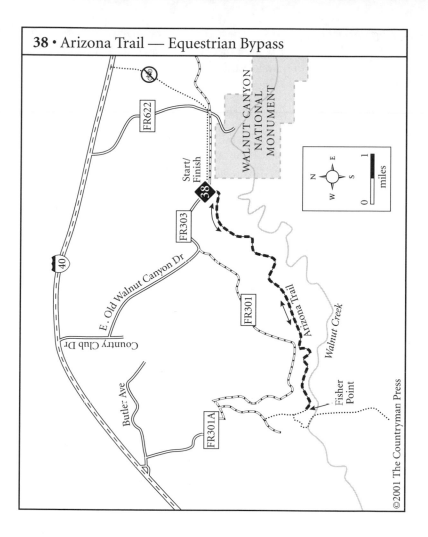

Difficulty: Moderate to difficult. This is a long, fairly strenuous ride if the entire distance is ridden. There are short but challenging climbs; sections of the singletrack are rocky and technical—use caution.

Scenery/highlights: Pretty scenery, great views into Walnut Canyon, and a good opportunity to see wildlife such as elk, deer, antelope, fox, and coyote. Great bird-watching.

The Arizona Trail offers many excellent opportunities for mountain biking throughout the state. The section of trail described here can be combined with another section that crosses the head of Walnut Canyon and extends south to Marshall Lake, through the Mormon Lake District of Coconino National Forest.

Best time to ride: Spring through fall.

Special considerations: Water and rest rooms are available at the Walnut Canyon Visitor Center. No water is available anywhere along this route, so be sure to bring plenty. If you plan to ride the entire distance you'd be wise to bring some high-energy snacks as well.

Directions for the ride: Head out from the trailhead and pedal due south. Within a few hundred yards the trail will swing around and head west, where it will begin to trace the rim of Walnut Canyon. Simply follow this well-marked trail, alternating between doubletrack and singletrack as you traverse through stands of ponderosa pine and along the Kaibab limestone ledges that form the canyon rim. Approximately 1.5 miles from the start, the trail becomes rocky as it drops into a side drainage. Most will want to dismount to safely negotiate this section. The trail then climbs back to the rim, but dips through several more side drainages over the next 2 miles, each requiring short but steep climbs and a few technical moves. The trail climbs almost imperceptibly as it heads west, arriving at Fisher Point, a prominent outcropping of Coconino sandstone, and a cave 9 miles from the start. If 18 miles is more than you're up for, ride out as far as you like and reverse your route when you've had enough.

CAMPING

Bonito Campground, located across from Sunset Crater Volcano Visitor Center, is a forest service campground that offers tent and RV sites (no hook-ups) for a fee. Call the Coconino National Forest's Peak Ranger District office for more information.

Nestled in the pines around Flagstaff you'll find at least ten private campgrounds; almost all have showers and tent sites. Leaf through the yellow pages or visit the Flagstaff Visitors Bureau to find out more.

There are almost unlimited opportunities for primitive camping in nearby Coconino National Forest; call or stop by a district office to get a list of regulations and site suggestions.

LODGING

There are dozens of lodging possibilities in the railroad and highway town of Flagstaff, where you'll find everything from historic downtown hotels built for Grand Canyon tourists at the beginning of the twentieth century to hostels, chain hotels, budget motels, and cozy B&Bs. Visit the Flagstaff Visitors Center at the chamber of commerce building for more information.

FOOD

The wide variety of choices includes French, Thai, Chinese, Middle Eastern, Mexican, even New Zealand food. **Macy's European Coffee House and Bakery** (914 S. Beaver St.) is one of the best places to get started in the morning with a good cup of coffee and an excellent selection of home-baked goods. They also serve lunch and dinner. Nearby **Beaver Street Brewery,** which also houses the **Whistle Stop Café** (11 S. Beaver St.), is a good choice for lunch, dinner, and a beer. The **Morning Glory Café** (115 S. San Francisco St.)

and **Café Espress** both specialize in vegetarian cuisine.

LAUNDRY

Being a college town, there are plenty of laundromats to choose from. Find the one closest to you in the yellow pages.

BIKE SHOP/BIKE RENTAL

Any of these should have everything you need.

Absolute Bikes, 18 N. San Francisco St.; 520-779-5969

The Bike Loft, 1608 N. East St.; 520-774-1582

Cosmic Cycles, 113 S. San Francisco St.; 520-779-1092

Loose Spoke, 1529 S Milton Rd.; 520-774-7428

Mountain Sports, 1800 S. Milton Rd.; 520-779-5156

Single Track Bikes, 12 N. Beaver St.; 520-773-1862

!

IT'S INTERESTING TO KNOW...

Sunset Crater is only one of nearly four hundred cinder cones in the San Francisco Volcanic Field and is the youngest but by no means the largest of the many extinct volcanoes dotting northern Arizona. Most of these volcanoes were formed during the Pliocene epoch of the Cenozoic era, between 2 and 4 million years ago. The reigning monarch of this volcanic field is the San Francisco Peaks, which formed between 2.8 million and 200,000 years ago. The peaks were at one time part of a single, large, stratovolcano similar to Japan's Mount Fuji and our own Mount St. Helens. Stratovolcanoes are composed of alternating layers of lava flows and volcanic ash that often take millions of years to accumulate. Like Mount St. Helens, the San Francisco volcano probably exploded sideways and then collapsed in on the empty magma chamber below. This collapse created what is now called the Inner Basin and the collection of peaks that form a semicircle around it.

Superintendent, Sunset Crater Volcano National Monument, Wupatki National Monument, Walnut Canyon National Monument, 2717 N. Steves Blvd., Suite 3, Flagstaff, AZ 86004

Sunset Crater Volcano National Monument: 520-526-0502; www.nps.gov/sucr/

Wupatki National Monument: 520-679-2365; www.nps.gov/wupa/

Walnut Canyon National Monument: 520-526-3367; www.nps.gov/waca/

Flagstaff Chamber of Commerce and Visitor Center, 1 E. Route 66 (at the Amtrak train depot), Flagstaff, AZ 86001; 1-800-842-7293 or 520-774-9541; e-mail visitor@flagstaff.az.us; www.Flagstaff.az.us and www.flagguide.com

Coconino National Forest, Peaks Ranger District Office, 5075 N. US Hwy 89, Flagstaff, AZ 86004; 520-526-0866; www.fs.fed.us/r3/coconino/

DON'T MISS

There is a wealth of interesting and informative places to visit while in the Flagstaff area. The Museum of Northern Arizona has excellent Native American exhibits and geological displays. At the historic Lowell Observatory, founded in 1894, you can look through a telescope and learn about the stars through interactive displays. The Pioneer Historical Museum has exhibits that portray early life in Flagstaff and the adjacent Art Barn has original works by local artists, including that of the area's Native Americans, on exhibit and for sale. See native and experimental plants at the Arboretum, or visit the charming Riordan Mansion and State Historic Park.

9

About 50 miles east of Phoenix as the crow flies is the Tonto Basin, a broad valley lying between the Superstition, Sierra Ancha, and Mazatzal Mountains. The basin was once coursed by the Salt River that brought life-giving water to this extremely rough, dry country, but is now filled by the dammed waters of Roosevelt Lake. In the cliffs above the lake are two large, masonry ruins protected as Tonto National Monument. The ruins were left by people who once farmed in the valley, collected cactus fruits and other wild plants from the hillsides, and hunted small game, birds, and even reptiles to supplement what they grew. Archaeologists have determined that the pottery, farming techniques, and other material artifacts of these people make them distinct from Arizona's other ancient cultures. They are called the Salado, in honor of the Rio Salado or Salt River that allowed their culture to flourish.

The first permanent settlements in the Tonto Basin were those of the Hohokam people more often associated with ruins further south. Beginning sometime around A.D. 750 they built pithouse villages near the river and farmed along its banks. Changes over time, reflected in settlement patterns, construction methods, pottery styles, and other traits reveal that by 1150 these people no longer adhered to Hohokam traditions or those of any other Southwestern culture. They now built pueblo

Looking out from the ruins at Tonto National Monument across Lake Roosevelt to the Sierra Ancha Mountains and the Salt River Wilderness.

villages along the river and irrigated corn, beans, pumpkins, amaranth, and cotton. They exchanged surplus crops with neighboring tribes for goods and decorative items, and were part of an extensive trade network stretching north to Colorado and south to Mexico. Starting around 1300, some of the Salado began to migrate into the surrounding hills. They chose eroded recesses in the siltstone cliffs to build apartment-style dwellings where they lived for the next 100 to 150 years. And then, for reasons that are not entirely clear, the Salado left their cliffside homes. Today these dwellings are all that remain of the Salado; the rest lies submerged beneath the waters of the lake.

Cycling in the Park

The acreage of Tonto National Monument is very small, steep, and rugged. There are no roads or trails in the park suitable for biking, but the surrounding terrain holds several possibilities. Road or mountain bikers can ride from the Roosevelt Ranger Station, Visitor Center, and Marina north along the lake on AZ 188 on an excursion that provides sweeping views of the Tonto Basin and a up-close look at the Roosevelt Dam. Mountain bikers that don't mind a good climb can ride a loop in the Three Bar Wildllife Area in the foothills of the Mazatzal Mountains and enjoy great views of the Tonto Basin and the distinctive collection of peaks in the west known as Four Peaks. You will find yourself surrounded here by the unique desert plants and animals that thrive in the Sonoran Desert environment.

Fall through spring is best for visiting and biking in the region surrounding Tonto National Monu-ment. Summer temperatures routinely soar well past 100 degrees and by mid-July, the start of the monsoon season, the air gets very humid. Temperatures throughout the winter are delightful, although nights are chilly. Stay properly hydrated in this climate during the warmer months by drinking plenty of water before, during, and after you ride. This will help you avoid fatigue, heat exhaustion, and many conditions that can become quite serious.

★ CYCLING OPTIONS

There are two possibilities described here; one along the lake shore on a paved road with wide shoulders that is a great opportunity for all kinds of cyclists to get out and pedal, and a loop in the foothills just west of the lake that fit and willing mountain bikers will enjoy. Tonto National Monument is too small and steep to offer much in the way of biking, but there are many possibilities in the surrounding Tonto National Forest; stop in and talk to the rangers at the Roosevelt Lake Visitor Center for more information.

39. ROOSEVELT LAKE TOUR (See map on page 226)

For road or mountain bikes. This ride is a great trip along the lake shore on a route that rolls slightly over 8 miles to Bermuda Flat Campground near the north end of the reservoir. If you get too hot there's always the opportunity to jump in the lake.

Starting point: Roosevelt Lake Visitor Center and Marina. To get there drive approximately 2 miles northwest on AZ 188 from the turnoff to the monument and go right on the short spur road heading toward the lake.

Length: 8.2 miles one-way, 16.4 miles out-and-back. Allow 2–3 hours to complete this ride.

FLORA

The presence of the tall, stately saguaro cactus is an indicator that this park falls within the Sonoran Desert habitat type. Several species of cholla, prickly pear, barrel, and hedgehog cacti can also be found on the slopes of the monument. These spiny creatures, while they may look unfriendly, put forth large, colorful blooms and supply desert wildlife with a bounty of nourishing fruit.

Honey mesquite and foothills paloverde can be found growing on the slopes and in drainages, but in water drainages you'll find Arizona sycamore and Arizona walnuts. Shrubs you might see include jojoba bean, hops, soapberry, brittlebush, and desert broom. Yucca, sotol, and agave are also abundant.

Wildflowers blooming in spring or again after it rains include gold poppy, Indian paintbrush, short-stemmed lupine, penstemon, Gooding's verbena, filaree, wild cucumber, globe mallow, and something called *chia*, a member of the mint family with a flower that looks like it might belong to a thistle. Mistletoe can be found growing on paloverde.

Riding surface: Pavement; nice, wide shoulders.

Difficulty: Moderate.

Scenery/highlights: Great views and scenery. Nice pedal. The Theodore Roosevelt Dam is the largest hand-built, masonry dam in the world at 284 feet high. The dam was constructed of stone blocks between 1905 and 1911 but was later covered with cement to reinforce it.

Best time to ride: Fall through spring.

Special considerations: Water, rest rooms, and all kinds of information are available at the forest service's Roosevelt Lake Visitor Center. Rest rooms and water are also available at Cholla Campground; vault toilets are available at Bermuda Flat.

Beware of the heat. Don't get dehydrated; drink plenty of water

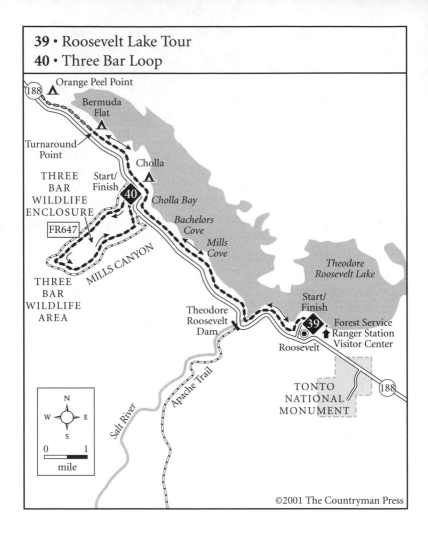

39 · Roosevelt Lake Tour
40 · Three Bar Loop

Orange Peel Point

Bermuda Flat

Turnaround Point

THREE BAR WILDLIFE ENCLOSURE

Start/Finish **40**

Cholla

FR647

THREE BAR WILDLIFE AREA

MILLS CANYON

Cholla Bay

Bachelors Cove

Mills Cove

Theodore Roosevelt Lake

Theodore Roosevelt Dam

Start/Finish **39**

Roosevelt

Forest Service Ranger Station Visitor Center

TONTO NATIONAL MONUMENT

Salt River

Apache Trail

N W E S

0   1
mile

©2001 The Countryman Press

before, during, and after your ride to prevent feeling sick and exhausted.

Directions for the ride: From the visitor center, ride 0.2 mile back out the spur road and go right. Simply follow this road as it gently rolls along, arriving at the junction with the dirt AZ 88, also known as the Apache Trail, just before the dam 1.6 miles from the start. Cross over the dam and continue heading northwest, pedaling along the lake shore. At approximately 6.4 miles from the start you will pass the turnoff to Cholla

Campground and Recreation Site; 1.6 miles beyond that is Bermuda Flat. This is your turnaround point. Have a dip and something to eat and then head back the way you came.

If you want to add some distance to your total mileage continue another 1.5 miles to Orange Peel Campground at the very end of the lake. This will give you a total distance of 19.4 miles.

---

40. THREE BAR LOOP (See map on page 226)

For mountain bikes. This 7-mile route begins near Cholla Campground and Recreation Site on the shore of Roosevelt Lake and makes a loop in the foothills of the Mazatzal Mountains, just east of the Four Peaks Wilderness Area. It traverses a portion of the Tonto National Forest specially managed as the Three Bar Wildlife Area. Views to the lake and to Four Peaks as well as beautiful, untrammeled Sonoran Desert scenery await you on this adventure.

Starting point: Cholla Campground and Recreation Site, just off of AZ 188, approximately 6.5 miles north of the Roosevelt Lake Visitor Center.

Length: A 7-mile loop. Allow 2 hours.

Riding surface: Dirt jeep roads. Trail surface is made up of decomposed granite which can be loose and gravelly in spots.

Difficulty: Moderate to strenuous. Although this ride isn't terribly long or technical, the elevation gain of almost 1,600 feet makes it challenging.

Scenery/highlights: The Three Bar Wildlife Area is managed by the Arizona Fish and Game department, who have conducted numerous studies on the animal species found in the Sonoran Desert. The area is known for its healthy populations of both mule and white-tailed deer, as well as javelina, or wild pigs. The route actually circumvents an enclosed study area.

Best time to ride: Fall through spring.

Special considerations: Rest rooms and water are available at Cholla Campground and Recreation Site. There is a fee for parking in the day-use parking lot.

FAUNA

Although this park is small, the terrain rough, and the climate harsh, it is home to a surprising amount of wildlife. No fewer than 142 bird species, 26 mammals, 32 reptiles, and 6 kinds of amphibians are documented residents.

The large body of water and constant supply of fish has begun to draw migrating bald eagles. Turkey vultures are quite common, as are ravens and red-tailed hawks. Many other hawk species come through but are difficult to identify. Canyon wrens, cactus wrens, curved-bill thrashers, black-headed grosbeaks, Gila woodpeckers, and Inca, rock, and mourning doves are all commonly seen. Bright red cardinals are very common, as are their less colorful cousins, phainopepla. Gambel quail are also very common. Finches, sparrows, warblers, and many other bird species are here either part of the time or year-round. Pick up a bird list at the visitor center if you are interested in getting a complete bird inventory and making identifications.

Small mammals include cliff chipmunks, rock squirrels, ground squirrels, desert cottontails, jackrabbits, and at least four kinds of skunks. Coatimundi, gray fox, coyote, javelina, bobcats, and mountain lions are all fairly common in this area. Both white-tailed and mule deer are also present.

Reptile species include four kinds of rattlesnakes: Western diamondback, Arizona black, black-tailed, and Mojave. Coral snakes, bull snakes, and several different types of racers are also seen from time to time. Gila monsters, who spend 98 percent of the time underground or moving around at night, are poisonous but rarely seen. Other lizards, including whiptails, zebra-tailed, and skinks are some of the most commonly seen wildlife in the park.

Don't forget your swimsuit; swimming is allowed in the reservoir and there's nothing like a cool dip after a hot, dusty ride.

Directions for the ride: This loop can be ridden in either direction but will described counterclockwise. From Cholla Campground head out onto AZ 188 and turn right. Ride northwest on this paved road for approximately 0.3 mile to Forest Road (FR) 647 and go left. You will begin to climb almost immediately and continue to climb over the next 3 miles as you travel up a ridge. A jumble of ridges and canyons rise up to meet Four Peaks in the west; Rock Canyon is the main drainage to the north, while Mills Canyon is the major drainage to the south. Follow the road as reaches its high point along the loop and then turns and heads northeast, contouring along the side of a drainage before descending along the spine of another ridge. In another 3 miles the route meets AZ 188 0.6 mile south of Cholla Campground and Recreation Site. Turn left and ride north to the campground. Take a dip to wash off the dust.

CAMPING

There are no campgrounds within the park but several developed ones along the shore of Roosevelt Lake are managed by Tonto National Forest. Both **Cholla** and **Windy Hill Campground** have water, rest rooms, and showers, but no hook-ups. **Schoolhouse**

and **Bermuda Flat Campgrounds** have fewer amenities. A fee is charged at all four. Inquire at the Roosevelt Lake Visitor Center about these campgrounds or about primitive camping elsewhere in the national forest. **Roosevelt Marina** also offers tent sites.

RVs needing hook-ups can look across the highway from Roosevelt Marina at **Lakeview Trailer Park,** at **Roosevelt Lake RV Park & Motel,** just over 10 miles south of the visitor center, and at **Roosevelt Lake Resort,** about 10.5 miles south of the visitor center.

LODGING

There is no lodging available within the park and few options nearby. The **Roosevelt Lake RV Park & Motel** and the **Roosevelt Lake Resort** are both about 8 miles south of the turnoff to the monument and offer rooms at reasonable rates. The **Punkin Center Lodge,** 22 miles northwest of Roosevelt, also has rooms. Other lodging options are located

IT'S INTERESTING TO KNOW...

The Salado were one of the only groups of Southwestern people to cultivate cotton, which they spun into thread and wove into cloth. Designs made with dyed threads are beautifully woven into items such as shirts and blankets, some of which feature artfully crafted, lacelike bands. Archaeologists examining the weaving traditions of modern Pueblo tribes suggest that weaving was an art practiced by men.

30 miles south in the twin towns of Globe/Miami, or 55 miles north in Payson. Both offer at least a dozen hotels and motels to choose from, including several chains.

FOOD

No food is available at the monument, but you will find a snack bar and a store that sells basic picnic items nearby at the **Roosevelt Marina.** About 10 miles south is a restaurant at the **Roosevelt RV Park & Motel** that serves three meals a day; groceries and gas are available at the nearby **Spring Creek Store.** The **Steak House** in Punkin Center serves lunch and dinner and has entertainment on busy weekends.

LAUNDRY

There isn't anywhere to do a load of laundry within 30 miles of this park. Your nearest option is in Globe.

BIKE SHOP/BIKE RENTAL

Bike shops are few and far between, although you are not far from the Phoenix area where there are dozens. Another option for repairs and bike service is 55 miles north in Payson.

FOR FURTHER INFORMATION

Tonto National Monument—Superintendent, HC02 Box 4602, Roosevelt, AZ 85545; 520-467-2241; www.nps.gov/tont/

Tonto National Forest, Tonto Basin Ranger District, Roosevelt Lake Visitor Center, AZ Highway 188, HC02 Box 4800; Roosevelt, AZ 85545; 520-467-3200

★ DON'T MISS

Don't miss the chance to hike to the Upper Ruin, a trip that requires some advance planning. Access to the larger ruin is permitted only on ranger-guided tours that run from November to April. The ranger answers questions and gives talks on the Salado people and the Sonoran Desert environment in which they were able to thrive. The hike is 3 miles long and climbs close to 600 feet. The tour takes about 3 hours. Call ahead to arrange to take one of these tours; you won't be disappointed.

10

When the Jesuit father Eusebio Kino and his entourage approached the village of Tumacacori in the winter of 1691 they found a people that Kino described as "docile—affable . . . [and] industrious." These were the Pima Indians, a sedentary people who lived in permanent settlements and farmed corns, beans, and squash along the banks of the Santa Cruz River. Kino called the land Pimeria Alta for the Upper Pima Indians that lived there. Here among the Pima Kino founded the mission San Cayetano de Tumacacori. Tumacacori served as the main mission post in the area until 1701, when it was supplanted by the Mission San Gabriel at Geuvavi, 15 miles to the south. At that time Tumacacori became a *visitas*, or mission outpost, visited from time to time by the presiding father based at Guevavi.

Mistreatment of Indians by the Spanish, who forced them to grow food, tend livestock, and labor in nearby mines, led to a widespread revolt in 1751, forcing many of the Pima living at Tumacacori to flee into the hills. As a result a *presidio*, or fort, was built at Tubac and a heavier Spanish presence reinstated. In 1767 King Charles III removed the Jesuits from the missions, which were then taken over by the Franciscans. Life wasn't any easier for the Franciscans, who simply inherited the problems that had plagued the mission before, including raiding Apache warriors, restlessness among the Pima, disease, unruly settlers, and a constant shortage of funds.

Sometime around 1800 Fray Narciso Gutierrez marshaled enough money and Indian labor to begin building a large church, one that would replace the simple structure originally built by the Jesuits. He made halting progress because of continuing Apache raids, lack of government support, and the Mexican wars for independence. The project was downsized several times and then abandoned in 1828 when Mexico ordered all Spanish priests to leave the missions. Work resumed under the direction of Mexican priests, but raiding Apache, a shortage of provisions, and one of the worst winters on record finally drove the residents of Tumacacori and Tubac to abandon the area for good in 1848.

CYCLING OPTIONS

There are two rides in this chapter, one an easy 7-mile out-and-back pedal on a paved frontage road that takes cyclists to the historic town of Tubac, now a thriving artist's colony. This route is suitable for any kind of bike and rider. The Elephant Head Trail is a strenuous adventure for even very fit and experienced mountain bikers but fat-tire fans of all abilities can make it easier by just riding a portion of the trail. There are several other good possibilities in the Santa Rita Mountains for off-road cyclists; check in with the Nogales Ranger District of the Coronado National Forest for more information.

Cycling in the Park

The minimal acreage surrounding the mission does not provide for any cycling opportunities within park boundaries, but there are a couple of worthwhile opportunities for doing some pedaling nearby. The short ride from Tumacacori to the historic presidio—now artist colony—at Tubac is a rewarding trip anyone on two wheels will appreciate. Many artists' wares are on display outside and the shopping for everything from Mexican clay pots to metal sculptures is great. The fit and adventurous mountain biker won't want to miss the Elephant Head Mountain Bike Trail, designed and built for mountain bikes by the forest service, in the nearby Santa Rita Mountains. There are many other mountain biking possibilities in the Santa Rita

Riding through the foothills of the Santa Rita Mountains south of Tucson.

Mountains; stop by to get more information on riding in the Coronado National Forest at the district station in Nogales, Sierra Vista, or Tucson.

---

41. TUMACACORI TO TUBAC (See map on page 235)

For road or mountain bikes. The short, almost 3.5-mile pedal to the artist's colony and historic presidio at Tubac is a great opportunity to do some sightseeing from the seat of your bike. The route travels along a paved frontage road and is suitable for riders of all ages and abilities.

Starting point: Tumacacori National Historical Park.

Length: 3.5 miles one-way, 7 miles out-and-back. Allow 2 hours to ride the distance and take in the sights of Tubac.

Riding surface: Pavement.

Difficulty: Easy.

Scenery/highlights: Tubac Presidio, the garrison village built after the Pima revolt of 1751, is considered the oldest European settlement in

41 · Tumacacori to Tubac

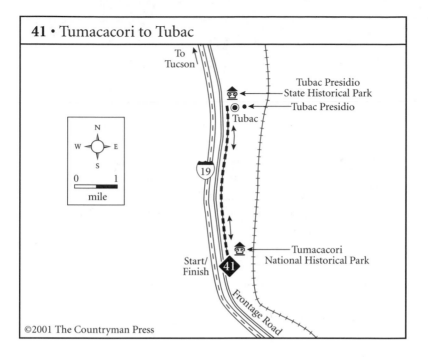

To Tucson

Tubac Presidio
State Historical Park

Tubac Presidio

Tubac

N
W — E
S

0   1
mile

19

Tumacacori
National Historical Park

Start/
Finish

41

Frontage Road

©2001 The Countryman Press

what is now Arizona. After the Spanish left in 1776 the fort was defended by Pima Indians and Mexicans against raiding Apache who made life extremely difficult. The residents of the presidio were repeatedly forced to flee and it was abandoned several times. By 1853, the year the United States acquired most of what is now Arizona and New Mexico in the Gadsden Purchase, the Tubac Presidio was mostly crumbled adobe ruins. The rebirth of Tubac began in 1948 when an artist's school opened there. Today there are dozens of galleries, studios, and shops selling the wares of some of the region's most accomplished artists and craftspeople.

Take some time to wander through the shops and galleries, and be sure to tour the Tubac Presidio State Historical Park while you are there.

Best time to ride: Fall through spring.

Special considerations: You may want to bring along a fanny pack or backpack to carry your wallet, camera, and a lock to secure your bike while wandering the streets and galleries of Tubac.

FLORA

Tumacacori is located within what is referred to as the Arizona Upland division of the Sonoran Desert, the ecosystem that covers the southern third of Arizona. Cacti are by far the most common kind of plants in this region, and one of the most common is cholla. Buckthorn, cane, jumping, teddy bear, and pencil cholla all thrive in the sandy soils of the valleys and slopes. Chollas are easy to pick out because of their spiny, jointed arms. These joints break off easily if you brush against them and are difficult to remove from skin and clothing. Barrel cactus appear as their name describes and have the curious habit of pointing southward. The saguaro, reigning monarch of the Sonoran Desert, towers over all other cacti, the tallest reaching 50 feet in height. A single saguaro can weigh as much as 8 tons and live to be 150 to 200 years old.

Shrubs that dot the landscape include creosote bush, bur sage, brittlebush, limber bush, and fairy duster or Apache plume. Soaptree yucca, foothill paloverde, desert ironwood, velvet mesquite, and ocotillo are some of the other tree and plant species found here. There are very few herbaceous wildflowers in this region, and the timing and number of blooms is entirely dependent on the amount of rain received in the previous season and when it fell.

Directions for the ride: From Tumacacori go left and ride north on the frontage road directly in front of the entry to the mission. Simply follow this road for 3.5 miles to the town of Tubac and reverse your route to return.

---

42. ELEPHANT HEAD TRAIL (See map on page 234)

For mountain bikes. This challenging route begins at the Whipple Observatory Visitor Center and skirts the edge of the Mount Wrightson Wilderness Area just below the high peaks of the Santa Rita Mountains.

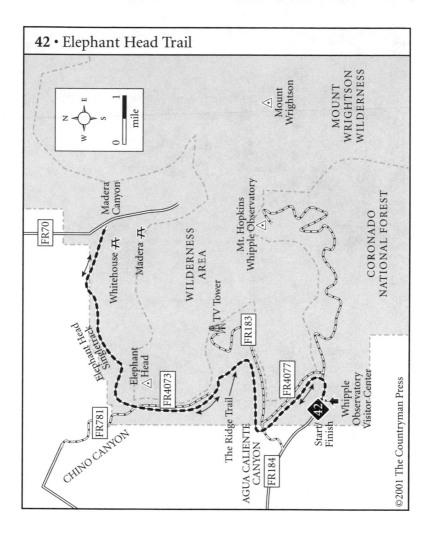

Avid mountain bikers from the Tucson area flock to this trail on the weekends but usually access it from its northern terminus at Madera Canyon and ride it south and west around the distinctive rock outcropping known as the Elephant Head. It is described traveling in the opposite direction here. Parking a second car, or arranging a pick-up so that you can begin at the Whipple Observatory Visitor Center and end at Madera Canyon is ideal.

Zipping along past forests of mesquite near Madera Canyon in the Santa Rita Mountains.

Starting point: The Smithsonian Institute's Whipple Observatory Visitor Center. To get there from Tumacacori drive north on I-19 approximately 11 miles to the Arivca-Amado exit. Continue north just over 2 miles to Elephant Head Road. Turn right and drive east, crossing over the Santa Cruz River. One mile east of the river turn right, onto Mount Hopkins Road. Drive 5.5 miles to the visitor center and park.

To access this ride from the Madera Canyon Trailhead, go north on I-19 about 20 miles to the Continental/Madera Canyon exit 63. Turn east on Continental Road and drive just over a mile to White House Canyon Road. Turn right onto this paved road, following signs for Madera Canyon. In 11.2 miles you come to Proctor Road, a dirt road on your right. Turn right onto Proctor Road and either park at the overflow parking area (and pay a fee if it is necessary), or continue another couple of miles on Proctor Road to the trailhead.

Length: 13 miles one-way. Because you lose so much elevation traveling this route, consider riding it only part of the way and back to shorten what would be a very long, grueling 26-mile ride. Total time and distance depend on your strength and stamina.

FAUNA

Because of the nearby Santa Cruz River and the food and vegetative cover it offers, this area has an enormous variety of migratory and resident bird species. Red-tailed hawks, American kestrels, and turkey vultures are year-round residents, as are a number of birder's favorites including pyrrhuloxia, its cousin the cardinal, and phainopepla. Gambel quail are often seen and always delight visitors. The softly cooing mourning dove is joined by Inca, ground, and rock doves spring through fall. No fewer than nine species of hummingbirds spend a good deal of their time here. Flickers, Gila and ladder-backed woodpeckers, vermillion flycatcher, mockingbird, curved-bill thrasher, and loggerhead shrike are also commonly spotted near the mission.

Desert cottontails and antelope jackrabbits, who regulate their body temperature through their ears, are some of the smaller mammals in the Santa Cruz Valley; javelina and coyotes are some of the larger ones.

Lizards are some of the most commonly seen wildlife in and around the mission and include side-blotched and whiptail lizards. The Gila monster, which can grow up to 2 feet in length, is North America's only poisonous lizard and is easy to spot because of the busy black-and-yellow design that covers its back. There are a few snakes in the area, most notable is the Western diamondback rattlesnake, which is not common but does occasionally turn up near human settlements.

Scorpions, which are actually members of the spider family, come in many different shapes, colors, and sizes in this area but are nocturnal and so not often seen. The large and hairy tarantula is a docile spider that will bite if threatened. Their sting is not unlike that of a bee.

Riding surface: Jeep trails and singletrack. Lots of loose, rocky sections and some gut-busting climbs.

Difficulty: Difficult. Very strenuous if ridden all the way to Madera Canyon and back. Mountain bikers of all abilities shouldn't be put off. Ride for as long as you like and turn around when you've had enough.

Scenery/highlights: Great views of the surrounding desert and mountains. Peaks of the Santa Rita Mountains rise immediately to the east. To the south and west across the Santa Cruz River Valley you'll be looking at the Tumacacori and Atascosta Mountains. To the northwest are the Sierrita Mountains and the Pima Mining District and sprawling open-pit copper mines. Surrounding Upper Sonoran Desert scenery is sparse but beautiful.

Allow yourself some time to check out the visitor center at the Smithsonian Institute's Whipple Observatory. The Multiple Mirror Telescope (MMT) on the top of nearby Mount Hopkins (8,550 feet) is the third-largest telescope in the world. There are several interesting displays and exhibits at the visitor center, which regularly holds Star Parties and other events celebrating the heavens.

Best time to ride: Fall through spring.

Special considerations: Water and rest rooms are available near the trailhead at the parking lot and inside the visitor center of the observatory.

This is a long, hot ride if it is ridden end to end and doubly so if it is ridden the entire distance out and back. Be sure to bring plenty of fluids and snacks with you if you plan to ride the whole thing.

Directions for the ride: From the parking lot ride up the road approximately 0.5 mile to Forest Road (FR) 4077, signed for the Elephant Head Mountain Bike Trail and turn left. Follow this jeep trail for just under 2 miles as it climbs, then descends in a northwesterly direction into Agua Caliente Canyon. Where the road reaches the drainage bottom it turns and heads nearly due east, up the canyon, becoming FR 183. The route climbs for the next 1.6 miles up this rocky jeep trail to the Ridge Trail, an almost mile-long singletrack that climbs up and over a saddle delivering you into Chino Canyon. (If you continue climbing straight on FR 183 you will reach a set of television towers in another 2 miles. This might be a good option if you do not want to lose a lot of elevation that will have to be negotiated on the return trip.)

In Chino Canyon you will pick up another rough, steep jeep road (FR

4073) and follow it as it careens downhill for 2.2 miles along the west side of the Elephant Head. Approximately 0.4 mile from the start of your descent down Chino Canyon on FR 4073 there will be a spring and a gate; do not drink the water. As you get past the nose of the Elephant Head look for a singletrack trail taking off to your right. This is the Elephant Head Trail, a fun, fast-paced section of trail that crosses open grasslands arriving at the Madera Canyon Trailhead 13 miles from the start. Return the way you came or look for your shuttle vehicle or pick-up.

CAMPING

There are no camping facilities within the historic park but several possibilities for staying at developed campgrounds or primitive camp sites in the nearby Coronado National Forest. Most are at least 20 miles from the interstate via dirt roads.

Inquire with the **Nogales Ranger District** north of Nogales for more information.

There are two RV parks in Tubac: the **Tubac Trailer Tether,** which specifies adults only, and **Mountain View RV Park** (north of Tubac on the frontage road). Mountain View RV Park has tent sites, a pool, and showers.

IT'S INTERESTING TO KNOW...

Father Eusebio Francisco Kino crisscrossed Pimeria Alta, a large area that included the Santa Cruz River Valley in Arizona and much of the present-day state of Sonora, Mexico, for 24 years, establishing as many as 20 missions. Kino arrived in Mexico in 1681 and was assigned to the Pima Indians by the Jesuit Order in 1687. Perhaps the most fantastic of the mission churches that arose from Kino's efforts is the Mission San Xavier del Bac south of Tucson. Kino first visited the site in 1692, but the First Chapel did not go up until 1700. Construction began in 1778 but was plagued with troubles, much like the mission church at Tumacacori. But today this whitewashed church stands in excellent condition, a marvelous example of the unique mix of Spanish baroque and Mexican and Indian folk influences that distinguish the architecture of Pimeria Alta missions. The San Xavier del Bac Mission, often referred to as the White Dove of the Desert, is located 10 miles south of Tucson off I-19 at exit 92. Signs from there will direct you to the church, which lies just over a mile northwest.

LODGING

There are a few lodging possibilities near Tubac but they tend to be more expensive. **Rancho Santa Cruz** is one of the more reasonable ones. The **Tubac Country Inn, Valle Verde Rand Bed & Breakfast,** and the **Burro Inn** all offer nice rooms in a Southwestern, ranch-style setting.

You'll find an assortment of cheap motels and a handful of chain hotels 20 miles south in Nogales, and dozens of choices 45 miles north in Tucson.

FOOD

Across the street from the mission the **Tumacacori Mission Restaurant** serves both Greek and Mexican food. North on the frontage road the **Wisdom's Café** serves American and Mexican food.

The **Montura Restaurant,** located at the Tubac Golf Resort, just off the interstate between exit 40 and Tubac, is more upscale and offers three meals a day. The **Burro Inn,** just a mile west of the resort, also has a restaurant serving mesquite-grilled items.

★

DON'T MISS

Don't pass up the chance to visit Tubac Presidio State Historical Park and view the ruins of the 18th-century Spanish fort that shared very close and important ties to Tumacacori. Tour the museum, where you'll find several excellent exhibits that portray the life of one of the West's earliest colonial towns, and watch the short film that provides insight into the role of the Spanish in settling this part of Arizona and the West. There is also an old church, an underground archaeological display, and living history demonstrations that portray Spanish colonial crafts, cooking, religious practices, and apothecary. These demonstrations run October to March. Also, the annual Anza Days Cultural Celebration, held every year around the third weekend of October, has food, crafts, and reenactments, and celebrates the departure of Tubac Presidio Captain Jaun Bautista de Anza, who led 240 colonists north and west to settle what is today San Francisco, California. The park is located just east of the artist's colony in Tubac.

LAUNDRY

There are no laundromats in the Tumacacori and Tubac area. Nogales, 20 miles to the south and Tucson, 45 miles north, have many to choose from.

BIKE SHOP/BIKE RENTAL

Your best bet for getting any bike repairs or supplies is in Tucson, where there are at least two dozen bike shops, many that specialize in one type of biking or another. Pick up a yellow pages, check out their advertisements and location, and decide which one is best for you.

FOR FURTHER INFORMATION

Tumacacori National Historical Park—Superintendent, 1891 E. Frontage Rd., P.O. Box 67, Tumacacori, AZ 85640; 520-398-2341; www.nps.gov/tuma/

Tubac Chamber of Commerce, P.O. Box 1866, Tubac, AZ 85646; 520-398-2704; www.tubacaz.com

Coronado National Forest, Nogales Ranger District, 303 Old Tucson Rd. (about 5 miles north of downtown Nogales), Nogales, AZ 85621; 520-281-2296; www.fs.fed.us/r3/nrd/

11

TUZIGOOT AND MONTEZUMA CASTLE NATIONAL MONUMENTS

Tuzigoot National Monument

Perched on the top of a hill in the middle of the Verde River floodplain, with commanding views in all directions, is a Sinaguan ruin called Tuzigoot (pronounced "Too-zee-goot"), Apache for "crooked water." This term probably identifies nearby Pecks Lake, a boomerang-shaped body of water that was once a bowed meander of the Verde River. The remnants of this stone village, built atop a ridge 120 feet above the valley floor, reveal that there were once three stories and at least 77 ground-floor rooms here. Like nearby Montezuma Castle, the bulk of this complex was built sometime between 1125 and 1400, although evidence suggests that the pueblo was erected around an older existing structure constructed at least a hundred years earlier, probably by the Hohokam. Here the Sinagua lived for over one hundred years, farming and irrigating the floodplain below, producing bountiful crops of corn, beans, squash, and cotton.

This pueblo was added onto repeatedly while it was inhabited, suggesting that there were successive years of plenty for the Sinagua. It is estimated that at least 50 people lived at Tuzigoot initially, but by 1200 the population had doubled, and then doubled again not long after. Because of the lack of exterior entryways to the pueblo, people had to climb ladders and enter into the maze of rooms through rooftops. The lack of doors, the location of the pueblo perched on a hill, and the evidence of rapid expansion of the dwelling suggest that Tuzigoot may have become a defensive structure. During this time the Sinagua became more centralized, possibly due to drought or hostilities from invading tribes. Bands of Yavapai Indians from the north and Apache from the south and east moved into the valley near the time the Sinagua left and were living there when the Spanish arrived a century and a half later.

Montezuma Castle National Monument

Nestled into a limestone cavern high above the burbling waters of Beaver Creek just 20 miles southeast of Tuzigoot is another pueblo, this one tucked into a cavern high in a cliff wall. This enchanting structure so impressed early settlers they mistakenly believed it belonged to the legendary Aztec leader Montezuma. In fact, this beautifully constructed and visually striking cliff dwelling was built by the prehistoric Sinagua people, who archaeologists believe first migrated into the Verde Valley sometime between A.D. 1125 and 1200.

As early as A.D. 600 the people who later became the Sinagua lived in pithouses among the foothills and plateaus to the northeast of the Verde Valley. They were dry farmers, completely dependent on seasonal rainfall to grow their crops. Archaeologists named these people Sinagua, a Spanish term that means "without water," for their ability to farm and thrive in an area almost completely devoid of surface water. By A.D. 1125 the Sinagua had migrated into the Verde Valley, onto land nourished by year-round streams previously inhabited by the Hohokam people.

Archaeological evidence indicates that the Hohokam vacated the Verde Valley and moved northeast, near present-day Flagstaff, to try their hand at farming the lands made fertile by Sunset Crater's ashfall. Soon after the Sinagua had relocated to the Verde Valley, they began building above-ground masonry villages and using irrigation systems that were built and then abandoned by the Hohokam. Montezuma Castle was built sometime in the 1300s and was occupied for about a hundred years. For reasons that remain unclear, Montezuma Castle, along with prehistoric villages throughout the region, were completely deserted by the early 1400s.

Just a few miles northeast of the ruins at Montezuma Castle is Montezuma Well, a partially filled sinkhole, or limestone "sink," that is

Coming down the rough and rocky Lime Kiln Trail in Dead Horse Ranch State Park, near Tuzigoot National Monument.

also protected as part of the monument. The sinkhole, 470 feet in diameter, formed when an underground cavern collapsed. Springs far below the surface continually feed the lake, filling the sinkhole to a depth of 55 feet. Both the Hohokam and Sinagua people irrigated the crops with water from the well. You can still see traces of their irrigation ditches that became coated with lime precipitating out of the water that ran through them. You can also see an early Sinaguan pithouse near the well, estimated to have been built sometime around A.D. 1100.

Cycling in the Parks

Because of the limited acreage of these monuments there are no roads or trails within their boundaries suitable for biking. There are, however, several excellent opportunities for both mountain and road biking nearby. Some of the state's best mountain biking trails just are 30 minutes away in the redrock paradise of Sedona. Dead Horse State Park, right next door to Tuzigoot National Monument, has developed a wonderful trail system where mountain bikers of all sizes and abilities can find a trail to

CYCLING OPTIONS

There are five rides listed in this chapter; one is best suited for experienced road riders and the others offer something for all levels of mountain bikers. Dead Horse Ranch State Park, immediately adjacent to Tuzigoot National Monument, has more than half a dozen trails ranging from paved loops around the park's wetlands to technical singletrack trails extending for several miles across surrounding national forest lands. The climb up US 89A from the Verde Valley to the historic mining town of Jerome and beyond to the top of Mingus Mountain will be a challenge for experienced road riders. The dirt Perkinsville Road, which heads north out of Jerome, is a great pedal for all levels of mountain bikers and offers spectacular views over the Verde Valley and beyond, to the red cliffs of Sedona. The easy mountain bike ride out to Loy Butte and Red Canyon takes cyclists to other Sinaguan ruins, nestled among cliff walls washed in striking hues of red, peach, and orange. The Cathedral Rock Loop also features gorgeous redrock formations and is just one of many five-star singletrack routes around Sedona that will cause serious fat-tire fans to rejoice.

suit their liking. Level trails that wind around Tavasci Marsh will be popular with the little folks, while bigger fat-tire fans may want to test their mettle on the sometimes steep and technically challenging Lime Kiln Trail. More serious road riders who relish a good climb will enjoy the trip up a winding road to the historic mining town of Jerome and the top of Mingus Mountain. Those who are less ambitious but want to stick to the pavement can make a short loop between Tuzigoot and the towns of Cottonwood and Clarkdale by using two different roads. A fairly easy ride out of Jerome along the dirt Perkinsville Road is suitable for most mountain bikers. Sedona is a mountain bikers' paradise, offering dozens of great singletrack rides. Two are featured here: the Cathedral Rock Loop, and an easy pedal out to see some ruins at Red Canyon and Loy Butte.

The climate from fall through spring is delightful for any kind of outdoor activity in this part of Arizona. But as spring turns to summer, temperatures soar, and exerting yourself outside begins to pose the risk of dehydration, heat exhaustion, and even heat stroke. Summer is also the time of year when this country receives most of its scant rainfall. It arrives in the form of intense thunderstorms that can flood drainages and low-lying areas within minutes. These supercharged storms also pose a danger due to lightning. Be sure to be well away from exposed areas and high points should one of these storms roll in. No matter what the temperature, the arid conditions of this desert mean that you will constantly need to replenish your body's fluids. Don't wait until you're thirsty to take in liquids.

43. DEAD HORSE RANCH STATE PARK
(See map on page 250)

For mountain bikes. The network of trails that wind around inside this park and extend beyond its boundaries offer riding possibilities for everyone, from the kids who want to stick to shorter, more level trails to the experienced mountain biker who wants a real challenge. These trails have been developed through the joint efforts of Arizona State Parks, the Verde River Greenway, and the National Forest Service, and are well marked and easy to follow. You can pick up a detailed map of the trails at the entrance station to the park, where you will need to pay a fee.

Starting point: Dead Horse Ranch State Park is right next door to Tuzigoot but must be accessed from Main Street in Cottonwood. From Main Street in Cottonwood turn north on 10th Street and drive almost a mile, following signs to the park. Pay a fee and pick up information at the entrance station.

Length: Total distance and time will vary depending on the trail, or combinations of trails, ridden.

Riding surface: Pavement, dirt road, and singletrack that features steep and rocky sections.

Difficulty: Easy to difficult.

Scenery/highlights: The trails within and just outside the park traverse

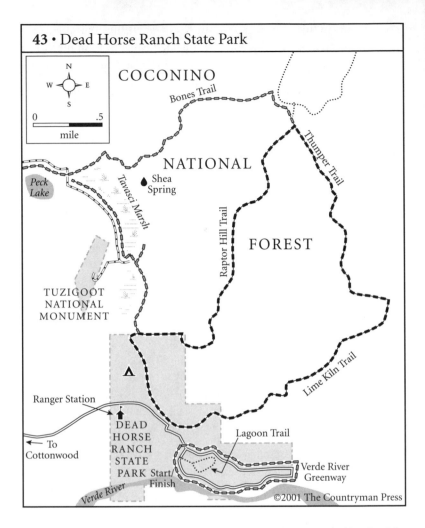

several different habitat types that support a wide variety of birds, fish, and wildlife. Here you'll find riparian woodlands, wetlands, and upper Sonoran Desert scrublands. The riparian woodlands along the Verde River give refuge to some of the highest densities of breeding birds anywhere in North America. The river itself supports three endangered fish species and nearly 20 threatened or endangered animal species. These include river otter, southwestern bald eagle, southwestern willow flycatcher, and the lowland leopard frog. Observing rare and common bird and wildlife species is one of the highlights of visiting this park, as is spending time on your bike on the park's multi-use trail system.

Best time to ride: Fall through spring.

Special considerations: Water and rest rooms can be found at the campgrounds, day-use areas, and several other sites around the park. Be aware of hikers and equestrians who also use the trails in this park.

Directions for the rides: Here are some of the trails best suited for biking and a basic description each:

Lime Kiln Trail (also Forest Trail, or FT, 82): This trail is for serious mountain bikers and can be picked up where it crosses over the North Campground Road directly across from the turnoff to the park's main campground. While the Lime Kiln Trail itself is only 2.1 miles long, it is usually combined with the 2.25-mile Thumper Trail and 2.85-mile Raptor Hill Trail to create a 7.2-mile loop. The Lime Kiln Trail starts out fast and smooth but soon begins to climb; as it does, you'll encounter sections that are steep and washed-out. Simply follow this trail as it rolls along, climbing gradually in elevation. There are several trails taking off the Lime Kiln Trail; stay heading northeast, arriving at the Thumper Trail (FT 131) 2.1 miles from the start. Sections of the Thumper Trail are very technical and should be walked by everyone except the most accomplished riders. The Thumper Trail rolls up and down considerably as it traverses the eroded drainages of Mesa Blanca, named for the white, limestone rock that abounds here. Approximately 4.5 miles from the start you come to the Raptor Hill Trail (FT 181). Turn left onto this trail and follow it southwest as it descends out of the foothills and reenters the park 7.2 miles from the start.

Bones Trail (FT 180): This 2.5-mile trail can be ridden in combination with the Raptor Hill and Lime Kiln Trails, but it ends outside the park boundaries near Pecks Lake. Riders can reverse their route or continue on to Cottonwood. Once in Cottonwood you can go left, ride a short distance, and then go left again back into the park. The last section of trail from Pecks Lake to Cottonwood traverses the private property of the Phelps-Dodge Corporation. A subdivision is planned for the area and access to this portion of the trail may change.

Tavasci Marsh: This 1.5-mile trail (one-way) traverses an old dirt road

A mountain biker cruises downtown Jerome before heading out on the Perkinsville Road.

and begins at the north end of the park. Paths bordered by railroad ties (off-limits to bikes) will take you out to platforms in the wetlands where you can enjoy an up-close view of birds and wildlife.

Verde River Greenway: This multiple-use trail is accessed from the West Lagoon parking lot and makes a sweeping 1.5-mile loop through the east segment of the park. The trail parallels the Verde River for part of the route and accesses several other trails along the way.

44. HIGHWAY 89A TO JEROME (See map on page 253)

For road bikes. The ride from Tuzigoot to the historic mining town of Jerome is not terribly long but it is a sustained climb that is best suited for riders in good condition who are experienced at sharing the road with cars. Superfit and adventurous riders may want to continue beyond Jerome, up to Mingus Mountain, almost 4,000 feet above the valley floor.

Starting point: Tuzigoot National Monument.

Length: 7 miles one-way to Jerome, 14 miles up and back. It is another 7

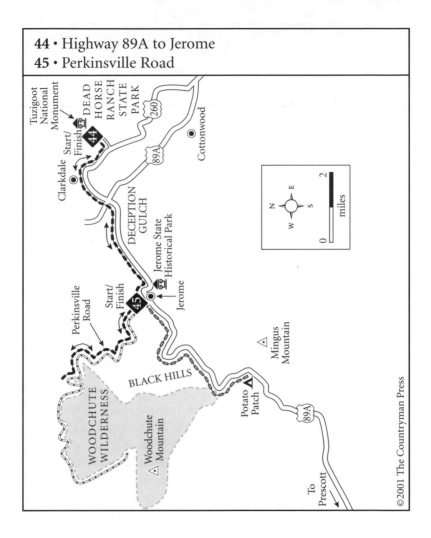

Tuzigoot National Monument

DEAD HORSE RANCH STATE PARK

Clarkdale

Start/Finish

44

260

Cottonwood

89A

DECEPTION GULCH

N
W — E
S

0 — 2 miles

Jerome State Historical Park

Perkinsville Road

Start/Finish

45

Jerome

Mingus Mountain

BLACK HILLS

Potato Patch

89A

WOODCHUTE WILDERNESS

Woodchute Mountain

To Prescott

©2001 The Countryman Press

miles beyond Jerome to the lookout at the top of Mingus Mountain.
Allow at least half a day to do the shorter version of this ride, with time
spent poking around Jerome and visiting Jerome State Historical Park.

Riding surface: Pavement. Sections of this road are narrow and winding;
stay to the right, ride in single file, and wear your helmet.

Difficulty: Difficult. There is a lot of climbing on narrow, winding roads

FLORA

Both Montezuma Castle and Tuzigoot are situated along riparian corridors in an Upper Sonoran lifezone, a habitat type that has all but disappeared in Arizona. These biological ecotones support a rich matrix of plant and animal life and are crucial to the diversity and health of life in desert environments. Over 90 percent of Arizona's riparian areas have disappeared over the last 150 years, because of diversion, development, and the gradual lowering of the water table.

Tuzigoot is located alongside the Verde River. Along Beaver Creek the beautiful Arizona sycamore dominates, but is joined by Arizona ash, desert willow, and Gooding willow. Present along the Verde River but not found along Beaver creek are Fremont cottonwoods. Black walnut is less common but was an important food source for the Sinagua. Soap tree, which also grows along the river, has a poisonous root and was used by the Sinagua to poison fish that they could then easily catch. Netleaf hackberry is also found in these riparian areas.

On the drier slopes false paloverde, honey mesquite, and catclaw acacia are common. They are joined by creosote bush, several types of yucca, and four-wing saltbush. Higher up one-seed juniper and Arizona cypress are sometimes found. Arizona cliffrose presents a profusion of creamy-yellow blooms in spring and is currently listed as an endangered species. Verde Valley sage and Ripley wild buckwheat thrive in the area's limestone soils and are listed as endangered.

Wildflowers blooming around either monument in spring include orange globe mallow and desert marigold. In the evening or early morning you may catch the large, white blooms of the sacred datura while they are open. Agave, Englemann's prickly pear cactus, and hedgehog cactus also bloom on the dry slopes of these areas. The agave sends up a tall spear covered with yellow blooms. Prickly pear bloom in shades from yellow to pink, while hedgehog blooms are usually hot pink. Tall, yellow snapdragon-like flowers called butter and eggs can be found around Beaver Creek near Montezuma Castle, and at the well you can find small, delicate golden columbine.

that demand your full attention. Elevation at the monument is 3,328 feet and at Jerome it is approximately 5,000 feet. Mingus Mountain rises to 7,100 feet.

Scenery/highlights: This route offers a tremendous perspective on both the land that stretches away beneath you as you climb toward the lofty haven of Mingus Mountain. You will ride through several habitat types, beginning with the Upper Sonoran of the Verde Valley and arriving in the ponderosa pine forests of Mingus Mountain. You also ride through history, beginning at the Sinaguan ruins of Tuzigoot and climbing to Jerome, rich in mining history. A visit to the Jerome State Historical Park, where the region's colorful past is explored and preserved, is a don't-miss stop.

Best time to ride: Fall and spring. Temperatures can hover around 100 degrees in summer in the Verde Valley, and in winter Mingus Mountain can get snow.

Special considerations: Water and rest rooms are available at Tuzigoot, in Clarkdale just up the road, and in Jerome. Beyond Jerome there are no facilities.

Directions for the ride: From the monument ride west on Tuzigoot Road to South Broadway, also AZ 260, and go right. Ride about 0.5 mile to Main Street in the town of Clarkdale and go left. Ride up Main Street, past the park, and go left on 11th Street. Follow 11th Street as it climbs to the junction with US 89A. Go straight onto 89A and begin the long, consistent climb up to Jerome. The road climbs west and south, angling its way up Deception Gulch, where miner's ghosts still curse their luck. It then begins a series of switchbacks as you climb into town. Just after the second switchback you come to Jerome State Historical Park, approximately 6.5 miles from the start. In another 0.5 mile you enter into the charming old mining town of Jerome. When you've had a look around and are ready to go, strap on your helmet and head back the way you came.

    Option: To continue up Mingus Mountain, follow 89A as it routes you through the one-way streets of Jerome and continues climbing for another 7 miles and 2,000 feet to the top of the mountain. A lookout at the top of the mountain is your turnaround point. An up and back trip to the top of Mingus Mountain will give you a total distance of 28 miles.

---

45. PERKINSVILLE ROAD (See map on page 253)

For mountain bikes. Riding out the Perkinsville Road from Jerome is a great opportunity to enjoy some fantastic views of central Arizona. The Perkinsville Road, County Road 72, is a well maintained dirt road that climbs only slightly over the first 5 miles as it contours its way around Woodchute Mountain and the Woodchute Wilderness. This ride is suitable for riders of all abilities and offers the chance to visit Jerome, see the old mining equipment at the Gold King Mine, and tour the ghost town of Haynes.

Starting point: Jerome. Park anywhere in town, or beyond the one-way loop through town near the fire station.

Length: A good turnaround point is about 5 miles along the road, where it begins dipping away to the west toward the Chino Valley. There is no time limit here; ride as far and as long as you like.

Riding surface: Graded dirt road.

Difficulty: Easy.

Scenery/highlights: Views looking east over the Verde River Valley and north to the crimson cliffs of Sedona are spectacular. The Sycamore Canyon Wilderness covers a vast amount of terrain in the north. The mountains above you are known collectively as the Black Hills, but are broad, plateau-like peaks. This route contours the east and north flanks of Woodchute Mountain and actually forms part of the Woodchute Wilderness Area's boundary.

Jerome is itself one of the highlights of this ride. This old mining town has been lovingly cared for, its storefronts now filled with boutiques and shops carrying the wares of many local artists.

You may want to bring your wallet along and stop in at the Gold King Mine and the ghost town of Haynes. Here you can see an extensive collection of old machinery and tools and see a replica of both a mine shaft and an assay office. There are numerous other curious objects and leftovers from mining days, and a souvenir shop offering rock samples and

The redrock cliffs of the Sedona area signal the southern terminus of the Colorado Plateau, as well as fantastic mountain biking and outdoor adventuring.

tacky doodads. Enter and pay at the gift shop. The mine and ghost town are located a mile from Jerome along the Perkinsville Road.

Best time to ride: Fall through spring. It will be cooler than the valley floor below in summer, although still hot. You are high up and very exposed along this route; don't get caught out up here when powerful summer storms unleash their electrical fury on the mountains.

Special considerations: Water and rest rooms can be found in Jerome.

Directions for the ride: At the north end of the one-way loop through town, go right, onto Main Street, riding a few hundred feet past the fire station and off the elbow of the switchback onto the Perkinsville Road (Forest Road 318). Follow this route, which in many places rests on old mine tailings, as it contours the steep slope of the Black Hills, so named for the Miocene lava flows that cap the tops of both Woodchute and Mingus Mountains. Ride as far as you like and reverse your route to return to Jerome. Approximately 5 miles from the start the road begins to descend along the northern flank of Woodchute Mountain on its way into the Chino Valley. Any loss of elevation past this point will have to be gained on the return trip.

46. LOY BUTTE–RED CANYON RUINS
(See map on page 259)

For mountain bikes. This ride is located in an area northwest of Sedona but can be accessed from Tuzigoot and the Cottonwood area in about 30 minutes. This is an easy pedal along dirt roads that takes you to two beautiful Sinaguan ruins tucked into the redrock cliffs characteristic of the Colorado Plateau.

Starting point: Begin at the intersection of Forest Road (FR) 525 and FR 152C, also called the Boyton Pass Road. To get there from the Verde Valley drive northeast on US 89A toward Sedona. Go approximately 10 miles from the town of Bridgeport and the intersection with AZ 279 to FR 525, a graded dirt road leaving on the left. Turn onto FR 525 and drive 5.3 miles to the junction of FR 525 and the Boyton Pass Road. Park off the road at this intersection.

Length: 10.5 miles total. Allow at least a half a day to ride the distance and spend time at the ruins.

Riding surface: Dirt road; hot and dusty in the summer. Can be washboarded.

Difficulty: Easy.

Scenery/highlights: Honanki Ruin at the base of Loy Butte and Palatki Ruin in Red Canyon are the two largest ruins in the Sedona redrocks area and are the work of the people known as the Sinagua. These ruins actually represent what archaeologists refer to as the "Honanki Phase," or prehistory of the Sinagua. When these sites were abandoned the inhabitants most likely moved to pueblos along the Verde River, such as Tuzigoot and Montezuma Castle.

Honanki, Hopi for "Bear House," originally contained 60 rooms and was occupied between A.D. 1280 and 1300. Tree ring data from a lintel above a window of the upper ruin suggest this pueblo was built around the year 1271. Dozens of pictographs and petroglyphs around Honanki have

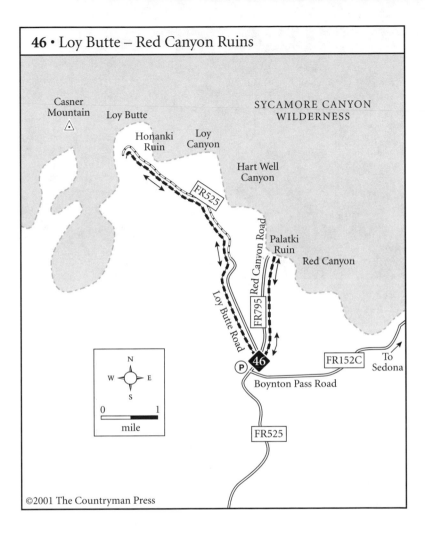

©2001 The Countryman Press

been identified as belonging to several different groups, including Archaic peoples (3,000 to 8,000 years ago), the Southern Sinagua (900–1,300 years ago) and the Yavapai and Apache (A.D. 1400–1875). An inscription above the main ruin at Palatki is credited to some of the first ranchers in the area. Palatki, Hopi for "Red House," is younger than Honanki, and was probably inhabited between 1100 and 1300.

These ruins are extremely fragile; do not climb or lean on ruin walls.

Tucked high into a cliff wall above Beaver Creek, Montezuma Castle looks as though it might have been built as a defensive structure.

Also, do not touch any pictograph or petroglyph, as the oil from your skin will permanently damage the image. It is a federal offense to damage, disturb, or collect artifacts on public land. These violations can result in harsh penalties. Take only pictures and memories; leave only footprints.

Best time to ride: Fall through spring. Despite the higher elevations of this area the summers are very hot.

Special considerations: There is a visitor center and book shop at Palatki where a fee is charged for entrance to the ruin. Make sure to bring your wallet to pay the fee and a lock for securing your bike while you are away.

Water and rest rooms are available at the visitor center, but nowhere else along this route. It can be very hot and dusty out here, so bring plenty of your own water and/or sport drinks.

Directions for the ride: From the junction where you parked ride northward, continuing on FR 525 for approximately 0.25 mile to another junction. Bear right onto FR 795 to Red Canyon and Palatki Ruin. For the next 2 miles the road rolls gently through a red landscape, the cliffs of

Supai Group sandstones and shales defining the northern horizon and your first destination. These cliffs are the southern boundary of both the Red Rock/Secret Mountain Wilderness Area and the raft of sedimentary rocks known as the Colorado Plateau.

Approximately 2.3 miles from the start you arrive at the Palatki Ruins and visitor center. When you are done here, ride the 2 miles back to the junction with FR 795 and FR 525 and go right, riding FR 525 north for 3 miles through more undulating red-hued terrain dotted with piñon and juniper, to Honanki Ruin. Along this route you will pass through the private property of the Hancock Ranch; stay on the main road and keep moving.

After spending some time inspecting the ruin and examining some of the many ancient petroglyphs and pictographs along the cliff face, remount and reverse your route, riding 3 miles back to the junction with FR 795, and another 0.25 miles back to your car.

---

47. CATHEDRAL ROCK LOOP (See map on page 262)

For mountain bikes. The ride out around Cathedral Rock combines of pavement, dirt road, and singletrack and includes a section of the Bell Rock Path, part of the larger Sedona urban trail system. Probably one of the most popular rides around Sedona, this loop begins near the town of Oak Creek and is only about 25 minutes away from Montezuma Castle. Sections of technical singletrack and the distance of this ride make it best suited for mountain bikers with some experience.

Starting point: Bell Rock Path Trailhead. To get there from Montezuma Castle and Well, go north on I-17 to exit 298, signed for Sedona and AZ 179. Go north on AZ 179 approximately 7 miles to Oak Creek. Continue heading north through town another mile to the Bell Rock Path Trailhead and parking area, just past a convenience store on the right.

Length: 12 miles round-trip. Allow at least 3 hours.

Riding surface: Pavement, dirt road, doubletrack and even a section of singletrack. A few steep, rocky sections; one sandy section called Buddha Beach.

Difficulty: Moderate to difficult.

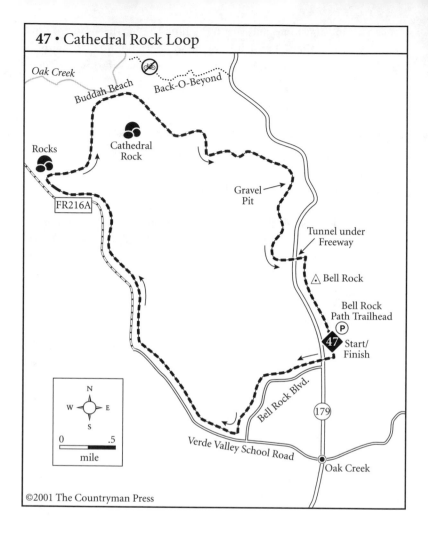

Oak Creek

Buddah Beach

Back-O-Beyond

Rocks

Cathedral Rock

FR216A

Gravel Pit

Tunnel under Freeway

⚠ Bell Rock

Bell Rock Path Trailhead
Ⓟ

47 Start/ Finish

Bell Rock Blvd.

179

N
W ✦ E
S

0 .5
mile

Verde Valley School Road

● Oak Creek

©2001 The Countryman Press

Scenery/highlights: Spectacular redrock scenery, intriguing rock formations, great views to red, peach, buff, and persimmon cliffs in nearby Munds Mountain Wilderness, excellent singletrack, and the opportunity to take a dip in Oak Creek and cool your heels on Buddha Beach all get this ride a five-star rating.

Best time to ride: Fall through spring.

FAUNA

Riparian areas in the desert southwest are magnets for all kinds of wildlife, especially birds. Both monuments offer comprehensive lists of migrant and resident birds that can be seen in the monument. Common year-round residents of both monuments include ravens, Gambel quail, mourning doves, cardinals, roadrunners, Gila woodpeckers, thrashers, belted kingfishers, and great blue herons. A variety of phoebes, sparrows, finches, towhees, and wrens also visit these areas, along with numerous other songbird species. American kestrels, ferruginous and red-tailed hawks, screech owls, and wintering bald eagles are also regularly seen here. Many other raptors pass through on their seasonal migrations. The marshy wetlands around Tuzigoot draw abundant waterfowl.

Common mammals around the monuments include rock squirrels, skunks, cottontail and jackrabbits, ringtail cats, coyotes, gray foxes, and javelina. Animals drawn to the watery environment of the creek and river provide include beaver, muskrat, and otter. Bobcats have been seen at both monuments, and mountain lions have been known to visit on occasion. Mule deer and whitetailed deer are regularly seen around both parks, while wintering elk sometimes come down from around the Mogollon Rim to visit the area around Montezuma Well. Several kinds of bats, including at least four species of myotis bats, live in the crevices and caves of the limestone cliffs near Montezuma Castle.

Lizards are everywhere at these monuments, scurrying among stones stacked long ago and sunning themselves on the pathways. Several species of rattlesnake, including the Western diamondback and black-tailed, are fairly common but are quite shy and rarely seen. Regal ringneck snakes, gopher snakes, bull snakes, black-necked garter snakes, kingsnakes, and sometimes coral snakes are seen around these monuments.

Special considerations: Get what you need at the convenience store near the trailhead.

Be extremely cautious when crossing the highway; cars drive very fast along AZ 179 and their drivers usually have one eye on the scenery.

Directions for the ride: From the Bell Rock Path Trailhead ride out onto AZ 179 and go left, heading south for just a few hundred yards to Bell Rock Boulevard. Turn right onto this paved road and follow it just over a mile to the junction with the Verde Valley School Road. Pedal northwest on this paved road for 2 miles until it turns to dirt. Continue on this dirt road, Forest Road 216A, for another mile to singletrack taking off on your right through some boulders. If you get to an S-curve sign you have gone too far. Follow the rolling singletrack for another mile to a gate. Go through the gate, leaving it as you found it, and find the burbling waters of Oak Creek and Buddha Beach waiting just beyond. Jump in, dry off, and continue along the creek on a 0.5-mile section of trail that winds around through the trees, becoming rocky and unrideable in spots. Go right, following the singletrack as it climbs steeply beneath a powerline. Sections of this uphill are very steep, studded with rock and roots, and will probably have to be negotiated on foot for most.

Approximately 5.5 miles from the start you will reach the top of the first climb and an excellent vantage point from which to take in views of Cathedral Rock and the surrounding country. Follow the singletrack as it winds around Cathedral Rock, crossing several sections of slickrock. The trail then comes to an intersection with the hiking trail to Cathedral Rock 6 miles from the start; continue straight. The route climbs, then dips slightly and climbs again. In another 1.5 miles look right for an old jeep track that begins to parallel a wash. Follow it, keeping an eye out for rock cairns leading to a tunnel that will take you under AZ 179. Once on the other side of AZ 179 ride a short distance to the Bell Rock Path and turn right. It is an easy 4.2 miles on this fun, easy singletrack back to the parking area where you left your car.

CAMPING

There is no camping at either monument in this chapter but plenty of choices nearby. **Dead Horse Ranch State Park** has spaces for tenters and RVs with or without hook-ups. Campsites are awarded on a first-come, first-served basis and tend to fill up quickly in spring and fall. A fee is charged.

There are a couple of private campgrounds in Cottonwood, including **Rio Verde RV Park,** located east of the intersection of US 89A and AZ 260, the **Turquoise Triangle RV Park,** on US 89A a block and a half east of the intersection with AZ 260, and the **Camelot RV Park,** at 651 Main St. in Cottonwood. All have showers and hookups. Rio Verde RV Park also offers tent sites. There are several more private campgrounds that provide for RVs and tenters located in nearby Camp Verde, and still more in the Sedona area. Check with local chamber of commerce offices for complete listings.

There are many opportunities for camping in the nearby Coconino and Prescott National Forests. District rangers for the Coconino National Forest can be found in Sedona and at Beaver Creek, about 3 miles east of I-17 at the Sedona exit. A district ranger for the Prescott National Forest, which includes national forest lands extending east of the Verde River, can be found in Camp Verde.

LODGING

In the towns of Cottonwood and Camp Verde you'll find a good selection of inexpensive motels and several moderately priced chain hotels. If you're looking for something different try Jerome, where you'll find several small inns and hotels housed in Victorian-era homes and historic buildings. Among them is the **Jerome Grand Hotel,** where the views are superb and the rooms more expensive. The hotel's **Grand View Restaurant & Lounge** is a fine dining establishment serving continental cuisine.

Northeast of the Verde Valley

IT'S INTERESTING TO KNOW...

Very little is known about the culture and customs of the people that once lived at Montezuma Castle and Tuzigoot, people that modern-day archaeologists call the Southern Sinagua. We do know that they were culturally flexible, adopting the irrigation practices and other traits from the Hohokam and the masonry skills of the Anasazi, or ancestral Puebloans. Pottery featuring black and white designs and other gray, textured vessels remain critical in identifying Sinaguan sites.

The Sinagua are also distinguished by their burial practices. Burial sites suggest the Sinagua people did not fear the ghosts of the dead, unlike the Navajo and Apache Indians. The Hohokam cremated their dead, suggesting the need to rid themselves of the presence of death. Sinaguan infants were buried in the floor of their parent's house. Adults, who rarely lived past the age of 40, were elaborately painted in green and blue dyes, their heads wrapped with woven reeds, dressed in cotton burial robes, and buried along with numerous arti-facts, including painted prayer sticks, quartz crystals, and medicine bags containing objects such as plant roots, feather bundles, pigment, and antelope hooves, perhaps to aid the dead in their travels through another world. In several instances objects found at these burial sites correlate to ceremonial objects that remain important to specific clans of the Hopi Indians.

in the trendy tourist town of Sedona you'll find dozens of pos-sibilities for lodging. Among the redrock formations and towering canyon walls that have made Sedona one of Arizona's hottest destination spots there is a hostel, at least a dozen B&Bs, a handful of inexpensive motels, hotels galore, resorts, spas, and even New Age retreats. Visit the Sedona Chamber of Commerce, go to their web site, or call their central reservations number for a com-plete list of lodging possibilities.

FOOD

For morning fare in Cottonwood try **Olde Town Bagel and Deli**

(705 N. Main St.), **Bellespresso** (1205 N. Main St.), or **Georgie's Café** (in the Verde Valley Plaza at the intersection of US 89A and Cottonwood St.). **Su Casa,** on Main Street in Clarkdale, is a good choice for Mexican food. **Gratella's Ristorante** (1075 AZ 260) serves Italian food, while **Ming House** (888 Main St.) and **Golden Dragon** (Sawmill Shopping Center) offer a variety of Chinese dishes. The **White Horse Inn** (east of the junction of 89A and AZ 260) and **Rosalie's Bluewaters Inn** (517 N. 12th St.) both offer prime rib, seafood, and other American favorites for dinner.

If your palate is more adventurous you might consider heading up to dine at one of Sedona's many fine cafés and restaurants. There you'll find Indian, Thai, Japanese, Oaxacan, Italian, and Swiss restaurants, as well as numerous cafes serving nouveau cuisine of every description.

LAUNDRY

Try these two in Cottonwood:

Poole's Maytag Equipped Laundry, 790 S. Main St.; 520-634-2488

Verde Village Laundromat, 2593 Union Dr.; 520-646-7342

BIKE SHOP/BIKE RENTAL

You don't have to go far to find some great bike shops in this area.

Mingus Mountain Bicycles, 418 N. 15th Street, Cottonwood; 520-634-7113

Round Trip Bike Shop (family oriented), 460 S. Main Street, Camp Verde; 520-567-1878

Mountain Bike Heaven, 1695 W. Hwy 89A, Sedona; 520-282-1312

Sedona Bike & Bean, 6020 Hwy. 179, Sedona; 520-284-0210

Sedona Bike & Bean Shoppe, 376 Jordan Rd., Sedona; 520-282-3515

FOR FURTHER INFORMATION

Montezuma Castle National Monument, Tuzigoot National Monument—Superintendent (both), P.O. Box 219, Camp Verde, AZ 86322; 520-567-3322 (Montezuma); 502-634-5564 (Tuzigoot); www.nps.gov/moca/; www.nps.gov/tuzi/

Cottonwood/Verde Valley Chamber of Commerce, 1010 S. Main St. (at the intersection of US 89A and AZ 260), Cottonwood, AZ 86326; 520-634-7468; www.chamber.verdevalley.com

Sedona–Oak Creek Canyon Chamber of Commerce, P.O. Box 478, On the corner of N. US 89A and Forest Rd. (one block north of the Y), Sedona, AZ 86339; 520-288-7336 or 520-282-7722; www.sedonachamber.com or www.sedona.net

Jerome Chamber of Commerce, Drawer K, 310 Hull Ave., Jerome, AZ 86331; 520-634-2900

Dead Horse Ranch State Park, 675 Dead Horse Ranch Rd., Cottonwood, AZ 86326; 520-634-5283

Coconino National Forest—Beaver Creek Ranger District, H.C. 64, P.O. Box 240, (Exit 289 off of I-17, 2.5 miles southeast on Forest Road 618), Rim Rock, AZ 86335 ; 520-567-7500 or 520-567-4121; www.fs.fed.us/r3/coconino/

Coconino National Forest—Sedona Ranger District, P.O. Box 300, 250 Brewer Rd., Sedona, AZ 86339; www.fs.fed.us/r3/coconino/

Prescott National Forest—Verde Ranger District, P.O. Box 670, 300 E. AZ 260, Camp Verde, AZ 86322; www.fs.fed.us/r3/prescott

DON'T MISS

If you are riding to Jerome or staying there while visiting these two monuments, be sure to set aside some time for a visit to Jerome State Historical Park. This park is mainly a museum housed in the enormous Douglas Mansion, built in 1916 by mining magnate James Douglas. Overlooking what was once the Little Daisy Mine, the mansion is now filled with mining memorabilia and fascinating exhibits explaining the methods used to extract copper, silver, and gold from the side of this mountain. Outside the building you'll see some of the old stone mills used for crushing rock and several other interesting remnants of this area's mining heyday, when Jerome was Arizona's fifth largest city. Take some time to wander around the town itself as well, where you'll find many of the original storefronts and buildings have been preserved. Jerome has become a magnet for artisans, many of whom maintain studios in old miner's homes and sell their wares in the shops and boutiques that line Jerome's narrow streets.

Part Two  NEW MEXICO

12

ocated in the lush Animas River Valley of northern New Mexico, not far from the Colorado border, lie the remains of what was once one of the largest Anasazi villages in the Southwest. Tree ring data show that Aztec was built between A.D. 1111 and 1115, a time when the Anasazi, or ancestral Puebloans, were flourishing throughout the Four Corners region. The architecture, masonry, and layout of the pueblo resemble that of the great houses of Chaco Canyon, the hub of Anasazi culture, and suggest Aztec may have been an outlier community. Roads connecting Aztec and nearby Salmon Ruins to Chaco Canyon, 50 miles to the south, as well as pottery styles and other artifacts also help to identify the builders of Aztec as Chacoan Anasazi.

Evidence suggests that Aztec was a center for trade and ceremony for some 60 years but was abandoned as Chacoan social and economic influences began to fade. Around 1225 Aztec once again came to life as another group moved in. Their pottery and textiles identify them as Anasazi from Mesa Verde, 45 miles to the northwest. This second group remodeled the large west pueblo, sealing doorways, adding rooms, repairing walls and roofs, and altering the kivas. They also built several other pueblos nearby with techniques similar to those found at the many sites atop Mesa Verde. These people lived at Aztec for only a few generations before they too moved on, probably to the well-watered Rio Grande Valley where their legacy endures among today's Pueblo Indians.

SARAH BENNETT ALLEY

The size, design, masonry styles, and date of construction all help to identify Aztec Ruin as a Chacoan outlier.

Why the ancestral Puebloans left Aztec is unclear, but prolonged drought, exhaustion of the area's resources, pressure from invading tribes, or a combination of these factors probably contributed to their eventual abandonment of the area.

Aztec Ruin, mistakenly attributed by early European settlers to the pre-Columbian Indians of central Mexico, includes at least six major sites, the largest being the West Ruin, the only fully excavated site. West Ruin is an enormous, E-shaped pueblo with over four hundred rooms and 28 kivas. Although the pueblo suffered several decades of looting in the late 1800s, the site was protected as private property early on, and was the focus of intensive archaeological research beginning in the early 1900s. Earl H. Morris, an archaeologist with the American Museum of Natural History, is credited with deciphering much of what we know about the Anasazi in the region, and was responsible for stabilizing and rebuilding the Great Kiva at West Ruin, the centerpiece of monument.

Cycling in the Park

The 300-plus acres encompassing the ancient ruins of this monument do not include any routes for road or mountain biking, but the beautiful high-desert country that surrounds the park offers several great riding opportunities. An active community of cyclists in the Farmington area and biking events offered throughout the season are an indication that there is good support for bikers and a wealth of biking possibilities. Avid riders who live at higher elevations nearby flock to this area in spring when their trails are still snow covered, and linger long into fall when temperatures here stay mild.

Riding from the monument on either road or mountain bike north on Ruins Road through the Animas River Valley is an outing riders of all abilities can enjoy. Mountain bikers of varying experience and fitness levels can find plenty to keep them busy on the Glade Mountain Bike Trails, just north of Farmington.

Summer temperatures are warm, often hovering right around 90°F at this latitude and elevation, while the nights are always cool. Afternoon thunderstorms, some of which can be quite violent with lightning, hail, and strong winds, are common through the summer and early fall. Fall is a great time of year for being outside when the autumn foliage is beau-

CYCLING OPTIONS

There are two rides listed in this chapter. One is best suited to road bikes but can be enjoyed by either; the other is for mountain bikes. Cyclists of all abilities and descriptions can ride out of the parking lot at the monument and enjoy a beautiful and not too demanding pedal north through the upper Animas River Valley. There are no time or distance requirements for this ride. The Glade Mountain Bike Trails, site of the annual Road Apple Rally Mountain Bike Race, offer miles of fun, fast-paced singletrack linked by a maze of dirt roads and trails. While riding a 28-mile race course loop through the Glade area, you can explore many options and create your own routes of varying lengths and difficulty.

There are more good riding options in this area—several for road riders—including a loop through the lower Animas River Valley on the Old Aztec Highway and South Side River Roads. Check in with the folks at Cottonwood Cycles for a complete list of both on- and off-road options.

tiful. While snowstorms are not uncommon, significant accumulations around the monument are rare. Daytime winter temperatures can be mild, reaching up into the 50s and even lower 60s, while nights dip below freezing.

---

48. RUINS ROAD (See map on page 274)

For road or mountain bikes. Riding up the Animas River Valley on the Ruins Road is a delightful pedal through beautiful Southwestern farm country. This narrow road is mostly level, rising and falling gently to where it meets busy US 516. You can make a loop by returning on this highway, but some experience riding with vehicle traffic is recommended. There are no distance requirements for this ride. If you would like to make it shorter simply turn around and head back the way you came when you've had enough.

Starting point: Aztec National Monument.

Length: 10 miles one-way (20 miles out-and-back) to US 516 or as far as you want to go. The optional loop ride is approximately 22 miles.

Riding surface: Pavement.

Difficulty: Easy to moderate. Length and elevations of around 6,000 feet above sea level will make this ride more difficult for some.

Scenery/highlights: The Animas River feeds into the fertile and historically rich San Juan Basin where it is joined by the San Juan and La Plata Rivers. It is not hard to imagine, as you glide up this valley, fields of corn and squash tended by the ancient peoples who once thrived here. The beautiful scenery and enchanting history of this landscape can't help but thrill the senses and stir the imagination.

Best time to ride: Spring through fall.

Special considerations: Ruins Road is narrow but doesn't see too much traffic. The posted speed limit is 30 mph. Making a loop and riding back via US 516 is recommended only for those who have experience riding with vehicle traffic. Heavy trucks and summer tourists can make riding on this road nerve-wracking.

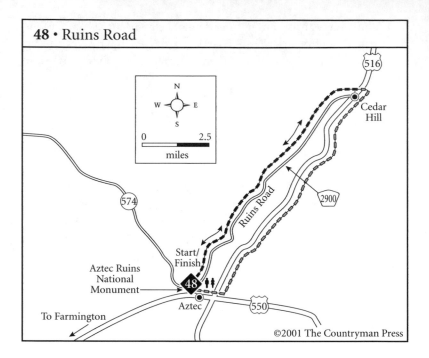

N
W — E
S

0   2.5
miles

516
Cedar Hill

574

Ruins Road

2900

Start/Finish

Aztec Ruins National Monument

48

Aztec

550

To Farmington

©2001 The Countryman Press

Rest rooms and water are available at the monument visitor center.

Directions for the ride: From the parking lot in front of the visitor center simply ride out to Ruins Road, County Road (CR) 2900, and go left. Follow the road as it heads northwest, up through the Animas River Valley. Large cottonwoods line your route and sandstone rimrock defines the valley on either side. The road curves and then climbs gently after 0.5 mile, then levels off but continues to roll along gently to where it meets US 516 (listed on maps printed before 2000 as NM 550), approximately 10 miles from the start. Turn around here and head back the way you came.

Option: If you would like to make a loop and ride US 516 back to the monument, go right onto the highway and follow it for just over 10 miles to the town of Aztec. Ride through the east side of town and go right, onto Ruins Road, just after passing over the Animas River. Ride just over a mile to reach the monument. Total distance for this loop option is approximately 22 miles.

49. GLADE MOUNTAIN BIKE TRAILS
(See map on page 276)

For mountain bikes. The more than 50 miles of dirt roads, doubletrack, and singletrack in this area provide mountain bikers of all abilities an excellent opportunity to get out and test their skills on a variety trails. The dirt roads were built to access the many oil wells that dot the hills and are linked by sections of singletrack. All roads connect to Glade Road running down the center of a gentle valley encircled by singletrack. This route has been used as the race course for the annual Road Apple Rally Mountain Bike Race for many years.

Starting point: Access for the Glade Trails is at Lions Wilderness Park, a community park for special events in Farmington. To get there from Aztec head southwest on US 516 approximately 10 miles to Piñon Hills Boulevard on the northern outskirts of Farmington. Go right onto

FLORA

While the surrounding juniper-dotted hills and mesas are indicative of a high desert, the environment of the valley where Aztec Ruins sit has been partially shaped by the presence of the Animas River. Water-loving Fremont cottonwoods found around the visitor center, picnic area, and West Ruin provide precious shade on a hot summer day. Slippery elm is another big tree found inside the monument. Sagebrush, greasewood, four-wing saltbush, and rabbitbrush, which blooms brilliant gold in fall, are shrubs common to the Four Corners region. Native to this valley are a variety of bunchgrasses that include Indian rice grass, alkali sakatone, blue and black grama, and needle and thread grass. The monument is currently trying to reintroduce the native grasses once abundant here. Agriculture and livestock grazing eliminated not only grasses but much of the valley's native vegetation shortly after settlement. Globe mallow, cinquefoil, curly dock, and Wood's rose are some of the native bloomers you are likely to see around the ruins in spring.

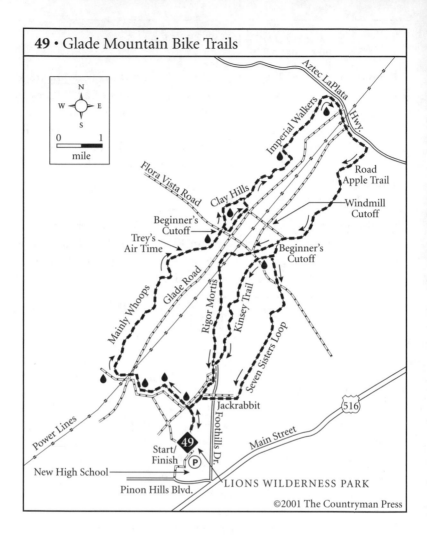

49 • Glade Mountain Bike Trails

N W E S

0   1

mile

Aztec LaPlata Hwy.

Imperial Walkers

Road Apple Trail

Flora Vista Road

Clay Hills

Windmill Cutoff

Beginner's Cutoff

Trey's Air Time

Beginner's Cutoff

Glade Road

Mainly Whoops

Rigor Mortis

Kinsey Trail

Seven Sisters Loop

Power Lines

516

Jackrabbit

Foothills Dr.

Main Street

49

Start/ Finish   P

New High School

LIONS WILDERNESS PARK

Pinon Hills Blvd.

©2001 The Countryman Press

Piñon Hills Boulevard and drive west 2 miles to College Boulevard. Turn right and drive north just under a mile, following signs for Lions Wilderness Park. Park in the main parking lot near the amphitheater.

Length: 28 miles for the entire loop used as the Road Apple race course. There are no distance requirements; ride for as long as you like, creating your own loops, using the network of trails that run in all directions.

SARAH BENNETT ALLEY

Whoop-de-doos on the fast-paced, super-fun singletrack of the Glade Trails just outside Farmington, New Mexico

Riding surface: Hardpacked dirt roads, doubletrack, and singletrack. Fast with few loose or really technical sections. Lots of whoop-de-doos.

Difficulty: Mostly moderate to advanced. Easy if you stick to dirt roads.

Scenery/highlights: Great riding through rolling, juniper-covered hills.

Best time to ride: Spring through fall.

Special considerations: There are rest rooms available near the amphitheater at Lions Wilderness Park. There is another set of rest rooms inside the park near a group of covered picnic tables. Bring your own water.

There are many possible routes and trail combinations out here and roads and trails heading in all directions. Because you are at a higher elevation on the trails that encircle the valley, and you will continually be crossing over dirt roads that connect to the central Glade Road and roads and trails on the far side of the valley, options for making shorter loops will be readily apparent. It is hard to get too lost out here but easy to get sidetracked and turned around. Detailed maps of the Glade Mountain Bike Trails are available at the Farmington Chamber of Commerce and at area bike shops. The following is a general description of traveling the main loop in a clockwise direction.

Directions for the ride: From the parking area near the amphitheater at Lions Wilderness Park head north on a maintained dirt road. After approximately 0.5 mile go right onto a singletrack immediately past a well site. Follow the singletrack past another well site to where it ends at a dirt road 1.9 miles from the start. Cross over this well-maintained road, onto another dirt road, passing another well site on the right. Head west and downhill for 1 mile to a T intersection. Go right, ride for another mile to another T intersection. Go left onto another maintained road and ride for a short distance to a major intersection at Brown's Spring. Go straight, across Glade Road, and ride uphill.

In 0.4 mile you reach the top of the hill where a singletrack takes off to the right. Go right and be prepared for some fun, fast-paced riding and stretches of whoop-de-doos. You will intersect several dirt roads perpendicular to the trail; ignore them and continue riding north on the singletrack. Approximately 7 miles from the start and 3 miles from the start of the singletrack you come to a fence at the top of a hill. Go right, following the main trail as it crosses through the fence and continues northward. Cross over another road and follow a section of rolling trail known as Trey's Air Time. Just past another well site, approximately 7.5 miles from the start, is an intersection; bear left on the main trail that goes around an area called the Clay Hills. Just past this intersection the trail crosses over the old Flora Vista Road—a good bailout for a shorter option. Continue north on singletrack as it jogs back and forth, crosses a few roads, and arrives at the paved La Plata Highway 15 miles from the start.

Go right and ride the pavement 1 mile east to the top of a hill where you will go right again, onto a dirt road at a BLM sign. Ride for a short distance on this maintained dirt road and then bear right onto a jeep road. In 1.5 miles, or 17.5 miles from the start, you pass a well site, bear right onto another road, and then pick up a singletrack on the left. In 2 miles continue straight onto a section of road, follow it to the top of a hill and go left onto singletrack again. In another mile you come to an intersection; bear right to continue south on the Rigor Mortis Trail, or bear left to ride the Kinsey Trail or Seven Sisters Loop. Both the Rigor

FAUNA

It is not uncommon to see both bald and golden eagles soaring in the skies above the monument or perched in trees nearby. The Animas River Valley is a wintering ground for bald eagles; they are more numerous during that time of year. Gambel's quail are year-round residents and can often be seen scurrying about. Mourning doves, northern flickers, Lewis woodpeckers, western kingbirds, and violet swallows are regular summer sights, as are the noisy and gregarious magpies, ravens, and scrub jays. Broad-tailed and black-chinned hummingbirds come through in summer, as do the white-breasted nuthatch and brown creeper. Black-capped and mountain chickadees are year-round residents, while western and mountain bluebirds visit mostly during winter.

Desert cottontails and chipmunks are common, while jackrabbits prefer the wide-open spaces of piñon and juniper forests nearby. Mule deer come right down to the monument in winter, but tend to keep their distance during the busier summer season. Red fox and coyotes are also regular visitors.

Whiptail, western side-blotched, and fence lizards are among the most commonly seen wildlife at the monument, and the presence of both bull snakes and racers is noted on a fairly regular basis.

Mortis and Kinsey Trails wind their way south, arriving at a trailhead at the end of Foothills Drive in approximately 4 miles; the Seven Sisters Loop exits onto Jackrabbit Road further south on Foothills Drive. From the trailhead where Rigor Mortis and Kinsey terminate, ride south 0.2 mile and go right onto County Road (CR) 3809. Follow it a short distance to an intersection and turn left onto CR 3807. Follow this road for 1 mile to an intersection where a singletrack takes off on the left. Follow this trail for just under 2 miles, arriving back at the trailhead and Lions Wilderness Park 28 miles from the start.

CAMPING

No camping facilities are available within the monument, but you'll find great campgrounds at **Navajo Lake State Park,** 25 miles east of Aztec. Caught behind Navajo Dam, the waters of the San Juan River have created a 13,000-acre lake that has become a haven for fisherman and campers looking to escape the summer heat. The first 3 miles of river below the dam provide some of this area's best trout fishing. There are several developed campgrounds, one of the nicest being **Cottonwood Campground** on the San Juan River west of the dam and lake. Most campgrounds have rest rooms and water but no showers. For more information call 505-632-2278 or visit their website at www.emnrd.state.nm.us/nmparks/pages/parks/navajo/navajo.htm.

You'll find **KOA Kampgrounds** in both Farmington and Bloomfield, offering RV hook-ups, tent sites, showers, and laundry.

IT'S INTERESTING TO KNOW...

The first Anglo of record to see the ruins was Dr. John S. Newberry, a geologist who was in the area surveying for the government in 1859. He reported ruin walls 25 feet high, but by the time anthropologist Lewis H. Morgan arrived to study the ruins 20 years later, more than a quarter of the stones had been carted away by settlers for building materials. The site came under the protection of the American Museum of Natural History in 1916 and was declared a national monument in 1923. Efforts to protect the ruins are ongoing. Recently, portions of the West Ruin have been either backfilled or reburied to prevent the decay of the walls, and even the stones themselves, that exposure to sun, wind, and weather eventually causes.

There is no lodging in the monument but at least half a dozen choices in the town of Aztec. There's a **Holiday Inn** and a **Super 8** as well as the **Step Back Inn,** a moderately priced hotel decorated in Victorian settler–era décor; the **Aztec Motel,** on Main Street; and the **Enchantment Lodge,** on Aztec Boulevard.

You'll find many more choices in Farmington, and still more in Bloomfield. Contact their chambers of commerce for a complete listing of lodging possibilities.

FOOD

Aztec is a small town with limited dining options. Start your day at the **Rio Grande Coffee Company** (606 S. Rio Grande), where you

---

★

DON'T MISS

If you are interested in the mystery of the Anasazi and the brief but brilliant flourishing of Chacoan culture, don't pass up the chance to visit Salmon Ruin just 2 miles west of Bloomfield on US 64, about 15 miles due south of Aztec. The community at Salmon Ruin was another outlier of Chaco Canyon, linked to the settlements there by an ancient system of roads. Salmon Ruin is older than Aztec, built sometime between 1088 and 1095. The original pueblo was built in the shape of a C and stretched over 430 feet along its back wall. At least 250 separate rooms, arranged around a central plaza and a great kiva, housed several hundred people.

George Salmon, for whom the ruins are named, settled in the area in the late 1800s and protected the ruin from pot hunters and vandals during a time when there were few protections for these ancient sites. In 1969 the property was purchased by San Juan County and shortly after a bond was passed for the construction of the San Juan County Archaeological Research Center and Library that now occupy the site. Extensive excavation of the pueblo was done throughout the 1970s, producing more than half a million artifacts, now housed in the museum. The museum and ruins are open to the public for a fee. Call the Research Center for more information at 505-632-2013.

can get a bagel and a cup of java. They also serve lunch and light dinners. The **Aztec Restaurant** serves three meals a day and offers basic American and tasty Mexican dishes.

Pick up a local phone book to check out your dining out choices in Farmington or Bloomfield.

LAUNDRY

Apache Queen Laundry, 204 E. Apache St., Farmington; 505-326-1916

San Juan Laundry, 3030 E. Main St., Farmington; 505-326-4933

The Wash Tub, 500 W. Broadway, Bloomfield; 505-632-2410

BIKE SHOP/BIKE RENTAL

Bicycle Express (BMX, family-type shop), 103 N. Main St., Aztec; 505-334-4354

Cottonwood Cycles, 3030 E. Main St., Farmington; 505-326-0429

Havens Bikes and Boards, 2017 E. Main St., Farmington; 505-327-1727

FOR FURTHER INFORMATION

Aztec Ruins National Monument—Superintendent, P.O. Box 640, 84 County Road 2900, Aztec, NM 87410-0640; 505-334-6174; www.nps.gov/azru/

Aztec Chamber of Commerce, 110 N. Ash St. (one block south of Aztec Blvd. on the west side of town), Aztec, NM 87410; 505-334-9551; www.cyberport.com/aztec

Farmington Convention and Visitors Bureau, 3041 E. Main St., Farmington, NM 87401; 505-326-7602 or 1-800-448-1240

13

The ruins found at Bandelier National Monument include both multi-storied freestanding pueblos on the floor of Frijoles Canyon and almost 2 miles of dwellings built along the base of the canyon's cliff. Together these ruins represent a period of Anasazi history identified by archaeologists as Pueblo IV, or the Rio Grande Classic period. These dwellings were constructed in the mid to late 1300s after what is called the Great Migration, the period when the Anasazi were abandoning sites throughout the upper San Juan River drainage and Four Corners area and moving into the upper Rio Grande River Valley. Tyuonyi Pueblo, the nearby cliff houses, as well as the ruins at Puye, on the Santa Clara Indian Reservation near Española, were all occupied simultaneously for about a hundred years, but were deserted by the time the Spanish arrived in the area in the early 1500s.

What makes the ruins at Bandelier and others nearby so unique is not only their size and number but the type of construction that utilized the soft volcanic tuff of the canyon walls. The series of events that made this type of construction possible began close to a million years ago. At this time an enormous mountain that probably looked a lot like Mount St. Helens stood immediately to the west of Bandelier. Like Mount St. Helens, this mountain exploded in at least two volcanic eruptions, spew-

SARAH BENNETT ALLEY

A well defined groove in soft volcanic rock is evidence of centuries of foot traffic along a path that took ancient Puebloans to their homes in the cliffs.

ing 100 times the volume of gases, pumice, ash, and broken rock material that Mount St. Helens did in 1980. As layer upon layer of superheated ash particles settled and cooled they bonded together to form a porous, relatively soft rock called tuff. The builders of the cliff dwellings at Bandelier were later able to carve away the tuff to form pockets for beam supports for their roofs, and even entire rooms connected by doors and passageways. Tyuonyi Pueblo, with more than 300 ground-floor rooms and three kivas, was built with rough blocks of lava and tuff cemented together with mud mortar.

The ruins in Frijoles Canyon and those nearby belonging to the same Rio Grande Classic period form a crucial link between the more ancient Anasazi who lived throughout the Four Corners region and modern Pueblo Indians who live today in the many pueblos scattered across northern New Mexico. The name Tyuonyi, identifying the large pueblo on the floor of Frijoles Canyon, is Keresan, a language spoken by the residents of nearby Cochiti Pueblo, who regard that ruin and the adjacent cliff dwellings as their ancestral home.

Cycling in the Park

Although Bandelier National Monument covers almost 33,000 acres, there are only 3 miles of road within park boundaries that are open to bicycles, and that is just the steep descent from the mesa top to the canyon floor. The vast majority of Bandelier is designated as wilderness and is traversed by foot trails open only to hikers and backpackers. The incredibly beautiful canyons and mesas of the surrounding Jemez Mountains, however, and the active, outdoor communities of Los Alamos and Santa Fe, combine to furnish plenty of biking opportunities and resources for those determined to take in the surrounding country from the seat of their bike.

Mountain bikers can start out with the short loop on the White Rock Canyon Rim Trail that will help you adjust to the high elevations and arid conditions here. This route also serves as a good introduction to the gorgeous scenery of this region, characterized by contrasting deep pine forests, cliff bands of light volcanic rock, shadowy canyons, and sprawling mesas. The trip out Sawyer Mesa and Obsidian Ridge just outside the northwest boundary of the monument is a ride that provides great views into upper Frijoles Canyon and a lesson in forest regeneration after wildfire. The Pines Canyon Trail is in the same general area and will provide fat-tire fans hungry for singletrack plenty to sink their teeth into. The road ride out to Tsankawi Ruins is a great destination ride for less-experienced road riders and features a good hike at the end. An option takes more serious road riders on a circuit of the Pajarito Plateau.

There are many more mountain bike routes worth exploring in the St. Peters Dome area, including Forest Road (FR) 501 and the road out to St. Peters Dome itself; both are dirt road adventures suitable for beginning and intermediate riders. The Dome Singletrack, Capulin, and Alamos are great trails for the more advanced rider. There are also dozens of singletrack trails and forest service roads in the area immediately outside of the town of Los Alamos, all of which were devastated by the Cerro Grande wildfire in the spring of 2000. At the writing of this book all roads and trails in the national forest north and west of Los Alamos were closed to prevent erosion. Inquire locally about trail openings; many trails will likely be redesigned and rerouted over the coming years.

CYCLING OPTIONS

There are four rides listed here; three for mountain bikes and one for road bikes. The loop around the White Rock Rim, and around the town of White Rock itself, is a good place to start and get acclimated to this region's high elevations and dry air. The pedal out along Sawyer Mesa and the knife-edge Obsidian Ridge is a ride mountain bikers of all abilities with a good level of physical fitness will enjoy. The nearby Pines Canyon Trail will thrill the more serious singletrack fan. There are many, many more trails and rides in this area and around the town of Los Alamos that avid fat-tire riders should plan on taking some time to explore. A road ride to Tsankawi Ruins, a separate unit of Bandelier National Monument, offers options for all levels. Those wanting a quick spin can start in White Rock, the more ambitious can start at the park entrance station, and the truly serious can make a 30-plus mile loop around the Pajarito Plateau after riding the spur out to the ruins.

Elevations around Bandelier are quite high, ranging from 6,500 to 9,000 feet above sea level. Those coming from lower altitudes should take a few days to acclimate before spending a long day in the saddle. Start out slow, don't overdo it, and drink plenty of water. Despite the high elevations, and often cool temperatures, you're in arid country here. The dry air will rob your body's precious fluids and zap your energy if you fail to replace them.

Also, like much of the Southwest, this part of New Mexico has a monsoon season that begins sometime in mid-July and can last into the middle of September. During this time moist air pushes north from the Gulf of Mexico. When it meets warm air rising off the mountainous landscape of this region, thunderstorms quickly develop. A day that begins clear and blue can turn dark and nasty by afternoon. Be aware of local forecasts and plan to be done with your ride, or at least well off high or exposed places, when one of these storms moves in.

The freestanding pueblos on the floor of Frijoles Canyon housed thousands of people on several floors stacked above the foundations that remain.

50. WHITE ROCK RIM TRAIL (See map on page 288)

For mountain bikes. This short 5.5-mile loop (with a spur) traverses the rim above White Rock Canyon while skirting the perimeter of the town of White Rock. Beginning and intermediate riders will enjoy the single-track portion of this trail, which offers little in the way of hills or technical challenges. There is a good amount of exposure in places where the trail snakes along almost 900 feet above the canyon floor; use caution.

Starting point: Begin this ride at the trailhead on Sherwood Boulevard in White Rock. To get there from the monument go right onto NM 4 and drive 8 miles to the town of White Rock. Turn right onto Sherwood Boulevard and head south 0.6 mile, past the intersection with Grand Canyon Drive, to the trailhead for the White Rock Rim Trail and parking area on the left side of the road.

Length: 5.5 miles. Allow 2 hours to complete this loop.

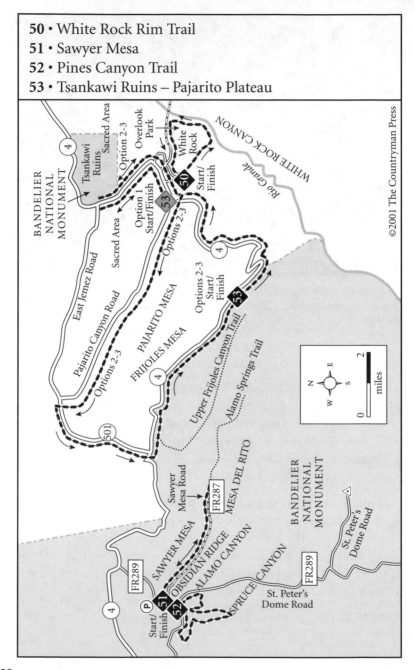

©2001 The Countryman Press

BANDELIER NATIONAL MONUMENT

Sacred Area

Tsankawi Ruins

Option 2-3

Overlook Park

White Rock

WHITE ROCK CANYON

Start/Finish

50

Option 1 Start/Finish

53

Options 2-3

Rio Grande

East Jemez Road

Sacred Area

Pajarito Canyon Road

PAJARITO MESA

Options 2-3 Start/Finish

53

FRIJOLES MESA

Options 2-3

Upper Frijoles Canyon Trail

Alamo Spring Trail

501

N E S W

0 miles 2

MESA DEL RITO

Sawyer Mesa Road

FR287

BANDELIER NATIONAL MONUMENT

St. Peter's Dome Road

FR289

SAWYER MESA

OBSIDIAN RIDGE

ALAMO CANYON

SPRUCE CANYON

FR289

St. Peter's Dome Road

Start/Finish

P 51 52

Riding surface: Singletrack and pavement.

Difficulty: Easy.

Scenery/highlights: Fun singletrack, great views, and beautiful scenery all make this a good introduction to the area's off-road riding.

Best time to ride: Spring through fall.

Special considerations: There are no facilities at or near the trailhead. Water and rest rooms can be found nearby in White Rock. Be sure to come prepared.

A good sense of direction is also helpful here as numerous trails take off in all directions, although the canyon rim provides a constant geographical reference point along the way so it is hard to get too lost. Please be careful near the rim. If you arc unstcady and nervous about the exposure don't hesitate to dismount and walk your bike.

Directions for the ride: From the trailhead, pick up the White Rock Rim Trail and begin pedaling in a southeasterly direction, following the edge of Pajarito Canyon. Stay on the main trail, ignoring the many trails taking off in all directions. In approximately 1 mile the trail hits the edge of White Rock Canyon and turns north and east. For the next mile it winds along between the rim and the neighborhoods of White Rock. For the next 0.8 mile the trail still hugs the rim but to the left is the wilder country of Overlook Park. At 2.8 miles the trail hits the pavement. Go right and ride the 0.25-mile spur out to White Rock Overlook. To continue back to the start, reverse direction and ride west on Overlook Road 0.7 mile to Meadow Lane. Go right onto Meadow Lane and follow it around 0.8 mile to Rover Boulevard. Turn left onto Rover Boulevard and head south a few hundred yards to Grand Canyon Drive. Go right on Grand Canyon Drive and ride west 0.3 mile to Sherwood Boulevard; ride south 0.2 mile to the parking area and your car.

---

51. SAWYER MESA (See map on page 288)

For mountain bikes. The dirt road out Sawyer Mesa, across Obsidian Ridge, and to the edge of Bandelier National Monument and Wilderness

FLORA

Elevations in the park range from about 6,000 feet to over 10,000 feet atop Cerro Grande. The dominant habitat type is termed high desert, supporting quaking aspen, Douglas fir, piñon pine, one-seed and Utah juniper, and dense stands of ponderosa pine. The majority of the park is covered in piñon and juniper and is accompanied by shrubs such as rabbitbrush (chamisa), sagebrush, Mormon tea (also called joint fir), and Apache plume. Cholla and prickly pear cactus grow on drier slopes at lower elevations. Along the canyon bottom near streams and springs you'll find riparian vegetation such as narrowleaf cottonwoods, box elder, thin-leaf ash, water birch, willows, currant, and horsetail reeds. Yarrow and the delicate purple blooms of harebells are also found in the wetter areas, while wildflowers such as desert four o'clock, several species of penstemon, Indian paintbrush, bee blam, scarlet gilia, globe mallow, western wallflower, and galardia commonly grow in drier areas. Evening primrose, cone flowers, false-pea lupine, mullien, New Mexico locust, and sacred datura are some of the other flowers you might expect to see.

Area is a great trip on a long, thin mesa separating Upper Frijoles and Alamo Canyons. Beginning and intermediate riders will enjoy this rolling trip with excellent views.

Starting point: Begin this ride from the start of Forest Road (FR) 287 north and west of the monument. To get there drive up and out the road from the visitor center to NM 4. Go left and drive north approximately 6 miles to the intersection with NM 501. Continue past this intersection, following NM 4 as it winds up into the Jemez Mountains, another 6.5 miles to the Dome Road, FR 289. Turn left and drive just over 2 miles to a parking area in a meadow called Graduation Flats. Park here.

Length: 5.5 miles one-way, 11 miles out-and-back. Allow 3 to 4 hours to complete this ride.

A gorgeous fall day somewhere high in the Jemez Mountains.

SARAH BENNETT ALLEY

Riding surface: Gravel and dirt roads with some rocky sections.

Difficulty: Easy to moderate. The relatively high elevations and the length of this ride may make this trip more difficult for some. You will descend almost 900 feet to the turnaround point, elevation that will have to be gained on the return trip.

Scenery/highlights: The dense ponderosa pine forests that dominate this area have been ravaged by fire in recent years. Evidence of the 1996 Dome Fire is abundant along this route, although the forest is now making an energetic comeback. Traversing Obsidian Ridge is a bit spine-tingling as it is extremely narrow—the mesa drops away into the canyons on either side. Obsidian flakes litter the ground. Views into the park and its canyons are excellent.

Best time to ride: Spring through fall. The ridges are usually free of snow by early to mid-May.

Special considerations: There are no facilities at the trailhead or anywhere along this route. Come prepared with plenty of your own water and any snacks you might want to munch on while enjoying the view.

Directions for the ride: From the parking area head east, across FR 289, to the start of FR 287, also called the Sawyer Mesa Road. Shortly after you begin pedaling down this gravel road you pass a spur road on the right that rejoins the Dome Road. In 0.5 mile you come to a gate blocking motorized vehicles from entering; go around it and continue on this rougher dirt road past several spurs on the left. The spur roads make loops out to the edge of Upper Frijoles Canyon. Approximately 2 miles from the start the ridge begins to narrow. At 2.4 miles from the start there is another old gate; go through it and begin to descend along the knife-edge of Obsidian Ridge. There are several rocky sections through here; use caution.

In just over 3 miles from the start the route emerges onto Mesa del Rito. Ignore a gated spur road on the right and continue on the main route, rolling out across the mesa, where views to the east and south get bigger. Just over 4 miles from the start you climb a low hill. Another 0.5 mile later you pass the Alamo Springs Trail on the right. After another mile of winding through stands of young ponderosa the trail ends atop a small hill. Take a minute and let your eyes sweep over the sprawling vistas that can be had from here. When you're rested head back the way you came.

---

52. PINES CANYON TRAIL (See map on page 288)

For mountain bikes. This trail, constructed over the last few years by ATV users, is a great, fast-paced singletrack that fat-tire fans will love. The trail winds around through pine forests and meadows on the top of the fingered mesas reaching into the upper drainages of Cochiti Canyon before dropping down into Pines Canyon and climbing back out. Beginning riders who might not be up for this much singletrack can explore FR 500, take in some great views, and experiment by creating some shorter loops.

Starting point: Begin this ride at the parking area at Graduation Flats. To get there drive up and out the road from the visitor center to NM 4. Go left and drive north approximately 6 miles to the intersection with NM 501. Continue past this intersection, following NM 4 as it winds up into the Jemez Mountains, 6.5 miles to the Dome Road, FR 289. Turn left and drive just over 2 miles to the parking area at Graduation Flats.

Length: 11.7-mile loop. Allow 3 hours to complete this loop.

Riding surface: Mostly singletrack with sections of graded dirt and gravel roads. A few rocky sections.

Difficulty: Moderate to difficult. Several steep climbs and technically challenging rocky spots.

Scenery/highlights: A fun trail that takes you through some of the Jemez Mountains' prettiest scenery.

Best time to ride: Spring through fall.

Special considerations: There are no facilities up here; come prepared with plenty of your own water for before, during, and after your ride.

Directions for the ride: From the parking area ride out onto FR 289, also known as the Dome Road, and go right, pedaling south. Ride a few hundred yards, looking for a trail taking off on the right side of the road immediately after passing FR 36, also on the right. Follow this trail as it heads into the woods and parallels the Dome Road. In a meadow approximately 0.5 mile from the start the trail meets an old road that splits; bear right, heading west as the trail winds through the trees across the top of the mesa. For the next mile the trail heads west, meeting a dirt road approximately 2.5 miles from the start. (An overlook awaits down this road to the left. Riding out-and-back to the end of this road will add approximately 0.5 mile to your total distance.)

Go straight across the dirt road, picking up the trail again and following it along the canyon rim. The trail goes north, following the rim of the canyon, and then turns, dropping into the top of Spruce Canyon 3.5 miles from the start. The trail switches back out of the canyon and heads south, following an old section of road before arriving at the east fork of FR 500 4.5 miles from the start. Go straight across the road, continuing on singletrack through open, grassy meadows, reaching the main fork of FR 500 a mile later. Cross over this road and turn right, heading north as you drop into Pines Canyon 6.5 miles from the start.

The trail continues heading north as it climbs up the far reaches of the canyon, emerging onto the mesa top 0.5 mile later. The trail parallels FR 500. You will pass a steep trail heading back down into the canyon just before your trail bears left and heads west around the top of the drainage, now paralleling FR 36 just to the north. The trail then drops into the canyon one more time, 8.5 miles from the start. You'll now head up the canyon, ending at a dirt road and a gravel pit. Follow this dirt road uphill for just over a mile, reaching FR 36 10.3 miles from the start. Turn right, riding this dirt road 1.3 miles to FR 289, the Dome Road. Then go left, arriving back at your car at Graduation Flats 11.7 miles from the start.

---

53. TSANKAWI RUINS–PAJARITO PLATEAU
(See map on page 288)

For road bikes. This route takes cyclists to the Tsankawi Section of Bandelier Monument where a loop trail leads to a largely unexcavated ruin sitting near the end of a long, thin finger mesa of volcanic ash. There are options for all levels of riders here; the shortest is to ride from the

A cyclist takes time off her bike to peer inside an ancient dwelling from a replica of the ladders the Puebloans once used to access their homes in the cliffs.

town of White Rock, the intermediate option is to start near the park's entrance station, and the most ambitious option is to ride a loop traversing the Pajarito Plateau using the Pajarito Road and NM 501 (West Jemez Road).

Starting point: Begin in either White Rock or just off to the side of the road near the park entrance station on top of the plateau. To get to White Rock from the visitor center simply drive up the access road and go right onto NM 4. Drive 8 miles to White Rock and park.

Length: 6 miles out-and-back from White Rock; 22 miles out-and-back from the park entrance station. The longest option is 33.2 miles, riding the spur to Tsankawi ruins and the loop. Adjust time needed for route.

Riding surface: Pavement. Much of the route is narrow with little shoulder.

Difficulty: Easy to more difficult. There is little shoulder along most of the roads described here. Experience riding with vehicle traffic will go a long way toward making this ride more enjoyable. Use caution, ride in single file, and stay well to the right.

Scenery/highlights: A steep, winding 1.5-mile hiking trail takes you past a series of caves and petroglyphs to a largely unexcavated mesa-top ruin. Tsankawi was a Pueblo IV village, consisting of the pueblo atop the mesa and the cliff dwellings that were secured into cliffs of volcanic tuff at the mesa's south end. Construction may have begun as early as 1150 but it wasn't until the 1300s that the Tsankawi community reached its peak. The layout of the pueblo—a series of room blocks surrounding a plaza with two kivas—can still be made out below the mounds of earth. Both the mesa and cliff dwellings were abandoned before Spanish contact. The San Idelfonso Pueblo Indians, whose reservation abuts the Tsankawi unit of the park, claim these ruins as their ancestral home. "Tsankawi" means "gap of the sharp, round cactus," in Tewa, the language spoken by the San Idelfonso tribe. An interpretive brochure available at the start of the trail can tell you more.

Portions of the trail leading up to the mesa are worn deep into the tuff, traversed for centuries by Indians traveling to and from their mesa-top home. Ladders like those once used by the mesa inhabitants access some of the caves and higher reaches. Please use caution on the ladders and near the edge of the mesa, which drops away precipitously in places.

Pottery shards litter the ground here; do not disturb or remove any natural or cultural object from this site! Every piece of pottery has a story to tell and removing them from where they lie is like stealing words off a page. Stiff federal penalties and fines await those caught with anything taken from park lands.

Best time to ride: Spring through fall.

Special considerations: Water and rest rooms are available just below the entrance station at Juniper Campground, but you must pay to enter the park to get there, unless you have a pass from entering the park previously. All conveniences can be found in White Rock.

The roads that loop around the mesa are all narrow and busy with vehicle traffic during commuting times. If you can, try to go when rush-hour traffic isn't an issue. Some experience sharing the road with cars is helpful here.

Bring a lock for securing your bike while you walk the trail and explore the mesa. It is also a good idea to wear or bring a sturdy pair of shoes for hiking up to the ruins.

FAUNA

In summer turkey vultures are everywhere, pinwheeling in the sky overhead as well as roosting in the cottonwoods near the visitor center. Ravens, year-round residents, also make their presence known. Wild turkeys also live here year-round and were domesticated by the ancient Puebloans who relied on them as a food source. Red-tailed hawks are commonly seen on the wing, hunting along the mesa tops or simply riding warming air currents. Steller's jays are higher up while scrub jays prefer piñon-juniper habitat. Other commonly sighted birds include northern flickers, hairy woodpeckers, western and mountain bluebirds, western and hepatic tanagers, pygmy and white-breasted nuthatches, rufous-sided towhees, black-headed grosbeaks, and a diminutive brown bird with a beautiful descending song—the canyon wren. Both rufous and broad-tailed hummingbirds frequent the area in summer, as do violet-green swallows and white-throated swifts.

Small mammals include desert cottontail rabbits, rock squirrels, and Abert's squirrel, easy to recognize because of its tufted ears and white underbelly. Over sixteen species of bats have been identified in the monument, of them the Mexican free-tail is perhaps the most common, having several large roosts in caves along the canyon walls. Raccoons are present and although there have been sightings of its relative, the ringtail cat, it is more rare. Gray fox, coyotes, bobcats, mountain lion, mule deer, elk, and black bear have all been seen from time to time in the canyons and on the mesas of Bandelier. Western coach whips and western diamondback rattlesnakes are the most common snake species. Lizard species include fence, skink, and prairie. The Jemez salamander, who lives in the highest reaches of Frijoles Canyon, is endemic to the area and is listed as an endangered species.

Directions for the ride, option #1: If you are riding from White Rock, simply head out onto NM 4 and turn right. Begin pedaling northwest, crossing onto the private property of the San Idelfonso Indian

Reservation within the first 0.5 mile. Just after the reservation boundary you pass a road on your right. Just past this road the main route, NM 4, swings around and heads northwest following the depression of Mortandad Canyon. For the next 2 miles the road crosses an area considered sacred to the San Indelfonso Pueblo tribe; please be respectful. It then climbs, passing East Jemez Road on the left just before arriving at the Tsankawi Unit and the trailhead for the ruins approximately 3 miles from where you started.

Option #2: If you are riding from near the park entrance station go right onto NM 4, descending as you pedal in a southeasterly direction. Approximately 1.5 miles from the start the route switches back, traversing the upper reaches of Ancho Canyon. After another mile the route climbs onto a finger terrace of the larger Pajarito Plateau, rolls along heading due north, and then descends and climbs, rolling through Water, Fence, and Portillo Canyons. After climbing out of Portillo Canyon the route levels and you begin passing a series of roads on your right accessing housing developments outside of White Rock. Approximately 7 miles from the start Pajarito Road is on your left; the center of White Rock is 8 miles from the start. Continue on to Tsankawi as described above.

Option #3: If you are interested in riding the long loop option, one that is a favorite of local road riders, go right onto Pajarito Road on your return trip from the ruins, about a mile past the center of White Rock. The road climbs for approximately 7 miles through Pajarito Canyon, gaining 900 feet to reach an elevation of 7,400 feet near the intersection with NM 501. When you reach NM 501, also called the West Jemez Road, turn left, heading west and then south 4 miles through stands of ponderosa pine, or what is left of them after the Cerro Grande fire, to a T intersection. Go left again, back onto NM 4, now heading southeast along the edge of Frijoles Mesa and the monument boundary. You will descend gently for the next 6.7 miles to the starting point at the monument entrance station.

CAMPING

There are two campgrounds at Bandelier. **Juniper Campground** is located on the mesa above Frijoles Canyon, has 94 sites, flush toilets, water, and can accommodate RVs. It is managed on a first-come, first-served basis and a fee is charged. **Ponderosa Campground** is located at the north end of the monument near the intersection of NM 4 and 501 and is a group campground available by reservation only.

There are numerous developed

IT'S INTERESTING TO KNOW...

Bandelier National Monument is named for Adolph Bandelier, who came to New Mexico in 1880 as an archaeologist sponsored by the Archaeological Institute of America. In one year Bandelier visited 166 ruins throughout the Southwest and Mexico, including those in Frijoles Canyon. He was brought to Frijoles Canyon by men from Cochiti Pueblo who identified the ruins there as their ancestral home. Bandelier worked to extract as much information as he could from the living, did extensive research into archival materials, and greatly advanced the discipline of Southwestern archaeology. Bandelier was fascinated with the ruins at Frijoles Canyon, so much so that he wrote a novel called *The Delight Makers,* published in 1890. Set among the canyons and dwellings of the monument, it depicted Indian life prior to Spanish contact as Bandelier imagined it. Edgar L. Hewett, an archaeologist who followed in Bandelier's footsteps, conducted several excavations in the canyon in the early 1900s, and realized the need for formal protection of the ruins. He was instrumental in having the area declared a monument in 1916 and honoring the man who loved the ruins and did so much toward understanding them.

campgrounds in the surrounding **Santa Fe National Forest,** as well as excellent possibilities for primitive camping. Stop in at the Los Alamos office of the Santa Fe National Forest for a complete list of campgrounds, availability, and regulations.

If you are looking for more campgrounds that accommodate RVs, head to Santa Fe where you'll find at least a half a dozen.

If you want a shower while in the area head to the YMCA in Los Alamos.

LODGING

Los Alamos is not a big tourist town and does not have much to choose from in the lodging department. The **Los Alamos Inn, Hilltop House,** and the **Holiday Inn Express** are all moderate to expensive, and are your best motel choices. There are also a handful of B&Bs. Try the **Orange Street Bed and Breakfast, Bud's Bed and Breakfast,** or the **Canyon Inn**.

You can also stay in White Rock, which is slightly closer to the monument. The **Bandelier Inn and Suites** has moderately priced rooms, or you can stay at the **Back Porch B&B.** Visit the White Rock information center to find out more about lodging options around the monument, or try the Los Alamos Chamber of Commerce.

There are dozens of hotels, motels, resorts, B&Bs, and even a hostel 50 miles away in Santa Fe. If you think you might want to stay there call their central reservations number: 505-983-8200 or 1-800-776-7669.

FOOD

In Los Alamos, get started at **Café Allegro** on Trinity Drive, where you can get a good cup of coffee and a fresh baked croissant. The **Hill Diner,** also on Trinity Drive, offers basic American fare but the food is fresh and the portions large. You can get a good salad at the **Central Avenue Grill,** or Szechwan Chinese at the **China Palace,** also on Central Avenue. The **Blue Window,** on Trinity Street, offers continental dining as well as Italian and Mexican dishes in a nice atmosphere and is slightly more pricey. **Café Sushi,** on Arkansas Avenue, and **Ashley's Restaurant and Pub,** on Trinity, are a two more you might want to try.

In White Rock your choices are few. **Katherine's Restaurant** offers a continental style menu, a nice atmosphere and the food is quite good, albeit slightly more expensive. There is also the **Chinshan Inn.** Both establishments are located on Longview Drive.

If you're looking for a culinary adventure you'll have to head to Santa Fe, the hub of art, culture, and cuisine in the Southwest.

LAUNDRY

Laundromats are few and far between in this neck of the woods; you'll need to go to Santa Fe.

BIKE SHOP/BIKE RENTAL

Land Of Oz Bicycles and Spin Studio, 208 DP Rd., Los Alamos; 505-661-6544

DOME Bicycle Tours Sales & Rentals, 3801 Arkansas Ave., Los Alamos; 505-661-3663

FOR FURTHER INFORMATION

Bandelier National Monument— Superintendent, HCR 1, Box 1, Suite 15, Los Alamos, NM 87544; 505-672-0343; www.nps.gov/ band/

Los Alamos Chamber of Commerce, P.O. Box 460, 109 Central Park Square (located on Central Ave. and 15th Street), Los Alamos, NM 87544; 505-662-8105; www.vla.com

Santa Fe National Forest, Los Alamos Office, 475 20th Street, Suite B, Los Alamos, NM 87544; 505-667-5120; www.fs.fed.us/r3/ sfe/

DON'T MISS

While in Los Alamos, home of the Los Alamos National Laboratories, the entity responsible for our country's nuclear capabilities, don't pass up the chance to visit the Bradbury Science Museum, named for nuclear physicist Norris Bradbury. The museum has excellent displays on the development of nuclear technologies at the labs, including World War II's Manhattan Project. Other kinds of technologies, including computer, laser, solar, and geothermal, are explored at the museum through interesting interactive exhibits, displays, and videos. Plan on taking a couple of hours to see all the fascinating displays and one or more of the films that are offered. The museum is located in downtown Los Alamos on Central Avenue and 15th Street. It keeps regular business hours and admission is free.

14

Natural "rooms" the size of concert halls, corridors that twist through the darkness descending to the depths of the cavern 750 feet below the earth's surface, and thousands of exquisite cave decorations hanging from the ceiling, growing from the cavern floor, and dripping from every surface, have made Carlsbad Caverns one of the most celebrated caves in the world. The cavern also serves a critical role for the million or more Mexican free-tail bats that migrate here each summer to roost and bear their young in a section of the cavern called Bat Cave. Every evening at dusk the bats put on a show that thrills visitors. As darkness falls the bats leave the cave for a night of hunting insects, erupting from the cave's entrance in great spiraling swarms before dispersing into the night air. The awesome beauty of the cave formations, the size of the caverns, and the fascinating dance of the bats, have all made Carlsbad Caverns one of New Mexico's most popular parks.

The story of the cave's formation reaches back over 250 million years to the Permian and Triassic periods, when the region that is now Texas and southeastern New Mexico was covered by a warm, shallow, nutrient-rich sea. Three large bays scalloped the edge of the continent and in them coalesced dense mats of algae. Other small marine creatures, including sponges, corals, and mollusks, took root in the algae and over time a massive coral reef formed. Referred to as El Capitan by geologists, the reef died as the ocean receded. Millions of years later the reef was uplifted by faulting, becoming riddled with fissures and cracks. A process of solution began as groundwater seeped in through the cracks, dissolving weak pockets in the limestone, forming the caves. With each uplift groundwater went to work, carving out a succession of caverns at each new level. The largest caves are evidence of periods when the water table remained fairly constant. Also during this time, hydrogen sulfide gas percolated toward the surface from large natural gas and oil deposits trapped beneath the ancient reef. Dissolved into the groundwater, the gas became sulfuric acid, a highly corrosive substance that no doubt played a role in the formation of these large caverns and passageways.

The fantastic decorations that ornament the cave did not begin to form until 500,000 years ago, after the cave had been created. During this period the climate of the area was much cooler and wetter. Carbon dioxide mixed with rainwater percolating down through the rock, making the water slightly acidic. As the water seeped downward it dissolved the limestone, carrying away its basic ingredient—the mineral calcite. Upon entering the cavern the water deposited its payload, a tiny calcite crystal, onto one of the many incredible formations. The result is stalactites, stone icicles that hang from the cave ceiling; stalagmites, formed when stalactites reach the cavern floor; flow stone; and massive rock draperies. More delicate formations—soda straws, cave popcorn, helictites, and lily pads, which form on the surface of ponds in the cave—are just some of the fascinating sights at Carlsbad Caverns.

Cycling in the Park

Besides the park's subterranean showpiece you'll find almost 47,000 acres of desert backcountry

CYCLING OPTIONS

There are two rides in this chapter: one for mountain bikes and one for either road or mountain bikes. Walnut Canyon Desert Drive is a scenic loop through the park's backcountry on a maintained dirt road that mountain bikers of all abilities will enjoy. An out-and-back route to Slaughter Canyon from Rattlesnake Springs can be ridden on either road or mountain bikes. This route traverses open country on a road that is paved except for the last 1.5 miles. Neither route sees much vehicle traffic.

A cyclist enjoys the solitude of the park's backcountry on Walnut Canyon Desert Drive.

and several good opportunities for exploring on two wheels, including the 12-mile Walnut Canyon Desert Drive and the road to Slaughter Canyon Cave. Along both routes you'll enjoy wide-open spaces, great views, beautiful Chihuahuan Desert scenery, and brilliant sunshine—a contrast to the cool, dark recesses of the caverns. Walnut Canyon Desert Drive is a rolling, one-way, unpaved loop. It is open to passenger cars but not recommended for campers or trailers. Sections can become washboarded but in general it does not see much traffic. The ride out to Slaughter Canyon is an easy, although somewhat lengthy, pedal for either road or mountain bikes across a gently sloping alluvial fan to the mouth of the canyon. Families can start at the picnic area at Rattlesnake Springs and ride out as far as they like before turning around.

Riding in the Chihuahuan Desert anytime fall through spring is delightful, and at this time of year you will find fewer crowds. Even in midwinter temperatures reach into the 50s and 60s, almost perfect for working up a sweat. Summer, on the other hand, can be beastly hot and biking then should be avoided. June through August the park sees the bulk of the almost 750,000 visitors that come annually, although most do not venture into the backcountry. Summer is also the time when the region receives most of its rainfall, usually in the form of intense thunderstorms. These storms pose a danger from lightning in higher areas and flash floods in washes and other low-lying areas.

54. WALNUT CANYON DESERT DRIVE
(See map on page 306)

For mountain bikes. This loop runs southwest and northeast, following Guadalupe Ridge, the ancient remnant of El Capitan Reef that forms the backbone of the park. Riders of all abilities will enjoy this nontechnical route, an excellent introduction to the Chihuahuan Desert and its creatures.

Starting point: Visitor center.

Length: 12 miles. Allow 2 to 3 hours to complete this loop.

Riding surface: Dirt road and 2 miles of pavement.

Difficulty: Easy to moderate.

Scenery/highlights: Desert scenery, views of the Guadalupe Mountains, and several historic and archaeological sites.

Best time to ride: Fall through spring. Evenings and early mornings are the best for catching a glimpse of wildlife. Birds are especially active in the morning.

Special considerations: Water and rest rooms are available at the park visitor center.

Be sure to pick up a free brochure at the visitor center before you head out. Descriptions of sights, plants, and geologic features along the way are numbered and correspond to posted numbers along the route.

Warning: The section of paved road between the end of Walnut Canyon Desert Drive and the visitor center is very narrow and has several blind curves. The park service recommends that cyclists dismount at the curves and walk off to the side of the road. In one place a rock wall comes down almost to meet the road and it may be prudent to cross the road and walk your bike along the gravel shoulder, facing oncoming traffic. If you do not want to dismount, at least make sure that

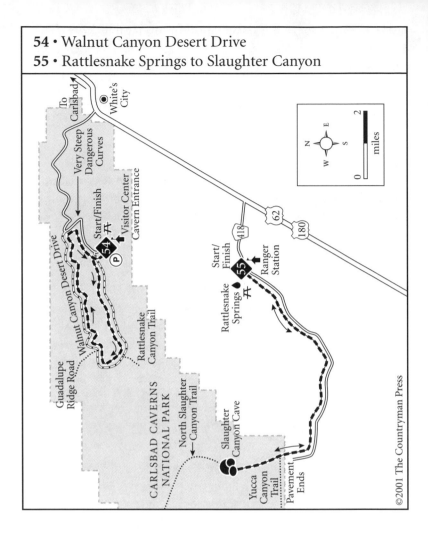

no vehicles are coming from behind before riding the curves.

Directions for the ride: From the visitor center pedal back the way you drove in approximately 0.5 mile, turning left when you come to the start of Walnut Canyon Desert Drive. As you begin pedaling west and slightly south, you'll be riding along the top of the Guadalupe Escarpment, formed by faults deep within earth. Within the first mile you'll pass a rock quarry where limestone was removed to build the amphitheater inside the cavern and create the walls that support the trail down into the caves.

Approximately 1.5 miles from the start you'll see the first of two storage tanks that collect water for the visitor center and its facilities from Rattlesnake Springs. Views that take in the sprawling Delaware Basin, to the southeast, and the spine of Guadalupe Mountains along this stretch are superb. The ancient El Capitan Reef, estimated to have risen 1,800 feet from the sea floor, forms the core of this range, while successive deposition of sediments that covered the reef are responsible for the layering in the cliffs that can be seen in the distance. The route continues its westward beat, arriving at the Rattlesnake Canyon Trailhead 4 miles from the start.

From here the road cuts across the head of Walnut Canyon and drops down to meet the canyon bottom. Just over 5.5 miles from the start you come to an intersection where a dirt road takes off to the west. This is the Guadalupe Ridge Road, called the Putnam Ridge Road on some maps. It extends all the way to the park boundary and beyond, and is currently open to mountain bikes but can be very rocky and rough. Past this junction the road continues east, winding its way down through Walnut Canyon, reaching the main paved road to the park 10 miles from the start. Go left onto this road, and get ready for a steep, 1.5-mile climb back to the top of the ridge. Be very careful around the blind curves on this hill. After passing the start of the drive it is another 0.5 mile back to the visitor center.

---

55. RATTLESNAKE SPRINGS TO SLAUGHTER CANYON (See map on page 306)

For road or mountain bikes. The 10-mile ride from Rattlesnake Springs to Slaughter Canyon is a relatively easy pedal up and across the gently sloping alluvial plain that drains the eastern side of Guadalupe Ridge. The overall length of the ride will make it more difficult for some, however, there are no time or distance requirements. While it is great to ride to the canyon itself, go as far and as long as you'd like, then turn around when you or the kids have had enough.

Starting point: Rattlesnake Springs Picnic Area. To get there drive

FLORA

Carlsbad Caverns National Park lies within the northern extremes of the Chihuahua Desert, a region loosely defined by latitude, elevation, rainfall, and the many intriguing plant and animal species that live in it. As part of the northern Chihuahuan Desert vegetation zone, the park consists mostly of shrub and grassland, but at highest elevations species common to the Rocky Mountains appear. Desert scrub is found mainly at lower elevations along Walnut Canyon Drive and the road out to Slaughter Canyon.

Indicator plants of the Chihuahua Desert include sotol, tarbush, algerita, and lechuguilla, a member of the agave family easily identified by its tightly bunched curved leaves. Like other agaves the lechuguilla sends up a tall flower spike covered with yellow blooms in early spring. Creosote bush, four-wing saltbush, banana yucca and Torrey yucca are all common to the park. There are few trees—catclaw acacia, white-thorn acacia, mescal bean, desert willow, soapberry tree, and Texas madrone, with beautiful, smooth, reddish bark found in the drainages of the Guadalupe Mountains. A grove of cottonwood trees at Rattlesnake Springs was planted by the Civilian Conservation Corps in the 1930s and is now considered a historic grove.

A variety of cacti exist in the park, including big spine and Englemann's prickly pear, claret cup, and turk's head, a kind of barrel cactus. Ocotillo, with its long, whiplike branches, tufted with red blossoms in spring, is not a cactus but a tree.

Most wildflowers in the Chihuahuan Desert wait to bloom until after cycles of rain. While rains can come in the spring, they most often arrive during the monsoon season in July and August. Prairie coneflower, skeleton-leaf golden-eye, Wright's verbena, and white-eye phlox, as well as Apache plume, desert four o'clock, desert marigold, and Mexican golden poppy are all wildflowers you are likely to see after a few weeks of rain.

FAUNA

Birds common to the park include turkey vultures and black vultures, which can be seen soaring along the ridges or pinwheeling in the sky almost anytime of year. Mockingbirds, western kingbirds, curve-billed and sage thrashers, Inca and mourning doves, woodpeckers, flickers, and roadrunners are other birds common in the park.

Skunks of several varieties, raccoons, and ringtail cats are very common as are desert cottontails and jackrabbits. Mule deer are also abundant and are hunted by a population of mountain lions who favor rocky ledges for hideouts. Bobcat and javelina, or wild boar, are also present.

As you might expect reptiles are numerous, including at least six species of rattlesnake. Rock rattlers and western diamondback rattlesnakes are the two most common and can often be seen in the evening, stretched out across the road soaking up the last bit of heat from the pavement. It is also not uncommon to see them slithering across the road when riding the Walnut Canyon Scenic Drive. Should you see a rattler out and about when riding on the back roads of the park, be sure to give it plenty of room and a few minutes to get moving and it will gladly slither out of your way.

The park's most famous bat species is the Mexican free-tail, but it shares the recesses of the cavern with at least six other species. A total of 16 different bat species have been identified at one time or another here. Be sure to pick up a bat list at the visitor center, or one of a number of books at the bookstore if you are interested in these fascinating creatures.

approximately 5 miles south on US 180/62 from White's City to County Road (CR) 418. Go right onto CR 418, and drive 2.5 miles to Rattlesnake Springs.

Length: 10 miles one-way, 20 miles total distance. Allow 3 to 4 hours to ride this out-and-back route.

Riding surface: Pavement with a short section of gravel road leading up to the parking area. The road is narrow.

Difficulty: Moderate.

Scenery/highlights: Wide-open desert spaces, with great views to Guadalupe Ridge and mountains. There are several good options for hiking from the Slaughter Canyon Cave parking lot. You can hike up the North Slaughter Canyon Trail, or head west 1.5 miles to the start of the Yucca Canyon Trail. If you are interested in exploring up any of these trails be sure to bring a lock to secure your bike while you are away.

Best time to ride: Fall through spring.

Special considerations: Water, rest rooms, and shady picnic grounds are all available at Rattlesnake Springs.

If you choose to go off exploring on any of the dirt roads that intersect CR 418 accessing Slaughter Canyon, beware of mesquite, cholla, and the other spiny plants that grow in this desert. Many of the rarely used roads are being reclaimed by thorny vegetation that can flatten your tires and leave you with nasty scratches.

Directions for the ride: From the picnic area at Rattlesnake Springs head back out onto CR 418 and go left. Follow the road as it angles south, then southwest, and then west before turning north and heading for Slaughter Canyon. As you approach the mouth of the canyon you'll notice several large limestone fins; one looks like an elephant's back. The pavement ends just before reaching the end of the road at the parking area. When you get to the parking area take a break, drink some water and have a snack, then get ready for the ride back. Reverse your route to return to Rattlesnake Springs.

CAMPING

There are no camping facilities within the park but there are several options nearby. **Carlsbad RV Park,** south of Carlsbad on the National Parks Highway, US 180/62, about a half a mile before the airport, has hook-ups, tent sites, a pool, showers, and laundry facilities. **Brantley Lake State Park,** located just north of Carlsbad, has over 50 developed sites with rest rooms, showers, swimming, and even a few short bike trails. For more information call 505-457-2384 or visit their website, www. emnrd.state.nm.us/nm parks/.

There are both developed campgrounds and primitive camping possibilities west of Carlsbad in the Guadalupe Mountains. Visit the **Lincoln National Forest** district ranger in Carlsbad for more information.

You will find two RV parks in Carlsbad: the **Queens Store & RV Park,** on the Queens Highway, and the **Windmill Shevron 28,** on US 180/62. Just outside the park entrance is the **AAA White's City RV Park.**

IT'S INTERESTING TO KNOW...

Like the other seven species of bats that roost in Carlsbad Caverns, the Mexican free-tail navigates and hunts using a natural sonar called echolocation. This sonar is also used by dolphins and whales, some of the earth's most intelligent creatures. As the bats fly they emit ultrahigh frequency sounds inaudible to humans. When the sound waves strike a flying insect, a low-hanging branch, or any other object, they are reflected back and heard by the bat. The bat then uses its superb agility and maneuverability in the air to zero in on its prey or avoid a collision.

LODGING

There is no lodging inside the park, but just outside in the touristy town of White's City you'll find the **Cavern Inn Best Western.** Further north along the highway to Carlsbad there are at least a half dozen inexpensive to moderately priced motels, as well as a **Motel 6,** a **Days Inn,** and a **Quality Inn.** In Carlsbad there are another half a dozen cheap motels, a **Holiday Inn,** and the **Best Western Motel Stevens** that has a pool, restaurant, and lounge.

FOOD

A restaurant at the visitor center offers a wide variety, including soups, salads, burgers, sandwiches, steaks, and tacos.

Just outside the park entrance in White's City is the **Velvet Garter Saloon and Restaurant**. They serve steaks, seafood, fried chicken, and burgers.

Other than the dozens of fast food joints in Carlsbad there's the **Cortez Restaurant** (508 S. Canal St.), **Ventana's Fine Dining Restaurant** (at the Holiday Inn, 601 S. Canal St.), and **Mel's Fish & Seafood** (516 S. Canal St.). **Lucy's Mexicali Restaurant** (701 S. Canal St.) seemed to be a favorite for Mexican food. There

---

⭐ DON'T MISS

Don't miss the chance to visit Living Desert State Park. Located just west of Carlsbad on a hill overlooking the Pecos River Valley, Living Desert State Park is an excellent place to familiarize yourself with the plant and animal species of the Chihuahuan Desert. This desert extends far south into Mexico but includes only part of Texas and southeastern New Mexico in the United States. Trails through the park take visitors through several different environments where plants and caged animals are identified. Besides the extensive plant collections, including one featuring cacti from around the world, you'll see eagles, hawks, rattlesnakes, lizards, bison, antelope, and even a gray wolf. The park serves as a rehabilitation center as well as a zoo. Animals that have been injured are nursed back to health, and, if possible, returned to the wild. The park is open every day. An admission fee is charged, but kids are free. Call 505-887-5516 for more information.

are at least another dozen or so restaurants in Carlsbad offering Chinese and Italian food, and chicken-fried steak served any way you like. Visit the chamber or pick up a phone book to find more dining options.

LAUNDRY

In Carlsbad:

Cavern Estates Laundry, 105 Old Cavern Highway; 505-887-0735

Lea Street Laundry, 1009 W. Lea St.; 505-885-3078

BIKE SHOP/BIKE RENTAL

Bike Doc, 304 W. Orchard Lane, Carlsbad; 505-887-7280

Carlsbad Bike & Hike Outfitter (rentals), 1028 N. Thomas St., Carlsbad; 505-885-4852

FOR FURTHER INFORMATION

Carlsbad Caverns National Park—Superintendent, 3225 National Parks Highway, Carlsbad, NM 88220; 505-785-2232; www.nps.gov/cave/

National Parks Information Center, 3225 National Parks Highway (US 180/62), Carlsbad, NM 88220; 505-885-8884

Carlsbad Chamber of Commerce, 302 S. Canal St., Carlsbad, NM 88220; 505-887-6516 or 1-800-221-1224

Lincoln National Forest, Guadalupe Ranger District, Federal Building, Room 159, Carlsbad, New Mexico 88220; 505-885-4181; www.fs.fed.us/r3/lincoln/

15

CHACO CULTURE NATIONAL HISTORICAL PARK

Cradled among several low mesas in a dry, almost treeless desert in northwestern New Mexico, are the ruins of what was once the most complex pre-Columbian society to exist north of the Mexican border. Scattered about the relatively small, 7-mile long confines of Chaco Canyon are the remains of 13 separate pueblos, stone cities that at one time served as the hub of Chacoan civilization. At least 30 outliers are connected to Chaco by a system of roads that extend in a spokelike pattern throughout the Chaco Basin and beyond. Occupied for some two hundred years, the great cities of Chaco were the social, religious, economic, and creative epicenter for an entire culture the likes of which the West had never seen before and would not see again.

Evidence indicates that Chaco Canyon was inhabited as early as A.D. 1–450, what archaeologists refer to as the Early Basketmaker Period. During this time the people living in the canyon were seminomadic hunters and gatherers, but by the Modified Basketmaker Period, (A.D. 450–750), they had begun to build pithouses, ceremonial kivas, and above-ground storage bins for the corn they were successfully cultivating on the canyon floor. During the next phase, the Developmental Pueblo Period (750–1100), Chacoan culture began to flourish. Pithouses were replaced with single-story communal dwellings made of rock, wooden

A cyclist pauses in front of another one of Chaco's Great Houses, perhaps considering the beehive of activity that once went on here.

supports, and mortar, more sophisticated canal and irrigation systems were put into use, black on white pottery typical of the Anasazi emerges, and cotton textiles began to appear, suggesting an expanding trade network with Indians to the south.

By the Classic or Great Pueblo Period (1100–1300) intricately constructed multistoried pueblos—Pueblo Bonito, Chetro Ketl, Casa Rinconada, and others—began to rise up off the canyon floor. It was also during this period that Chaco began to boom as a trade center. Seashells from the Pacific Ocean, remains of brilliantly colored macaws from southern Mexico, and copper bells from even further south suggest that Chaco was part of an extensive trade network that included the highly advanced cultures of Mesoamerica.

The architecture of Chaco's great pueblos and kivas is divided into three distinct phases. The Bonito Phase, lasting from 920 to 1120, represents the height of Chacoan ingenuity and accomplishment. Most of the pueblos in Chaco Canyon were built during this phase, including Pueblo

Bonito, or Beautiful House, the largest and most impressive of the ruins in the canyon. Pueblos built during this era were laid out in D- or E-shaped patterns and were undoubtedly designed and erected according to detailed plans.

During the Hosta Butte Phase (1040–1110), Casa Rinconada and several other small pueblos were built. The architecture of these structures is more random, with blocks of roughly finished rooms and kivas built into the room blocks. The final phase of building at Chaco, the McElmo Phase (1050–1154), is typified by structures resembling those found on Mesa Verde and in the Montezuma Valley region. These last two phases suggest an influx of outsiders into the Chacoan community, outsiders who lived simultaneously alongside the traditional Chacoans, but retained some degree of separation. By 1100 it is estimated that close to 6,000 people lived in Chaco Canyon, and that during the peak of building in the early Bonito Phase, the population of the valley was likely twice that. For reasons that are still unclear, the pueblos of Chaco Canyon, like those throughout the Four Corners region, were deserted by 1300.

The fascinating architecture, beautiful masonry and elaborate construction of the pueblos, the intriguing layout of the ceremonial kivas, and the clearly defined phases of building make the ruins at Chaco Canyon some of the most important in the American Southwest. The system of roads stretching away from Chaco Canyon, laboriously dug down to bedrock, as well as the stone stairs carved into the sandstone walls leading in and out of the canyon add to the mystery of this place and leave many unanswered questions. The Sun Dagger site on Fajada Butte, pointing to the Chacoan's use of astronomy, and their floodwater irrigation system, unequaled by their peers in the region, are testament to the creativity and intelligence of these people. Pueblo, Hopi, Zuni, and Navajo tribes all claim ties to the people who once lived here and for them this place remains sacred.

Note: Many of the ruin walls are unstable; please do not climb or lean on any part of these structures. Do not pick up, move, or take away any artifact you might find lying on the ground, including pottery shards or stone flakes. These fragments are important clues to life in the canyon, and how and where they occur is as important as the object itself. Please treat these magnificent ruins with the care and respect they deserve.

Cycling in the Park

Chaco Culture National Historical Park is slightly more difficult to get to and has fewer conveniences than other parks, but it well suited to seeing from the seat of your bike. Although the main loop that circles the valley floor accessing most of the ruin sites is paved, it is still rough. The rest of the roads in the park are dirt and the nearest paved highway is 20 to 26 miles away, making a mountain bike the best choice for getting around and seeing the ruins. Although there aren't any technical singletracks, big climbs, or thrilling descents, there is great cruising on gently undulating dirt roads winding through an open, pastel-hued desert landscape. Bikers of all ages and abilities will find enjoyable routes here. The short 3-mile ride out to Wijiji Ruin and back is a good choice for families with kids. Pedal around the main paved loop on the valley floor to see the major sites and ride a spur road out to still more ruins, or make the longer 12-mile trip out to Kin Klizhin Ruin. A free backcountry visitation permit is required for visiting Wijiji, Kin Klizhin, and sites along the spur road beyond the end of the loop. Be sure to stop in at the visitor center and obtain the proper permit before you head out on your ride.

CYCLING OPTIONS

There are three rides listed in this chapter; two are for mountain bikes, and one can be ridden on either a road or mountain bike. The ride out to Wijiji Ruin is a short, 6-mile adventure the whole family will love. The 9-mile loop around the floor of Chaco Canyon that accesses all the major sites is paved but the road is narrow and rough in spots. A spur road open to hikers and bikers but closed to vehicle traffic extends beyond the end of the loop and accesses still more ruins. There is a lot to see and riders should plan on bringing food and spending most of the day out here. The longer 24-mile out-and-back trip to Kin Klizhin Ruin, a Chacoan outlier, is a ride that will appeal to those who like wide open spaces and want more time in the saddle.

Elevations at Chaco Canyon are around 6,200 feet; the air is thin and dry. Start out slow and be sure to drink plenty of water before, during, and after you ride. The sun is strong and hot out here in summer, with temperatures averaging about 95 degrees. Winters are cold and windy with nighttime temperatures often dipping below zero. This desert receives only about 10 inches of moisture a year, most of it coming in July and August in the form of brief, sometimes violent thunderstorms. Because of the clay content of the soils the dirt becomes a sticky, gooey mess when saturated. If there have been thunderstorms in the area, you may want to wait a day or so until things dry out.

As mentioned earlier, Chaco Canyon is fairly remote and conveniences such as gas stations, hotels, restaurants, and bike shops are at least an hour and a half away. Camping at the park campground is comfortable, convenient, and a great way to enjoy these archaeological treasures and their serene desert setting. Whether you plan to stay the night or not, come prepared and well supplied. Bring extra water and clothing, a cooler full of food and drinks, and spare tubes and a few tools for making basic repairs to your bike.

---

56. WIJIJI RUIN (See map on page 319)

For mountain bikes. The ride out to Wijiji Ruin from the visitor center is an easy pedal on level terrain that beginning riders and families with children on bikes can enjoy. The dirt road portion of this ride is closed to vehicles but can be rutted and slightly rough in spots. The route heads east, up Chaco Wash between Wijiji and Chacra Mesas, gaining only slightly in elevation. Be sure to stop in at the visitor center and acquire a backcountry permit for visiting Wijiji Ruin before you go.

Starting point: Visitor center.

Length: 3 miles one-way, 6 miles out-and-back. Allow at least an hour to ride the distance and spend time at the ruin.

Riding surface: The first mile is pavement, the rest is a dirt road.

Difficulty: Easy.

Scenery/highlights: Wijiji is a Navajo term that means "greasewood," a

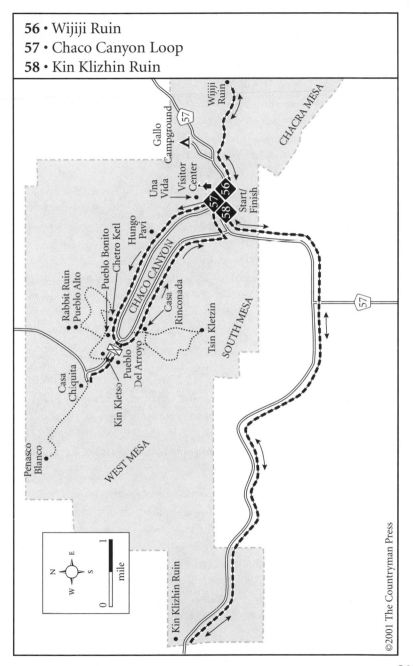

56 · Wijiji Ruin
57 · Chaco Canyon Loop
58 · Kin Klizhin Ruin

Wijiji Ruin

CHACRA MESA

Gallo Campground

57

Una Vida

Visitor Center

57 56

58

Start/Finish

Hungo Pavi

Chetro Ketl

Pueblo Bonito

CHACO CANYON

Rabbit Ruin
Pueblo Alto

Casa Rinconada

Tsin Kletzin

SOUTH MESA

57

Casa Chiquita

Kin Kletso

Pueblo Del Arroyo

Penasco Blanco

WEST MESA

N
E
S
W

0   1
mile

Kin Klizhin Ruin

shrub common to this area. Wijiji Ruin is a classic Bonito Phase pueblo built sometime between 1055 and 1083, the height of construction activity in Chaco Canyon. This village once had 92 first-floor rooms and two great kivas.

The road to the ruin follows the old Sargeant Ranch Road, built by the wealthy sheepman Edward Sargeant. Sargeant lived in Chama but used the canyon for grazing large herds of sheep during the winter months. For at least two hundred years prior to that both Puebloans and Navajos migrated through this canyon herding their sheep, farming, and building "pueblitos," small rock shelters for protection from the weather and other native groups wanting to steal their livestock. The arrival of Sargeant and his sheep caused unrest among the Indians and conflict that eventually boiled over into violence, livestock rustling, and murder.

The ruins of Wijiji exist in the former homeland of the Navajo people and figure prominently in their legends of how they came to be in this land. Oral traditions tell of a Pueblo woman living here long ago who taught the Navajo people how to weave. Today Navajo rugs are prized for their exquisite craftsmanship and collectors pay thousands of dollars to acquire them.

Best time to ride: Spring through fall.

Special considerations: Rest rooms and water are available at the visitor center. Avoid riding out this way if the ground is saturated and muddy. Although this park is remote and crime is not usually a problem, bringing a lock to secure your bike while you are away seeing the ruins is a good insurance policy.

Directions for the ride: From the visitor center ride out onto the paved road and go left. Follow this paved road as it heads east and then swings north toward the campground. One mile from the start the turnoff for Gallo Campground will be on your left. Continue past that turnoff another 100 yards to a dirt road on the right, the old Sargeant Ranch Road. Go right onto this road and follow it for just under 2 miles to Wijiji Ruins. Leave your bike in the rack and take a short walk over to the ruins. Reverse your route on the way back.

57. CHACO CANYON LOOP (See map on page 319)

For road or mountain bikes. The main scenic drive at Chaco Canyon is a narrow, paved loop that heads west across the canyon floor. This one-way loop route is open to bicycles and vehicle traffic in a counterclockwise direction only. At the far end of the loop a spur road extends another 1.5 miles west, accessing Pueblo Del Arroyo, Kin Kletso, and Casa Chiquita. This spur road is actually part of the old road to Chaco Canyon, and is now open to bikers and hikers but closed to vehicles. Hiking trails accessing still more ruins atop the mesas are accessed from this spur road. A permit is required to travel this road and visit the backcountry sites. Pick one up at the visitor center for free.

Starting point: Visitor center.

Length: The loop is 9 miles along. The spur road out to Casa Chiquita is 1.5 miles. If the loop and spur are ridden a total distance of 12 miles is possible. Plan on spending at least a half a day to ride the distance and spend time walking among the ruins, more if you plan to hike to any of the sites on top of the mesas.

Riding surface: Pavement; rough in spots.

Difficulty: Easy to moderate. Overall distance will make this route more difficult for some.

Scenery/highlights: Eight major ruin sites, including Pueblo Bonito, can be visited along the loop and spur, and three others can be accessed by short hiking trails. There is much to see and comprehend in this otherwise unremarkable desert canyon. Here an ancient people blossomed, built beautifully constructed stone villages housing hundreds, conducted elaborate ceremonies, honored their gods, laughed with friends, played with their children, and then abruptly, and somewhat mysteriously, departed. The canyon floor, now traversed by a paved roadway, was once covered by corn, beans, and squash, and crisscrossed with elaborate irrigation channels and canals. Scholars have spent entire careers studying these ruins, unmatched in their sophistication and artistry by any other ancient culture known to have existed in North America outside of Mexico.

FLORA

The environment of the entire Chaco River Basin can be termed high desert, receiving only a scant 10 inches of rain per year. Piñon and juniper are the only trees that thrive in these conditions. Shrubs such as big sagebrush, greasewood, four-wing saltbush, cliffrose, and rabbitbrush, or chamisa, as it is called in New Mexico, are the most common types of vegetation. Joint fir, also called Mormon tea, narrowleaf yucca, and Apache plume are also quite common in and around Chaco Canyon. Bunchgrasses, including Indian rice grass, which had an important place in the diet of the Chacoan Anasazi, are also present. In spring you might see the beautiful dark red blooms of claret cup cactus, the only cactus in the Chaco area. Other flowers such as sky rocket, or scarlet gilia, larkspur, globe mallow, beeplant, and blazing star appear in the spring and then sometimes after summer rains.

Before heading out for your ride, spend some time at the visitor center seeing the exhibits and collecting any information that will make your trip among these ancient wonders more rewarding. You will find brochures stored in information boxes at each ruin.

Best time to ride: Spring through fall.

Special considerations: Water and rest rooms are available at the visitor center. If you are interested in hiking to any of the mesa-top ruins be sure to bring a lock to secure your bike while you are away.

Directions for the ride: From the visitor center ride out onto the paved road and go right, staying right as you pass the intersection with County Road (CR) 57. As you begin you have a good view of Una Vida Ruin, accessed from the visitor center by a short trail. Continuing west along the loop another 1.8 miles you come to Hungo Pavi. Beyond Hungo Pavi the road continues through Chaco Canyon along the north wall, arriving at Chetro Ketl in 2 miles. Chetro Ketl is a major site in the canyon and is well worth stopping for. There is a gate on the right-hand side of the road

The angled sunlight of early morning and evening is best for photographing Chaco Canyon's spectacular ruins.

approximately 0.4 mile beyond Chetro Ketl. It marks the beginning of the spur road and the halfway point in the loop. Pueblo Bonito, near the start of the spur road, is the biggest and most important ruin in the canyon. Take some time here before heading out the spur road or continuing around on the loop.

Continuing west on the spur road from the gate it is approximately 0.3 mile to Pueblo Del Arroyo, on the left-hand side of the road.

At this parking area you will also find the trailhead for the 5.4-mile Pueblo Alto Trail. This trail takes you to Pueblo Alto and Rabbit Ruin on the mesa top north of the canyon, providing spectacular overlooks of Pueblo Bonito and Chetro Ketl. One mile from the gate, and 5.5 miles from the start you will come to Kin Kletso Ruin on the right. It is another 0.5 mile from there to the Casa Chiquita Ruin and the trailhead for Penasco Blanco Ruin, the furthest west of the pueblos in the canyon.

When you are ready to continue, return to the start of the spur road at the gate and go right. In a short distance you come to Casa Rinconada and the start of the trail taking you up to South Mesa and Tsin Kletzin Ruin. Casa Rinconada is your last stop, beyond here it is a straightforward 4-mile cruise along the canyon's south side to the intersection with CR 57. Go left at this intersection and ride 0.5 mile to return to the visitor center.

---

5 8 .   KIN   KLIZHIN   RUIN (See map on page 319)

For mountain bikes. The ride out to Kin Klizhin Ruin is a longer pedal, perhaps better suited to those with a solid level of physical fitness accustomed to spending a few hours at a time in the saddle. This route has no technical challenges, rolling easily out across a series of broad valleys before arriving at this former outlier settlement. The route follows a series of roads that are used infrequently by vehicles.

Starting point: Visitor center.

Length: 12 miles one-way; 24 miles out-and-back. Allow 3 to 4 hours to ride the distance and spend time at the ruin.

Riding surface: 6 miles of pavement, 18 miles of irregularly maintained dirt road. Can be rough and rutted after rain or snow.

Difficulty: Moderate.

Scenery/highlights: Kin Klizhin, Navajo for Black House, is identified as a Chacoan outlier because it is tied both visually and physically to the canyon. It has both a prehistoric road feature and is perched on a hill enabling a line of sight to Tsin Kletsin. Tsin Kletsin sits atop South Mesa and, in turn, has visual links to the pueblos in the canyon. Kin Klizhin is one of the great houses built during the Bonito Phase and is distinguished by its tower kiva, massive construction, and banded masonry. At one time fields of corn, beans, and squash likely stretched across surrounding flats, fed by water that was stored behind dams like the one you can see here.

Best time to ride: Spring through fall.

Special considerations: Water and rest rooms are available at the visitor center. This is a longer ride so be sure to bring plenty of water and a few snacks.

Directions for the ride: From the visitor center ride out of the park, heading south on CR 57. Follow this paved route approximately 3 miles

FAUNA

Ravens, among the most curious of birds, scrub and piñon jays, and Gambel quail are among the year-round residents at the park. Wild turkeys, domesticated and kept in pens by the people of Chaco, also live in the area year-round. In summer turkey vultures can often be seen pinwheeling in the sky overhead, when mourning doves, mockingbirds, western meadowlarks, horned larks, brown-headed towhees, and sage, black-throated, and song sparrows are present. White-throated swifts and barn, cliff, and violet-green swallows, the "top guns" of the bird world, also come to the canyons in summer where they hunt for insects caught in the updrafts along canyon walls. Screech owls can sometimes be heard at the campground at night, and the narrow-winged nighthawk is often seen zigzagging through the air at dusk. Great horned owls have been spotted in the park and golden eagles have been known to nest in alcoves on the canyon walls.

Desert cottontails, jackrabbits, kangaroo rats, and a variety of field and pocket mice inhabit the canyon floor and mesa tops. Mule deer are quite common, as are coyotes. Less common are bobcats and mountain lions. Black bear have been known to visit on occasion.

Whiptail lizards and the sometimes colorful collared lizard are some of the most visible wildlife in the park. Less visible, but critters to watch out for, are the prairie rattlesnakes that like to warm themselves on roads and trails in the mornings. Bullsnakes and whipsnakes are more commonly seen than rattlers.

to where it bends around, making an almost 90-degree turn. Go right onto a dirt road leaving from the elbow of this turn and head west. Continue on this road for 6 miles as it traverses the private property of the Navajo tribe. Please be respectful and do not ride off the main road. As you near the ruin you will cross back into the park, ride across Kin Klizhin Wash, pass a road on your left, and take the next left signed for Kin Klizhin. Reverse your route to return to the visitor center.

CAMPING

Gallo Campground, the only campground in the park, is located 1 mile east of the visitor center. It has 48 sites offered on a first-come, first-served basis. The campground is open all year and can fill up by early afternoon from April through October. Each campsite has a picnic table and a fire grate; you must supply your own wood or charcoal for cooking. Collecting firewood is prohibited. Rest rooms and non-potable water are available. Drinking water is available at the visitor center parking area. Trailers over 30 feet can not be accommodated. Group campsites for more than ten people are also available. To make a reservation for a group site call 505-786-7014.

Private campgrounds with both RV and tent sites as well as shower and laundry facilities can be found in the towns of Gallup or Grants to the south, or in Farmington or Bloomfield to the north.

LODGING

There is no lodging in the park. The nearest lodging is a B&B located 21 miles north in the town of Nageezi. You'll find a good selection of inexpensive motels to choose from in Gallup or Grants to the south, and in Farmington to the north. All three host a number of chain hotels as well. For more information on lodging in Gallup and Grants, see the El Malpais/El Morro National Monuments lodging, page 348.)

FOOD

No food of any kind is available at the park. The nearest supermarkets or restaurants can be found in Farmington, Gallup, or Grants. A convenience store near Nageezi sells a few basic items, as does **Seven Lakes Trading Post,** located 20 miles to the south. Go prepared when you head out to Chaco Canyon with enough supplies for a few meals plus drinks and snacks.

IT'S INTERESTING TO KNOW...

Archaeologists have determined that there was little new construction at Chaco Canyon after 1120. The McElmo people were the last to build or add to existing pueblos in the mid-1100s, but it is clear that by that point, the Chaco Phenomenon had ended. Mesa Verdean Anasazi inhabited the dwellings for a time after that, but by 1300 all Anasazi had disappeared.

Where did they go? What happened at Chaco? There is much speculation and debate and several intriguing theories. One of the most widely accepted is that a prolonged drought lasting from 1130 to about 1190 meant crop failures and a shortage of food. The social and political cohesion needed to weather the drought may have collapsed under such stress. Families may have decided that enough was enough, packed their belongings and left.

Another theory suggests that Athabascan-speaking peoples (Navajo and Apache) moving into the area may have driven the Anasazi out. While there is evidence of defensive additions when some of the structures were remodeled, without the horse (introduced in the 1500s by the Spanish), Athabascans would have found it difficult to successfully raid such well-fortified structures.

The final, perhaps most convincing theory is that the Chacoans simply exhausted their resources. It is estimated that at least 215,000 logs were carried into Chaco Canyon for the pueblos' construction. The road system was probably built to facilitate their transport. Wood was also constantly needed as a source of fuel. Collecting firewood likely denuded the landscape, increasing erosion and the loss of arable land. The limited confines of the valley floor, farmed for perhaps a thousand years, probably became exhausted of the nutrients needed to maintain crop production.

Most likely the Chacoans filtered away in families and small groups over time, moving southeast into the Rio Grande Valley, south into Zuni country, and west to the Hopi Mesas. Most of today's Pueblo, Hopi, and Zuni tribes have clans that trace their ancestry to Chaco.

DON'T MISS

Be sure to spend some time at Pueblo Bonito, the largest and most thoroughly excavated ruin credited to the Anasazi. Regarded by archaeologists as an extraordinary architectural achievement for a people who did not have use of the wheel, metal tools, or beasts of burden, it is one of the largest ancient ruins in America. The long outer walls were undoubtedly a community effort, while the construction of interior rooms and kivas were likely the responsibility of family groups.

It is estimated that Pueblo Bonito could have housed as many as a thousand people in six hundred rooms but the configuration and size of the rooms suggest that this pueblo had special ceremonial, social, and economic roles as well. In addition to the more than 30 small clan or family kivas, there are two great kivas, forty to fifty feet in diameter. A third great kiva may have existed on upper levels that collapsed prior to excavation. Pueblo Bonito was built in four stages, beginning around A.D. 920. This early structure was built on the site of a pithouse village that had been occupied for a hundred years. Each phase of construction can be identified by masonry styles and techniques, each one more elaborate than the next.

Lieutenant James H. Simpson of the U.S. Army was the first of record to visit and describe the ruin in 1849. Richard Wetherill was the first to excavate the ruin but was shot and killed by a Navajo shortly after he began. The Hyde Exploration Expedition spent four years excavating the ruin, beginning in 1896. They removed countless pots and jars as well as a huge number of turquoise beads, the Chacoans' primary trade item. Most of these artifacts were then shipped to the East Coast and sold to private collectors and museums. Many subsequent excavations have been carried out at the pueblo, the last major one conducted by the University of New Mexico and the park service in the 1970s.

LAUNDRY

The nearest laundromats or laundry services are found in Farmington, Gallup, or Grants.

BIKE SHOP/BIKE RENTAL

Cottonwood Cycles, 3030 E. Main St., Farmington; 505-326-0429

Havens Bikes and Boards, 2017 E. Main St., Farmington; 505-327-1727

FOR FURTHER INFORMATION

Chaco Culture National Historical Park— Superintendent, P.O. Box 220, Nageezi, NM 87037; 505-786-7014; www.nps.gov/chcu/

Farmington Convention and Visitors Bureau, 3041 E. Main St., Farmington, New Mexico 87401; 505-326-7602 or 1-800-448-1240

Grants/Cibola Chamber of Commerce, 100 N. Iron Ave., Grants, NM 87020; 505-287-4802 or 1-800-748-2142

Gallup Convention and Visitors Bureau, 701 Montoya St., P.O. Box 600, Gallup, NM 87305; 505-863-3841 or 1-800-242-4282

16

El Malpais National Monument

El Malpais ("ell-mal-pie-EES"), or the Bad Country, was the name given to this rough, lava-strewn region by early Spanish explorers as they passed through more than four hundred years ago. Showcased within the boundaries of El Malpais National Monument and the adjacent El Malpais National Conservation Area are a wonderland of volcanic formations that include cinder cones, spatter cones, ice caves, lava tubes, and a chain of at least thirty craters stretching north and south for 20 miles through a high-desert landscape. Covering an area roughly 40 miles long and 5 to 15 miles wide, El Malpais is regarded by geologists as one of the most important volcanic fields in the United States.

Within the 114,000-acre monument and the 262,600 acres of surrounding conservation area lands managed by the Bureau of Land Management there is evidence of at least five major eruptions and close to 75 vents that periodically spewed gas and lava. The oldest lava flow was produced by El Calderon Volcano and is estimated to be close to two hundred thousand years old, although much older flows and vents probably lie below. The youngest flow was produced by McCarty's Crater between two and three thousand years ago. Faults penetrating deep into the earth, fanning away from the southeastern boundary of the Colorado

Plateau and running along the Zuni Uplift to the west and the Lucero Uplift to the east provided escape routes for pressurized magma at the earth's core to travel upward and radically change this landscape.

There are at least four different kinds of volcanoes in the El Malpais volcanic field: cinder cones, basalt cones, shield volcanoes and composite, or stratovolcanoes. Cinder cones, formed by frothlike cinders that build up around a vent, are the most common. Although cinder cones like Cerro Bandera can grow to be several hundred feet high, the spongy, poorly consolidated cinders that give it shape allowed the lava to seep out around its base or from its side, rather than being forced up in the middle. Basalt cones are smaller than cinder cones and produce lava that is less viscous and so spreads easily. Lava Crater is an example of a basalt cone. Shield volcanoes, as their name suggests, are low and mounded, and produce gentle but more numerous eruptions. Cerro Rendija, Cerro Hoya, and McCarty's Crater are all shield volcanoes. Composite, or stratovolcanoes are the largest and potentially the most destructive. They add layer upon layer over time, eventually exploding in great clouds of gases, ash, lava, and broken rock. The infamous Mount St. Helens is a composite volcano, as is Mount Taylor (11,301 feet) rising just to the north, a slumbering giant who may some day awake in a fury of fire.

There are many other natural and cultural wonders in and around El Malpais, among them the La Ventana Cliffs, a beautiful series of towering sandstone walls that flank El Malpais to the east along NM 117. Views from Sandstone Bluffs Overlook, perched atop these cliffs, across the lava flows and craters in the distance, are spectacular. There is access to good hiking trails at the overlook, one taking you to three natural arches. La Ventana Arch, tucked into these cliffs just south of the overlook, is the second largest arch in New Mexico, rising over 125 feet and spanning 165 feet. Several historic homesteads and Anasazi ruins nearby round out the list of things to see and do while visiting El Malpais.

El Morro National Monument

Etched into the beautiful frosted white sandstone cliffs dubbed El Morro, Spanish for the Bluff, not far from the sprawling lava fields of El Malpais, is a fascinating record of travelers who passed through this country. These sandstone walls served for centuries as a sort of graffiti travel log, unrivaled in kind or importance to the history of the American West.

Built atop the bluff at El Morro, this pueblo, called A'ts'ina, and another one nearby, are identified by the Zuni Indians as their ancestral home.

Also translated as the Headland, the shining cliffs of El Morro undoubtedly leapt out of the landscape, signaling water and rest to the parched and travel-weary who had come several days across rugged, dry terrain to reach here. A spring at the base of the cliffs still forms a pool, which first drew archaic hunters thousands of years ago. The Anasazi, Spanish conquistadors, American soldiers, and eventually American migrants, all followed, leaving their mark on the cliffs of El Morro.

The first to carve their thoughts into the cliffs were the Anasazi, who came and settled here during a time when they were migrating off the Colorado Plateau and heading south and east toward the Little Colorado and upper Rio Grande Valleys. They built two pueblos atop the cliffs. One of them, called A'ts'ina by the local Zunis, was a large, multistoried dwelling of 850 rooms that may have housed as many as fifteen hundred people by the early 1300s. Along the cliff walls they pecked images of birds, humanoid figures, a herd of sheep, and myriad other forms and symbols that archaeologists have yet to decipher.

Although he did not leave his mark on the cliffs, records indicate that on March 11, 1583, Antonio de Espejo, a conquistador sent to look for two Franciscan fathers who had been two years missionizing in the area, rested at El Estanque del Penol, "the pool at the great rock." Espejo thus established El Morro as a favorite Spanish camp. In 1598, Don Juan de Onate became the first governor of New Mexico and officially began efforts to colonize and expand the Spanish frontier. Returning from one of his last, disappointing efforts to find riches in the New World, he left the first known European inscription at the rock which reads: "Passed by here, the Adelentado Don Juan de Onate from the discovery of the Sea of the South, the 16th of April, 1605." Seeking to establish some kind of success, Onate claimed discovery of the Gulf of California fifteen years before the pilgrims landed at Plymouth Rock. Numerous other Spanish inscriptions were left in subsequent years by priests, governors, and soldiers on their way to resupply at Zuni and other pueblos. Simple records of passage as well as tales of battle, revenge, and murder indicate the hazards of life on the Spanish frontier.

Later, during the Mexican-American War of 1846–1848, American soldiers marked their passage by El Morro. One of them, Lt. J.II. Simpson, had artist Richard Kern copy the inscriptions in 1849. This record remains one of the most complete, as vandalism in recent decades totally erased some of the inscriptions and made others illegible. Emigrants on their way to California, and later railroad surveyors, also took time to chisel evidence of their visit to the rock before rails were finally laid across Campbell's Pass 25 miles to the north and the route that took travelers by El Morro was abandoned.

Cycling in the Parks

There are many excellent riding opportunities for both fat- and skinny-tire fans in and around these parks. The four rides offered here will give you just a taste of what might fill a week of two-wheel adventuring in this beautiful and enchanting corner of New Mexico. Although the limited acreage and nature of the resources at El Morro do not provide for potential biking routes, the monument's proximity to El Malpais makes it an excellent destination for more fit and experienced road riders starting from the El Malpais Information Center on NM 53. Mountain bikers might want to spend all day on the loop out around Cerro Rendija, taking time to explore the Big Tubes and clamber around on several old lava flows. Those who don't want to tackle the distance may choose to shorten the route by driving to a different starting point. The route out around Cerritos de Jaspe is not quite as long but might be more than little mountain bikers are up for. An option here allows families to park at that picnic area and ride a short distance out to El Calderon Crater, explore Junction Cave, the Double Sinks, and inside the Bat Cave. NM 117, which runs north to south along the eastern edge of the Malpais, is an incredibly scenic, lightly traveled route that is sure to delight those who prefer the pavement.

There are many more rides, too many to be included here, for both road and mountain bikers. The Brazo Canyon area south and east of the Cebolla Wilderness and the extensive road system running through the Chain of Craters region just west of the monument, both inside the El Malpais National Conservation Area, hold numerous possibilities for exploring by mountain bike. Mountain bikers should also look into riding possibilities in the Cibola National Forest just north of these monuments and in the Mount Taylor area, north of I-40.

Elevations around El Malpais and El Morro range between 6,500 and 8,300 feet. This is high-desert country where the air is thin and dry and the sun is strong. Those coming from lower altitudes may experience shortness of breath and fatigue after exerting themselves. Start out slow, drink plenty of water, and allow your body to acclimate to this environment.

Weather in northwestern New Mexico is notoriously unpredictable so it's a good idea to come prepared for anything. Summers are generally warm, with temperatures often reaching 90 degrees and above; nights are cool. Winter snowstorms are common and nighttime temperatures frequently dip below zero. Violent summer thunderstorms are a regular occurrence and pose a significant hazard to hikers and bikers in open, exposed areas. These storms can also turn dirt roads into a slimey goo that will stick to your tires and make forward progress all but impossible. Listen to local forecasts and stay off back roads if they are saturated.

If you are interested in scrambling around in any of the caves wear good, sturdy shoes and gloves, and bring a flashlight. Most serious cavers bring at least two sources of light. One other note of caution: do not be tempted to ride off established roadways in this area; the sharp and broken lava will quickly shred your tires.

![star icon]

CYCLING OPTIONS

There are four rides in this chapter; two for mountain bikes and two for road bikes. The 8-mile loop around Cerro Rendija is an easy trip around an extinct shield volcano that takes you to several other interesting volcanic formations in the Big Tubes Area. An option here takes advanced riders out a spur to Cerro Encierro and a view of the Hole in the Wall, a *kipuka* or area of ground surrounded but not covered by lava. The loop in the El Calderon area around Cerritos de Jaspe is another great ride through the lunar landscape created by this region's volcanic activity. It is slightly longer but there are options for a shorter ride as well. The road ride along NM 117 is an incredibly scenic tour along a north-south route that is flanked by the lava flows of El Malpais to the west and towering, honey-colored sandstone cliffs to the east. There is much to see and do along this route. The pedal to El Morro from the El Malpais Information Center is another excellent road ride that is longer and will be more challenging for most.

There are many good routes and areas for riding not discussed here, especially for mountain bikers. Talk to the El Malpais BLM rangers about riding in the Brazos Canyon area or out along the Chain of Craters west of the monument, or contact the Cibola National Forest's Mount Taylor Ranger District about riding in the Zuni Mountains or around Mount Taylor.

---

59. CERRO RENDIJA LOOP (See map on page 337)

For mountain bikes. The loop around Cerro Rendija is an excellent introduction to the gorgeous backcountry and many volcanic wonders of this region. Along the way you can visit Big Skylight Cave, see a collapsed lava tube called the Catepillar Collapsc, and marvel at a lava wall over a hundred feet high. It is a good idea to wear or bring sturdy hiking shoes and a flashlight. Beginning riders will have few problems with the 8-mile dirt road around Cerro Rendija. More advanced riders should consider an option out across a lava flow to Cerro Encierro at the edge of West Malpais Wilderness and to a *kipuka*, an island of ground encircled by lava flows.

Starting point: Begin this ride at the intersection of County Road (CR) 42 and the East Rendija or Big Tubes Road. To get there drive approximately 3.3 miles west of the El Malpais Information Center on NM 53 to CR 42. Turn left onto this dirt road and drive 4.5 miles to the intersection of CR 42 and the East Rendija or Big Tubes Road. Park off to the side of the road.

Note: CR 42 is a dirt road that can be rough with rocks and deep potholes, especially after winter snows and summer rains. A high-clearance, four-wheel-drive vehicle is best for accessing this trailhead. If you are in a low-slung passenger car you might consider parking at the start of CR 42 and riding from there.

Length: 8 miles. If you ride from the start of CR 42 and do the loop your total distance will be 17 miles. It is approximately 6 miles out Cerro Encierro from the Big Tubes parking area, which will add 12 miles to your total distance. Allow at least a half a day to ride the distance and spend time exploring the volcanic wonders along the way.

Riding surface: Dirt road and doubletracks. Roads out here can be rough but are generally easier to negotiate on a bike than in a car. Sections of the road out to Cerro Encierro cross lava flows and are quite rough.

Difficulty: Moderate.

Scenery/highlights: Cerro Rendija, Spanish for Crevice Hill, is a shield volcano created by a series of explosions that excavated a line of craters along its crest, some crowned by red cinders with a high iron content. A fairly easy 2.2-mile trail leads to the top from the Big Tubes parking area. On the way out to the Big Tubes you pass a lava wall that is over 100 feet tall in places, the highest in the Malpais. Plants and trees, such as aspens, appear in places they are not normally found because they are able to capitalize on small pockets of moisture that collect in the lava along the wall.

The 1-mile hike out to Big Skylight Cave, Four Windows Cave, and the Caterpillar Collapse is very rough, taking you over jumbled lava flows along a faint trail marked by rock cairns. Good shoes are a must for mak-

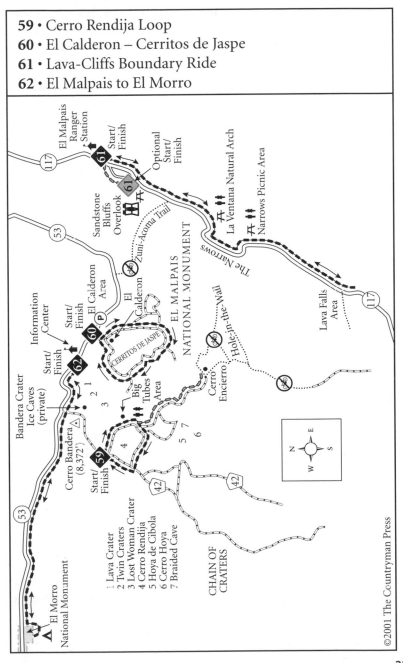

59 · Cerro Rendija Loop
60 · El Calderon – Cerritos de Jaspe
61 · Lava-Cliffs Boundary Ride
62 · El Malpais to El Morro

El Malpais
Ranger Station

117

61 Start/
Finish

Optional
Start/
Finish

6

La Ventana Natural Arch

Narrows Picnic Area

Sandstone
Bluffs
Overlook

Zuni-Acoma Trail

53

El Calderon
Area

EL MALPAIS

The Narrows

NATIONAL MONUMENT

Information
Center

Start/
Finish

60 P

El
Calderon

117

Start/
Finish

62

CERRITOS DE JASPE

Lava Falls
Area

Bandera Crater
Ice Caves
(private)

Cerro
Encierro

Hole-in-the-Wall

Big
Tubes
Area

Cerro Bandera
(8,372')

2 1

3

5 7

6

N

E

Start/
Finish

59

S

53

4

W

42

42

El Morro
National Monument

1 Lava Crater
2 Twin Craters
3 Lost Woman Crater
4 Cerro Rendija
5 Hoya de Cibola
6 Cerro Hoya
7 Braided Cave

CHAIN OF
CRATERS

© 2001 The Countryman Press

ing the trip out to these tubes, but the trip is well worthwhile. Beyond enormous, moss-covered cave openings light pours in where rock has fallen from the ceilings and created skylights. A long, sinuous section of collapsed tube called the Caterpillar Collapse is a canyon filled with a jumble of boulders.

Best time to ride: Spring through fall.

Special considerations: Rest rooms and water are available at the information center on NM 53. Bring plenty of your own water and some snacks to allow you the time to do some exploring out here. It is also a good idea to bring a flashlight for entering the caves and a lock to secure your bike while you are away.

Travel on these back roads should be avoided after heavy rains. Also, there are many roads heading in all directions; it is a good idea to bring supplementary topographic maps. It is also difficult to find your way out to the caves. A detailed handout available at the information center can help you discover these interesting volcanic features.

Directions for the ride: From the intersection of CR 42 and the East Rendija Road, go left, riding south and east toward the Big Tubes Area. The road rolls along the edge of the steeper north side of Cerro Rendija Volcano. A lava field stretches away to your left. Approximately 2 miles from the start you pass the highest part of the Lava Wall. Another 0.7 mile past that is the parking area and trailhead for the Big Tubes. When you are done hiking and exploring, continue heading south on East Rendija Road. The route climbs and descends over a low saddle, and then swings around and heads west, passing several roads on the left. About 2 miles from the tubes you'll pass an old car by the side of the road as you cruise along the southern flank of the volcano. The road then rejoins CR 42 almost 6 miles from the start. Turn right on to CR 42 and ride 2 miles back to your car at the intersection with the East Rendija Road.

Option: If you are up for the 5.7-mile side trip (11.4 miles out and back) to Cerro Encierro, continue heading south on East Rendija Road from the Big Tubes Area, around the eastern side of Cerro Rendija. Approximately 0.5 mile past the Big Tubes, just past the easternmost point in the loop around the volcano, there is a road on the left. Take this road and follow it as it heads south and then east tracing the edge of a lava flow. You will come to a junction 1.8 miles from the East Rendija Road. To the right a road to Braided Cave, Hoya de Cibola Crater, and Cerro Hoya will eventually loop back around and rejoin the East Rendija Road.

Stay left here to continue on to Cerro Encierro. The route crosses open piñon and juniper country mixed with stands of ponderosa for another 1.2 miles before hitting an old lava flow. It is another 2.7 bone-jarring miles across the lava to the end of the road at Cerro Encierro and the trail to the top of the volcano. Fantastic views of the *kipuka*, land surrounded by lava called the Hole in the Wall, can be had from here. Reverse your route to return to the East Rendija Road, and turn left to complete a circuit of the volcano. Go right when you reach CR 42 and return to your car.

---

60. EL CALDERON–CERRITOS DE JASPE LOOP
(See map on page 337)

For mountain bikes. The El Calderon area and circuit of Cerritos de Jaspe, the Little Mountains of Jasper, have something for everyone and several fascinating volcanic wonders. Little riders and their folks can pedal the 1-mile road out to El Calderon and spend some time exploring Junction Cave and the Double Sinks. Intermediate riders will enjoy the route that heads south and east from the junction cave, looping around Cerritos de Jaspe.

Starting point: El Calderon Picnic Area and trailhead. To get there from the El Malpais Information Center drive east on NM 53 approximately 2.5 miles. Turn right onto a dirt road signed for the El Calderon Area and drive 0.3 mile to the picnic area.

Length: 11 miles round-trip. A shorter option out to El Calderon crater and back is a total of 2 miles. Allow 3 hours to do the loop.

Riding surface: Dirt road that has mostly deteriorated to a doubletrack. Pretty rocky in spots.

Difficulty: Moderate. The shorter option is easy.

Scenery/highlights: There is much to see, especially if you have the time to get off your bike and walk around. Junction Cave is the first point of interest, located just beyond the parking lot. It extends for 3,000 feet just

FLORA

The region surrounding El Malpais and El Morro is high desert, receiving only 10 inches of rain per year. Piñon pine, one-seed and Utah juniper are common, as is ponderosa pine. Rocky Mountain Douglas fir and alligator juniper also occur here with some frequency. Unique growing conditions are created by the lava: air and water are trapped microclimates are created that support vegetation that would not normally grow here. Stands of aspens growing at the perimeter of the flows in several places are evidence of this effect. An astounding variety of mosses and lichens also take advantage of these microclimates. Volcanic soils seem to create conditions that favor tree longevity. One of the oldest known living Douglas firs grows northeast of Cerro Rendija. Gambel oak and mountain mahogany are other trees occurring around the monument.

A healthy variety of shrubs and grasses grow in this area. In the drier areas greasewood, banana yucca, four-wing saltbush, Apache plume, and bear grass are more common. In the more wooded areas you can expect to see wax currant, New Mexico privet, skunkbush sumac, ninebark, gooseberry, and raspberry. Rabbitbrush, or chamisa, as it is called in New Mexico, becomes covered in a mantle of golden blooms in fall and is everywhere. Big sagebrush is common and a telltale sign of overgrazing in the Southwest. Undisturbed ground in the kipukas show an excellent representation of the natural matrix of species before the introduction of livestock.

Wildflowers include the Rocky Mountain beeplant, yellow wallflower, evening primrose (whose big white petals often look like Kleenex caught in a bush), and locoweed, deer vetch, and lupine, which all bloom pink to purple and are in the pea family. Globe mallow, wild geranium, Indian paintbrush, a variety of penstemeons, blue flax, scarlet gilia, desert marigold, and several types of asters also bloom in and around these monuments. There is some bloom in spring, but often the most vigorous bloom occurs in late summer after monsoonal rains.

below the surface and was created by a channel of hot lava that flowed south and west from La Tetra vent, about 3 miles to the northwest. The Double Sinks, near Junction Cave, are collapsed portions of tubes connected by a lava bridge. The sinks are at least 60 feet deep; the larger of the two is close to 90 feet across.

Past Junction Cave is a trail leading to Bat Cave, so named for the thousands of Mexican free-tail bats that live here from June through October. Mexican free-tailed bats live in segregated communities— pregnant and nursing females inhabit some caves and males inhabit others. This cave is a roost for male bats. Please do not disturb them; their numbers have fallen drastically in recent years and they need all the peace and quiet they can get. If you're interested you can visit the Bat Cave in the evening and watch them come swirling out as they leave their roost for a night of hunting. Stand to the east of the cave so you can see the bats silhouetted against the evening sky.

El Calderon, the Cauldron, is the oldest volcano at El Malpais. Its flows have been dated to almost to 200,000 years ago.

Best time to ride: Spring through fall.

Special considerations: Water and rest rooms are available at the information center. Vault toilets are available at the El Calderon parking area. If you plan on entering and exploring either of the caves along this route, bring along a flashlight for each person. You may also want to bring a lock to secure your bike.

Directions for the ride: From the parking area follow the doubletrack that angles off to the right. In a short distance you will come to the trail leading to Junction Cave. Hop off your bike and check it out or save it for your return trip. Follow the sometimes rocky road southwest for approximately 0.8 mile from the parking lot to where the route splits. Bear left and begin the climb around the flank of El Calderon Volcano, taking in great views to the east as you go. The route then descends and comes to a gate 1.7 miles from the start. At the next intersection, 2.5 miles from the start, two roads come together. Bear right a short distance later, following a southwesterly route up and over the toe of the Cerritos de Jaspe. Approximately 3.5 miles from the start the route crests a ridge. Stay left of a fenceline as you descend. After riding downhill about a mile there is

Jumbled lava flows, collapsed lava tubes, barren craters and numerous other volcanic features prompted early Spanish explorers to call this region "El Malpais," or "bad country."

another intersection; go right and begin climbing up a fairly steep and rocky road. Continue along the western flank of the Cerritos de Jaspe with lava fields stretching away to your left, following the main route as it rolls up and down. Ignore the multitude of tracks taking off to either side of the road. Three miles from the last major intersection the road splits; stay right, arriving at a gate 0.2 mile later. Go through the gate, leaving it as you found it, and follow the route as it bends around and heads northeast. At 8.5 miles stay right at a junction and head south, then bear left, 0.5 mile later at another intersection where you will climb again for a short distance. In another mile you will arrive back at the junction where you began the loop. Bear left and ride 0.8 mile back to the parking lot.

Option: Beginning riders or families with kids may want to explore this route as far as El Calderon and then return. Go further if you like then turn around when you have had enough. The Double Sinks can be accessed by a hiking trail that heads south past Junction Cave 0.25 mile. The Bat Cave is another 0.5 mile past the sinks on the same hiking trail.

61. LAVA-CLIFFS BOUNDARY RIDE
(See map on page 337)

For road bikes. There are several different starting points for this ride, allowing cyclists of varying fitness and ability levels to choose how far they want to pedal along this incredibly scenic, lightly used state road. NM 117 winds north and south between the extensive lava flows of El Malpais to the west and the beautiful sandstone cliffs inside BLM wilderness and the Acoma Indian Reservation.

Starting point: The more serious road rider may want to start along NM 117 at I-40, but most will want to begin at either the El Malpais BLM Ranger Station, approximately 10 miles south of I-40, or at Sandstone Bluffs Overlook, another mile south of the ranger station. It is 1.6 miles from NM 117 in to the overlook.

Length: From the ranger station to Lava Falls at the southernmost end of the monument is 20 miles (29 miles from I-40), making an out-and-back 40 miles total. One of the best options is to ride south from the ranger station to La Ventana Arch, an out-and-back distance of 16.8 miles. For those wanting an even shorter ride, one that perhaps the kids could handle, the trip out to Sandstone Bluffs Overlook from the ranger station and back gives a total distance of just over 5 miles.

Riding surface: Pavement with nice, wide shoulders.

Difficulty: Moderate to difficult.

Scenery/highlights: Views, scenery, and the arches. You may want to start and finish your ride at the overlook and take time to hike the trail to at least three arches. Further south on NM 117, La Ventana Arch, besides being the second largest in New Mexico, is also one of the most beautiful, tucked high into the cliffs painted in beautiful shades of buff, honey, and salmon.

This is a great place to get out push on the pedals, enjoy the wind in your face, and take in some stunning desert scenery.

Best time to ride: Spring through fall.

Special considerations: Rest rooms and water are available at the BLM ranger station. Vault toilets are available at Sandstone Bluffs Overlook, La Ventana Arch, and the Narrows Picnic Area. You will also find picnic tables for your use at these spots.

Directions for the ride: From your desired starting point simply head out onto NM 117 and go south. Ride the 1.6 miles out to Sandstone Bluffs Overlook and take some time there to absorb the view. Continue on, passing over the ancient Zuni-Acoma Trail that connected the Indians of these pueblos to trade networks reaching as far away as Mexico. Don't miss La Ventana Arch, approximately 8.4 miles from the lookout or 10 miles from the ranger station, just a short walk away from the road. Past the arch the road passes through an area referred to as the Narrows, where the road pushes right up against the cliffs and the lava pushes right up against the road on the other side. Past the Narrows Picnic Area it is another 8 miles to Lava Falls, where you can walk a 1-mile trail out to the terminus of an ancient lava flow and see several sinkholes. When you have had enough simply reverse your direction and enjoy a new perspective on this beautiful landscape on the return trip.

---

62. EL MALPAIS TO EL MORRO (See map on page 337)

For road bikes. NM 53, which makes a loop south of I-40 around the Zuni Mountains between Grants and Gallup, offers road riders a great opportunity to get out and see the beautiful and historically rich region many refer to as Zuni Country. The 18-mile stretch between El Malpais and neighboring El Morro National Monument is one of the best choices along this route for a day ride. Great scenery, several interesting natural and historic sites, and a traverse of the Continental Divide add to the outing. Intermediate- and advanced-level road riders who are in good condition and acclimated to the higher altitudes of this area will find this route challenging but rewarding.

Starting point: El Malpais Information Center.

Length: 18 miles one-way, 36 miles total distance.

Riding surface: Pavement. Improvements to this road are underway as

FAUNA

The number of different habitats in these monuments result in a healthy variety of bird life. Some of the most common birds are the jays, which include Stellar's, western scrub, and pinyon. Ravens are year-round residents that like to nest in cliffs and tall trees. Turkey vultures soaring on warm air currents are a common sight in summer. Common residents from the raptor family include northern harriers, red-tailed hawks, and American kestrels. Numerous migrant raptors also pass through but are difficult to identify. Black-chinned, broad-tailed, and rufous hummingbirds can often be seen and heard zipping about in summer, and near the cliffs of El Morro or along NM 117 you're likely to see cliff and barn swallows as well as white-throated swifts. Chickadees, white-breasted nuthatches, northern flickers, Cassin's kingbirds, western and mountain bluebirds, spotted towhees, and dark-eyed juncos prefer the woodlands but can also be spotted at the perimeter of grasslands. Horned larks and western mead-owlarks are usually found in open grasslands, while rock wrens and canyon wrens favor canyons and crevices along the cliffs.

Blacktail jackrabbits, desert cottontails, rock squirrels, Abert's squirrels, porcupines, raccoons, striped skunks, ringtail cats, and bad-gers all inhabit this high-desert environment. The smaller rodents are prey for gray fox, coyote, and bobcat. Mountain lions prefer mule deer, an easier target than trying to bring down an elk or speedy pronghorn. Black bear also ramble through these monuments from time to time but are uncommon. At least 12 species of bats inhabit the caves and cliffs.

Both western diamondback and prairie rattlesnakes are known to haunt these areas, but they are shy, slow, and easy to avoid. Keep your eyes peeled for them sunning themselves on trails or roadways in the morning and evening. Gopher snakes, western garter snakes and desert striped whip snakes also inhabit this high desert, as do a host of lizards, including earless lizards, collared lizards, eastern fence lizards, short horned lizards, side-blotched lizards, and at least two varieties of skinks.

this book goes to press. Sections that are finished are smooth with wide shoulders.

Difficulty: Moderate to difficult. The length, high altitudes, and rolling sections of this route will make it more difficult for most.

Scenery/highlights: You'll pedal through shady forests of ponderosa pine, wind through rolling piñon- and juniper-dotted hills, and enjoy intermittent views of wide-open grasslands where pronghorn antelope often play. The lava beds of El Malpais at times appear as a lunar landscape, an otherworldly place that is sometimes difficult to comprehend.

Not long after you start out you'll pass the turnoff for Bandera Crater Ice Caves where you might want to stop and have a look around. Then again, you might want to save this stop as a place to cool off toward the end of your ride. The ice in the cave, some 14 feet thick and 50 feet across, exists because of a unique combination: the orientation of the cave opening (south), its depth, and the insulating properties of basalt. There are actually six ice caves in El Malpais. This cave has long been sacred to the Zunis, and was not visited by a non-Indian until the 1880s. Local ranchers carted ice away from the cave for decades until the land fell into private hands and was managed as a tourist attraction. It is still privately owned and you must pay a fee to visit. It is a short 0.4 mile hike to the cave and a descent down 75 stairs to see the ice.

El Morro National Monument, as described in the introduction, is a fascinating glimpse at the history of this area. Take time to hike the Mesa Top Trail, taking you on top of the bluffs, and to A'ts'ina, the large pueblo now in ruins that local Zunis claim as their ancestral home. Views from the mesa top are outstanding.

Best time to ride: Spring through fall.

Special considerations: Water and rest rooms are available at the information center and at the El Morro Visitor Center.

This is a long day out so go prepared with plenty of snacks and some extra clothes. Plan on wearing or bringing shoes suitable for making the 0.5-mile walk along El Morro to see the inscriptions and the 2-mile hike to the mesa top and pueblo ruin. Bring a lock to secure your bike while away.

Directions for the ride: From the El Malpais Information Center saddle up and ride out onto NM 53 heading west. After 2 miles you will begin to climb, passing the turnoff for Bandera Crater Ice Caves on your left shortly before you crest the hill. At the top of the hill you cross the Continental Divide, the geographical delineation that sends runoff either west, to the Gulf of California, or east, to the Gulf of Mexico. Not quite 1 mile past this point is CR 42 and access to the Chain of Craters, also traced by the Continental Divide. Past CR 42 the road descends gently and for a time rolls along below Oso Ridge, the main spine of the Zuni Mountains. Eventually the route angles away from the mountains and crosses open, grassy flatlands where it is not uncommon to spot antelope. Approximately 18 miles from the start you arrive at the turnoff for El Morro National Monument. It is close to 1 mile to the visitor center. After spending time seeing the inscriptions and hiking to the mesa top, return to your bike and head back the way you came.

CAMPING

There are no campgrounds at El Malpais but there is one nine-site campground at El Morro that has rest rooms, water, picnic tables, and fire grates. The campground is open May through October and a fee is charged.

IT'S INTERESTING TO KNOW...

The centuries-old Zuni-Acoma Trail, a section of which traverses the El Malpais National Monument and passes by El Morro, is part of a network of ancient Indian trails that once connected the people of this area to cultures as far away as Mexico and probably beyond. The 8 miles of trail that cross El Malpais wind around and over old lava flows and through stands of ponderosa; rock cairns mark the route. Lichens growing on the cairns indicate that some may be as old as the trail itself.

There are many excellent choices for camping at developed national forest campgrounds, the nearest being **Ojo Redondo Campground** in the Zuni Mountains. There are also many possibilities for primitive camping in this area.

Another good choice is **Blue-water Lake State Park,** located about 7 miles south of I-40 between Gallup and Grants off exit 63. They've got sites with hookups as well as tent sites and rest rooms with showers. **Cibola Sands RV Park,** just a mile south of I-40 on NM 53 has tent sites and shower facilities, as does **Lavaland RV Park** at exit 85 off I-40.

LODGING

Because both Gallup and Grants are located on I-40 they are host to a full compliment of chain hotels and cheaper, budget-friendly motels. Ask to see the rooms at some of the really cheap motels, there are some real dives in these towns. In Grants you'll find a **Days Inn,** a **Motel 6,** a **Holiday Inn Express,** and a **Best**

Western Inn and Suites. You'll find all the same in Gallup, plus a **Super 8** and the **Red Rock Best Western Inn.** The **El Rancho Hotel** in Gallup is somewhat of a landmark. Built in the 1930s in Southwestern ranch-style, the hotel housed numerous Hollywood stars during the era when Westerns were being filmed in the surrounding redrock desert. Signed photos decorate the walls throughout.

FOOD

Besides a plethora of fast-food restaurants there are a number of

---

⭐

DON'T MISS

While in the area don't pass up the chance to visit Acoma Pueblo, the home of the Acoma Indians since the middle of the 12th century. Built atop an isolated mesa over 350 feet above the surrounding desert floor, Acoma Pueblo, along with Taos Pueblo, is considered the oldest continually inhabited human settlement in the United States. Coronado visited Acoma in 1540 and remarked in his journal that the pueblo rose three and fours stories high and the people had "abundant supplies of maize, beans, and turkey."

The Acoma became ever more familiar with the Spanish in the decades after Coronado's visit, much to their sorrow. In 1598 they, along with other Pueblo Indians throughout the region, submitted to the Spanish rather than fight. Later, they became unhappy with the cruel treatment they suffered and in retaliation attacked Don Juan de Zaldivar, who had come to Acoma to resupply. Don Juan de Onate, the first governor of New Mexico, then attacked the pueblo with 70 of his men. The men of the pueblo were murdered and thrown over the cliffs, except for those the Spanish kept as slaves. These men were hobbled by removing a foot. Women and girls were also carted off to serve as slaves to Spanish families along the Rio Grande River. Acoma was the last pueblo to surrender to the Spanish after the Pueblo Revolt of 1680 and the Acoma Indians have remained a force for independence among the native peoples of New Mexico ever since.

greasy cafés in Grants; the **Uranium Café** (519 W. Santa Fe) has a few dishes that are sure to leave you glowing. The **Canton Café** and the **China Gate Restaurant,** both located on Santa Fe, serve Chinese, while good Mexican fare can be found at **El Cafecito,** the **Monte Carlo,** or at **Grants Station,** where you can also get good, basic American dishes. All are located along Santa Fe, the main drag through town. **La Ventana** (110 ½ Geiss St.), serves continental fare such as steaks, ribs, and seafood in a slightly more upscale atmosphere.

There are similarly oodles of fast-food restaurants in Gallup, probably some you've never even heard of, as well as a good many greasy-spoon cafés. **El Rancho Restaurant** in the El Rancho Hotel on Route 66 is a good place for breakfast and you can get it starting at 6 AM. They also serve seafood, steaks, a variety of barbecued meats, and New Mexican specialties daily for lunch and dinner. **Earl's Family Restaurant,** also on 66, is a good bet for standard American food and a few good New Mexican dishes. **Panz Allegra** is a newer restaurant serving some excellent New Mexican creations and good Mexican food as well.

Fresh Scent Laundromat, 749 E. Roosevelt Ave., Grants; 505-876-2257

In Gallup: There are more than a half dozen laundromats in Gallup; here are just a few that are centrally located.

Busy Bee Laundry East, 2010 E. Hwy 66; 505-863-2237

Pronto Laundromat, 2422 E. Hwy 66; 505-863-2207

Wash & Save Laundry, 201 Marguerite; 505-722-9827

Bike shops are scarce in this corner of New Mexico but this shop can take care of most of your biking needs, including rentals.

Fantasy Lowrider Bicycle Inc., 107 W. Coal Ave., Gallup; 505-722-2459

El Malpais National Monument —Superintendent, P.O. Box 939, Grants, NM 87020; 505-783-4774; www.nps.gov/elma/

El Malpais National Conservation Area, Bureau of Land Management, P.O. Box 846, Grants, NM 87020; 505-240-0300

El Morro National Monument—Superintendent, Route 2, Box 43, Ramah, NM 87321; 505-783-4226; www.nps.gov/elmo/

Northwest New Mexico Visitor Center (multi-agency visitor center), 1900 East Santa Fe Ave., Grants, NM 87020; 505-876-2783

Cibola National Forest, Mt. Taylor Ranger District, 1800 Lobo Canyon Rd., Grants, NM 87020; 505-287-8833

Grants/Cibola Chamber of Commerce, 100 N. Iron St.; Grants, NM 87020; 505-287-4802 or 1-800-748-2142

Gallup Convention and Visitors Bureau, 701 Montoya Ave., P.O. Box 600, Gallup, NM 87305; 505-863-3841 or 1-800-242-4282

GILA CLIFF DWELLINGS NATIONAL MONUMENT

Surrounded by 3 million acres of wilderness at the end of a long, winding road 2 hours from the nearest town are a series of cliff dwellings credited to people belonging to the Mogollon culture. The Mogollon were counterparts to the Anasazi of the Four Corners region but inhabited a broad area further south that included southwestern New Mexico, southeastern Arizona, and the northern portions of Chihuahua and Sonora, Mexico. The Mogollon were most concentrated along the Gila and Mimbres Rivers of southwestern New Mexico and it is high in the cliffs along the West Fork of the Gila River, among a tangle of canyons, low mesas, and piñon- and juniper-dotted foothills that some of their most impressive village ruins are protected inside Gila Cliff Dwellings National Monument.

Pithouse structures built between A.D. 100 and 400 in the vicinity of the cliff dwellings were the first permanent shelters constructed by the Mogollon. Several hundred years later, rectangular, above-ground, free-standing structures began to appear on the canyon floor. Sometime in the late 1200s, whether it was for defensive reasons or simply because the alcoves and caves in the cliffs offered better protection from the elements, construction began on the cliff dwellings. Treering data show that they were completed in the late 1270s and early 1280s. Five of the seven caves along the canyon wall contain pueblo-like structures that probably housed no more than 10 to 15 families at one time.

Like the Anasazi, the Mogollon farmed corn, beans, and squash, but also grew amaranth, cotton, and tobacco. These crops were supplemented by hunting small game and deer, and gathering wild plants and fruits. What scant evidence has been collected suggests that they practiced a religion imported from Mesoamerican Indian cultures. Trade items such as shell beads, obsidian that was made into spear points, and certain kinds of pottery reveal that the Mogollon, like the Anasazi, belonged to an extensive trade network that reached far to the south and extended west to the shores of the Pacific. After only 30 years, the span of a single generation, the Mogollon left their cliff dwellings for reasons that are still unknown. Archaeologists theorize that the Mogollon, like the Anasazi who left their homes at approximately the same time, migrated toward the Rio Grande and melded with those who eventually became today's Pueblo tribes.

Cycling in the Park

Because of the park's small acreage there are no roads or trails suitable for biking. The 44-mile road between Silver City and the monument, however, is a favorite of seasoned road bikers who are fit enough to tackle the rolling terrain and long distance. Most of this route is included in the annual Tour of the Gila road race as a long-distance event. Those who prefer the pavement but are not up for the time and distance commitment of riding this incredibly scenic route can choose from one of several optional starting points for a shorter ride. The wilderness status of the vast amount of national forest lands surrounding the monument means that mountain bikes are not allowed on nearby trails. Fat-tire enthusiasts will need to head south to the area around Pinos Altos and Silver City, where dozens of trails invite exploration. A great place to start is the Fort Bayard Trail System, where you can ride historic wagon roads and create a number of different loops. This area is also a game preserve, home to a healthy herd of Rocky Mountain elk. The ride through the old mining district north of Silver City traverses part of Arroyo Rico and takes you to the Cleveland Mine, now a federal Superfund site. This ride offers a loop option sure to please the more adventurous. A loop that takes riders up and around Signal Peak and the

CYCLING OPTIONS

There are four rides in this chapter; three for mountain bikes and one for road bikes. Because of the enormous amount of wilderness area surrounding the monument and the small size of the monument itself, mountain biking opportunities are located 35 to 40 miles south of the monument around the towns of Pinos Altos and Silver City. Begin by exploring the historic Sawmill and Wood Haul Wagon Road Trails, both designated as National Recreation Trails. They wind their way north into the foothills of the Pinos Altos Mountains and a national elk preserve behind Fort Bayard. A route through the heavily mined region north of Silver City takes mountain bikers to the Cleveland Mine, an old mine in the Arroyo Rico area that is now a Superfund site. The adventurous can try an excellent loop option on the Continental Divide Trail. A loop around Signal Peak and the Twin Sisters area has a great section of somewhat technical singletrack and rounds out the list of trail offerings. A road ride from Lake Roberts to the cliff dwellings is well suited for experienced road riders, but a good option for the less ambitious begins at Gila Hot Springs, where cyclists can soak after their ride.

The Canada-to-Mexico Great Divide Mountain Bike Route runs right through Silver City, and is an excellent long-distance adventure for those interested in a multiday or multiweek excursion. A map of this trail, developed by the Adventure Cycling Association in Missoula, Montana, can be acquired by calling them at (406) 721-8719. Section 6 details the area around Silver City.

Twin Sisters out of Pinos Altos offers sections of pavement, dirt road, and technical singletrack best suited for intermediate- and advanced-level riders in good condition. There are options here as well. There are many more great riding opportunities in this area, especially for experienced mountain bikers. Inquire about riding the Continental Divide Trail, the Signal Peak Challenge Race Course, or riding south of Silver City in the Burro Mountains.

The Silver City area's climate furnishes almost ideal conditions for exploring by bicycle anytime of year. Daytime temperatures during the winter are often in the 50s and 60s and the nights are cold. Snowstorms are not uncommon, but what falls usually does not stick around for very long. Summers are warm, with daytime temperatures frequently reaching up into the mid- to high 90s. Higher up in the mountains temperatures will be cooler. Elevations are relatively high to begin with, ranging between 5,500 and 9,000 feet above sea level. Like much of the Southwest, this region receives the bulk of its moisture during the summer months when moist air pushes up from the Gulf of Mexico, boils up off the mountains, and then rains down in violent thunderstorms.

Because of the extensive mining that has gone on in the area surrounding Silver City there is a maze of roads taking off in all directions. Carrying supplementary forest service or topographic maps or both is strongly recommended when heading into the hills for two-wheeled adventuring.

---

63. FORT BAYARD TRAIL SYSTEM (See map on page 356)

For mountain bikes. The historic National Recreation Trails that wind through the foothills of the Pinos Altos Mountains north of Fort Bayard offer excellent opportunities for all levels of mountain bikers to get out and pedal. You can ride north and visit a National Elk Refuge, ride to the Big Tree, purportedly one of the biggest juniper trees known, or traverse the old roads once traveled by wagons bringing lumber to the fort.

Starting point: There are three main trailheads for the Fort Bayard Trail System. The first is located west of the fort in Arenas Valley. To get there drive east of Silver City on US 180 3.5 miles to Arenas Valley Road. Go left onto this road and follow it just over a mile to the intersection with Elias Road. The Arenas Valley Trailhead is located on the east side of this intersection.

The second trailhead is located just north of the fort itself. To get there drive east from Silver City on US 180 approximately 8 miles to the Fort Bayard/Central turnoff. Go left and drive north through Fort Bayard 1.3 miles, past the medical center. The main road will fork; stay right to get to Forest Road (FR) 536. At the end of the pavement FR 536 begins; fol-

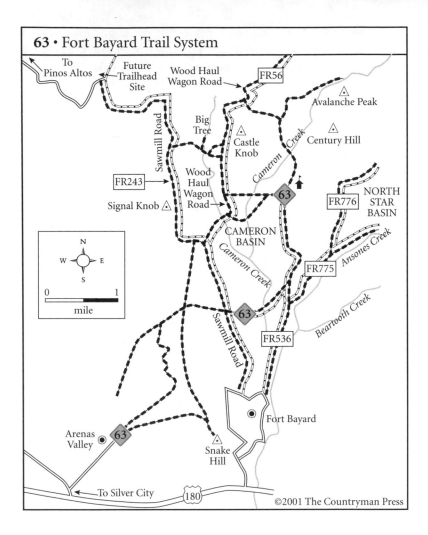

63 • Fort Bayard Trail System

To Pinos Altos

Future Trailhead Site

Wood Haul Wagon Road

FR56

Avalanche Peak

Big Tree

Castle Knob

Century Hill

Cameron Creek

FR243

Wood Haul Wagon Road

Signal Knob

63

FR776

NORTH STAR BASIN

CAMERON BASIN

Cameron Creek

FR775

Ansones Creek

N
W   E
S

0   1
mile

63

Sawmill Road

FR536

Beartooth Creek

Fort Bayard

Arenas Valley

63

Snake Hill

To Silver City   180

©2001 The Countryman Press

low it 1.5 miles, past Asones Creek Road (FR 775) leaving on the right, to a road on the left a few hundred feet farther. Go left onto this dirt road and drive west approximately 1 mile to a trailhead at the Sawmill National Recreation Trail.

The third trailhead is north of the second. Follow directions as above to get to Fort Bayard. Continue on FR 536, past the turnoff for the second trailhead, another 1.5 miles to a forest service outpost. Go left on the road directly across from these buildings and drive a short distance to the trailhead for the Sawmill and Wood Haul Wagon Road National Recreation Trails.

The old Sawmill Road can be picked up from the cemetery road at the north end of the fort, and a singletrack trail can be picked up near Snake Hill. A future official trailhead will be located just east of Pinos Altos at the end of Cross Mountain Road. It is still possible to access the Fort Bayard Trails from this point, although it is not marked.

Length: There are several possibilities here, one of the best is riding a short, 4.5-mile loop using the Wood Haul Wagon Road. You can also ride north almost 7 miles on the old Sawmill Road to the Twin Sisters area, or stay on the Wood Haul Wagon Road, riding it north and east into Bear Canyon and beyond, to where it intersects Trail 100 near Signal Peak (about 6 miles).

Riding surface: Dirt roads, doubletrack, and singletrack.

Difficulty: Easy to more difficult, depending how far and how long you choose to ride. Not all the trails and intersecting roads are well marked out here; route finding adds an element of difficulty.

Scenery/highlights: The open country and rolling hills of the Pinos Altos Mountains are lovely. Fort Bayard is a former military reservation and has a unique place in Western American history. Built in 1866, the fort served as headquarters during a campaign against several Apache bands who were making life unbearable for the early settlers and miners of the area. Fort Bayard was home to the Ninth and Tenth Cavalry division, also known as the Buffalo Soldiers, African-American men who had distinguished themselves as fearless fighters during the Civil War. It was believed that they were perfectly suited to fighting the wily Apache, an assignment most soldiers regarded with a mixture of fear and dread. Many Buffalo Soldiers died during the long, and bitterly fought skirmishes and are buried at the Fort Bayard National Cemetery, along with veterans from every major conflict in U.S. history. Fort Bayard was maintained as a military reservation until the early twentieth century, when it became a hospital for war veterans suffering from tuberculosis.

The land directly behind Fort Bayard is managed jointly by the Gila National Forest and the New Mexico Division of Wildlife Resources as a

Heading home from somewhere in the Gila.

National Elk Refuge. The Big Tree is nationally recognized as the second largest alligator juniper known to exist. It is 63 feet tall, over 18 feet in diameter, and has a crown spread of 62 feet.

Best time to ride: Spring through fall.

Special considerations: There are no rest rooms or water at any of these trailheads so come prepared. As mentioned earlier, many of the trails in this area are not well marked. It is a good idea to bring supplementary maps. Stop by the forest service office in town and pick up a map of the Fort Bayard trails and Gila National Forest. Even better, supplement both with a USGS topographic map.

Directions for the ride: Ride from any trailhead or access point you wish and explore one or a combination of routes. You might want to head north on the Sawmill/Wood Haul Wagon Road and make a loop using the trail that accesses the Big Tree and connects the two roads after they divide. Another loop option heads north from the trailhead at the end of FR 536 and goes north, connects with the Wood Haul Wagon Road, and then comes south, past the spur to the Big Tree. You can get back to the start by picking up a singletrack that heads east about 0.5 mile past the trail to Big Tree. Several bigger loops requiring endurance and good route-finding skills are possible to the north; check in with the folks at either of the bike shops in Silver City or the forest service office for more information and guidance.

64. ARROYO RICO TO CLEVELAND MINE
(See map on page 361)

For mountain bikes. This route traverses a heavily mined area north of Silver City and west of Pinos Altos. Riders will cross a portion of Arroyo

FLORA

The Gila Cliff Dwellings sit at the apex of three different life zones: the Chihuahuan, Great Basin, and Sonoran Deserts. Trees you are likely to see along the road to the ruins and around the monument include piñon pine, one-seed and alligator juniper, ponderosa pine, mountain mahogany, and Gambel and Emory oak. On north-facing slopes Douglas fir mixes with ponderosa pine and on the hotter, drier south-facing slopes you'll find piñon and juniper. In the riparian areas of Cliff Dweller Canyon several species of willows and the stately cottonwood dominate. Shrubs include Apache plume and rabbitbrush, or chamisa as it is called in New Mexico. It is easy to identify in the fall with its golden crown of blooms. Birch-leaf buckthorn, gooseberry, and lemonade bush, a member of the sumac family, all produce fruit that attract a host of birds and wildlife to the canyon bottoms. Lemonade bush was and still is the basket-making material preferred by Native Americans throughout New Mexico.

Some of the most common wildflowers include the yellow, daisy-like rudebeckia or cutleaf coneflower, prickly poppy, milkweed that comes in shades of orange and lavender, tall evening primrose, a magenta-colored four o'clock locally called maravilla, and sacred datura, or jimsonweed, easy to identify by its enormous, white, trumpet-shaped flowers and thorny fruits.

Rico, Spanish for "rich drainage," on their way to the Cleveland Mine, an old gold and silver mine identified as a federal Superfund clean-up site. The route follows an old jeep road that is badly deteriorated and impassable to vehicles in places. There is a excellent option for creating a loop with the Continental Divide Trail here that avid fat-tire fanatics who are fit and willing should seriously consider.

Starting point: The town of Pinos Altos.

Length: 5.25 miles one-way to the Cleveland Mine, 10.5 miles out-and-back. The loop option using Continental Divide Trail is approximately 18.3 miles round-trip. Allow at least 3 hours for the out-and-back, twice that to complete the optional loop.

Riding surface: Jeep road; rough, washed out, with rocky sections. The optional loop includes almost 6 miles of singletrack.

Difficulty: Moderate. The loop option is difficult.

Scenery/highlights: Arroyo Rico bears the scars of many who came and toiled here hoping to strike it rich. The Cleveland Mine was one of those efforts, reaching its production peak around the turn of the twentieth century. The mine's operation was short-lived and turned out only modest amounts of gold and silver. The acrid smell that hovers around the mine and the burnt orange color of the rocks and water seeping from the old works is caused by arsenic and other heavy metals. These heavy metals are toxic and have earned this site Superfund status. At some point in time federal dollars will be put to use to try to clean up this mess, but in the meantime, don't touch the sticky, orange rocks or drink the water.

Best time to ride: Spring and fall.

Special considerations: Water and rest rooms can be found in Pinos Altos at several places; the Buckhorn Saloon is a favorite watering hole among locals and visitors alike. They would appreciate your patronage if you are using their facilities.

Use extreme caution around the old mine sites. Do not approach or go into old mine shafts, because they may collapse or contain poisonous gases that can quickly overwhelm. The old buildings are unstable and should not be entered or climbed on. Also, there is private property along this route; please respect all private property signs.

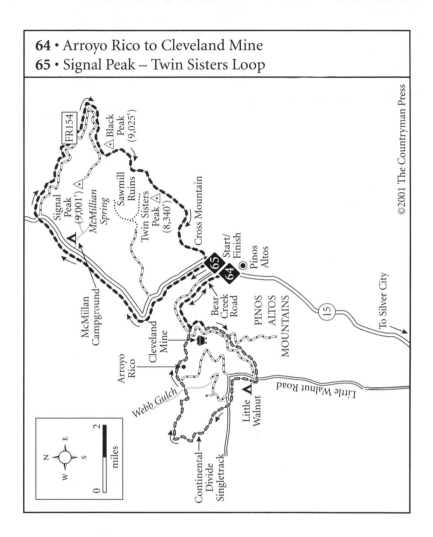

64 • Arroyo Rico to Cleveland Mine
65 • Signal Peak – Twin Sisters Loop

FR 154

△ Black Peak (9,025')

Sawmill Ruins △

Signal Peak (9,001') △

McMillian Spring

Twin Sisters Peak △ (8,340')

Cross Mountain

Start/ Finish

Pinos Altos

65 64

©2001 The Countryman Press

McMillan Campground

Bear Creek Road

PINOS ALTOS MOUNTAINS

15

To Silver City

Arroyo Rico

Cleveland Mine

Webb Gulch

Little Walnut Road

Little Walnut △

Continental → Divide Singletrack

N W E S

0 ▮ 2 miles

Directions for the ride: From Pinos Altos head north out of town on the gravel Bear Creek Road. This road leaves from the northwest corner of the paved loop that swings through town off NM 15. As you head north the road descends toward Bear Creek, then climbs, then continues a gentle descent, passing several gated spur roads before reaching an intersection with a lesser-used dirt road approximately 1.5 miles from the start. Go left onto this dirt road, passing an access to the Continental

Divide Trail on your right a short distance later. In 0.3 mile you come to another intersection; turn left again. Continue on this main road, heading west now, passing a road on your right. This spur road accesses the Continental Divide Trail and will be the point where you rejoin the main trail if you do the loop option.

Past the spur road 0.4 mile is a major intersection; go left and descend into the Arroyo Rico drainage (the road to the right is also part of the loop option). You will cross over Arroyo Rico, which is dry a good part of the time, and pass a spur road on the left 0.5 mile later that goes to an old mine building. Bear right and climb out of Arroyo Rico drainage, enjoying the views as you go. Over the next 2 miles you pass several old mine workings, dilapidated structures, and open shafts. Just over 5 miles from the start is a spur road on the left leading to the Cleveland Mine. Ride up to the mine, spend some time marveling at the mess it left behind, and then reverse your route to return to Pinos Altos.

Option: If you are interested in the loop option continue heading south and west on the main road past the mine. This turns into a gravel road in 0.5 mile. In another 0.6 mile is an intersection with Forest Road (FR) 506. Go right onto FR 506, the continuation of Little Walnut Canyon Road. Follow it 1.5 miles, looking for the Continental Divide Trail to cross the road. It is marked with small CD signs nailed to trees. South is to the left; north is to the right. Turn right to ride the north section in a loop that will take you back to Pinos Altos.

The trail begins as a doubletrack, but soon swings west and becomes a singletrack. Follow this trail 1.5 miles to a gate; go through it and leave it as you found it. The trail then heads north around some low mountains before swinging east. Approximately 3 miles from FR 506 you dip across Webb Gulch. Climb out of this drainage as you head north another 0.5 mile to an intersection with a dirt doubletrack. Go right, following this lightly used road for almost 2 miles, much of it uphill, to the next section of Continental Divide singletrack leaving from the left-hand side of the road. Follow this next section for approximately 1.2 miles until it ends at a doubletrack road. Go right; this doubletrack joins the main road from Pinos Altos in a few hundred feet. Turn left when you reach this dirt road and follow it almost 3 miles back to Pinos Altos.

65. SIGNAL PEAK–TWIN SISTERS LOOP
(See map on page 361)

For mountain bikes. This 19-mile loop can also be ridden from Pinos Altos and covers miles on paved roads, dirt roads, and another section of Continental Divide Trail singletrack. Advanced and intermediate riders in good condition who don't mind a few road miles or stretches of rocky trail will love this circuit of some of the really pretty country the Gila is known for. Beginning riders might want to consider riding up the dirt road to Signal Peak Lookout for a good workout and excellent views.

Starting point: Pinos Altos.

Length: 19 miles. Allow at least 4 hours to complete this loop.

Riding surface: Pavement, graded dirt road, and singletrack.

Difficulty: Moderate to difficult. Length, climbs, technical sections of singletrack will make this ride more difficult for most.

Scenery/highlights: Good views of surrounding country, some great singletrack, some good choices for ride options, and a chance to visit the ruins of a historic sawmill.

Best time to ride: Anytime, but spring and fall are best.

Special considerations: Refreshments and rest rooms can be found in Pinos Altos but be sure to bring plenty of water and snacks along with you on the ride.

Directions for the ride: From Pinos Altos head out onto NM 15 and go north. The road descends gently toward Bear Creek for about 3 miles, makes a switchback, and then heads northeast, climbing along Cherry Creek for the next 4 miles to FR 154 on the right. Go right onto this dirt road, following it as it climbs, winding up, up, up through forests that become increasingly dominated by pines. Approximately 2.5 miles along the dirt road you come to a fork; bear right and continue climbing toward Signal Peak Lookout. Stay on FR 154 another 3 miles, riding beyond a switchback that heads west, looking for the start of the Continental Divide Trail, Forest Service Trail (FT) 74, on the left. (Beginning riders not interested in singletrack can ride past the start of the

FAUNA

The Gila River's three forks converge near the monument and are a magnet for wildlife in this dry, mountainous environment. Numerous waterfowl species are drawn to the riparian areas, including the great blue herons that maintain a rookery inside monument boundaries. Bald eagles are rare, while golden eagles, red-tailed hawks, and American kestrels are common. Turkey vultures are ever-present during the summer months; the curious, noisy raven is always about. Gambel quail and mourning doves are commonly sighted, as are northern flickers and acorn and hairy woodpeckers. Violet-green and cliff swallows are drawn to the cliffs, as are canyon, rock, and house wrens. Steller's, scrub, and pinyon jays are often seen around the campgrounds, and the whir of hummingbird wings is almost constant in summer. Say's phoebe, rufous-sided towhees, western bluebirds, yellow-crowned kinglet, yellow-rumped warbler, and solitary and warbling vireo are common songbirds.

Desert cottontails, Abert's squirrel, raccoons, ringtail cats, coatimundi, badger, javelina, coyote, gray, kit, red fox, and beaver are all regular visitors. Bobcats are quite shy but sometimes seen; mountain lions are common. Both lions and bears are frequently seen along the rivers during recent years of drought. Desert bighorn sheep, pronghorn antelope, mule deer, and elk are some of the area's grazers.

One of the most famous residents of the Gila is the recently reintroduced Mexican gray wolf, struggling back from the brink of extinction. They have found a less-than-warm reception in the ranching communities of eastern Arizona and western New Mexico and many have turned up shot or disappeared altogether.

Blacktailed rattlesnakes are very common on the trails around the dwellings in the early morning when they come out to warm themselves. They are easy-going and fairly small for rattlesnakes. Give them plenty of room and they will be happy to slither away. You'll find lots of lizards skittering about but don't expect to see any Gila monsters; they prefer lower elevations and are found only along the eastern extreme of the region that they are named for.

Continental Divide Trail and continue on FR 154 up to the top of Signal Peak and the Lookout. When you are done, reverse your route.) Turn left and begin the push toward Black Peak. In approximately 0.5 mile you will gain Black Peak where you might want to take a minute to absorb the view, catch your breath, and check to make sure your helmet is snug and securely fastened. It is a technical descent for the next mile to the saddle between Black Peak and the Twin Sisters. At this saddle you will find a four-way intersection; go straight and continue around and over Twin Sisters. (To the left is the historic Sawmill Wagon Road Trail, a National Recreation Trail that connects to the Fort Bayard trail system. The old Sawmill ruins are west of Twin Sisters along Cherry Creek.) From the saddle it is approximately 3 miles of rolling, descending, sometimes technical singletrack heading southwest to where the trail comes out on a dirt road. Follow this road as it descends, making several switchbacks for 1.5 miles to the graded Cross Mountain Road. Go right and ride 0.5 mile to Pinos Altos and the Buckhorn Saloon for some refreshment—you've earned it!

---

66. GILA CLIFF DWELLINGS (See map on page 366)

For road bikes. While the serious road biker in peak condition might want to consider riding from Silver City to Gila Cliff Dwellings (44 miles one-way), tackling several mountain passes en route, most of us will be happy to start at Lake Roberts, still a challenging pedal. During the Tour of the Gila annual road race series some of the country's top cyclists ride a 100-mile loop that includes the road to the monument and NM 35, which heads east and south to Mimbres before circling back to Silver City via NM 152 and US 180. Those looking for an even easier option should consider starting at Gila Hot Springs, 4.3 miles south of the monument, where you can spend some time soaking at the end of your ride.

Starting point: Lake Roberts or Gila Hot Springs. Lake Roberts is located 3 miles east of NM 15 on NM 35. Gila Hot Springs is located just over 4 miles south of the monument on NM 15.

Park and start riding from either the gas station or from one of the campgrounds at Lake Roberts. At Gila Hot Springs you'll want to start at the trading post/gas station/grocery store/café.

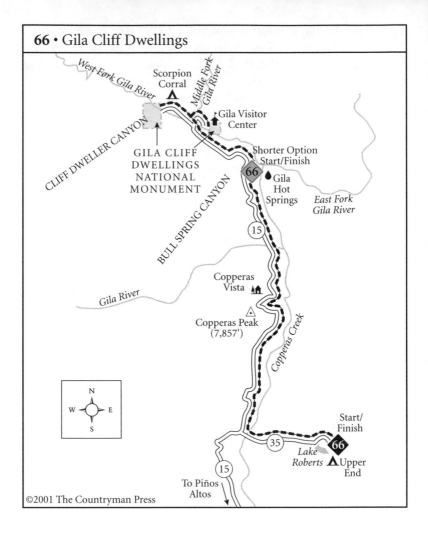

66 · Gila Cliff Dwellings

Length: From Lake Roberts to the monument and back is approximately 42 miles. From Gila Hot Springs to the monument and back is 10 miles. Allow all day for the longer ride, and half a day for the shorter.

Riding surface: Pavement.

Difficulty: Easy to difficult. The ride from Gila Hot Springs is easy. Riding from Lake Roberts is challenging because of the length and rolling terrain.

Like other ancient peoples of the Southwest, the Mogollon eventually built their pueblos in cave recesses for protection from the elements and perhaps hostile invaders.

Scenery/highlights: The mountain scenery along this route is quite beautiful and has a uniquely different flavor from other Southwestern mountain ranges. This is the country that inspired Aldo Leopold, a pioneer in environmental thinking, to write so eloquently and convincingly of the intrinsic worth of wilderness. His lobbying efforts resulted in the designation of the Gila Wilderness, the first wilderness area in the country.

The cliff dwellings, some 180 feet above the canyon floor, are fascinating and can be accessed by a 1-mile loop trail. The hot springs found along the Middle Fork of the Gila, accessed via a hiking trail near the visitor center, and those back at Gila Hot Springs are evidence of this region's volcanic past and add to the overall experience.

Best time to ride: Spring through fall.

Special considerations: Water and rest rooms are available at the campgrounds or at the gas station at Lake Roberts. All of the same, including snacks and burgers, are available at the trading post at Gila Hot Springs. Be sure to bring a lock to secure your bike while you are hiking the loop trail in the monument or enjoying one of the hot springs.

Directions for the ride: From Lake Roberts ride west along Sapillo Creek on NM 35 approximately 3 miles to the intersection with NM 15. Go right onto NM 15 and pedal north along Copperas Creek, climbing gently from approximately 5,835 feet near the intersection of NM 15 and 35 to almost 7,500 feet near Copperas Vista, 9 miles from the start. From there you descend to Gila Hot Springs and then the monument, just over 4 miles beyond. After hiking the trails seeing the ruins and taking some time to enjoy their beautiful natural setting, saddle up and ride back the way you came.

From Gila Hot Springs it is 3 miles of pedaling to the turnoff for the eastern unit of the monument and the visitor center. Go left and ride the 0.4 mile to the visitor center, examine the displays, collect whatever information you need, and continue 1.5 miles on to the main part of the monument and the cliff dwellings. Ride back to Gila Hot Springs, jump into your swimsuit, and soak.

CAMPING

While there is no camping in the monument itself there are many excellent choices at developed campgrounds and primitive campsites in surrounding Gila National Forest. Located on the river between the visitor center and the ruins is **Scorpion Campground** with 17 sites, drinking water, rest rooms, grills, and picnic tables. **Forks** and **Grapevine Campground** are semideveloped campgrounds with vault toilets and grills located 1 and 2 miles south of Gila Hot Springs respectively. There are at least 3 campgrounds around Lake Roberts, where you can take a dip and cool off after your ride or do a little fishing in the evening. They are equipped with rest rooms and drinking water. Two other cool, shady campgrounds, **Cherry Creek** and **McMillan,** are located north of Pinos Altos and have rest rooms but no drinking water.

At Gila Hot Springs you'll find tent and RV sites with full hook-ups at **Doc Campbell's Post and Vacation Center.** They have showers and laundry facilities as well as a gas station, gift shop, and hot pools for soaking. **Sapillo Crossing,** at the intersection of NM 15 and 35, has a dozen RV sites. **Continental Divide RV Park,** located about 6 miles north of Pinos Altos on NM 15, has 30 sites with hook-ups and showers. They also have a café open spring through fall. The **KOA Kampground,** located 5 miles east of Silver City just off US 180, has RV and tent sites as well as cabins, showers, laundry, and a pool. The **Silver City RV Park** is in town behind Furr's grocery store and has tent sites, showers, and laundry.

LODGING

At Gila Hot Springs you'll find the small but charming **Wilderness Lodge,** where meals are made from scratch. Breakfast is included, lunch and dinner are available by prior arrangement. They've also got hot springs, horseback riding, and a great location for exploring the area. **Sapillo Crossing Lodge,** at the intersection of NM 15 and 35, has 16 rooms and a restaurant next door. At Lake Roberts you'll find cabins for rent through the general store and a motel with six units that have kitchenettes. **Spirit Canyon Lodge** is located at the south end of Lake Roberts, is moderately priced, has a café, and welcomes pets. You'll find several more lodging possibilities along NM 35 and in the town of Mimbres. Closer to Silver City is the rustic **Bear Creek Motel and Cabins,** located outside the hamlet of Pinos Altos.

There are several good, moderately priced motels in Silver City, including the **Copper Manor,** the **Drifter Motel,** and the **Holiday Motor Hotel.** The **Palace Hotel,** right downtown, is a restored Victorian building from the Wild West days. It is moderately priced. **Carter House** is a B&B that also serves as the area's youth hostel. If you are looking for a unique

---

!

IT'S INTERESTING TO KNOW...

One of the Mogollon's most notable achievements was their skill in crafting black-on-white and brown-on-white pottery. The Mimbres, a branch of the Mogollon, are especially well known for their pots and bowls with highly decorative geometric designs featuring animal figures, hunters, and sometimes mythical man-animal figures. The bowls are the most striking and were likely cherished family objects. When the person owning the bowl died it was ceremonially "killed": a hole punched in the bottom released the bowl's spirit and allowed it to accompany its owner to the afterlife. The many Mimbres bowls that have been recovered from burial sites almost always have these holes and are often found covering the face of the deceased. Mimbres pueblos, scattered along the river that bears their name, were early targets for pot hunters, and many were leveled by bulldozers looking to unearth burial sites located beneath the structures' floors. The Silver City Museum has a good collection of Mimbres pottery and tools and the visitor center at the monument has a few pieces as well.

lodging experience that is slightly off the beaten path and you don't mind paying a bit more try **The Cottages,** offering private cottages with all the amenities near the Continental Divide on Cottage San Road.

FOOD

At **Doc Campbell's Post** in Gila Hot Springs you'll find a few groceries and a snack bar. Further down the road at **Sapillo Crossing** is a restaurant serving three basic meals a day. East on NM 35 you can find groceries at the **Lake Roberts General Store** and a café at **Spirit Canyon Lodge** at the south end of the lake. South along NM 15 in Pinos Altos is the **Buckhorn Saloon,** where you can get steaks, seafood, and burgers. They have been serving up

DON'T MISS

There is much to see and do in the Silver City area, including hiking to hot springs, visiting Pinos Altos and its historic Hearst Church, or taking the self-guided Billy the Kid tour through the outlaw's boyhood home. If you are interested in the area's mining history don't pass up the chance to visit Old Tyrone and the remains of the Phelps-Dodge open-pit copper mine, or travel east for a gander at the Santa Rita/Chino open-pit copper mine, the oldest mine in New Mexico. Worked by the Spanish as early as 1800, the pit wasn't begun until 1910 but now spans 1.5 miles and is over a thousand feet deep. You can peer into the pit from NM 152 about 15 miles east of Silver City. Scrambling through twisted rocks at the City of Rocks State Park, about 30 miles south of Silver City, is a worthwhile side trip, as is traversing the Catwalk through Whitewater Canyon near Glenwood, about 60 miles to the north. Catwalk was the name given to a pipe that snaked through the canyon, feeding water to an ore mill. In order traverse the canyon and make repairs workers had to gingerly walk on top of the pipe. Now a fenced walkway is suspended along the canyon wall, allowing visitors safe passage through the canyon.

drinks and basic grub to miners, ranchers, and tourists for more than a hundred years.

In Silver City there are quite a few restaurants to choose from, too many to list here. Try the **Corner Café** (corner of Bullard and Broadway) for breakfast or lunch; they have legendary cinnamon rolls. **Jalisco Café** (103 S. Bullard) is another local favorite that serves Mexican dishes for lunch and dinner. The **Silver Café** (514 N. Bullard) emphasizes New Mexican–flavored dishes for lunch and dinner that are delicious. The **Health Food Shoppe** (303 E. 13th St.) has fresh juices, smoothies, and a deli and makes for a great stop after a ride.

LAUNDRY

Other than the laundry facilities at the RV parks listed (often reserved for guests only) try **Laundryland USA,** 407 N. Hudson, Silver City; 505-538-2631

BIKE SHOP/BIKE RENTAL

Gila Hike & Bike (rentals), 103 E. College Ave., Silver City; 505-388-3222

Twin Sisters Cycling and Fitness, 303 N. Bullard St., Silver City; 505-538-3388

FOR FURTHER INFORMATION

Gila Cliff Dwellings National Monument—Superintendent, Route 11, Box 100, Silver City, NM 88061; 505-536-9461 or 505-536-9344; www.nps.gov/gicl/

Silver City–Grant County Chamber of Commerce, 1103 N. Hudson St. (NM 90), Silver City, NM 88061; 505-538-3785 or 1-800-548-6106

Gila National Forest, 3005 E. Camino Del Bosque, Silver City, NM 88061; 505-388-8201

18

Pecos National Historical Park

Located at the southern end of the Sangre de Cristo Mountains, 25 miles southeast of Santa Fe, are the ruins of Pecos, once called Cicuye by the Pueblo people who lived here. A Spanish mission church, built sometime between 1621 and 1640, also shares the site. Perched atop a small hill, these visually striking ruins are testament to the more than a thousand years of human history in this area.

As early as A.D. 800 pre-Puebloans were living in pithouses scattered along Glorieta Creek and the Pecos River, farming the usual trio of corn, beans, and squash. By 1100 they were building freestanding stone villages, adding cotton to their crops, producing artfully crafted pottery, and participating in a trade network that stretched far to the south, west, and east. Sometime in the 14th century, smaller individual family or clan villages were abandoned and the pueblo atop the hill rapidly expanded. By 1450 Pecos had reached its maximum size, standing four to five stories high, with 660 rooms, 22 kivas, and somewhere between two thousand and twenty-five hundred people. Archaeologists have theorized that the reason behind Pecos' centralization was the growing threat posed by Plains Indians. The Pecos people became increasingly powerful because of their numbers, their location at the eastern edge of the Pueblo world,

Claret cup cactus blooms are a deep crimson and are a delight to find in the foothills of the Santa Fe Mountains where they thrive.

and their ability to supply crops and trade goods, such as pottery and clothing, to Apaches, Comanches, and others. In return they received buffalo hides, slaves, and flints for points and cutting tools. These items were often traded west or south for turquoise beads, pottery, parrot feathers, or other desired goods. The Spaniards would later participate in this trade.

The Indians of Pecos had a long history of Spanish contact, beginning in 1540 when Francisco Vasquez de Coronado came through in search of riches similar to those of the Aztecs and Incas to the south. After attacking the Zuni's pueblos and seizing their food stores, Coronado continued on to Pecos, accompanied by an army of twelve hundred men. Before they could attack, however, the Indians rushed out to greet them with food and gifts, eliminating the need for domination. After an unsuccessful foray onto the plains of western Kansas, Coronado turned back. Sixty years later the Spanish returned, this time seeking to establish their influence and secure the frontier through settlement and missions. In 1598 Don Juan de Onate claimed the region of the Rio Grande for Spain and quickly dispatched a friar to Pecos, the richest and most powerful pueblo in the region. The mission church was built under the direction of Fray Andres Juarez sometime after he arrived in 1621 and was the most impressive of frontier's mission churches, featuring towers, buttresses, and enormous log beams hauled out of the mountains.

Over the next two hundred years there were periods of peace and prosperity mixed with periods of resentment. The Pecos joined with other pueblos and revolted against the Spanish in 1680, but welcomed Diego de Vargas back twelve years later when he came to reclaim the lost province. Subsequent years of unrest punctuated by outbreaks of disease, raids by Comanches, and migration left Pecos little more than a ghost town when the Santa Fe Trail began bustling with travelers and traders in 1821. The last inhabitants of Pecos left to join their Towa-speaking relatives at Jemez Pueblo in 1838.

Fort Union National Monument

About an hour's drive from Pecos is another important historic site, significant for its role in an entirely different chapter of Western American history. After the Mexican War of 1846–1848 and New Mexico became a part of the United States through the Treaty of Guadalupe Hidalgo, garrisons were established up and down the Rio Grande to protect trade and travel routes as well as the area's settlers. But in 1851 Lt. Col. Edwin V. Sumner saw the need to revise the territory's defensive strategy, ordering garrisons relocated closer to "problem" Indians. He also wanted the army's headquarters and supply depot moved from Santa Fe, a place he referred to as a "sink of vice and extravagance," to a location near the junction of the Mountain and Cimmaron branches of the Santa Fe Trail. This was the order that gave birth to Fort Union, which first rose from the grassy plain east of the mountains as a ramshackle collection of log buildings.

For the next decade the fort served as a base for military operations, a way station for those traveling along the Santa Fe Trail, and the principle quartermaster depot of the Southwest territory. Campaigns were launched against several Indian tribes, including the Jicarilla Apache, the Utes of southern Colorado, and later the Kiowas and Comanches who were raiding the plains east of the fort. At the outbreak of the Civil War, in 1861, most troops and officers were withdrawn from Fort Union and replaced with volunteer regiments while regulars were concentrated fur-

Piñon, juniper, and ponderosa pine interspersed with an understory of short-grass prairie grasses are a common sight in the foothills of the Santa Fe Mountains.

ther south at Fort Craig on the Rio Grande. Col. R.S. Canby, in charge of defending the New Mexico territory, sensed a Confederate invasion and sent Fort Union troops east to patrol the Santa Fe Trail while ordering the construction of a second Fort Union, this one characterized by a star-shaped layout and massive earthwork fortifications. This second fort never saw battle, thanks to a force of Colorado and New Mexico volunteers who turned back an assault on Santa Fe at the battle of Glorieta Pass in March, 1862.

By the following year New Mexico was free from Confederate threats, prompting the new regional commander, Brig. Gen. James H. Carleton, to begin construction of the third and final Fort Union. This sprawling complex of adobe buildings took six years to complete and included a military outpost, a quartermaster depot, warehouses, corrals, a mechanic's shop, stores, offices, and living quarters for a population of civilian workers and their families that eventually outnumbered military personnel. Operations against hostile Indians continued until about 1875, when most tribes were forced onto reservations or relocated. The fort continued to help maintain law and order in the region while the supply

CYCLING OPTIONS

There are three rides in this chapter: one can be ridden by either road or mountain bikers and the other two are for mountain bikes only. All riders who have the fitness to tackle the mileage can pedal part of the Santa Fe Trail's Mountain Branch from I-25 to Fort Union along the now lightly traveled road that dead ends at the park. More serious road riders can also choose a route that follows the Cimarron Cutoff of this historic trail. Both branches converge at the freeway exit where the ride begins. The ride across Glorieta Mesa is another historic route, one that was taken by a Union officer and his men attempting to surprise Confederate forces hoping to take Fort Union after capturing the territorial capital of Santa Fe. This is an easy pedal on dirt roads across an open landscape. The ride up to Barillas Peak is more strenuous, taking mountain bikers 10 miles to a lookout atop a peak with commanding views of the Pecos River Valley and the surrounding Sangre de Cristo Peaks.

There are many, many more possibilities both on- and off-road in this area and around Santa Fe. Several good bike shops and a healthy community of cyclists provide excellent resources for those wishing to stay longer and see more of this beautiful and historically rich area.

depot flourished. That all changed in 1879, when the Santa Fe Railroad replaced the Santa Fe Trail as the Southwest's main avenue of travel and commerce. The fort was completely abandoned by 1891, its adobe buildings left to melt away in the wind and weather.

Cycling in the Parks

The ruins that are the focus of these parks, and the limited acreage that surrounds them, means that there are no real riding possibilities within park boundaries. There are, however, excellent riding opportunities immediately adjacent to both parks. A great ride that locals have discovered and drive to get to is the 8-mile pedal from the interstate exit to Fort Union National Monument along a lightly traveled road that dead-ends

Wooden floor and beam supports like these surviving in the ruins of the mission church at Pecos allow archaeologists to use tree-ring dating to pinpoint the exact date structures were built.

there. The road to the monument follows the Mountain Branch of the Santa Fe Trail north. I-25, and a frontage road that parallels it, follow the Cimmaron Cutoff northeast to Wagon Mound. This presents an option for the serious road riders who might want to cover more distance. Glorieta Mesa, rising to the southwest of Pecos, features open meadows rimmed by ponderosa pine forests and rolling terrain traversed by dirt roads that mountain bikers of all abilities can enjoy. The ride up to Barillas Peak is physically demanding and requires intermediate riding skills. Views from atop the lookout at the peak are superb. There are many more riding opportunities in the region for both road and mountain bikers and a good selection of shops in Santa Fe where you can get more ideas and any other bike needs.

Elevations are relatively high, about 7,000 feet. The climate is semi-arid and the sun shines a good deal of the time. Winters can be cold and snowfall is not an uncommon event. Spring through fall is the best time to explore on two wheels, although summertime can be hot, with temperatures reaching into the 90s. The summer months are also the busiest season, and if you are planning to visit then it's a good idea to secure hotel and campground reservations well in advance. Summer is also the time for frequent, often violent thunderstorms due to moisture in the upper levels of the atmosphere moving north from the Gulf of Mexico. Be aware of stormy weather patterns during this time of year and plan to be well off high ridges or exposed areas by mid- to late afternoon when these storms usually hit.

67. SANTA FE TRAIL TO FORT UNION
(See map on page 380)

For road or mountain bikes. The 8-mile trip from the junction of the Santa Fe Trail's Mountain and Cimarron Cutoffs to Fort Union is a pedal through time that almost all types and abilities of cyclists will find to their liking. The route undulates across an open, grassy landscape that provides sweeping views up to the Sangre de Cristo Mountains just a few miles to the west. A longer option is provided for more serious road riders.

Starting point: Begin this ride just off of I-25 at exit 366. Park off to the side of the road.

Length: 8 miles one-way, 16 miles out-and-back. Allow at least 4 hours to complete this ride and spend time seeing the exhibits at the visitor center, cruising the great selection of books, and walking the trails around the ruins. The longer road option is 21 miles one-way.

Riding surface: Pavement.

Difficulty: Moderate. Distance and elevation will make this more difficult for some.

Scenery/highlights: This is a great pedal along a route that once served as the main artery of commerce and transportation for the entire Southwest but now sees only a few cars traveling back and forth to the monument. The pretty, rolling country that surrounds the fort looks much the same as it did 150 years ago when the first fort was built here, but instead of a single road coming in from the south there were rutted wagon roads and trails coming in to the fort from all directions.

Best time to ride: Spring through fall. It can be windy in the spring.

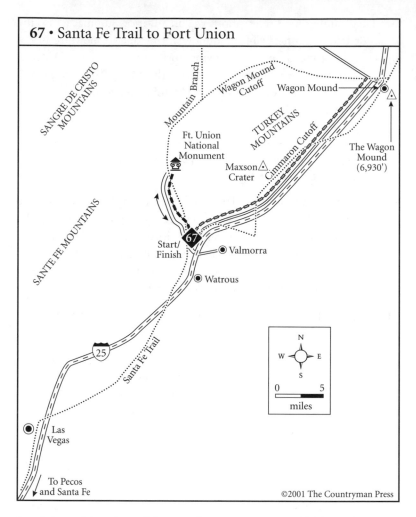

67 · Santa Fe Trail to Fort Union

Special considerations: Water and rest rooms are available at the monument. Bring a lock to secure your bike outside the visitors center.

Directions for the ride: From your starting point just off of I-25, which parallels the Cimmaron Cutoff, head north on NM 161, the only access to the fort. Follow this road as it climbs gently, rolling across several drainage depressions before arriving at the fort 8 miles from the start. There are no side roads to worry about and the road ends at the monument.

The long, low brow of Glorieta Mesa defines the Pecos River Valley for miles in either direction, as seen from the ruins at Pecos.

Option: Serious road bikers looking for more of a workout may want to head northeast to Wagon Mound along a frontage road running along the left side of the freeway. It is 21 miles to the town of Wagon Mound, named for the oddly shaped butte that rises just behind the town. The butte served as an important landmark for travelers and pioneers on the Santa Fe Trail.

68. GLORIETA MESA (See map on page 383)

For mountain bikes. This is a casual, 5-mile pedal out across the long, low expanse of Glorieta Mesa to its northeast rim where you can peer down on the ruins of Pecos and imagine the bustle of life that once went on there. You will also be looking down on the Glorieta Pass Battle site, where Union and Confederate troops fought during the Civil War.

Starting point: Begin this ride at the forest service boundary on the west side of Glorieta Mesa. To get there from the town of Pecos go west on

FLORA

The two dominant habitats in and around these monuments are piñon-juniper woodlands and Southwestern grasslands or shortgrass prairie. Areas of mixed conifer forests and riparian wetlands exist at Pecos. Other trees coexisting with piñon and Rocky Mountain and one-seed juniper include wavyleaf and Gambel oaks and mountain mahogany. There are no trees within the boundaries of Fort Union National Monument but there are many types of grasses, including blue grama, ring muhly, hairy grama, western wheatgrass, Russian wild rye, and Kentucky bluegrass.

Shrubs you are likely to see include big sagebrush, wax and golden currant, wild rose, four-wing saltbush, snakeweed, and chamisa. Yucca, Spanish dagger, pincushion cactus, Fendler hedgehog, cholla, and four other species of cactus can be found blooming in spring. Again, most of these are found at Pecos only. Wildflowers that grow in one or both parks include butterfly milkweed, asters, blanketflower, oxeye daisy, prairie coneflower, wallflower, silvery lupine, purple geranium, western blue flax, red globe mallow, trailing four o'clock, evening primrose, and Indian paintbrush.

NM 50 toward the town of Glorieta and get on I-25 heading south and west. Drive approximately 8 miles to exit 290, signed for Lamy/Vaughn. Go right onto a frontage road, and go right again, heading back north and east. Continue on the frontage road for just over 2 miles, to County Road (CR) 51, which is dirt. Go right onto CR 51 and drive 3.5 miles to a fork. Bear left onto Forest Road (FR) 326. Drive 1 mile to a boundary fence marking forest service property and park here.

If you do not want to drive your vehicle on the dirt road or want to lengthen your ride you can park at the start of CR 51. This will add 9 miles to the total distance of your ride.

Length: 10 miles. Allow 2 to 3 hours to complete this ride, more if you park and begin at the start of CR 51.

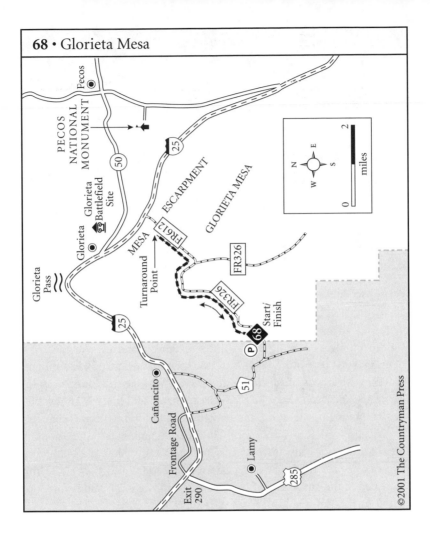

Riding surface: A dirt road that can get pretty beat-up in places, especially after heavy rains.

Difficulty: Easy to moderate.

Scenery/highlights: In 1861 Gen. Henry Hopkins Sibley approached Confederate President Jefferson Davis with a plan to invade the West, capture its vast mineral wealth, and take shipping ports in southern

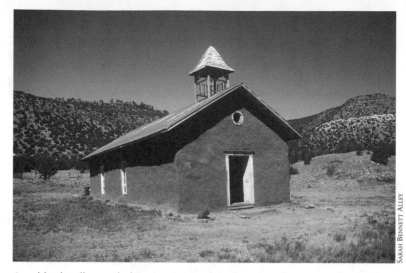

An old schoolhouse belonging to an abandoned settlement in the Santa Fe Mountains not far from Pecos.

California, thus securing trade routes to Europe and the Far East. The plan involved recruiting Utah Mormons, sympathetic Colorado miners, and New Mexicans of Mexican and Spanish heritage still bitter from the Mexican-American war. The plan was approved and in early 1862 Sibley began moving up the Rio Grande with three thousand Texas Riflemen.

Col. Edward R.S. Canby, the Union commander for operations in New Mexico, quickly learned of Confederate invasion plans but was without needed troops, who had been called to fight in the east. Canby appealed to the governors of New Mexico and Colorado and before long had four thousand volunteers at the ready.

The first battle came at Valverde, near Fort Craig, about 100 miles south of Albuquerque. Confederate troops pounded the Union troops, forcing them to retreat to Fort Craig. Sibley pushed on, intent on taking Santa Fe. The Fifth Texas Regiment took the undefended city, hoisting the Confederate flag at the Palace of the Governors on March 13, 1862. As the disorganized and demoralized troops at Fort Craig regrouped and began to move north, another 950 men from the First Regiment of Colorado Volunteers was pushing south, and camped at Kolzlowski's Station just south of Pecos on March 26.

Over the next two days Union and Confederate forces would clash in two major battles just below the northern tip of Glorieta Mesa; one on the west side at Cañoncito, a few miles farther east of CR 51, the other on the northeast side, at Pigeon Ranch near the town of Glorieta. Union Maj. John Chivington and his troops crossed Glorieta Mesa along the same route described here, but in the opposite direction, surprising and destroying a critical Confederate supply train at the mouth of Apache Canyon, almost where CR 51 crosses under I-25. These battles were hard fought, killing over a hundred men on both sides and wounding almost twice that. The result was the retreat of Confederate troops from New Mexico, and the elimination of Confederate threat in the West for the remainder of the Civil War.

Best time to ride: Spring through fall.

Special considerations: There are neither water nor conveniences along this route. Come prepared with plenty of whatever you will need.

There are tempting side roads taking off in all directions; a Santa Fe National Forest map or USGS topographic map will help with route finding and exploring.

Directions for the ride: From the forest boundary simply follow FR 326 as it rolls out along the mesa top, traversing open, grassy expanses dotted by grazing cows and stately stands of ponderosa pines. The road traverses the mesa in a northeasterly direction for almost 3 miles before bending around and heading east, then south. Approximately 4.2 miles from the start there is an intersection with another dirt road on the left; this is FR 612. Turn left onto this road, negotiating a short, steep section of downhill before the route levels out again. Continue along this road another mile to where it plunges over the side of the mesa, dropping down to the town of Glorieta. This is your turnaround point and the point at which you are directly above the Civil War battle site of Glorieta. Retrace your route back to your car.

---

69. BARILLAS PEAK (See map on page 387)

For mountain bikes. The ride up to Barillas Peak (9,371 ft.) and lookout in the Sangre de Cristo Mountains can be accessed from the town of

Fort Union served as a strategic command post during Civil War battles, campaigns against raiding Plains Indians, and as a commercial hub along the Santa Fe Trail, but was abandoned with the coming of the railroad in 1879.

Pecos. The route is not super-technical but there are steep spots with loose rock and gravel that can be challenging. The ride's distance and the vertical gain of almost 1,400 feet means you'll want to be physically fit to tackle this one.

Starting point: Begin from the intersection of FR 83 and 203 on Ruidoso Ridge. To get there drive east out of the town of Pecos on NM 223 for just over 3 miles before turning right onto CR B44A, also FR 83. This will be a gravel road. Continue driving on FR 83 for almost 6 miles past the settlement of Lower Colonias. FR 83 bears left at a fork just below Lower Colonias, crosses over Cow Creek, and begins climbing up onto Ruidoso Ridge. Drive another 4 miles past this fork to the intersection with FR 203 on Ruidoso Ridge. Park here, off to the side of the road.

Length: 18 miles up and back with a loop around the peak and a spur to a lookout.

Riding surface: Dirt road; steep, loose, and rutted in spots.

Difficulty: Moderate to difficult.

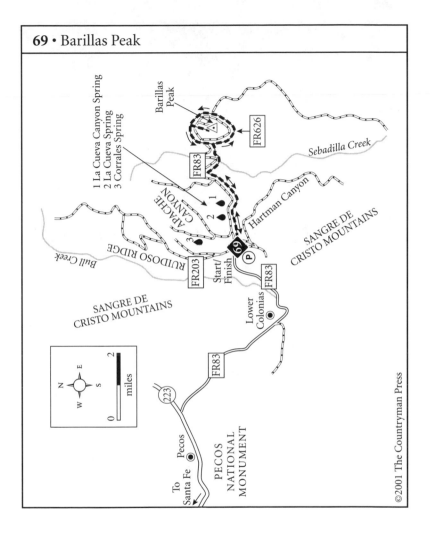

1 La Cueva Canyon Spring
2 La Cueva Spring
3 Corrales Spring

Barillas Peak

FR626

FR83

Sebadilla Creek

APACHE CANYON

Hartman Canyon

SANGRE DE CRISTO MOUNTAINS

Bull Creek

RUIDOSO RIDGE

FR203

Start/ Finish

FR83

69

P

Lower Colonias

SANGRE DE CRISTO MOUNTAINS

N E S W

miles

0   2

FR83

223

To Santa Fe

Pecos

PECOS NATIONAL MONUMENT

©2001 The Countryman Press

Scenery/highlights: As you pedal upward the high-desert mix of piñon, juniper, and Gambel oak gives way to ponderosa pines and then mixed conifer and aspen. Keep your eyes open for wild raspberries growing along the side of the road; they're pretty thick and start to ripen around the first of July.

Views are fantastic from the lookout. To the north you will see the

FAUNA

Birds you are likely to see here include turkey vultures, red-tailed hawks, American kestrels, Gambel's quail, Cassin's kingbirds, northern flickers, scrub and piñon jays, roadrunners, and ravens. In summer mourning doves, broad-tailed hummingbirds, Say's phoebes, ash-throated flycatchers, golden-crowned kinglets, western and mountain bluebirds, solitary vireos, yellow warblers, black-headed grosbeaks, rufous-sided towhees, land lesser goldfinches are common.

Desert cottontails, blacktail jackrabbits, least chipmunks, rock squirrels, pocket gophers, porcupines, ringtail cats, raccoons, long-tailed weasels, badgers, and several species of skunks are all known to exist in this area. Most are more common at Pecos. Collared peccary, bobcats, mountain lions, and coyotes are larger mammals that once again prefer the cover found in the woodlands near Pecos. White-tailed and mule deer, elk, pronghorn antelope, and occasionally bighorn sheep are spotted around Pecos as well. Pronghorns are sometimes spotted on the grassy plains around Fort Union.

Reptiles include western box turtle and desert tortoise, regal horned lizard, Great Plains skink, and a variety of snakes, among them gopher snakes, regal ring-neck snakes, western hognose snakes, black-neck garter snakes, lots of prairie rattlesnakes and the western diamondback rattlesnake.

prominent shape of Elk Mountain, rising to 11,659 feet. This peak, which can also be summited on a mountain bike, and much of the surrounding area was badly burned during the Pecos Fire in June, 2000. Rosilla Peak (10,637 ft.) is just below it and to the west. Beyond the Cow Creek and Upper Pecos drainage you may be able to see Santa Fe Baldy (12,622 ft.), Pecos Baldy (12,500 ft.), and Truchas Peak (13,103 ft.), all within the Pecos Wilderness. To the south you'll be looking along the central spine of the more humble El Barro Peaks, into Apache Canyon, the Pecos River Valley, and beyond to Glorieta Mesa.

A valley view of Fort Union and the beautiful New Mexico countryside.

Best time to ride: Mid-spring through fall.

Special considerations: There are no water or conveniences at the trail-head so be sure to come prepared with everything you'll need to sustain your energy during and after your ride. Also, this is a long day out; it's not a bad idea to bring a shell or extra piece of clothing should the weather change suddenly, as it so often does in New Mexico.

This is a popular area for deer hunting in the fall; be aware of hunting schedules and locations before heading out. If you are here during hunting season wear a bright piece of clothing to alert hunters to your presence and be prepared for more road traffic than normal.

Directions for the ride: From the intersection where you parked continue straight ahead on FR 83. Approximately 0.7 mile from the start you will pass a road to Hartman Canyon on your right, and shortly after pass a road on your left—FR 82 leading up into Apache Canyon and Cañon Corrales. Continue climbing on FR 83, up Cañon de La Cueva, past La Cueva Canyon Spring, ignoring several dirt roads taking off on either side of the main route. The road traverses Sebadilla Creek drainage, approximately 5.3 miles from the start, and then makes a series of switchbacks up a steep, rocky section toward the peak. You arrive at the loop portion of the ride 6.7 miles from the start. Go right, heading south on FR 626. This road makes a circuit of Barillas, rejoining FR 83 on the southeast side of the peak approximately 2.4 miles later. Go left when you reach FR 83, climbing for 0.4 mile to an intersection. Go left to make the final push up to the lookout 10 miles from the start. After spending some time at the lookout, head back down the road and go left, down FR 83 all the way to your car.

CAMPING

There is no camping inside the park but there are more than a dozen developed campgrounds located directly north of the town of Pecos along NM 63. Several of these are state-run recreation sites, the remainder are under the supervision of the Santa Fe National Forest. Some of the prettiest are at the very end of the road, some 20 miles north of Pecos and include **Jack's Creek, Iron Gate, Winsor Creek, Gowles,** and **Holy Ghost,** at the end of FR 122. Most of these campgrounds, which are a favorite of equestrian groups riding into the wilderness area, have rest rooms, drinking water, picnic tables, and spaces for RVs. Check with the Pecos Ranger District office just north of the monument for more information.

IT'S INTERESTING TO KNOW...

Alfred V. Kidder is responsible for excavating the South Pueblo, mission church, and convento—the heart of the mission, containing the priest's quarters, kitchen, dining room, workshops, and stables—at Pecos between 1915 and 1929. Kidder is credited with pioneering a method of Southwestern archaeology using stratigraphic dating of debris found in pueblo trash mounds. Because Pecos had been occupied for so long, the trash piles at its edge were enormous. Kidder knew that the bottom layers were the oldest and that he could date successive layers from pieces of pottery and other remains. In 1927, a gathering of archaeologists, convened by Kidder, agreed on the identification of stages in Anasazi development based on his findings. Still in use today, those stages are Basketmaker I, II, and III, followed by Pueblo I through V. The Pecos Conference remains an important annual meeting for people devoted to the study of Southwestern archaeology.

For RV parks you'll need to head toward Santa Fe. The two closest to Pecos are **Rancheros de Santa Fe Camping Park** and the **Santa Fe KOA,** both located west of Pecos off the frontage road between exits 290 and 294. Both have tent sites and shower facilities.

In the town of Las Vegas, situated between Pecos and Fort Union, there are two RV campgrounds: the **Las Vegas KOA,** just off I-25 at exit 339, and the **Vegas RV Park,** at 504 Harris Road. There are at least another half-dozen great forest service campgrounds just northwest of Las Vegas along Gallinas Creek. To get to these drive out of Las Vegas on NM 65/FR 263. **El Porvenir Campground** can accommodate RVs, while many of the others are more primitive, with vault toilets and picnic tables only. Stop in at the Las Vegas Ranger District offices for more information.

LODGING

There is no lodging available in or directly adjacent to either of these parks. In Santa Fe, 25 miles from Pecos, you'll find at least a hundred lodging choices including B&Bs, resorts, spa retreats, historic hotels in old downtown, and every kind of chain hotel. Contact the Santa Fe Convention and Visitors Bureau for more information.

Las Vegas, located between the monuments right off I-25, is not so overwhelming and expensive as Santa Fe and is a good place to stay if you're not interested in the shopping and galleries that the capital city has to offer. The **Plaza Hotel,** on the old plaza in the center of Las Vegas is a classic Western inn that was first built in 1882 and has been fully restored. This charming hotel has wonderful ambiance and is on the National Register of Historic Places. Live music is often featured on weekends. It is moderately priced, as is the **Carriage House Bed & Breakfast,** housed in a hundred-year-old Victorian house just a few blocks from downtown. At the north end of town, near the freeway entrance, you'll find close to a dozen budget motels and several chain hotels, among them a **Super 8,** a **Days Inn,** and a **Comfort Inn.**

FOOD

There is a drive-in, a Dairy Queen, a Mexican restaurant, and a café serving basic American food in Pecos. In Santa Fe you will find every kind of restaurant

DON'T MISS

While in the area, don't pass up the chance to visit the historic city of Santa Fe, the oldest capital city in the nation. It was founded in 1607, more than a dozen years before pilgrims from England established their colony at Plymouth. Santa Fe de San Francisco de Asis originally existed as a Spanish fort and outpost, one of a series of missions and forts aimed at converting the Pueblo Indians to Catholicism. It later became headquarters for the colony's political and military operations. No fewer than 60 New Mexican governors ruled from the fortress at Santa Fe, which eventually came to be known as the Palace of the Governors. After it was completed in 1610, the fortress became the epicenter of change and upheaval in New Mexico. First occupied by Spanish soldiers, it became the home of Popé, the Indian leader who led the Pueblo Revolt of 1680 and drove the Spanish completely out of New Mexico for 12 years. Later it housed American infantrymen under the command of Gen. Stephen Kearney, who took the city without incident and claimed the New Mexico territory for the United States during the war with Mexico in 1846. Still later, the Confederate flag flew over the fort for several weeks after the city was taken by a regiment of Texas Riflemen during the Civil War. Confederate forces were later defeated near Glorieta Pass, ending their campaign for the West.

The colorful history of Santa Fe figures prominently in the history of the American West and the nation and is worth delving into while visiting the historically important parks at Pecos and Fort Union. In addition to the history of Santa Fe there is the art. More than 130 galleries display the works of artists who have long been drawn to this town and its enchanted aura. The Museum of Fine Arts has numerous exhibits that reveal this city's support of both the visual and performing arts and is a highly recommended stop.

you've ever dreamed of, including several of critical acclaim that regularly lure chefs away from famous eateries on both coasts. If you are serious about exploring the culinary scene in Santa Fe stop in at the visitors bureau where you can get an up-to-date list of all the latest, greatest, and best-loved restaurants.

In Las Vegas, the **Landmark Grill** at the Plaza Hotel serves Mexican and New Mexican entrees, seafood, and steak for dinner, and also serves breakfast and lunch everyday. **El Rialto** (141 Bridge St.) is a favorite for Mexican fare, while **La Concina Restaurant** (211 Plaza) and **La Fiesta** (411 Grand Ave.) serve dishes with more of a New Mexican flavor. For more dining ideas inquire at the chamber of commerce.

LAUNDRY

There are many self-service laundries in Santa Fe. In Las Vegas there is just one, **Trujillos Laundromat** (802 N. Grand Ave.).

BIKE SHOP/BIKE RENTAL

In Santa Fe:
The Bicycle Zone, 100 N. Guadalupe St.; 505-992-0549

Rob and Charlie's, 1632 Saint Michael's Dr.; 505-471-9119

Santa Fe Mountain Sports, 607 Cerrillos Rd.; 505-988-3337

SMR Inc., 1241 Calle De Comercio; 505-473-3033

FOR FURTHER INFORMATION

Pecos National Historical Park— Superintendent, P.O. Box 418, Pecos, NM 87552; 505-757-6032; www.nps.gov/peco/

Fort Union National Monument, P.O. Box 127, Watrous, NM 87753; 505-425-8025; www.nps. gov/foun/

Santa Fe Convention & Visitors Bureau, 201 W. Marcy, Santa Fe, NM 87501; 505-984-6760 or 1-800-777-2489; www.santafe.org

Las Vegas Chamber of Commerce, 727 Grand Ave., Las Vegas, NM 87701; 505-425-7504 or 1-800-832-5947

Santa Fe National Forest, Pecos Ranger District, P.O. Drawer 429, Pecos, NM 87552; 505-757-6121; www.fs.fed.us/r3/sfe/

Santa Fe National Forest, Las Vegas Ranger District, 1926 N. 7th Street, Las Vegas, NM 87701; 505-425-3534; www.fs.fed.us/r3 /sfe/

19

Defining the western skyline west of the Rio Grande Valley, just outside the city of Albuquerque, is a long, low tableland of volcanic rock. Lava first oozed out of cracks in the ground and began altering the landscape here during Permian times, about 250,000 years ago. Layers of lava built up on one another, smothering the sedimentary rock below. Then in one last burst of activity, close to 110,000 years ago, five volcanic cones erupted atop the mesa, sending still more lava flowing across the tablelands. As time passed the softer, sedimentary rock underlying the lava at the edges of the flow began to erode, causing large chunks of the black rock to fall off and tumble away. A well-defined escarpment running north to south eventually emerged along the edge of the mesa, presenting a blackboard of sorts, an irresistible invitation to those who would pass through and settle here to etch their ideas and beliefs in stone. Along a 17-mile stretch of this escarpment a remarkable concentration of more than twenty thousand petroglyphs are now protected as a national monument.

As long as three thousand years ago people discovered they could create images on the rock face by chipping away the "varnish," a coating on the rock created when iron and manganese oxides in the lava became exposed to the elements. Archaic hunting and gathering peoples were the

Just a few of the thousands of intriguing petroglyphs easily accessed from the trails inside the monument.

first to leave their mark, mostly abstract patterns and lines. Crosses and sheep brands were later chipped into the rock by 17th-century herders and priests, and by those who were the beneficiaries of the 1692 Atrisco land grant, presented to colonists by the Spanish Crown. The bulk of the petroglyphs, however, were left by ancestors of the Pueblo Indian people over a period that lasted four to seven hundred years.

What do these images mean? Why were they left here? Why are they etched into surfaces facing only certain directions? These are just a few of the many questions the petroglyphs evoke. We know that chipping these images into the rock was not an easy process, requiring forethought as to placement and design, and took many hours, perhaps even days, to create. Images of things such as parrots, birds native to Central America far to the south, may have communicated that the people living here belonged to an extensive trade network that gave them both power and influence. Humanoid figures may represent gods in Indian cosmology and were left here as guardians or as a form of worship. The Pueblo tribes of the Rio Grande Valley consider these images sacred and still use the area for religious ceremonies.

Cycling in the Park

Petroglyph National Monument was established in 1990. Prior to that it was a state park with many trails and dirt roads open to bikers. As this book goes to press some of those roads—the ones around the volcanoes on the west side of the park—remain open but it is likely there will be future restrictions. In the meantime mountain bikers of all abilities can enjoy making several loops out around the volcanoes and the fantastic views of the Rio Grande Valley, the Sandia Mountains that define the valley to the east, and to other landmarks farther in the distance. Rio Grande Valley State Park, just east of the monument, encompasses 25 miles of the river corridor and includes many miles of paved bike trails, dike roads, and bike lanes along city streets, allowing cyclists of all varieties to pedal north and south along the river for as long as suits them. Singletrack and dirt dike roads run through Corrales Bosque, a beautiful river woodland of stately Rio Grande cottonwoods. A cherry-stem loop on the Foothills Trail System is the only ride listed on the east side of the

★ CYCLING OPTIONS

Five rides are offered here; one is for road bikes, one is for road or mountain bikes, and three are for mountain bikes. All except one are located on the west side of Albuquerque. A ride around the volcanoes inside the monument presents a number of options for riders of all abilities. Views from atop this mesa are excellent. The paved bike paths of Rio Grande Valley State Park run for miles along the Rio Grande and are fun for all ages and types of bikers. The singletrack that winds along the river in the Corrales Bosque is slightly more difficult but still a great choice for mountain bikers of varying abilities. Several places where the trail meets the river on this route make for great picnic spots. The Foothills Trail System on the east side of the valley inside Albert G. Simms City Park offers a network of singletrack trails serious fat-tire fans won't want to miss. A loop route for road riders that can be ridden from the monument visitor center rounds out the offerings in this chapter.

city. This trail system offers five-star singletrack riding and options for creating your own routes. A loop route for road bikers heads north from the monument and travels through the charming old hamlet of Corrales. A shorter option that avoids traffic near the monument begins and ends in the town of Corrales.

These are just a few cycling possibilities among the dozens of on- and off-road routes in the Albuquerque area. More serious road riders often head out of the city to ride secondary roads linking some of the smaller nearby towns. NM 44, which heads northwest toward Jemez Pueblo and the Jemez Mountains, is popular, as is NM 14 east of Albuquerque, running through the towns of San Antonio, Golden, Madrid, and Cerillos. Mountain bikers generally head east to Otero Canyon, the Cedro Peak area, the eastern and northern slopes of the Sandias, or up to Sandia Peak Ski Area, where you'll find a whole system of singletrack trails serviced by chairlifts.

Albuquerque sits about a mile above sea level and has a wonderful year-round climate. Summertime can be hot, with temperatures reaching well into the 90s. Winters remain mild, with daytime temperatures often climbing into the 40s and 50s. Enough snow falls atop Sandia Peak to entertain skiers but rarely accumulates on the ground around Albuquerque. Like most of the Southwest, this region receives much of its scant annual moisture in the summer months during the desert monsoon season; plan to be done riding by midafternoon or at least be away from open or exposed areas.

---

70. VOLCANOES TOUR (See map on page 399)

For mountain bikes. This is not so much a ride as it is a delightful cruise among the extinct volcanoes that dot the mesa to the west of the escarpment where the petroglyphs are found. Mountain bikers of all ages and abilities can pedal the dirt roads and sections of trail that wind around the volcanoes and crisscross the mesa while enjoying spectacular views over the city to the east, and to massive Mount Taylor looming in the west. While there is no set route, it is hard to get lost among the distinctive shapes of the volcanoes and more distant landmarks.

Starting point: Begin this ride at a dirt parking lot on the west side of the

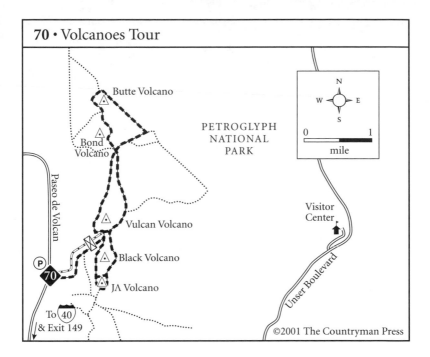

Butte Volcano

Bond Volcano

PETROGLYPH NATIONAL PARK

N
W — E
S

0   1
mile

Paseo de Volcan

Vulcan Volcano

Visitor Center

P
70

Black Volcano

JA Volcano

Unser Boulevard

To 40 & Exit 149

©2001 The Countryman Press

monument. To get there from the visitor center go out the road into the monument and turn right onto Unser Boulevard. Travel south on Unser Boulevard 3.5 miles and get on I-40 west. Go about 4 miles to exit 149, get off the freeway, and head north on Paseo del Volcan. Drive 4.8 miles north to a dirt parking lot on the right.

Length: The loop around Vulcan Volcano is about 3 miles. Spinning up and around Butte Volcano, the farthest volcano to the north is close to 7 miles. Riding south around Black and JA Volcanoes totals about 4 miles. Ride one loop or all three. There are no distance or time requirements here; ride for as long and as far as you like.

Riding surface: Dirt road, doubletrack, and a few stretches of single-track.

Difficulty: Easy. A few stretches of trail are rocky and steep where they traverse the sides of the volcanoes.

FLORA

The habitat type at Petroglyph National Monument is loosely defined as a transitional desert grassland or Southwest desert grassland. The monument exists at the boundary of three different biomes: the Great Basin Desert, the Chihuahuan Desert, and the Great Plains. There are two other life zones in the monument as well, one created by conditions along the escarpment face and rocky outcrops along the mesa's edge and base, and one created by conditions atop the mesa. They are generally hotter and drier than the surrounding terrain because the black rocks tend to gather heat.

There are few trees in the monument. One-seed juniper exists on the mesa top in a few places; desert willow is found in drainages at the south end of the park. Sand sage, broom dalea, four-wing saltbush, lemonade berry, and Apache plume are all generally found in the sandy conditions along the base of the mesa. Indian rice grass, several species of grama grass, galleta grass, and needle and thread grass are found in abundance atop the mesa and along its base. There is a limited spring bloom dominated by scorpionweed and spectacle pod on this arid landscape. The large, white flowers of sacred datura can be found at the north end of the park in early summer and wild sunflowers are blooming by midsummer along roadsides. The park's showiest bloomers go on parade in fall and include purple aster and chamisa, or rabbitbrush.

Scenery/highlights: The five cones atop this mesa are evidence of the last burst of volcanic activity here 110,000 years ago. These cones built up around fissures or cracks in the ground that alternately oozed lava and sprayed a mixture of rock and gases into the air. Hundreds of archaeological sites scattered across the mesa in the vicinity of the volcanoes suggest that this was a significant area for the ancient cultures who lived here for thousands of years. Please respect the delicate nature of this landscape and hidden archaeological treasures by staying on the main roads and trails.

Views from atop the mesa are excellent. It is a great place to watch the weather, sunset or sunrise, or even balloons lifting off during the annual fall Albuquerque Balloon Fiesta.

Best time to ride: Year-round, provided the ground is not saturated from recent rain or snow.

Special considerations: There are no rest stops or conveniences so come prepared.

It's easy to see what the weather is doing from up here, but few places to find shelter. If you see a thunderstorm approaching beat a hasty retreat to your vehicle; don't get caught out in the open during an electrical storm.

Directions for the ride: From the parking lot head east on a dirt road. You'll come to another parking lot and a gate in a few hundred yards; go around the gate and proceed to an intersection of several different trails. Go straight ahead or left to make a loop around Vulcan Volcano and access roads that loop around Bond and Butte Volcanoes farther north, or go right and explore the loops around Black and JA Volcanoes to the south.

---

71. RIO GRANDE VALLEY STATE PARK
(See map on page 402)

For road or mountain bikes. The paved hiking and biking trails of this city park stretch for 25 miles along the Rio Grande and provide a great opportunity for both road and mountain bikers of all ages and abilities to get out, enjoy the river's unique environment, or travel about town. Pick up the bike trail from the Rio Grande Nature Center where there are displays and information about the Rio Grande bosque (pronounced "bos-KAY"), or river woodlands, and ride as far and as long as you like. Paved roads and dirt dike roads that parallel the river on the west side can be linked together with the bike path to create a number of routes.

Starting point: Begin this ride at the Rio Grande Nature Center. To get there from the monument drive out the road to the visitor center and go left onto Unser Boulevard. Drive 1.3 miles north and turn right onto Montano Road. Head east, crossing over the river, for 3 miles to Rio

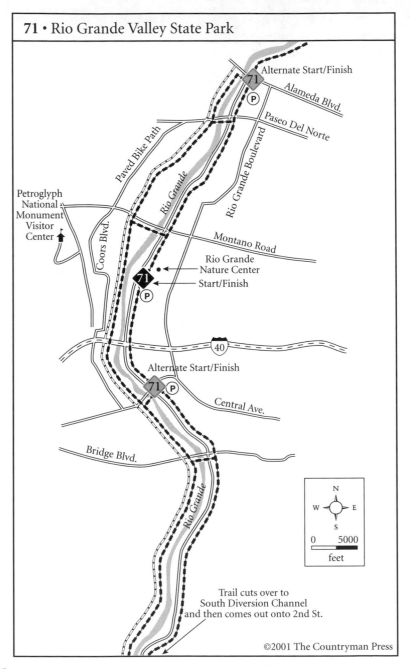

71 • Rio Grande Valley State Park

Alternate Start/Finish

71

Alameda Blvd.

Paseo Del Norte

Paved Bike Path

Rio Grande

Rio Grande Boulevard

Petroglyph
National
Monument
Visitor
Center

Coors Blvd.

Montano Road

Rio Grande
Nature Center

71

Start/Finish

40

Alternate Start/Finish

71

Central Ave.

Bridge Blvd.

Rio Grande

N
W — E
S

0   5000
feet

Trail cuts over to
South Diversion Channel
and then comes out onto 2nd St.

©2001 The Countryman Press

One of the craters responsible for the lava flows that created the escarpment on which generations of ancient people chiseled their thoughts and marked their passing.

Grande Boulevard. Go right onto Rio Grande Boulevard and follow it south for 1.4 miles to the Rio Grande Nature Center entrance on your right.

Note: Parking is limited here and is discouraged for those not visiting the nature center. The parking lot closes at 5:00 PM. Alternate access points for the park's bike trail are at Alameda Boulevard and the river, about 5.5 miles north of the nature center, and at Central Avenue and the river, just west of Old Town about 3 miles south of the nature center. Another access point is 1 mile south of Central Avenue at Tingley Park.

Length: There are no distance or time requirements here. Spend an hour or most of a day riding along the river or creating loop routes using dike roads and city streets. The Aldo Leopold Trail, a short, 1.25-mile paved trail at the nature center, is great for little cyclists.

Riding surface: Pavement. Some dirt sections along dikes.

Difficulty: Easy to more difficult, depending on how long and how far you ride.

Scenery/highlights: Rio Grande Valley State Park includes 25 miles of the river corridor and almost 6,000 acres of bosque. The park shares its northern boundary with Sandia Pueblo and its southern boundary with Isleta Pueblo. Created in 1984, its primary responsibility is the protection of the cottonwood forest, considered to be the largest in North America.

The Rio Grande is the third-longest river in North America behind the Mississippi and the Yukon. It rises in the San Juan Mountains of Colorado and stretches 1,878 miles to the Gulf of Mexico. Several endangered species inhabit the park, including the jumping meadow mouse, black hawk, southwestern willow flycatcher, and Rio Grande silvery minnow.

The Rio Grande Nature Center is an excellent place to learn about the riparian woodlands of the river and the five other life zones of the Albuquerque area. There are over 20 self-guiding displays along trails through the center's 170 acres, a children's educational room, and a bookstore and gift shop. A wetland pond created near the visitor center provides critical habitat for some 260 species of migrating and resident birds and a home for creatures such as muskrat and beaver.

Best time to ride: Anytime of day or year.

Special considerations: A nominal fee is required for visiting the nature center; rest rooms and water available there.

Directions for the ride: From the Rio Grande Nature Center, or wherever you have parked your vehicle, pick up the paved bike trail and ride north or south. Ride for as far and as long as you like and when you have had enough return to the nature center by either retracing your route or by crossing over the river at Alameda Boulevard, Paseo Del Norte, or Bridge Boulevard and looping back on dike roads or via bike lanes along city streets. Coors Boulevard has a bike lane from I-40 to Paseo Del Norte.

---

72. CORRALES BOSQUE PRESERVE (See map on page 405)

For mountain bikes. This ride is an easy pedal through the beautiful river woodlands of the Rio Grande on dirt roads and singletrack. The route is completely level and is suitable for rank beginners but can be enjoyed by all off-road riders. This riparian woodland, or bosque, is unique to the Rio Grande, supporting enormous, centuries-old cotton-

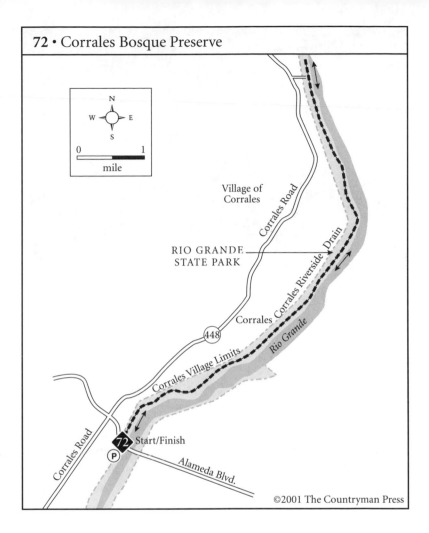

Village of
Corrales

Corrales Road

RIO GRANDE
STATE PARK

Corrales Riverside Drain

Corrales

448

Corrales Village Limits

Rio Grande

Corrales Road

72 Start/Finish

P

Alameda Blvd.

©2001 The Countryman Press

wood trees, lush undergrowth, and a rich variety of bird and wildlife. Cruising along beneath these giant trees in fall, when their heart-shaped leaves have turned brilliant yellow, is magical.

Starting point: Begin this ride just south of the town of Corrales at a parking area off Alameda Boulevard next to the river. To get there from the monument go out the main road and continue heading east on

Taking time to study an especially large and detailed panel of petroglyphs.

Western Trail Road. Drive less than a mile to Coors Boulevard, also NM 448, and go left. Drive north on Coors Boulevard approximately 6.8 miles to Alameda Boulevard and go right. Head east on Alameda almost 0.8 mile, crossing the river, looking for a parking area on the right side of the road signed for Rio Grande Open Space. Park here.

Length: 7.25 miles one-way, 14.5 miles out and back. There is no time or distance requirement for this route; ride out as far as you like and turn around when you have had enough.

Riding surface: Singletrack dirt trail with short sections of dirt road running along canals. Some stretches of both road and trail can be sandy.

Difficulty: Easy to slightly more difficult if you ride the entire distance. You may encounter a few spots of loose sand, and several gates that come up quickly will require you to dismount.

Scenery/highlights: The Corrales Bosque is a fantastic example of a mature riparian woodland habitat now very rare in the Southwest. The matrix of plant and animals species that make up the bosque, dominated by the giant Rio Grande cottonwood, nearly disappeared because of wood harvesting, dikes, and river diversion. Early settlers in the Rio Grande Valley depended almost entirely on the cottonwood for their material needs, including utensils, tools, building materials, and fuel. The dikes and channeling that came with settlement and agriculture reduced the periodic flooding the cottonwood depends on for nourishment and seed dispersal. The rich, silty floodplain of the "Big River" that sprawled across the valley floor is no more, but the abundant life that once thrived here is making a comeback along the Corrales Bosque. Hundreds of species of birds now inhabit the river forest and are joined by other creatures such as raccoons, gray foxes, muskrats, and beavers. To learn about life in and along the river, visit the Rio Grande Nature Center described in the Rio Grande Valley State Park ride.

The almost 8 miles of riverfront property traversed by this trail was purchased decades ago by the Nature Conservancy in an effort to preserve this beautiful and important piece of New Mexico's natural heritage. It is now part of Rio Grande State Park and is jointly managed by Albuquerque Open Space Division and the village of Corrales.

Best time to ride: Anytime. This trail is great year-round.

Special considerations: There are no facilities at this trailhead so come prepared with whatever you might need, including a pair of binoculars, a bird book, and a picnic.

Directions for the ride: Pick up the paved path on the right (west) side of the parking lot and ride north, under Alameda Boulevard. Go left and cross a small bridge over a canal ditch to get to a bigger bridge that will take you across the Rio Grande. Immediately after you cross the river go right onto a dirt dike road. In approximately 0.5 mile you can pick up a singletrack trail on your right. Continue pedaling northeast along the canal ditch, going right at a ramp for the ditch just over a mile from the start. Bear left almost immediately onto another singletrack trail and continue following the main route as it alternately parallels the canal ditch, crossing it several times, and then swings toward the river and courses through the bosque. In places where the trail emerges from the trees and arrives at the river's edge you can enjoy excellent views of the Sandia Mountains. Just under 4 miles from the start you encounter a series of metal gates, some requiring bikers to dismount. Just over 7 miles from the start the trail emerges from the bosque and ends at a flood-control channel. Head back the way you came.

73. FOOTHILLS TRAIL SYSTEM (See map on page 409)

For mountain bikes. This system of multiple-use trails winds along the base of Sandia Peak on the east side of the Rio Grande Valley through an area managed jointly by the city of Albuquerque's Open Space Division and the Cibola National Forest. The loop trail described here is best suited for intermediate riders, but fat-tire fans of all abilities should not pass up the chance to pedal these fun, fast-paced trails. Shorter loops are possible among the many trails that traverse the piñon- and juniper-dotted foothills just outside the Sandia Mountain Wilderness.

Starting point: There are several places to access the Foothills Trail System; two of the best are Embudito Trailhead at the end of Trailhead Road and Elena Gallegos Picnic Area inside Albert G. Simms City Park. You will need to pay a nominal day-use fee to get into the park but there are facilities such as rest rooms, picnic tables, and water available. There are no facilities at Embudito Trailhead.

To get to Embudito Trailhead from the monument go out the access road to the visitor center and turn left, heading north on Unser Boulevard for approximately 1.3 miles to Montano Road. Go right onto Montano Road and take it east, across the river and through town. Montano Road turns into Montgomery Boulevard as it passes under I-25. Continue heading east on Montgomery Boulevard 6.5 miles to Tramway Boulevard. Go straight at the intersection and continue heading east for 0.5 mile to Glenwood Hills Road. Go another 0.5 mile and turn right onto Trailhead Road. Drive a short distance to the trailhead and park.

To get to Albert G. Simms Park from Petroglyph National Monument follow directions as above to Tramway Boulevard, then turn left, and drive 2 miles to Simms Park Road. Go right and drive into the park.

Length: Starting at Embudito Trailhead gives a total distance of approximately 10 miles. From Elena Gallegos Picnic Area this loop is 7.8 miles.

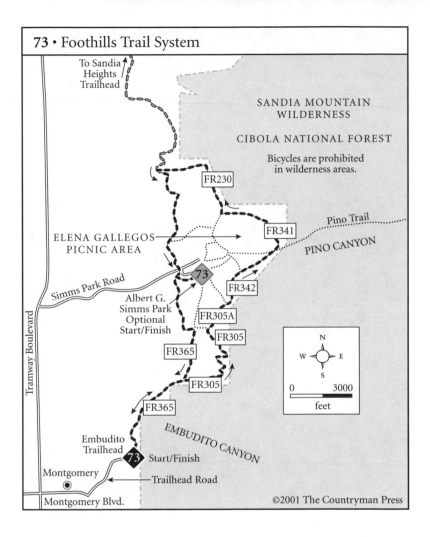

To Sandia Heights Trailhead

SANDIA MOUNTAIN WILDERNESS

CIBOLA NATIONAL FOREST

Bicycles are prohibited in wilderness areas.

FR230

Pino Trail

FR341

PINO CANYON

ELENA GALLEGOS PICNIC AREA

Simms Park Road

73

FR342

Albert G. Simms Park Optional Start/Finish

FR305A

FR305

N

W · E

S

FR365

FR305

0   3000

feet

FR365

Tramway Boulevard

Embudito Trailhead

EMBUDITO CANYON

73 Start/Finish

Montgomery

Trailhead Road

Montgomery Blvd.

©2001 The Countryman Press

Riding surface: Singletrack; mostly smooth and fast except where the trail dips through arroyos. Expect loose, rocky, and sometimes sandy conditions in arroyos.

Difficulty: Moderate. Strength and technical skills needed for negotiating arroyos and several steep climbs make this route difficult in spots.

Scenery/highlights: This is a five-star singletrack that is hugely popular

A fat-tire enthusiast relishes the fun, fast-paced trails of the Foothills Trail System.

among Albuquerque's fat-tire riders. Views over the city to the west and up to the steep, west-facing granite cliffs of the Sandia Mountains inside the Sandia Mountain Wilderness are excellent.

Best time to ride: Year-round. Get an early start if you're riding during the summer months so you won't get cooked by the afternoon sun. This is also a good time to avoid the crowds of bikers that flock to these trails daily. Conversely, a later afternoon ride during the cooler months will surely warm you up and you'll have the trails to yourself. Weekends are usually pretty busy any time of year.

Special considerations: As mentioned above, rest rooms and water are available at Elena Gallegos Picnic Area, but no facilities at Embudito Trailhead.

Numerous route options are possible, allowing riders to create shorter loops. A spur out to a trailhead at the north end of the trail system will add 5.6 miles to your total distance.

Directions for the ride: From Embudito Trailhead pedal east and then north on Forest Trail (FT) 365. Follow the trail for just over a mile as it skirts the edge of the wilderness boundary and comes to a forked intersection. Go right onto FT 305 and ride east for 0.4 mile before the trail swings and heads north. Approximately 2 miles from the start the trail dips across Bear Canyon arroyo. At 2.5 miles from the start you will come to another trail junction; stay right here, continuing north on 305A. Stay right again 0.5 mile later, continuing on FT 342. At the next junction 0.3 mile later, go right onto FT 341. Continue heading northeast on FT 341 for 0.5 mile to the junction with FT 140. FT 140 goes left to the picnic area and to the right into Pino Canyon, which it is off-limits to bikers.

Descend past Pino Canyon, following the trail as it swings northwest and begins to roll, sometimes dramatically, over rockier terrain. Approximately 4.8 miles from the start FT 341 meets FT 230; bear right, hugging the wilderness boundary as the trail climbs northward, traverses Cañon de Domingo Baca, and then turns and heads west. Approximately 5.9 miles from the start FT 230 rejoins FT 365. Turn left and begin your return trip south on FT 365. (You can go right here and ride north almost 3 miles to Sandia Heights Trailhead if you have the time and the energy.) Follow FT 365 south, crossing over the paved road into Elena

Gallegos Picnic area in 0.5 mile. Stay right at any trail intersections, arriving at the beginning of the loop 9 miles from the start. Ride 1 mile back to Embudito Trailhead.

---

74. CORRALES–RIO RANCHO LOOP
(See map on page 413)

For road bikes. This almost 30-mile loop takes you north on Coors Boulevard through the historic town of Corrales and then swings south through the newer subdivisions of Rio Rancho. It is a route popular with local road riders and is best-suited for more serious skinny-tire fans who are used to riding with vehicle traffic. Shorter and longer options are suggested.

Starting point: Petroglyph National Monument Visitor Center.

Length: 33 miles. Shorter option is 12.5 miles.

Riding surface: Pavement.

Difficulty: Moderate. Long-ish but mostly level. Shorter option is easy and stays away from heavier traffic areas.

Scenery/highlights: This loop takes you through the charming and fairly old town of Corrales where you will find art galleries, boutiques, and a couple of good restaurants. Nicer adobe-style homes surrounded by green pastures with well-bred horses grazing in them flank the old town. On the way back you'll ride through the newer, upscale neighborhoods of Rio Rancho, slide by several golf courses, and get a peek at where Albuquerque's well-heeled live and play.

Best time to ride: Anytime of year as weather and temperatures permit.

Special considerations: Water and rest rooms are available at the visitor center and at numerous spots along the way.

Directions for the ride: From the visitor center ride 0.3 mile out the entrance road and go straight onto Western Trail Road. Ride east for approximately 0.8 mile to the intersection with Coors Boulevard, NM 448. Go left onto Coors Boulevard, a four-lane divided highway with bike lanes, and begin pedaling north. You'll pass under Paseo del Norte

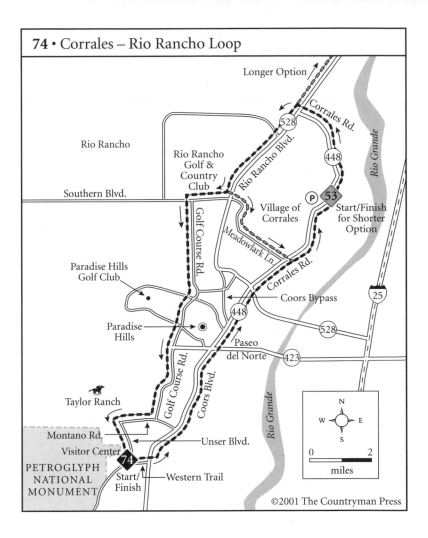

74 · Corrales – Rio Rancho Loop

4.3 miles later, and another 1.2 miles beyond that you'll come to the intersection with the Coors Bypass Road accessing NM 528. Stay right and continue pedaling north on NM 448, which has become Corrales Road. Another 1.3 miles past this intersection, almost 8 miles from the start, you come to an intersection with NM 528. Again, stay straight on NM 448/Corrales Road, now two lanes, cross over the town line, and begin to swing through Corrales proper.

FAUNA

There is little water in the monument so bird species are few. Those you might expect to see soaring above include red-tailed hawks, northern harriers, and American kestrels. Ravens are common, as are rock wrens, canyon towhees, white-crowned sparrows, house finches, western meadowlarks, and horned larks. Great horned owls are known to hunt along the escarpment and atop the mesa but you won't see them unless you are out at dusk or have good night vision. Your likely to hear the cooing of mourning doves in the morning and evening, and the whir of black-chinned hummingbirds zooming by in summer. Ash-throated flycatchers, Say's phoebe, barn swallows, blue-gray gnatcatchers, green-tailed towhees, and crissal thrashers are some of the other birds seen at the monument. The ferruginous hawk and loggerhead shrike, two birds listed as "Species of Concern" by the U.S. Fish and Wildlife Service, are sometimes spotted here.

Desert cottontails, blacktail jackrabbits, ground squirrels, and rock squirrels are quite common and comprise most of the coyote's meals. There are ten species of snakes; bull snakes, striped whip snakes, and coach whips are most common, but western diamondback and prairie rattlesnakes are fairly common as well. New Mexico whiptails, fence, side-blotched, and collared lizards thrive in the rocky face of the escarpment. One creature that you often see and is unique to this environment is the desert millipede. These are big bugs, growing 6 to 8 inches in length. The slate millipede also lives in the park and is considered a threatened species. Millipedes are nature's recyclers, consuming any kind of organic matter lying on the ground.

Continue riding north, looping through Corrales for 7.7 miles until reaching a T intersection where Corrales Road meets NM 528 again, 15.7 miles from the start. Turn left, and begin riding south on this two-lane road also called Rio Rancho Boulevard the town of Rio Rancho. Pedal south for 3.7 miles to Southern Boulevard. Go right onto Southern Boulevard and ride 1.3 miles to Golf Course Road. Go left onto Golf

Course Road and head south. In 4 miles you enter the Paradise Hills area, and 0.5 mile later pass the Paradise Hills Golf Course. Continue heading south, through a segment of the monument. The volcanic escarpment of the mesa is now to your right. Much of the escarpment is monument property surrounded by private ranch property. Approximately 0.7 mile past Paradise Hills Boulevard, Golf Course Road grows to four lanes and continues south another 3.6 miles to Montano Road, 29.5 miles from the start. Turn right onto Montano Road and ride west for 1.5 miles to Unser Boulevard. Go left onto Unser Boulevard and follow it south 1.7 miles to the intersection with Western Trail Road. Go right at Western Trail Road into the monument and arrive back at the visitor center approximately 33 miles from the start.

Option #1: For a shorter ride that avoids the busier four-lane roads, begin in the village of Corrales along Corrales Road (5.5 miles in length between Meadowlark Lane and NM 528) and ride north, to the T intersection with NM 528, Rio Rancho Boulevard. Ride south on Rio Rancho Boulevard 3.7 miles to an intersection. Go left at this intersection onto Meadowlark Lane and head east and south 3.3 miles to where it meets Corrales Road. Go left and ride back to your starting point.

Option #2: More ambitious road riders might want to continue heading north on NM 528 past the junction with Corrales Road another 5 miles to NM 44. NM 44 heads northwest over rolling country toward the Jemez Mountains and is frequented by serious cyclists looking for a good workout and time in the saddle. You might want to consider starting at Coronado State Park and Monument near the intersection of NM 528 and NM 44 and riding this scenic route from there.

CAMPING

There is no camping available at this city-side park but there are options for pitching a tent at several private campgrounds in town or in the Cibola National Forest. There are two campgrounds at the base of the Sandia Mountains in the foothills, but at least a dozen campgrounds on the east, or backside of the Sandia Mountains and the Manzanita Mountains just to the south. Visit the Sandia District Ranger Station about 20 miles east of the monu-

!

IT'S INTERESTING TO KNOW...

Unlike the Colorado River, which had to chisel its way down through solid rock to create its access south to the sea, the Rio Grande's course was created for it by a rift. A rift is a geologic feature described as a narrow block of the earth's crust that subsides between two parallel faults. The Rio Grande rift runs the length of the state of New Mexico. It formed when two fault blocks began pulling away from each other about 30 million years ago. In some places the distance between the rift valley floor, now covered over by miles of sediment, and the top of the adjacent fault block is almost 30,000 feet. Another feature of a rift is that the faults run extremely deep, often tapping into the earth's molten mantle. The volcanic eruptions responsible for the lava of Petroglyphs National Monument are the result, as are many of the volcanic features in northern New Mexico. The pulling apart of the earth's crust responsible for the rift is ongoing and is likely due to an upward movement, sometimes called "boiling," of the earth's mantle material. This feature is most often seen along rifts on the ocean floor. This means that the rifting going on in New Mexico might be setting the stage for the encroachment of the sea.

ment on I-40 in the town of Tijeras for information.

There are at least four private RV campgrounds in Albuquerque, including two **KOAs.** Almost all have tent sites, showers, and laundry facilities but are generally geared towards the motorhome traveler and aren't that nice for tent campers. They also tend to be more expensive than their small town counterparts.

LODGING

As a city over six hundred thousand, located at the intersection of two major interstate freeways, Albuquerque has a multitude of lodging possibilities. On the west side, closest to the monument, you'll find two **Motel 6s,** one on Coors Road and one on Iliff Road. There is also a **Holiday Inn Express** on Iliff Road. Founded in 1706, Old Town Albuquerque is the historic heart of the city, is not far from the monument, and is a good place to look for lodging and glimpse of this region's past. The **Best Western Rio Grande Inn, Sheraton Old Town,** and **Hyatt Regency** are all within walking distance of Old Town and are all more expensive. **La Posada de Albuquerque** is a historic hotel, built in the 1930s by

Conrad Hilton, that is also close to Old Town. This distinctively Southwestern establishment is elegant and slightly more expensive. **Casa de Suenos Country Inn** has some beautiful gardens and is also a good choice if you don't mind paying a bit more. If B&Bs are more your style try the historic **Bottger-Koch Mansion, Old Town B&B,** or **Sarabande B&B,** all located near Old Town. These are just a few possibilities; for a complete list of lodging options contact the Albuquerque Convention and Visitors Bureau. Many Albuquerque lodging establishments also have web sites that you can visit at your leisure.

Note: The Annual Albuquerque Balloon Fiesta in October is the largest gathering of balloonists in the world, attracting tens of thousands. Finding a hotel room during the festival can be extremely difficult. If you are planning to visit during the balloon festival make sure to make reservations well in advance.

FOOD

As you might expect, there are a multitude of eateries to choose from in Albuquerque. Of course there are many restaurants that feature New Mexican and

Mexican food, but you'll also find restaurants offering Italian, Native American, Thai, Chinese, Vietnamese, Japanese, and other ethnic foods as well.

If you're looking for something to get you started in the morning on the west side of town try the **Gourmet Bagel & Coffee Co.** (9311 Coors Blvd. NW) or **Wolfe's Bagels** (10701 Coors Blvd.). **La Hacienda** and **La Placita,** both just off the plaza in Old Town are well-known

---

★

DON'T MISS

There are several excellent museums near Old Town Albuquerque, among them the New Mexico Museum of History and Science; the Albuquerque Museum of Art, History, and Science; the intriguing Turquoise Museum, with displays of turquoise from around the world; and the American International Rattlesnake Museum, boasting the largest collection of live rattlesnakes in the world—sure to be a hit with the kids! There is also the National Atomic Energy Museum, the Maxwell Museum of Anthropology, and the Art Museum of New Mexico; the latter two are located on the University of New Mexico campus. One that shouldn't be missed, especially if you are visiting other parks and monuments in New Mexico, is the Indian Pueblo Cultural Center. Here you can learn about the 19 different Pueblo tribes that call northern New Mexico home, the three different languages spoken among them, and the migration patterns that brought them here. You can learn about the prehistory of the peoples who have lived in this state, from Clovis man who roamed the area hunting giant sloths, woolly mammoths, and other extinct creatures, to the Indians who first made contact with the Spanish. Exhibits also explain the history of each pueblo and the rituals and material crafts that make each one unique. Excellent displays of works by modern Native Americans can also be seen. During the summer live Pueblo dances take place both midmorning and mid-afternoon. Call ahead for more information; 505-843-7270 or 1-800-288-0721.

---

favorites for lunch or dinner. **Sadie's Dining Room** (6230 4th NW), north of Old Town, is a local favorite and reputedly serves some of the best New Mexican food in town. If you're looking for something special head north to the historic and charming hamlet of Corrales to **Rancho de Corrales** on Corrales Road, a quick 10-minute drive from the monument. The hacienda that houses the restaurant was built in 1801 and has a colorful history that includes romance, intrigue, and murder. You'll find the whole story on the menu along with Mexican and New Mexican specialties, steaks, and seafood. Nightly entertainment adds to this dining experience.

LAUNDRY

There are close to three dozen self-service laundries scattered throughout town; pick up a yellow pages to find one closest to you.

BIKE SHOP/BIKE RENTAL

Albuquerque is home to more than 30 bike shops specializing in everything from road bikes and mountain bikes to recumbent bikes and handmade frames. The incredible number of cyclists, biking clubs, and great shops is due to a combination of things including a great climate, excellent opportunities for outdoor recreation nearby, and city-wide system of bike trails and lanes.

Albuquerque Bicycle Center, 3330 Coors Blvd. NW; 505-831-5739

Old Town Bicycles, 2209 Centrale Ave. NW; 505-247-4926

Recreational Equipment Inc., 1905 Mountain Rd. NW; 505-247-1191

Rivertrailz Bikes & Blades, 6200 Coors Blvd. NW; 505-792-4708

FOR FURTHER INFORMATION

Petroglyph National Monument—Superintendent, 6001 Unser Blvd., Albuquerque, NM 87120; 505-899-0205; www.nps.gov/petr/

Albuquerque Open Space Division, P.O. Box 1293, Albuquerque, NM 87102; 505-873-6620

Albuquerque Convention & Visitors Bureau, P.O. Box 26866, 625 Silver Ave. SW, Albuquerque, NM 87125; 505-243-3696 or 1-800-284-2282 , www.abqcvb.org/

Albuquerque Chamber of Commerce, P.O. Box 25100, Albuquerque, NM 87125, 505-764-3700

Cibola National Forest—Headquarters, 2113 Osuna Road, Suite A, Albuquerque, NM 87713-1001; 505-761-8700; www.fs.fed.us/r3/cibola/

Cibola National Forest, Sandia Ranger District, 11776 NM Highway 337; Tijeras, NM 87058-8619; 505-281-3304

20

Before Spanish contact, the Indian pueblos at Abo, Quarai, and Gran Quivara, the three sites included in the monument, were thriving, tightly knit agricultural communities where ritual observance of natural cycles yielded bountiful harvests of maize, beans, cotton, and squash. Archaeological evidence suggests that two ancient cultures—the Anasazi and the Mogollon—came together in the Salinas Valley to create a major trade center and one of the most populous parts of the Pueblo world, perhaps supporting as many as ten thousand people by the 17th century. Situated along the eastern boundary of Pueblo territory, the people living in the Salinas Valley were both middlemen and producers of goods sought by tribes of the south and central Great Plains. The Puebloans traded surplus crops, piñon nuts, salt gathered from the dry basin lakes to the east, and cotton goods, such as decorative blankets to Plains Indians in exchange for buffalo meat, hides, and flints.

The salt that the Puebloans seem to have and trade in abundance, and the dry salt lakes to the east, prompted the Spanish to collectively call these pueblos Las Salinas. Having found little in the way of mineral wealth in the Southwest and poor conditions for productive agriculture, both the Catholic Church and Spanish Crown felt the best use of their resources, and perhaps the only way to profit in New Mexico, was to con-

The Franciscan padres who settled among the Indians at Salinas often forbade the use of their ceremonial kivas; this one was excavated from beneath debris.

vert Indians to Christianity and put them to work establishing a new Spanish colony. Because they were some of the most populous and powerful Indian villages in New Mexico the Salinas pueblos were attacked and subjugated as early as 1601. Two or three Franciscan fathers were immediately assigned to each pueblo and construction of the massive churches began. Indian hearts and minds were transformed as their bodies labored. The Spanish governors relied on the profits from Indian labor and goods and exploited their trade networks whenever possible, including those that involved sale of slaves captured in raids from Plains tribes.

Conflict with the Franciscan padres who destroyed kivas and burned sacred objects caused a good deal of resentment and prompted many Indians to abandon their pueblos. Increasingly hostile raids by the Apache in retribution for slave raids encouraged by the Spanish, along with repeated epidemics of European diseases such as smallpox and influenza against which the Indians had no immunity, also caused many Indians to flee the Salinas Pueblos. A severe drought in the 1660s and 1670s resulted in widespread famine and even starvation for some, and was perhaps the final blow to the life of these pueblos. By the Pueblo Revolt of 1680 there were few Indians left living at the missions. Those who remained, including the entire population of Tompiro speakers, left with the Spanish fathers, escaped the unrest, and settled near El Paso, Texas, where they disappeared among other groups of displaced Native Americans.

Cycling in the Park

The three different ruin sites that make up this monument are scattered around the edge of the sprawling Estancia Basin east of the Manzano Mountains 55 miles southeast of Albuquerque. The town of Mountainair is situated between all three ruin sites and is home to the monument's visitor center. Gran Quivira, the southernmost of the three, sits between Chupadera Mesa and Mesa Jumanas 25 miles south of Mountainair. Abó Ruins are 9 miles southwest of town; Quarai Ruins are 8 miles north. Each ruin site sits on just a few acres and is surrounded by private property, meaning there are no possibilities for riding within the park boundaries and limited possibilities for riding off-road nearby.

Those who favor skinny tires, however, will be pleased with their riding choices. Although US 60, which runs east to west and accesses Abó Ruins, gets more traffic, NM 55, accessing both Quarai and Gran Quivira, is much more lightly traveled and makes for some great road riding. This empty, wide-open country of low mesas and piñon- and juniper-dotted foothills is quite beautiful and can be stunning

CYCLING OPTIONS

There are two rides listed in this chapter; one is for road bikes and one is for mountain bikes. Both are fairly long, nontechnical rides that cyclists of all abilities who are in good physical condition will enjoy. The loop from the town of Tajique up to Fourth of July Campground and down to Torreon traverses graded and more primitive dirt roads and is best done in the fall when the foliage is ablaze. The half-century road ride, best started from Quarai Ruins, heads north along the eastern toe of the Manzano Mountains before making a loop out through the Estancia Basin. This is a great road ride that can be windy in the spring.

when the sky above is filled with billowing white clouds or lit in shades of pink and gold at sunset. A half-century loop that can be ridden either from Mountainair or from Quarai takes riders along the foothills of the Manzano Mountains and then heads east and south, through the town of Estancia and the Estancia Basin, before heading west back toward the mountains. A shorter option allows the less ambitious to simply ride along the base of the Manzano Mountains through the rustic villages of Punta de Agua and Manzano before turning back, or pedaling on to Torreon and Tajique. Physically fit mountain bikers of all abilities will enjoy the loop that can be ridden up into the Manzano Mountains and back between the towns of Torreon and Tajique. This route is spectacular in fall when stands of Rocky Mountain or big-tooth maples cloak the mountainsides in firey hues of red and orange.

The ruins of Salinas are all about 6,500 feet above sea level and enjoy a wonderful year-round climate. Summertime can be hot, with temperatures reaching well into the 90s. Winters remain mild; daytime temperatures often climb into the 40s and 50s. You'll want to cover up as much as possible to keep the fierce rays of the sun from exposed skin spring through fall, but hold on to your hat in springtime when gusty winds are common. Like most of the Southwest this region receives much of its scant annual moisture in the summer months during the desert monsoon season. Plan to be done riding or at least away from open or exposed areas by midafternoon if this type of weather pattern is dominant.

---

75. TAJIQUE-TORREON LOOP (See map on page 425)

For mountain bikes. This ride is a scenic trip up into the Manzano Mountains around a loop known for its fall foliage. The small towns at the beginning and end of this dirt road are ethnically Spanish and have histories reaching back to 17th century, when families settled land granted them by the Spanish Crown. There are few technical challenges along this route and lots of gorgeous scenery. All levels of mountain bikers should give this one a try provided they're physically fit.

Starting point: Begin this ride in the town of Tajique. To get there drive north from Mountainair on NM 55 approximately 21 miles, past the

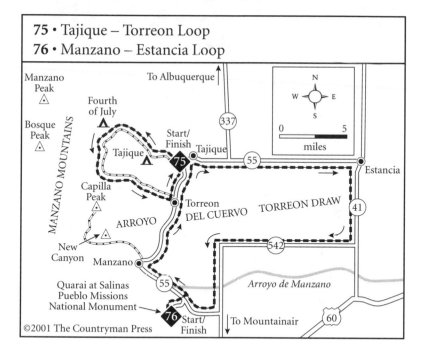

75 • Tajique – Torreon Loop
76 • Manzano – Estancia Loop

Manzano Peak

Bosque Peak

Fourth of July

MANZANO MOUNTAINS

Tajique

Capilla Peak

ARROYO

New Canyon

Manzano

Quarai at Salinas Pueblo Missions National Monument

©2001 The Countryman Press

To Albuquerque

337

Start/ Finish

Tajique

Tajique

55

N
W ———+——— E
S

0   5
miles

Estancia

Torreon DEL CUERVO

TORREON DRAW

41

542

55

Arroyo de Manzano

76 Start/ Finish

To Mountainair

60

hamlet of Torreon. Park in town, making sure you are not on private property.

Length: 20 miles. This outing takes most of the day.

Riding surface: Maintained and unmaintained dirt roads; 2.5 miles of pavement.

Difficulty: Moderate to difficult. Although there is 1500 feet of elevation gain the grades are gentle and it is an easy middle-chain-ring climb. The length of this ride will make it more difficult for some.

Scenery/highlights: "Manzano" means apple in Spanish and you will find them in abundance around these towns during the autumn harvest. Roadside stands often have several varieties for sale, and sometimes fresh cider too. Much like sugar maples of the east, the Rocky Mountain maples put on a spectacular show, turning shades of flaming orange and watermelon red at the end of September through the first few weeks in

FLORA

The habitat surrounding the three ruins sites is a mixture of Southwestern desert grasslands and Great Plains biomes. One-seed and alligator juniper are the dominant trees, although piñon pines are more abundant around Quarai. Shrubs such as sagebrush, chamisa, one-leaf yucca, and four-wing saltbush are common, and are joined by a shrubby cholla cactus that blooms purple to burgundy in June. There are numerous types of grasses around each ruin site, several species of grama grass being the most abundant. Brilliant purple desert sand verbena, which grows low to the ground, desert four o'clock, desert primrose, skyrocket, snakeweed, and orange globe mallow are just a few of the wildflowers you might see in spring. Common sunflowers bloom in midsummer and in fall purple asters and the golden blooms of chamisa put on a fantastic show.

October. Maples are not common in New Mexico and the brilliant fall colors along this route draw numerous gawkers from nearby Albuquerque.

Best time to ride: Spring through fall. Fall is best, although sightseer traffic can be heavy.

Special considerations: There are vault toilets at both campgrounds along the way and drinking water available at Fourth of July Campground. Ray's Store in Tajique is a good place to pick up any snacks you might need for your ride and a drink when you're done.

Directions for the ride: From Tajique pick up Forest Road (FR) 55 heading west toward the mountains just beyond Ray's Store. Pedal this graded dirt road as it climbs gradually through stands of piñon and juniper, winding its way up Cañon de Tajique. Approximately 2 miles from the start you will cross the forest service boundary, and in another mile reach Tajique Campground. You will pass FR 322 0.5 mile past the campground, heading up Cañon del Apache on the left. Just beyond that the road crosses through private property; please stay on the main road.

Continue climbing through the canyon passing FR 321 on the right in another mile, and then pass several other dirt roads before reaching Fourth of July Campground 7 miles from the start.

Continue past the turnoff for Fourth of July Campground, staying on a rougher, lesser-used FR 55 as it climbs the upper reaches of Cañon de Tajique where it drains of Manzano and Bosque Peaks to the west. You are now heading south and will come to a picnic area and the trailhead for the Bosque Trail, accessing those peaks, just over 2 miles past the campground and 9 miles from the start. In another mile you will reach the high point in this loop and begin to descend through upper Cañon de Torreon.

Approximately 11.5 miles from the start you pass Forest Trail 176 (Trail Canyon), which climbs up Cañon de la Vereda to a junction with the Manzano Crest Trail, which traverses the entire length of the range. Continue following FR 55 as it descends through the canyon, alternately passing through private property and forest service lands, until reaching the hamlet of Torreon and paved NM 55 17.5 miles from the start. Go left and ride 2.2 miles to Tajique.

---

76. MANZANO-ESTANCIA LOOP (See map on page 425)

For road bikes. This half-century circuit take road bikers north along the eastern foothills of the Manzano Mountains, through the towns of Manzano, Torreon, and Tajique, before heading east to the town of Estancia. Estancia is located at the edge of the Salt Lakes in the Estancia Basin that for centuries supplied the inhabitants of nearby pueblos with salt and contributed to their wealth and power. While this loop tour is best suited for seasoned road riders, the less experienced should consider riding out-and-back through the small Spanish towns along this route, or perhaps riding to Quarai from Mountainair.

Starting point: Quarai Ruins Contact Station.

Length: 53 miles. Allow 4 to 5 hours to complete this loop.

Riding surface: Pavement.

Difficulty: Moderate to difficult. Although there is not a lot of climbing, the length of this ride makes it more difficult.

A cyclist heads out to ride from the mission and pueblo at Abó to those at Quarai.

Scenery/highlights: The Manzano Mountains are a beautiful backdrop to Quarai Ruins and fill the western skyline with gently undulating ridges and shadowed canyons. Fall foliage is spectacular. The small towns situated along the mountains' eastern flank are centuries old and have roots reaching back to Spain.

Best time to ride: Spring through fall, although spring can be windy.

Special considerations: Water and rest rooms are available at Quarai.

Directions for the ride: From Quarai Ruins, ride out the access road just over a mile to NM 55. Go left onto this paved road and begin pedaling northward, through rolling piñon- and juniper-dotted hills, climbing gently toward the small town of Manzano. After reaching Manzano 4.5 miles from the start you continue to head north, along the foot of the mountains, descending toward the hamlet of Torreon, 15 miles from the start. Just over 2 miles from Torreon, enter the town of Tajique. Follow NM 55 as it bends around and heads east through Tajique, arriving at an intersection with NM 337 almost 3 miles later. Continue straight through this intersection, riding due east on NM 55 to the town of

FAUNA

Because it is located closer to the mountains, water sources, and is more wooded, the area around Quarai supports a greater abundance of both bird and wildlife than is found at the other two sites. Not commonly seen, but present at all the ruin sites is the New Mexico state bird—the roadrunner. If you are lucky you may catch a glimpse of one dashing across the road in pursuit of a lizard or some other quarry. Much more commonly seen are ravens, crows, and pinyon and western scrub jays. Black and Say's phoebes, house finches, and, occasionally, beautiful blue grosbeaks are spotted near the ruins. Red-tailed and Coopers hawks soar in the skies above the ruins, while the fairly common great horned owl is out and about at dusk and later; they have been known to nest in the church ruins at Quarai.

Desert cottontails, blacktail jackrabbits, and rock squirrels are the most common small mammals, but now and again you might see a raccoon or a porcupine. Mountain lions exist closer to the mountains, along with bobcats, coyotes, and mule deer. Reptile inhabitants include western diamondback rattlesnakes, bull snakes, and numerous lizards, the collared and whiptail being the easiest to identify. South around Gran Quivira, prairie rattlesnakes are more common. Keep an eye out for rattlers warming themselves on the trails around the ruins in the morning. Back away slowly while making some noise and the rattlesnake will gladly get out of the way.

Estancia in 10 miles. Upon reaching the small, sleepy town of Estancia on the plains of the Estancia Basin you come to a T intersection; go right onto NM 41 and begin pedaling south. Continue south for 6 miles to an intersection with NM 542 and go right again, now traveling west toward the mountains. Ride this road straight west for 10 miles, then follow it as it makes a 90-degree turn and heads south. In another 5 miles you will arrive at an intersection with NM 55. Go right and ride 3 miles to the turnoff for Quarai and another mile to the contact station and parking lot.

Options: Less ambitious road bikers might want to consider riding north to the town of Manzano and back (9 miles round-trip), or riding as far as Tajique and back (35.4 miles round-trip). For those staying in Mountainair, another option is to ride approximately 16 miles from town to Quarai and back. If there are long-distance types looking for more ideas, consider riding from Mountainair to Gran Quivira and back—another half-century ride.

★

DON'T MISS

The church ruins at Quarai are the most complete and some of the most visually arresting at the monument. Built with blocks of bright red sandstone and set against the foothills of the Manzano Mountains to the west, the remains of the church, with its massive walls and Spanish colonial architecture form a classic Southwestern scene. Visiting these ruins early in the morning or at dusk when long shadows and golden light play along the walls of the church is breathtaking. Many of the local, ethnically Spanish families who have roots in the area continue to use this church for weddings and other important occasions.

While the pueblos and mission churches of both Quarai and Abo are built of the same red sandstone, the ruins at Gran Quivira are built of out of a light gray limestone. The sites are all worth visiting but those at Quarai are especially memorable. Be sure to take some time to wander around, see the ruins, and absorb the special ambiance these pueblo and mission sites have. There is a museum at Quarai with a good collection of pre-contact Puebloan and Spanish colonial artifacts.

CAMPING

There are no campgrounds at any of the three units of this monument. There are however, excellent opportunities for camping just north of Mountainair in the Cibola National Forest. **Red Canyon, New Canyon,** and **Capilla Peak Campgrounds** can all be accessed from Manzano and Tajique; the popular **Fourth of July Campground** can be accessed from Tajique. **Manzano State Park,** located just outside Manzano, is also a good choice for tenters and those in RVs. **Tilly's Inn** in Mountainair also has RV sites. For other campgrounds that can accommodate RVs head north and west to Albuquerque.

LODGING

The closest lodging to the park is in Mountainair, where you'll find the **El Rancho Motel** and **Tilly's Inn Motel,** both located on US 60. Other lodging possibilities

can be found 35 miles to the west along I-25 at Belen or in Moriarity, 28 miles north on I-40. Both towns have the standard selection of interstate chain motels. All kinds of lodging possibilities can be found in Albuquerque, 65 miles northwest of Mountainair.

FOOD

There are really no dining choices in Mountainair. The few cafés that were open have closed since the writing of this book. You can pick up a few snacks and picnic supplies at **Dave's Deli Mart,** but if you are heading out to visit the ruins and spend time riding pack a cooler with food and drinks so you can stop and have a healthy meal whenever you get hungry.

LAUNDRY

Laundromats are few and far between; head to Albuquerque if you're in need of doing some laundry.

IT'S INTERESTING TO KNOW...

The relationship between the Spanish colonial government of the late 16th and early 17th century and the Indian pueblos of the Salinas area functioned through the encomienda system. In this arrangement, Spanish settlers of high ranking, called *encomenderos,* were appointed by the governor to provide education, aid, and protection for the pueblos. In return, the encomenderos were allowed to collect tribute in the form of crops, goods produced by the Indians or acquired through trade, and labor. But there was little oversight—too few government officials and too great an area to cover. As a result the encomenderos abused their power and exploited the Indians, much to the dismay of the Franciscan missionaries, who also required the labor and goods of the Indians. The encomenderos refused to give up the profitable arrangement granted them, often putting the mission fathers and the Spanish government at odds. Frustration and resentment continued to build among the Pueblo people, forcing many to abandon their ances-tral homes and escape an existence that had become intolerable. The pueblos at Salinas were occupied for as many as five hundred years before the arrival of the Spanish; the joint tenancy of the Spanish and the Pueblos at the missions lasted for less than 50.

In spite of these troubles, the Spanish did contribute to Pueblo life in some positive ways. Fruit trees such as apples were introduced, along with grapes, wheat, cattle, goats, and sheep, all of which have become staples of Pueblo existence. The Spanish also introduced silver and other metals quickly adopted by Puebloan craftsmen, now renowned for their metal smithing.

BIKE SHOP/BIKE RENTAL

The nearest town supporting bike shops is Albuquerque, where there are dozens.

FOR FURTHER INFORMATION

Salinas Pueblo Missions National Monument— Superintendent, P.O. Box 517 (at

Broadway & Ripley Streets), Mountainair, NM 87036; 505-847-2585; www.nps. gov/sapu/

Cibola National Forest, Mountainair Ranger District, P.O. Box E, Mountainair, NM 87036; 505-847-2990

Manzano Mountain State Park, P.O. Box 224, Mountainair, NM 87036; 505-847-2820; www.emnrd.state. nm.us/nmparks/

21

Located in south-central New Mexico in the middle of the expansive Tularosa Basin—a flat, almost waterless plain surrounded by high mountain peaks—is a natural wonder that dazzles the senses and invites exploration. Over 300 square miles of brilliant white gypsum dunes rise and fall across this landscape in waves of sugar-white sand as they march forward with prevailing winds. Intricate patterns and shapes created by wind, light, shadow, and the few hardy creatures who survive here are constantly changing with the wind and the angle of the sun.

The largest gypsum dunefield in the world, now protected as White Sands National Monument, evolved here because of three important factors: steady winds, a source of sand, and topography that causes the wind to deposit what it carries in a specific location. From February to April strong, almost constant winds whip across the Tularosa Basin from southwest to northeast. As the wind crosses the playas, the ancient lake beds of Lake Otero and Lake Lucero, it picks up fine white grains of gypsum sand. There are two main sources of the sand: gypsum-saturated groundwater drawn toward the surface where it crystallizes and is then broken down by the elements, and the Permian rocks of the San Andres Mountains to the west.

The gypsum was originally deposited across this region in a shallow sea some 250 million years ago. This sea was surrounded by Sahara-like deserts and may have been landlocked. Over the eons the sea repeatedly

SARAH BENNETT ALLEY

A group of fat-tire fans take time out for flat repair on the Rim Trail.

evaporated, leaving behind thick deposits of gypsum, salt, and other soluble minerals. Eventually these sediments were buried. During Cenozoic times when the Rocky Mountains were forming to the north, an enormous anticline, spanning both the present-day San Andres Mountains in the west and the Sacramento Mountains in the east, was pushed skyward. This was followed by a subsidence along parallel fault lines that caused the central core of the anticline to drop thousands of feet, much like the Rio Grande's rift valley. This subsidence of the earth's crust simultaneously worked to create the basin and the San Andres and Sacramento Mountain ranges that flank it on either side. The exposed rocks in the mountain ranges then began eroding, filling the Tularosa Basin with sediments. Some of these sediments dissolved and seeped into groundwater only to recrystalize at the surface later.

As the prevailing southwesterly winds lift over the Sacramento Mountains they drop their payload, forming four different kinds of dunes. Dome dunes, found at the leading edge of the dunefield where winds are strongest, can travel up to 30 feet per year. Barchan dunes form in areas with limited sand and are crescent-shaped with arms trailing downwind. Tranverse dunes are found in areas with ample sand and are really barchan dunes that have joined together to form long ridges. At the edges of the dunefield parabolic dunes form when plants begin to anchor the arms of barchan dunes, causing them to become inverted.

Cycling in the Park

The broad, almost completely flat Tularosa Basin, mountain ranges on either side, and a great route through the park means there is plenty of riding for all kinds of cyclists in and around White Sands National Monument. The 8-mile-long Dunes Drive, a paved road that snakes northwest through the dunefield, is an excellent ride for both road and mountain bikers. The park encourages cyclists to ride their scenic drive, and even hosts moonlight rides on summer nights when the moon is full.

CYCLING OPTIONS

There are three rides listed in this chapter; one is for either road or mountain bikes, one is for mountain bikes, and one is for road bikes. Two of the rides are 35 miles northeast of the monument near the small, recreation-oriented town of Cloudcroft. Dunes Drive is the one scenic drive in the park, taking riders 8 miles into the heart of the dunes. Those not wanting to go the entire distance can simply drive out and park at a pullout and ride from there; families with small children or trailers can drive out to the nature center and ride the 2-mile loop at the end of the drive. The Rim Trail is a 14-mile long singletrack that stretches north to south along the spine of the Sacramento Mountains and is one of southern New Mexico's classic mountain bike trails. This ride begins just outside Cloudcroft and will thrill advanced and intermediate mountain bikers. The road ride from Cloudcroft out to Sunspot and the National Solar Observatory is a wonderful pedal on the paved Sunspot Highway, also parallelling the ridge of the Sacramento Mountains. The last two rides are at relatively high elevations, so riders should plan on spending some time acclimating before attempting the entire distance.

Riding the loop at the end of the drive is a good option for families with little riders. Around the town of Cloudcroft in the Sacramento Mountains 35 miles east of the monument, cyclists can enjoy cooler temperatures, beautiful mountain scenery, and a host of trails and routes. The Rim Trail begins just south of Couldcroft and traverses the spine of the Sacramento Mountains, providing excellent views over the Tularosa Basin and the white sand dunes while thrilling mountain bikers with fast-paced single-track. Road bikers have some great opportunities from Cloudcroft as well, including the paved road out along the main ridge of the mountains to the Sacramento Peak Solar Observatory on the Sunspot Highway. There are many, many on- and off-road routes in the vicinity of Cloudcroft that serious cyclists who have the time can discover.

The climate of this region can be harsh, with hot summers, freezing winters, blistering winds, and dry conditions. At elevations just above 4,000 feet, summer temperatures in the Tularosa Basin average 95 degrees, and frequently soar well past the century mark. While the mountains surrounding the basin receive enough snow to entertain skiers at higher elevations, the basin floor receives a scant 8 inches of rain per year. Winters are generally mild, with daytime temperatures reaching into the 50s and even 60s. Nighttime temperatures can dip below freezing. From February to May expect strong winds out of the south and southwest. Winds of gale force can blow for days at a time in spring, making it difficult to get out of your car, much less enjoy cycling. It is during these windstorms that the dunes move the most.

---

77. DUNES DRIVE (See map on page 438)

For road or mountain bikes. Dunes Drive is the main scenic drive through the sand dunes and the only road in the park, paved or otherwise. Both road and mountain bikers will enjoy this level route as it slips between the stunning, sugar-white dunes, but both should be wary of sandy stretches of road. Riders who do not wish to ride the entire length out-and-back can simply drive to a pullout along the road and ride from there. A short ride suitable for small cyclists or parents with trailers is also suggested. This park is bike-friendly and annually sponsors full-moon rides; if you are interested call in advance to register.

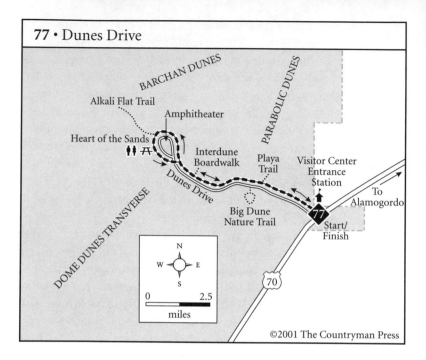

BARCHAN DUNES

PARABOLIC DUNES

Alkali Flat Trail

Amphitheater

Heart of the Sands

Interdune
Boardwalk

Playa
Trail

Visitor Center
Entrance
Station

To
Alamogordo

Dunes Drive

DOME DUNES TRANSVERSE

Big Dune
Nature Trail

77

Start/
Finish

N

W   E

S

70

0   2.5

miles

©2001 The Countryman Press

Starting point: White Sands National Monument Visitor Center, located just off I-70 at the start of Dunes Drive.

Length: 7.25 miles one-way, 14.5 miles out-and-back. Parking at the Nature Center and riding around the loop at the very end of Dunes Drive will give you a total distance of just over 2 miles.

Riding surface: Pavement; covered with packed sand in places.

Difficulty: Easy to moderate. The route is level but the distance will make it more difficult for some.

Scenery/highlights: The brilliant white shapes of the dunes contrasted against the deep blue New Mexican sky, the patterns that the wind creates in the sand, and the few hardy creatures that are able to survive in this harsh environment all make for a fascinating pedal through one of the West's great wonders. Be sure to take some time at the visitor center, browse through their museum and bookstore, and walk the short Playa

FLORA

White Sands National Monument falls within the Chihuahuan Desert region, but the presence of the gypsum dunes creates conditions that define a unique environment. Harsh climatic conditions prevalent at this latitude and elevation become even harsher in the dunes. Rainfall quickly drains away; surface temperatures soar well past 150°F in summer and plummet below freezing in winter. Periods of strong, unrelenting winds quickly bury anything that has taken hold and the gypsum sand and soils hold little in the way of nutrients. The closer you get to the heart of the dunes the fewer plants you will find.

The Rio Grande cottonwood is the only tree species; it survives by sending out an enormous root system that anchors it to the sand and often leaves it clinging to an exposed mound. Cottonwoods, desert willows, tamarisk, and even cattails are found near sinks and depressions among the dunes, places that catch water from time to time. Common shrubs include four-wing saltbush, creosote bush, skunkbush sumac, Mormon tea or ephedra, rubber rabbitbrush, and Russian thistle, also known as tumbleweed. Shrubs like sumac, saltbush, and rosemary mint are able to form nets with their roots that hold the soil underneath, creating the pedestals that support them above the shifting sands. The soaptree yucca has developed another coping strategy: when the wind blows and begins to bury the plant, it grows at hyper-speed, elongating roots and lengthening stems in an effort to stay on the surface.

Springtime wildflowers include the magenta-colored sand verbena, which has a lilac-like fragrance, soft globe mallow, trailing four o'clock, and yellow evening primrose. Sand milkweed, Englemen daisy, woolly paperflower, yellow cryptantha, spectacle pod, and white sands mustard, a plant endemic to the dunes, are also commonly found. Cholla, several species of prickly pear, and at least two different kinds of hedgehog cactus, including claret cup, are present, as well as ocotillo, blue barrel cactus, and in some places the night-blooming cereus.

Heading into the heart of White Sands National Monument on Dunes Drive.

SARAH BENNETT ALLEY

or Big Dune Nature Trails to get an up-close look at the dunes. You can also walk around the Interdune Boardwalk, or out along the 2-mile Alkali Flat Trail at the very end of the loop if you've got the time and energy.

Best time to ride: Any time of year, provided temperatures are comfortable for riding. Fall is best; spring is often windy.

Special considerations: Water, rest rooms, drinks, and snacks are available at the visitor center. A rest room is also available at the Heart of Sands Picnic Area at the end of Dunes Drive. Bring a lock to secure your bike if you are interested in hiking out among the dunes.

Whenever the full moon coincides with a Saturday night the park hosts a Moonlight Bicycle Ride. These happen about once a year and are a don't-miss opportunity to experience the dunes under the ethereal light of the moon. If you are thinking about visiting White Sands and are interested in participating call the visitor center. Advance registration and a small fee are required.

Directions for the ride: From the visitor center ride out the driveway, go right and turn immediately onto Dunes Drive. In a hundred feet or so you come to the park entrance station where you will need to pay your entrance fee. Continue past the entrance station, pedaling west with the dunefield on your left. The route traces the edge of a portion of the field for approximately 2 miles before arriving at the Playa Trail. The 0.3-mile trail leaves from the right side of the road and takes hikers to a small basin surrounded by the dunes on three sides. Another 0.5 mile past this trail the Big Dune Nature Trail leaves on the left side of the road and makes a 1-mile loop through an area of parabolic dunes. At this point the road enters the dunefield. For the next 1.5 miles you pass through parabolic dunes before entering a large area of transverse dunes. Approximately 5 miles from the start the Interdune Boardwalk Trail will be on your right. It is now just over a mile to the nature center and the start of the loop. Bear right past the nature center to ride the loop in a counterclockwise direction. In a mile you come to the park amphitheater, the end of Dunes Drive, and the start of the 2.3-mile Alkali Flats Trail. Continue around the loop, arriving back at the main route 8.2 miles from the start. Head back on Dunes Drive to the visitor center 14.5 miles from the start.

---

78. THE RIM TRAIL (See map on page 442)

For mountain bikes. This singletrack trail runs north and south, just west of the main ridge of the Sacramento Mountains, for a distance of close to 14 miles. It winds in and out of cool, shadowy stands of pine, fir, and spruce and brighter glades of quaking aspen and oak that every now and then allow for breathtaking views to the west, over the Tularosa Basin 5,000 feet below and the San Andres Mountains beyond. This twisting trail rolls up and down, providing plenty of excitement with technical sections that feature roots, rocks, and other trail users. Although best suited for advanced riders in good physical condition, less experienced riders should give it a try. Options for making shorter loops are possible by using the numerous side trails accessing the Sunspot Highway.

Starting point: The parking lot at the entrance to the Slide Group Campground in Lincoln National Forest, just south of Cloudcroft. To get

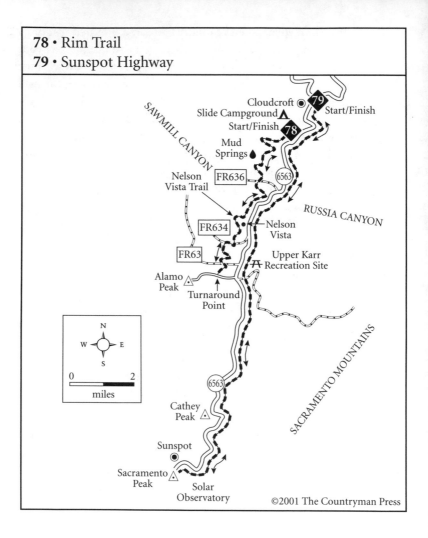

SAWMILL CANYON

Cloudcroft ◉ **79** Start/Finish
Slide Campground ▲
Start/Finish **78**

Mud Springs ◆

FR636 — 6563

Nelson Vista Trail

RUSSIA CANYON

FR634 — Nelson Vista

FR63

Upper Karr Recreation Site

Alamo Peak △

Turnaround Point

N
W — E
S

0 — 2
miles

6563

SACRAMENTO MOUNTAINS

Cathey Peak △

Sunspot ◉

Sacramento Peak △

Solar Observatory

©2001 The Countryman Press

there from town take NM 130 south for just under 2 miles before bearing right onto the Sunspot Highway, NM 6563. Go approximately 0.2 mile to the Slide Group Campground entrance.

If this parking lot is full there is also a paved pullout and trailhead on the right side of the road just before the campground entrance.

Length: 14 miles one-way to Alamo Peak Road. There are no time or distance requirements; ride as far and as long as you want, loop back on the pavement, or simply reverse your route and head back the way you came.

Riding surface: Singletrack with both fast, smooth sections and technical sections filled with natural hazards.

Difficulty: Difficult; strenuous if the entire length of the trail is ridden out-and-back, more moderate if only portions of the trail are ridden.

Scenery/highlights: The Rim Trail traverses the steep, west-facing edge of the Sacramento Mountains, formed when the fault block that created the Tularosa Basin subsided. The trail is comprised of old Indian trails, homesteader trails, railroad beds from this area's logging days, and portions of new trail built during the 1960s. It is the longest trail in the Lincoln National Forest and a designated National Recreation Trail. It is legendary among mountain bikers in this state and one of New Mexico's finest mountain bike trails. The Rim Trail continues past the turnaround point described here for another 14 miles, ending at Forest Road (FR 90). Portions of the trail beyond Alamo Peak Road are very rough and not well suited for mountain bikers, however, the forest service is constantly working to improve the trail and has plans to reroute some of the roughest sections.

Changing mountain scenery is beautiful up here, especially in fall, and views are fantastic.

Best time to ride: Spring through fall. Usually the trails are free of snow and dry by the first of May, but if you are here in the spring inquire with the forest service or the folks at High Altitude Outfitters about trail conditions before you go. Stay away if the trail is wet and muddy. Fall foliage is spectacular.

Special considerations: There are vault toilets at Slide Group Campground but no drinking water. Bring plenty of your own.

Elevations along this route are quite high, ranging between 8,800 and 9,400 feet. You may want to give yourself a day to ride some of the shorter trails around town to acclimate to the dry, thin air. Weather can change rapidly at these elevations; go prepared.

Directions for the ride: From the parking lot pick up the trail and begin pedaling south and west. For most of the first mile the trail closely par-

A ruin in a canyon of the Sacramento Mountains, somewhere below Cloudcroft.

allels the paved Sunspot Highway, staying mostly level. The route then heads west, descending to a point on a ridge above Mud Spring almost 2 miles from the start. The trail hugs the contour of the ridge for the next mile before beginning a climb up and over a finger ridge, making several switchbacks along the way. About 5 miles from the start, the trail crosses over FR 636 (a possible bailout) before arriving at a high point above a thickly timbered ravine. At this point the trail bends around to the left heading east, reaching the paved road in just under a mile. It again parallels the Sunspot Highway, arriving at Nelson Vista, where a trail comes in from the road close to halfway along this route—another good bailout for a shorter ride.

From here the trail jogs south, west, and eventually north as it contours the top of the drainage above Seven Springs. After winding around along the edge of the rim for more than a mile it heads due south for another mile. It then dips into the top of the drainage and climbs out before crossing through a densely forested plateau dotted with small meadows. Along this stretch you will intersect and cross over FR 634 heading out to an overlook almost 11 miles from the start. After winding through the forest the trail descends slightly to meet FR 63 in Upper Karr Canyon. Cross over Karr Canyon Road and climb up to the Alamo Peak Road about a mile later. This is your turnaround point. Return the way you came, or ride back to Cloudcroft on the Sunspot Highway.

---

79. SUNSPOT HIGHWAY (See map on page 442)

For road bikes. The 16-mile trip out along the Sunspot Highway to the National Solar Observatory at Sacramento Peak is a great pedal along the spine of the Sacramento Mountains on an excellent road surface. This route rolls, twists, and winds through alpine forests at elevations ranging between 8,600 and almost 10,000 feet. At the end of the road you can take yourself on a self-guided tour of one of the world's largest solar observatories.

Starting point: Cloudcroft.

Length: 16 miles one-way, 32 miles out-and-back.

Riding surface: Paved road with nice, wide shoulders.

Difficulty: Moderate to difficult. The distance, elevation, and climb will make it more difficult for all but the seasoned road rider in excellent physical condition.

Scenery/highlights: Pedaling through the cool, pine-scented air along the spine of this desert mountain range is an incredibly scenic tour on a lightly traveled road that road riders of all levels of experience can't help but enjoy. Not only is this a great ride along a National Scenic Byway, it has the added attraction of visiting one of the worlds most important solar observatories. The National Solar Observatory at Sacramento Peak welcomes visitors and has a fairly new visitor center featuring displays and exhibits about the science of studying the sun. Visit the Vacuum Tower Telescope, rising 13 stories above the ground and extending 20 stories below, where visitors are allowed to observe scientists hard at work, studying their instruments and trying to predict the sun's behavior. Take a self-guided tour or, if you are here on a Saturday, try a guided tour. To learn more about the observatory call 505-434-7000 or visit their web site, www.sunspot.noao.edu/.

FAUNA

Life is not easy for animals in and around the dunes, although a surprising number of them manage to survive here. Those that exist among the dunes have developed fascinating strategies for coping with the challenges posed by this harsh environment.

Raptors include Swainson's and red-tailed hawk, northern harriers, and American kestrels. The Chihuahuan raven is quite common as is the great-tailed grackle. The roadrunner, mourning dove, western kingbird, horned lark, northern mockingbird, eastern meadowlark, and loggerhead shrike are all common, as are Say's phoebe, yellow-rumped and Wilson's warbler, lark bunting, cactus wren, and pyrruhloxia.

Desert cottontails, blacktail jackrabbits, desert pocket gophers, and a host of different kangaroo rats, and pocket mice are all on the menu of the kit fox, the park's main predator. The kit fox is joined occasionally by gray fox, coyote, and badger. Many of these animals avoid hot temperatures by burrowing during the day.

The Apache pocket mouse and the bleached earless lizard have evolved into distinct species as a result of their efforts to survive in the dunes' environment. Their particular survival strategy is adaptive coloration. Instead of the normal brownish coloring of mice and lizards, these creatures are almost completely white, to better hide from their predators and absorb as little of the sun's heat as possible. Desert pronghorn used to roam this basin but were shot out by sport hunters long ago. Mule deer are joined by the oryx, an African antelope, introduced to the area as a game animal.

Commonly seen reptiles include the Sonora gopher snake, the western coachwhip, and both prairie and western diamondback rattlesnakes. Collared, Cowles prairie, desert side-blotched, round-tailed horned, and Texas horned are some of the more common lizards. Several varieties of spadefoot toads, a few different species of tarantulas, and a handful of scorpions round out the list of creepy, crawly things here.

Best time to ride: Spring through fall.

Special considerations: Water and rest rooms can be found both in Cloudcroft and at the observatory. You may want to bring some snacks as this can be a long day and there is no food available at the observatory. Bring a lock to secure your bike if you want to spend some time visiting the observatory facilities.

Directions for the ride: From Cloudcroft head south on NM 130, bearing right onto NM 6563 in just under 2 miles. For the first 6.5 miles this route twists and winds as it climbs toward the high point in the ride near Russia Canyon. From here the road rolls south along the spine of the Sacramento Mountains until reaching the observatory 16 miles from the start. When you are done having a look around, remount and pedal back the way you came.

CAMPING

White Sands National Monument offers only one backcountry campground. For those who don't mind hiking in a mile from Dunes Drive, it offers plenty of solitude and a chance to camp among the dunes. This is a primitive campground with no water or toilet facilities; you will need to carry in your own water and carry out all biological waste. Stop at the visitor center between 8 AM and 4 PM to obtain a permit. The campground is managed on a first-come, first-served basis and a fee is required.

Your best choice for camping is in Lincoln National Forest near Cloudcroft. Just outside of this small town you will find more than a half a dozen developed forest service campgrounds. **Silver, Saddle,** and **Apache Campgrounds,** about 2 miles northeast of Cloudcroft on NM 244, are part of a larger "recreation site" that has facilities for RVs, drinking water, showers, and a fishing pond for the kids. The **Scenic Canyon RV Park** is located 6.5 miles east of Cloudcroft off NM 82.

There is a **KOA** in Alamogordo, just a block east of I-70 on 24th Street, but you will find a nicer setting and good facilities at **Oliver Lee Memorial State Park.** The park and campgrounds are situated at the mouth of Dog Canyon at the foot of the Sacramento Mountains, about 10 miles south of Alamogordo.

LODGING

There is a good selection of chain hotels in Alamogordo; they include **Days Inn, Hampton Inn, Holiday Inn Express, Motel 6,** and **Super 8**. Most are located on White Sands Boulevard, the main street through town. You may also want to give the less expensive **Ace Motel, Satellite Inn,** or **White Sands Inn** a try. They are all located on White Sands Boulevard. In Cloudcroft there are a few choices, the best of these being **The Lodge.** The Lodge has rooms for different budgets, a golf course, and an excellent restaurant. The **Summit Inn** is less expensive and has rooms with kitchenettes. The **Aspen Rose Motel** is also less expensive. If B&Bs are more your style, try the **Crofting Bed and Breakfast,** where each room has a private bath, or the **Burro Street Boarding House.** There are also close to a half a dozen outfits that rent cabins, among them **Cabins at Cloudcroft, Heritage A-frames,** and **Spruce Cabins.** Contact the Cloudcroft chamber of commerce for more information.

IT'S INTERESTING TO KNOW...

Between 1969 and 1977 the New Mexico Department of Game and Fish released 93 oryx gazella, a large African antelope, onto the White Sands Missile range that surrounds the monument. Their intent was to introduce a large game species suitable for hunting, since the area was not supporting any such animals. The desert pronghorn previously lived in the Tularosa Basin but was shot out by unregulated hunters. The oryx, imported from the Kalahari Desert, has done quite well, now numbering around one thousand animals. Annual hunts began in 1974 and continue today.

The oryx has been successful in the region because it is so superbly adapted to desert life, happily dining on yucca, buffalo gourds, mesquite bean pods, and tumbleweeds, fodder many other grazers won't touch. The oryx is also able to reproduce at just two years of age and bear young continually throughout the year. They can weigh up to 450 pounds, stand 6 feet at the shoulder, and live to be 20 years old. Although the tawny brown body, black-and-white face mask, and long, sharp horns that can grow to be 3 feet long are striking, the animals actually remain well camouflaged among the desert scrub.

The oryx have created management problems for the monument because they frequently enter the park through the south boundary and forage on delicate desert plants. Because it is a nonnative species, the park is taking action to remove oryx when they enter the park, mostly through nonlethal means.

DON'T MISS

One of the very best ways to experience the magic of these white gypsum dunes is to ride and hike among them at dusk. If you miss the park's one or two annual full moon bike rides, or even if you are able to go on one, don't miss seeing White Sands at sunset. Dunes Drive is open every evening until 10 PM, allowing visitors to spend the evening and twilight hours exploring the fading patterns, deepening shadows, and the exquisite sunset hues reflected in the white sands. This is also the best time of day to observe wildlife; you might catch a glimpse of a kit fox trotting across a distant dune or see a tarantula amble out from its daytime hide-away in search of a meal. It is also the best time of day to take pictures. Take a picnic dinner, don't forget your camera, and be prepared to spend a few hours enjoying the spectacular evening light show.

FOOD

Among the dozens of fast-food joints common to any town at the intersection of major highways, you'll find a good selection of eateries to choose from in Alamagordo, including those that serve Chinese, Japanese, Italian, Mexican, and New Mexican, of course, and Southern barbeque. **A-Wok** (1200 White Sands Blvd.) is one of the best for Chinese; **Taiwan Kitchen** (110 N. White Sands), serving tempura and Szechuan, is good too. **Hatsue Japanese Kitchen** (804 N. New York Ave.) is good, and **Angelina's Italian Restaurant** (415 S. White Sands Blvd.) seemed to be pretty popular with the locals. For Mexican and New Mexican try **Maria's** (604 E. 10th St.), **Ramona's** (2913 N. White Sands Blvd.), or **Margo's** (504 1st St.). For meat lovers there are lots to choose from, including **Freddie's Mississippi Cooking and Bar-b-que** (20733 Interstate 70).

In Cloudcroft try the **Far Side** (right downtown on Burro Ave.) for excellent soups and sandwiches, the **Western Bar & Café** (also on Burro Ave.) for good Mexican and American dishes, and **Rebecca's** in the Lodge for something closer to a fine dining experience. Then again there is always **Dave's Café,** where you can get a good burger.

Busy Bee Laundry, 1334 East 10th Street, Alamogordo; 505-437-9637

There are a couple of good shops close by. Both of these rent, and have a good selection of gear and knowledgeable staff that can give you more riding ideas or take care of any service needs.

Outdoor Adventures, 1516 E. 10th, Alamogordo; 505-434-1920

High Altitude Outfitters, downtown Cloudcroft; 505-682-1229

White Sands National Monument Superintendent, P.O. Box 1086, Holloman AFB, NM 88330; 679-2599 or 505-479-6124; www.nps.gov/whsa/

Alamogordo Chamber of Commerce, 1310 White Sands Blvd., P.O. Box 518, Alamogordo, NM 88311-0518; 505-437-6120

Cloudcroft Chamber of Commerce, located on the east side of town on NM 82; 505-682-2733; www.cloudcroft.net

Lincoln National Forest—Main office, 1101 New York Ave., Alamogordo, NM 88310-6992; 505-434-7200

Lincoln National Forest, Sacramento Ranger District, P.O. Box 288, Cloudcroft, NM 88317; 505-682-2551